RUSSIA'S GREAT REFORMS, 1855–1881

RUSSIA'S GREAT REFORMS, 1855–1881

Edited by

BEN EKLOF, JOHN BUSHNELL, AND
LARISSA ZAKHAROVA

INDIANA UNIVERSITY PRESS

Bloomington and Indianapolis

© 1994 by Indiana University Press

The paper used in this publication meets the minimum requirements of American
National Standard for Information Sciences—Permanence of Paper for Printed
Library Materials, ANSI Z39.48-1984.

Manufactured in the United States of America

Library of Congress Cataloging-in-Publication Data

Russia's great reforms, 1855–1881 / edited by Ben Eklof, John
Bushnell, and Larissa Zakharova.
    p.   cm. — (Indiana-Michigan series in Russian and East
European studies)
    Includes bibliographical references and index.
    ISBN 0-253-31937-4. — ISBN 0-253-20861-0 (pbk.)
    1. Russia—History—Alexander II, 1855–1881. I. Eklof, Ben, date.
II. Bushnell, John, date. III. Zakharova, L. G.
(Larisa Georgievna) IV. Series.
DK221.R87 1994
947.08′1—dc20   93-26586

1 2 3 4 5   99 98 97 96 95 94

CONTENTS

INTRODUCTION   vii
     Ben Eklof

ABBREVIATIONS   xvii

  I. The Great Reforms and the Historians since Stalin   1
     Abbott Gleason

Part I   State and Reform

  II. Autocracy and the Reforms of 1861–1874 in Russia   19
     Choosing Paths of Development

     Larissa Zakharova   TRANSLATED BY *Daniel Field*

 III. The Year of Jubilee   40
     Daniel Field

 IV. Interest-Group Politics in the Era of the Great
     Reforms   58
     Alfred J. Rieber

  V. The Meaning of the Great Reforms in Russian
     Economic History   84
     Peter Gatrell

 VI. A Neglected Great Reform   102
     The Abolition of Tax Farming in Russia

     David Christian

VII. The Russian Navy and the Problem of Technological
     Transfer   115
     Technological Backwardness and Military-Industrial
     Development, 1853–1876

     Jacob W. Kipp

VIII. Miliutin and the Balkan War   139
     Military Reform vs. Military Performance

     John S. Bushnell

Part II   State and Society

IX. Accountable Only to God and the Senate   161
     Peace Mediators and the Great Reforms

     Natalia F. Ust'iantseva   TRANSLATED BY *Ben Eklof*

X.   Municipal Self-Government after the 1870 Reform   181

     Valeriia A. Nardova   TRANSLATED BY *Lori A. Citti*

XI. Crowning the Edifice   197
     The Zemstvo, Local Self-Government, and the Constitutional
     Movement, 1864–1881

     Fedor A. Petrov   TRANSLATED BY *Robin Bisha*

XII. Jurors and Jury Trials in Imperial Russia, 1866–1885   214

     Alexander K. Afanas'ev   TRANSLATED BY
     Willard Sunderland

XIII. Popular Legal Cultures   231
     The St. Petersburg *Mirovoi Sud*

     Joan Neuberger

XIV. The University Statute of 1863   247
     A Reconsideration

     Samuel D. Kassow

XV. The Rise of Voluntary Associations during the Great
     Reforms   264
     The Case of Charity

     Adele Lindenmeyr

BIBLIOGRAPHY   281
     COMPILED BY *Abbott Gleason*

CONTRIBUTORS   289
INDEX   291

INTRODUCTION

Ben Eklof

In the aftermath of the Crimean War (1853–56), the Russian autocracy was in a parlous state. Popular discontent was mounting, the country's finances were in ruin, and the military had been bloodied. On his deathbed, Nicholas I is reputed to have told his heir that he was leaving the Empire in sorry condition, that all he had devoted his life to was in ruins. For decades the autocracy had temporized on the vital issue of serfdom, and under Nicholas little progress had been made in addressing rampant corruption. Since 1848, in the celebrated words of one Russian contemporary, Russia had been marked by "the quiet of the graveyard, rotting and stinking, both physically and morally."[1] Little wonder, then, that when Alexander Nikolaevich, who was known to be quite as conservative as his father, came to the throne as Alexander II, few expected decisive initiatives. But in fact, over the next decade or so Alexander II launched a series of reforms quite remarkable for their breadth, comprehensiveness, and daring. These measures amply merit the appellation of "Great Reforms" which history has bestowed upon them.

The present collection of essays, based largely on papers presented at a conference held at the University of Pennsylvania in May 1989, before the breakup of the Soviet Union, is the first attempt to examine within a single compass the abolition of serfdom in Russia, the many other reforms associated with that historic act, and the social and economic environment with which the reforms interacted. There have been studies of individual reforms—some by contributors to this volume—and one recent volume on the reform process.[2] But as a whole, the Great Reforms, which the American historian Geroid T. Robinson long ago called the most important episode in Russian history between the Petrine and 1917 revolutions and Terence Emmons more recently labeled the "greatest single piece of state-directed social engineering in modern European history before the twentieth century," have occupied something of an historiographical vacuum.[3]

Thus the time for a careful assessment of the Great Reforms is more than ripe. The essays in this volume offer both a map of the major landmarks and a variety of contrasting perspectives from which to view them. Some basic questions must be confronted. In general, how did *these* reforms emerge out of *that* regime? What alternatives were or might have been considered? If, as most historians seem to agree, there was no master plan to the Great Reforms, what were the implicit values and understandings shaping the legislation? What path of national development did the reforms mark out? How were the individual reforms conceptualized, and what was their interrelationship? How deeply did the reforms get to what was fundamental in the structures of daily life, the political process, the national economy?

Russian scholarship on the reform era has, with few exceptions, been of low quality. Before the 1917 Revolution, few professional historians studied "recent history"; among those who did, Daniel Field has identified a predominant tendency which "smiled upon reform and reformers, the rule of law, and public opinion as a political force."[4] Later, Soviet scholarship was slowed by "attitudinal constraints" and ideological restrictions, which included the prevailing determinist current and emphases on a crude variant of labor history, the peasant movement, and economic change. Political and institutional history was long regarded as derivative and secondary, hardly worthy of serious attention. It is only recently that Russian scholarship has begun to pay close attention to the reform period; Abbott Gleason's introductory essay deals with this body of work.

American historical writing on the Great Reforms is also of relatively recent origin. This requires some explanation; after all, Western historians of Russian history, deeply influenced by liberal Kadet interpretations, were, unlike Soviet historiographers, prone to treat ideas and politics as autonomous spheres rather than as part of the superstructure of reality. Logically, then, the Great Reforms, which represented a landmark in political history, would attract considerable attention. Nevertheless, despite a general consensus that the Emancipation and accompanying reforms were major events, or at least represented a great missed opportunity in Russian history, little original American research was conducted on the Great Reforms before the 1960s. Instead, historians concentrated their attention on the emergence and evolution of the revolutionary movement, its organization and ideology as well as its links to the Bolsheviks. Essentially this was history designed to describe and explain the tragedy of the Russian Revolution or the failure of the liberal alternative. The Great Reforms emerge only as the primary example of this failure. Intended to provide the beginnings of societal participation in the processes of governing Russia and, implicitly, to limit the powers of the autocrat, the reforms were truncated and ultimately even aborted by the militant actions of radical revolutionaries, who drove the autocracy into repression and retreat. The assassination of Alexander II in 1881 on the very day he was purportedly to introduce constitutional limitations on his power was, according to this interpretation, a turning point in Russian history.[5]

In the 1960s the American historical profession underwent significant changes. The influence of the Annales school, the turbulent events in U.S. politics, and the expansion of higher education, which significantly democratized graduate training, brought social history to the fore and challenged the reigning liberal historical paradigm. Younger historians turned to issues of race, class, and gender and showed a new interest in conflict, mass movements, dominance, and exploitation.[6] These changes were reflected in a new agenda of research in Russian history, which was complemented by occasional access to archives in the Soviet Union.

A few scholars took up the Great Reforms or related issues. In addition to studies of the politics of reform by Rieber, Emmons, and Field (discussed in this volume by Abbott Gleason), Heide W. Whelan and Theodore Taranovski took up the counterreforms,[7] and W. Bruce Lincoln, Walter Pintner, and Daniel T. Orlovsky began to study the "deep structure" of the Russian bureaucracy in the nineteenth century.[8] Throughout this period, isolated reformers continued to find their biographers. Finally, while largely rejecting the notion of a "revolutionary crisis" defining the reform era, Abbott Gleason, Richard Wortman, and Daniel R. Brower advanced the study of the revolutionary movement by carrying it into the realms of sociology, cultural history, and psychohistory.[9] The general trend of the new writing in history, however, was to bypass the Great Reforms. Interested primarily in long-term social developments, historians leapfrogged from a study of revolutionary elites and ideology to the problem of the viability of the Old Regime and questions germane to that issue: conflicts between masses and elites, the solidarity of elites, and the tensions caused by social and economic development in late Imperial Russia.

The shift in the research agenda reflected changes in political consciousness among Western historians. Whereas earlier studies had focused critically upon revolutionary groups in order to discover the intellectual origins of the Bolshevik revolution and to understand the usurpation of power, now historians largely studied mass movements and social conflicts, if not to celebrate at least to explain, in far more sympathetic terms, why the revolution happened and why it enjoyed broad-based support.

While the Great Reforms were not central to this research agenda, recent currents in historical writing have suggested new ways of looking at the period. The interest in "civil society" visible in all the American contributions to this volume reflects the popularity among Western historians of the ideas of Jurgen Habermas, who pioneered the study of the emergence of societal opinion independent of the state and freed from aristocratic tutelage. The concept has moved from Western historical science to the study of Russian history. It has been reinforced both by the current fascination with the emergence of a civil society in the era of perestroika and by its links with earlier liberal and émigré historiography, which was structured around a fundamental opposition between *obshchestvennost'* and *vlast'* (educated society and the state). A renewed interest in politics and a concern with reform as an alternative to revolution have led Western historians to question old assumptions.[10] Among economic historians, a lively discussion over "proto-industrialization" has brought to the fore the debate over whether Russian economic development can best be understood in terms of gradual change or of sharp discontinuities.

Current events pose other questions, especially about the relationship of the Great Reforms to the revolution now under way in Russia. To many Western historians the Great Reforms are a pivotal moment in Russian history, but in the former Soviet Union—preoccupied with current reforms that are radically altering every facet of social, economic, and political life—the Great Reforms are of immediate and pressing interest. We are now also confronted with the issue of generational change. Today the *shestidesiatniki,* or people of the sixties in Russia, play a major role in pushing the country toward reform. These are people who, in their youth, were deeply affected by the early enthusiasm and later disillusionment of the Khrushchev era.[11] Similarly, *shestidesiatniki* of an earlier age carried their hopes, fears, and memories of the Great Reforms right up to the turn of the century.[12] Yet no one has studied these people as a group; we do not know what the reforms meant to them or how they applied the "lessons" of these reforms to their later lives.[13]

The contributors to this collection attend to history, not to current events. Ben Eklof and Larissa Zakharova first discussed the idea of a conference on the Great Reforms in 1983, two years before Mikhail Gorbachev acceded to power and long before it could have occurred to anyone that a collection of articles on the subject might have contemporary relevance. But it would reveal a remarkable lack of self-examination to claim that our concerns and approaches have not been shaped by the tumultuous events of recent years as well as by an evolving historiographical tradition. For example, an important legacy of the era of perestroika was to reintroduce the notions of contingency and alternative paths *(alternativy)* into Soviet historical discourse: what might have happened had circumstances been slightly different? Were there turning points, "plastic moments" at which, had different choices been made, the tragedy (and note, tragedy rather than triumph is the dominant interpretive note today) of twentieth-century Russian history might have been avoided? Similarly, Western historians, particularly those trained in the tools of social history, have been forced once again to deal with contingency. In this light, the Great Reforms take on a different hue, and the collapse of the Tsarist autocracy in 1917 is no longer seen as proof incontestable of the ultimate or inevitable failure of these reforms.[14]

Five years in the planning, the Great Reforms conference and this publication are themselves products of a specific historical moment. Fruitful collaboration between Russian and U.S. historians of the Great Reforms is not new. As an important case in point, many of the contributors to the conference and this volume, Russian and American both, were taught or assisted in their research by Professor Peter Andreevich Zaionchkovskii of Moscow University. Several of the U.S. contributors were aided in their early endeavors at research in Soviet archives by Larissa Zakharova, one of the editors of this volume and perhaps the leading authority on the politics of the reforms.

Nevertheless, the new reform era associated with Gorbachev made collaboration much easier than in the past. Certainly the publication of this collection jointly by Indiana University Press and Moscow University Press would have been impossible just a few years ago. Moreover, it is now natural for us to think of ourselves not as representatives of two sides with conflicting historical predispositions but as individuals who happen to be from different countries yet share a common interest in Russia's history.

Still, it must be admitted that the differences in historical approach or style that have long existed between Soviet and Western historians persist today. With the collapse of official Soviet Marxist ideology, Soviet historians were stripped of an "official" interpretive framework. In reality, a separation between research and grand—or, perhaps more important, middle-level—theory took place long before Gorbachev came to power and opened the door for the historical profession to deal with controversial issues in an open manner and to search for the truth, however unpalatable it was. Formerly, many of the best Soviet historians pursued their research within narrow boundaries, demonstrating a remarkable knowledge of primary sources but leaving conclusions and linkages to the reader (or the editor). Pursuing narrowly empirical issues was the only appropriate strategy for avoiding conceptual entanglements with prescribed interpretations. Western historians, on the other hand, often addressed larger issues of development, causality, and consequence but were prevented by their limited access to archives from following the evidence in an unimpeded fashion or from looking into the internal workings of the political or administrative process. This volume reflects these different legacies.

The editors have divided the volume into two sections: state and reform and state and society. The political process is treated by several historians. Larissa Zakharova argues that a concern for Russia's reputation and prestige abroad pervaded the considerations of policymakers. She emphasizes the absence of a general plan or program of action among the reformers. She sees the reforms as a watershed but also asserts that a fatal shortcoming of the reforms was the way they were carried out, and specifically the failure to institutionalize the decision-making process or to move toward constitutional reform. Alfred J. Rieber eschews constitutional issues and insists that traditional ideological labels, as well as the terminology of West European political experience in general, obscure as much as they reveal about the Russian political process. He finds that the Great Reforms were the crucible of modern Russian politics and argues that the institutional setting of politics evolved, the patterns of political communication changed, and the legislative process grew more complex—though no more systematic. Rieber concludes that in the second half of the nineteenth century the autocrat was transformed into a managerial tsar who had lost control over the governing process. At the same time, like Zakharova, he emphasizes that social forces or interest groups were too fragmented to extract concessions.

Other essays in this volume examine the new public institutions created by the Great Reforms that provided the forum for civic involvement. Fedor A. Petrov gives a useful introduction to the zemstvo reforms, then turns to the efforts of the zemstvos in the political arena toward the end of Alexander II's reign, a period which he treats as the incubator of the basic zemstvo liberal political program. His essay is part of a late trend in Soviet historiography offering a more positive estimate of the role of the zemstvo in Russian public life. Valeriia A. Nardova looks at the municipal reforms which followed six years after the zemstvo statute and which created similar institutions in the cities. She emphasizes that the lengthy discussions accompanying the eight-year preparations for the municipal reform reflected in miniature the changing fortunes of the reforms as a whole, the progressive hardening of the autocracy's position, and the shifting boundaries between state and society. Nardova demonstrates, through the first investigation of duma voting lists, that while the dumas were profoundly undemocratic in composition, they were not inactive. Nardova believes not only that they succeeded in improving municipal conditions but also that their ongoing friction with the central government over jurisdiction ultimately stimulated the rudiments of a political consciousness, a corporate identity.

Adele Lindenmeyr considers the "new spirit of voluntarism" which accompanied the Great Reforms and set it apart from the era of Nicholas I. The diverse associations which arose in the twenty-five years following the law of 1862 reflected a new civic consciousness and demonstrated sufficient vitality to survive the less auspicious climate after 1881. Focusing on private charitable associations, Lindenmeyr, like Nardova, demonstrates that autocratic lenience evolved out of a series of ad hoc decisions in response to societal pressure, but also that such lenience was bestowed only when it involved shifting the financial burden for low-priority projects from the state to the public. Samuel D. Kassow considers the troubled relationship between the state and the university and the uneasy—indeed, "unprincipled"—compromise achieved by the 1863 statute. He argues that the period leading up to the university legislation was a "plastic moment" but that the legislation failed to establish a proper balance of power among state, faculty, and students.

If the essays just referred to deal primarily with internal policy formulation and with relations between state and society, others, by Joan Neuberger, Alexander K. Afanas'ev, Natalia F. Ust'iantseva, and Daniel Field, deal with the relations between educated society and the *menu peuple*. In a lucid survey, Field emphasizes that while serfdom was abolished the servile economy was retained, and he specifies the hegemonic aspects of the social arrangements prevailing in the post-Emancipation countryside. Ust'iantseva deals with the mechanisms of implementation of the Emancipation Statute, the peace mediators responsible for negotiating between lord and peasant within the limits set by local statutes. She devotes the bulk of her essay to a collective biography of the nine thousand individuals who served during the thirteen-year life of the institution. Although the peace mediators have long been a subject of interest to historians, Soviet and Western, none have looked closely at the selection process, qualifications, and backgrounds of those who served; the popularity of the position among educated society;

or the degree of autonomy and glasnost obtaining in this area. Ust'iantseva treats the legislation on the peace mediators as a "trial balloon for the new bourgeois legislative norms" and regards the legislation ultimately as a failure in terms of consistency and irreversibility. In her mind, its main weakness was that it relied heavily on heroic personal sacrifice, or *podvig,* rather than on the institutionalization of rational norms of bureaucratic behavior and accountability.

Two essayists treat aspects of the new judicial system. Afanas'ev looks at another group brought together by the Great Reforms: jurors serving on the new courts of Russia. He studies the composition of juries, looking for changes over time and differences between the capital cities and the provinces. Finding widespread evasion of jury duty by the privileged classes, hence a numerical preponderance of peasants on juries, Afanas'ev concludes that through these peasant juries, customary law exerted a significant impact upon the outcome of formal trials. Neuberger scrutinizes the justices of the peace established during the era of the Great Reforms and inquires about their impact on popular legal culture in Russia. The notion of equality before the law embodied in the practices of these courts was indeed a radical departure, but subtle forms of deference and distinction remained, and, as Afanas'ev shows with the jury courts, severe underfinancing hobbled the progress of legality.

Peter Gatrell employs a formidable array of statistical data, much of it previously untapped for such purposes, to demonstrate that the Great Reforms produced no discontinuity, or rupture, in economic terms. In this he is reinforcing Olga Crisp's notion of a "continuous stream," which emphasizes the spontaneous patterns of economic growth over state-induced change. In addition, Gatrell emphasizes that the search for a take-off period of industrialization may be unwarranted; recent European economic history has discovered instead a gradually increasing growth curve. The Russian example conforms to this pattern. David Christian, on the other hand, sees the legislation bringing about major changes in the way vodka was manufactured and sold in Russian society as a landmark in Russian economic history, signaling a transition from a tributary to a contractual nexus.

Jacob W. Kipp's essay deals with a unique moment in Russian military and economic history, when Russia's navy had been destroyed and had to be reconstructed during a period of rapid technological change. With this essay as with many others, it is difficult to resist comparisons to the present. Russian leaders at the time of the Great Reforms were, according to Kipp, seeking a happy medium between economic autarky and overdependence upon foreign technology; they hoped to overcome inferiority by borrowing technology, harnessing private industry, and counting on the greenhouse effect of carefully nurturing selected industries or enterprises. Kipp shows how technological transfer and private enterprise replaced government orders, then how this brief but successful initiative was aborted. John Bushnell, who played a major role in organizing the conference, addresses the issue of the success of the military reforms, employing a simple test: how well did the reformed army perform in the field? Bushnell artfully describes the course of the Russo-Turkish War and the lamentable conduct of Russian forces. He concludes that because the emperor insisted on being warlord and picking his own generals, the highly successful administrative reforms launched by Dmitri Miliutin were not reflected in military practice. Is this emblematic, he hints, of what went wrong with the reforms as a whole? Most of the contributors to this collection would agree: the failure to limit the autocracy, to eliminate *proizvol* (arbitrary or lawless behavior), to provide for institutionalized decision-making processes at the higher level or for governmental accountability were all significant, perhaps fatal, flaws.

Thus these essays provide a map of the new political groupings emerging during the reforms, trace the shifting boundaries between state and society and between society and *narod,* and link issues of conceptualization and design with problems of implementation. A nuanced treatment is offered of the balance between continuity and change in the reform era. The political process as a whole is subject to detailed scrutiny, but without losing sight of the larger social forces impinging upon that process. To be sure, the original goal set for the conference of producing a new synthesis or overview of the reforms proved premature. Instead the participants discovered vast areas of uncharted terrain; we found ourselves groping for the right questions and terminology, searching for the proper comparative framework, and ultimately trying to set a new agenda for research. This is not, after all, surprising: an era as momentous as that of the Great Reforms will probably always defy attempts to establish consensus or to summarize in neat formulae or generalizations. The editors are pleased with the results achieved. We hope this volume will serve as a point of departure and will encourage further efforts to understand this richly complicated era.

We owe a great deal to many scholars whose contributions to the conference we could not include in this volume because of limitations of space and the need for thematic balance: Elizabeth Ballantine, Harley Balzer, Daniel Brower, Eduard Dneprov, Vladimir Fedorov, Cathy Frierson, Leonid Gorlanov, Gary Hamburg, Allan Kimball, Daniel Moran, Elliott Mossman, Igor Orzhekovskii, Louise McReynolds, Theodore Taranovski, Charles Timberlake, and Frank Wcislo. The English and Russian versions of this volume differ slightly, as some essays were judged appropriate for one potential readership, others not. We are happy to report that many of the papers are being published elsewhere. Other scholars served as commentators, and we greatly appreciate the time and effort they devoted. Without the generous support of the National Endowment for the Humanities we could not have held the conference at all.

We owe special thanks to Alfred J. Rieber for extending the offer to hold the conference at the University of Pennsylvania and to Elliott Mossman for serving as a genial and efficient host in his capacity as Director of that university's Russian and East European Center. The Center's grant to the conference and the work of its staff made the conference the success that it was. In particular, the efforts of Jean Gurley, Olga Rubenchik, and Alexei Dmitriev and Abby Schrader were vital to the success of the conference. The editors are also profoundly grateful to Indiana University graduate students Robin Bisha, Lori Citti, Willard Sunderland, and Eli Weinerman for their contributions as translators or research assistants and to the staff of Indiana University Press. Needless to say, none of the foregoing should be held responsible for those errors of fact or judgment which may remain in the text.

NOTES

1. Nikolai Pogodin, cited in Cynthia Whittaᴋer, *The Origins of Modern Russian Education: An Intellectual Biography of Count Sergei Uvarov, 1786–1855* (DeKalb, Ill., 1984), 238.

2. The recent attempt to provide a synthesis of the reform process is W. Bruce Lincoln, *The Great Reforms: Autocracy, Bureaucracy and the Politics of Change in Imperial Russia* (DeKalb, Ill., 1990).

3. Terence Emmons, "*'Revoliutsiia sverkhu'* v *Rossii:* Reflections on Natan Eidel'man's Last Book and Related Matters," paper presented to the Conference on Reform in Russia and the Soviet Union, Kennan Institute, June 1990.

4. Daniel Field, "The Reforms of the 1860s," in S. H. Baron and Nancy Heer, eds., *Windows on the Russian Past* (Columbus, Ohio, 1977), 94.

5. See Richard Pipes, *Russia under the Old Regime* (New York: Scribner, 1974), 281–315.

6. See Peter Novick, *That Noble Dream: The "Objectivity" Question and the American Historical Profession* (Cambridge, England, 1988).

7. Heide W. Whelan, *Alexander III and the State Council: Bureaucracy and Counterreform in Late Imperial Russia* (New Brunswick, N.J., 1982); Theodore Taranovski, "The Aborted Counter-Reform: The Murav'iev Commission and the Judicial Statutes of 1864," *Jahrbücher für Geschichte Osteuropas* 29 (1981): 161–84.

8. W. Bruce Lincoln, *In the Vanguard of Reform: Russia's Enlightened Bureaucrats, 1825–1861* (DeKalb, Ill., 1982); Walter McKenzie Pintner and Don Karl Rowney, eds., *Russian Officialdom: The Bureaucratization of Russian Society from the Seventeenth to the Twentieth Century* (Chapel Hill, N.C., 1980); Daniel T. Orlovsky, *The Limits of Reform: The Ministry of Internal Affairs in Imperial Russia, 1802–1881* (Cambridge, Mass., 1981).

9. Daniel R. Brower, *Training the Nihilists: Education and Radicalism in Tsarist Russia* (Ithaca, N.Y., 1975); Abbott Gleason, *Young Russia: The Genesis of Russian Radicalism in the 1860s* (New York, 1980); Richard Wortman, *The Crisis of Russian Populism* (London, 1967).

10. One example of this concern with reform is Robert O. Crummey, ed., *Reform in Russia and the USSR: Past and Prospects* (Urbana, Ill., 1989). This volume is the product of a conference held at the University of Michigan in April 1986. Another conference on reform in modern Russian history was held at the Kennan Institute in Washington, D.C., in 1990. Still another, on middle-class identity in late Imperial Russia, was held at Purdue University in 1989 and resulted in a volume edited by Edith W. Clowes, Samuel D. Kassow, and James L. West: *Between Tsar and People: Educated Society and the Quest for Public Identity in Late Imperial Russia* (Princeton, N.J., 1991).

11. Fittingly, one of the participants in the conference on which this volume is based, Eduard Dneprov, became a "great reformer," serving as minister of education (1990–1992) for the RSFSR. Dneprov, by training a specialist on the history of Russian education, published on the role of *Morskoi sbornik* in the reform era. Widely regarded as one of the most consistent and systematic of Boris Yeltsin's reform group, Dneprov repeatedly described himself in print as a *shestidesiatnik*. See, for example, an interview with him conducted by Ol'ga Marinicheva: "Vlast' svalilas' na nas sluchaino," *Komsomol'skaia pravda,* May 25, 1991.

12. For examples, see D. C. B. Lieven, *Russia's Rulers under the Old Regime* (New Haven, Conn., 1989), esp. 231–55.

13. For an attempt to analyze the issue of generational politics and the *shestidesiatniki,* see L. Anninskii, "Shestidesiatniki, semidesiatniki, vos'midesiatniki: k dialektike pokolenii v russkoi kul'ture," *Literaturnoe obozrenie,* 1991, no. 4, 10–14.

14. For a different perspective which emphasizes the limited scope of the Great Reforms and the reactive nature of government policies after 1861, when societal forces outstripped the ability of the state to shape or direct them, see Crummey, ed., *Reform in Russia and the USSR,* esp. the essays by Walter M. Pintner, "Reformability in the Age of Reform and Counterreform, 1855–1894," 86–99, and William G. Rosenberg, "Conclusion: On the Problem of Reform in Russia and the Soviet Union," 277–89.

ABBREVIATIONS

TsGIA	Central State Historical Archive
TsGAOR	Central State Archive of the October Revolution
ORGBL	Manuscript Division, Lenin Library
SbIRIO	Sbornik Imperatorskogo russkogo istoricheskogo obshchestva
GPB	Saltykov-Shchedrin Library
LGIA	Leningrad State Historical Archive
TsGIAM	Moscow State Historical Archive
PSZ	Polnoe sobranie Zakonov
TsGALI	Central State Archive of Literature and the Arts
ORIGIM	Manuscript Division, State History Museum

RUSSIA'S GREAT REFORMS, 1855–1881

I

THE GREAT REFORMS AND THE HISTORIANS SINCE STALIN

Abbott Gleason

National histories have usually been the work of historians from the nation in question—insiders, one might say. The history of France has been largely the work of French *savants,* the history of Germany mostly the work of German *Gelehrte.* They know the language, culture, and usually the archives best. They usually create the research paradigms, or at least mediate demands from elsewhere that lead to the creation of those paradigms. At the same time, there has often been a useful role for outsiders, who have frequently challenged the national establishment on issues and in ways that the dominant group might prefer to ignore. Elie Halévy played a useful part in creating the historiography of modern England. English-speaking historians have argued fruitfully with German-speaking ones over the course of German history since Bismarck.

The latter example suggests that the relationship between the insiders and the outsiders can become an adversarial one. There was, of course, a contest between the older generation of German historians and a group of foreigners for hegemony over German history. But it took two world wars and the attendant issues to bring about such a bitter confrontation between insiders and outsiders.

The German example notwithstanding, I know of no other case where the differences between the insiders and outsiders have been so deep, the contest so bitter, as that between Soviet and non-Soviet scholars—predominantly Americans—over how Russian history should be written. That contest has been going on for more than forty years, although its bitterness has dramatically diminished since the late 1980s. The political developments of the present time give us hope that many wounds may be healed and divisions overcome in the coming generation, among them, perhaps, the struggle between insiders and outsiders over Russian history.

But creating a single historiography instead of two, even during the era of *glasnost'* and *perestroika,* will not be easy. Methodological issues and

I

issues of historical culture still divide the two communities. As Soviet scholars have been increasingly willing to accept an ideal of "objectivity"[1] in historical inquiry (rather than excoriating it as "bourgeois"), American scholars have found the possibility of objectivity much more problematical.[2] Perhaps even more serious, the histories of the Soviet historical profession and the American have been very different and may be diverging in new ways even now. Americans have moved away from institutional history in recent years and show little sign of reinteresting themselves in it. And one may guess that the ideas and the intellectual circles of late Imperial Russia will continue to be more interesting to Soviet scholars than its state institutions. Still, the recurrent efforts to construct what is now universally referred to as civil society links the turn of the 1990s with what non-Soviet scholars still call the era of the Great Reforms.

American historians began to devote themselves to the serious study of Russian history only at the outset of the Cold War, and what they produced was much conditioned by this conflict. It was first of all the enormous task of explaining the Russian Revolution that engaged these novice historians of modern Russia—liberals, conservatives, and a few radicals. The work produced was of an extremely varied quality, but just as Soviet historians were attempting to work out how it happened so that they could make their version hegemonic, Western historians began to construct counterversions of how it had *really* happened. Whether their starting points were liberal, conservative-conspiratorial, Freudian, or nonparty Marxist, the fact of the Cold War powerfully and sometimes subtly pressured them toward common views. As they became engaged in this task, they tended to leap backward over work done in the Soviet period and base themselves on the populist-tinged liberal historiography of the late Imperial period that had devoted so much attention to the struggle against the Tsarist regime. Serious study of Russian history in the United States was insignificant until after 1945, but at that point young American and émigré historians began to familiarize themselves with the historiography of late Imperial Russia. As they set out to investigate the opposition to the Old Regime, which led to the Revolution, they steeped themselves in the work of historians such as V. I. Semevskii, A. I. Pypin, and A. A. Kornilov. Studies of radicalism and the revolutionary movement soon came to dominate European and especially American historigraphy and continued to do so until recently.

In the past two decades, American and to a lesser extent German scholarship has finally turned its attention toward the institutions and personnel of the Old Regime.[3] The Great Reforms had always been thought to be a topic of importance, an opinion inherited from the "liberal" historiography of late Imperial Russia. They were always an important subtheme of the history of the Russian Revolution; since the imaginations of many American historians were engaged by the consideration of alternative possibilities to the actual outcome of the Revolution, it was natural to place the Great Reforms, like the First World War, at the heart of such meditations. "Tsar Alexander II's emancipation of the serfs in 1861," wrote Arthur Adams in 1965, "may legitimately serve as the starting point for an investigation of Russia's march toward its twentieth-century revolutions. . . . In the longer view, the revolutions occurred because Russia failed to adjust rapidly and completely enough to the pressures for change that piled up after 1861."[4] American historians of nineteenth-century Russia were also impressed by the mere accomplishment of such an enormous task as the Emancipation, despite its ultimate lack of success. "The Emancipation," wrote another American scholar, "was probably the greatest single piece of state-directed social engineering in modern European history before the twentieth century."[5]

In the Soviet Union, the forces promoting the study of the reforms, as well as those inhibiting them, have been quite different.[6] It may be that no victorious Marxist regime is initially disposed to pay much attention to the political history of the defeated class enemy. Certainly when Soviet historians have turned to the eighteenth and nineteenth centuries, they have been interested largely in how the present was born out of this recent past. This has meant defining and studying the birth of "progressive" social groups, classes, or formations—the intelligentsia, workers, or capitalism itself. It has entailed studying the privation and oppression suffered by the peasantry and when possible their heroic struggle against that oppression: the "peasant movement." It has meant showing the development of "progressive" intellectual tendencies, linked either to economic development or the oppositional activity of new classes.[7] And it has led to what seems to outsiders an excessive preoccupation with periodization: the precise moment when "feudalism" gave way to "capitalism," for example.[8]

The political history of the Old Regime is in some respects the polar opposite, considered as a historical subject. Normally the study of the institutional past of one's nation entails certain feelings of relatedness, even piety. One ordinarily needs to think of past institutions, like personages of the past, as one's predecessors, in order to create the volume and intensity of study that one associates with national historiographies in the "bourgeois" world. But in Soviet historiography those institutions initially seemed dead and gone in a way which was different from that in which, say, Bismarck and the Reichstag were dead and gone in Germany. The tsars and their governing institutions, their world of exploitation, were ended by the march of history. What was defined as a proletarian revolution separated past from present in a way that had no parallel in the West. Even if Soviet historians never entirely believed in or felt such a total separation, the fact of the Revolution seriously inhibited the study of the institutions of tsarism, particularly during the first twenty years after 1917.

Especially since World War II, however, the state-sponsored recrudescence of Russian patriotism and nationalism steadily altered the initial "revolutionary" orientation of Soviet historiography. But only certain aspects of the Tsarist past have been fully rehabilitated, at least until the very most recent times. Patriotic indoctrination growing out of the wartime experience dictated above all that in condemning the Tsarist past an exception be made for the history of war, conquest, and diplomacy.

Since the discrediting of Pokrovskii's sociologism in the 1930s, what one might broadly call the creation of the Russian Empire, from its infant dependency to its glorious present, became legitimized. The more Tsarist Russia came to be seen as the precursor of Soviet Russia, the more its triumphs could be celebrated. Despite continued glorification of the October Revolution, this stress on continuity has subtly diminished its status as the point at which a new era was born.

But the increasingly desperate efforts at reform, over the last sixty years of the Imperial regime, do not comprise any such glorious chapter as the creation of a Russian *imperium*.[9] In contrast to Western historians, Soviet scholars have believed that since the feudal world *had* to give way to the bourgeois world, the failure of the reforms to achieve their purpose was inevitable. Daniel Field has shrewdly pointed out that within Soviet culture generally, the achievements of the reforms of the 1860s have been less highly valued than in our "bourgeois" world:

> We attach great importance to legal norms, and therefore see in the reforms of the 1860s principles analogous to the milestones of progress in our own past. . . . the substitution of civil freedom for bondage, trial by jury, elective local government and equal liability for military service . . . [but] advances and reversals in Soviet life are not considered dependent upon enacted constitutional principles.[10]

In the Soviet historical schema, by contrast, the real interest of the Great Reforms has turned on the way they fitted into the larger picture of the transition from feudalism to capitalism. Since the ruling class was bound to try to stave off that change, the reforms have inevitably had, for Soviet historians, the quality of an epiphenomenon. It was easy to go one step further and say that if the Old Regime in Russia made a determined effort to reform itself under such an unenlightened and stubborn monarch as Alexander II, that regime must have felt itself compelled to do so by external forces. If one really wants to understand the reforms of the 1860s (the argument would continue), one must study the underlying economic and social developments of the period and the pressures which those developments ultimately placed on the Imperial regime. It was general considerations like these which gave rise to the "revolutionary situation" paradigm, which until the most recent past was a powerful factor in the way Soviet scholars approached the reforms.

Non-Soviet scholars usually see the present as developing out of the past without such a serious break. They have often interpreted the Soviet Union as a peculiar but ultimately quite intelligible successor state to the Imperial Russian autocracy. It is natural for them to ask whether studying the reforms of Alexander II might be relevant for understanding the reforms of Mikhail Gorbachev, to see Alexander II's reforms as meriting comparison with those of Peter the Great, Count Witte, and Gorbachev.[11] For Soviet scholars, the requisite continuities which would make this sort of comparison intelligible have not existed until very recently, although they are now developing rapidly. The late N. Ia. Eidel'man's lively and engrossing "'Revoliutsiia sverkhu' v Rossii," which appeared serially in the last three issues of *Nauka i zhizn'* for 1988 and the first three in 1989, is a case in point. Popular history at its best, Eidel'man's essay is an examination of Russia's complex traditions of authoritarian "revolution from above" and their legacy of subjects who are still less than citizens. It is clearly aimed at the present situation of the Soviet Union.

Gavriil Popov, until recently an academic economist but now the embattled mayor of Moscow, published a lively, brief, popular account of the Emancipation in *Eko* early in 1987. Popov still saw a crisis of Russia's feudal system but understood that crisis to have manifested itself in the Crimean defeat and in the country's inability to compete economically with the "progressive countries of Western Europe." Alexander II, fearing "for his throne," was forced to act. In his conclusion, Popov used Lenin's critical words about "reforms made by serf owners" to suggest the need for radical reform in the contemporary Soviet Union.

More serious still is Larissa Zakharova's "1861: Reforma i reformatory. Iz istorii otmeny krepostnogo prava v Rossii," which appeared in mid-1989. Her essay, a condensation of a longer piece published in *Voprosy istorii,* is explicitly comparative, in its use not only of glasnost and perestroika but also of the thaw metaphor and the heavy burdens carried over from a previous era of stagnation and repression. In her conclusion, Zakharova suggests that the weakness and disorganization of the proreform social forces in the succeeding period made it possible for the old-style bureaucrats and pro-autocratic personnel to recover. It is obvious that she is not just making a point about the nineteenth century.[12]

Although pasts are more clearly demarcated from the present in the intellectual universe of Soviet scholarship than they are in the West, a straightforward, bipolar contrast between Soviet and American scholars would be much too simple. There are many reasons why historians everywhere repeatedly connect some individuals and historical developments more directly to the present, thus making them nearer in time, while others remain further away, their connections to the present left obscure or unexplored. Soviet historical practice has merely been more systematic and purposeful and open about establishing such preferential links. When Soviet historians studied the revolutionary past of their country in the mid–nineteenth century, that past was almost invariably brought very near the present.

But if 1861 has been quite close for Soviet historians when they studied the revolutionary movement, it has been much further away when they turned to how Imperial statesmen struggled to preserve feudal Russia by reforming it. Until Zakharova's 1984 study, at least, Chernyshevskii has been closer to the present in the Soviet Union than Nikolai Miliutin, while among

Western historians the difference is less great.[13] But great leaps and dramatic changes in historical perspective are more possible in the Soviet Union than they are in the West, because Soviet scholars have been clearer and more forthright than their Western colleagues about how the historians' present circumstances influence their interpretations of the past. Although the era of the Great Reforms has been further away in the Soviet Union than in the West, if the Soviet commitment to a pluralistic and interest-driven "civil society" endures, the 1860s will gain rapidly in interest for Soviet scholars.[14]

Because of the Marxist historical schema, the feudal past has also been regarded as more retrograde than it has in the West. The closer one gets to the glorious present, the better the world becomes, despite the continuing power of reactionary formations. Much of Soviet Marxism has been the ultimate in Whig history.[15] And its scholarship has clearly set itself against studying retrograde, nonprogressive historical phenomena, perhaps less because doing so teaches the wrong lessons than because there is nothing important for the present, nothing instrumental to be learned in studying such subjects as the unsuccessful efforts of feudal or quasi-feudal institutions to reform themselves. The concern of such regimes is not the masses, their historical victims, but perpetuating their long reign of oppression. "I must say," wrote Academician N. M. Druzhinin in his argument with Franco Venturi a quarter of a century ago, "that I do not consider the reform of 1861 'great.'"[16]

Given the differences, then, in how Soviet and Western scholars have approached the study of the Great Reforms, it is notable and perhaps surprising that a single Soviet scholar could have had a major impact on the study of the reforms in both the Soviet Union and the United States. But it is so. That scholar was Petr Andreevich Zaionchkovskii. It is easier to perceive the magnitude of Zaionchkovskii's influence, however, than to understand it. To what degree, for instance, was Zaionchkovskii really a figure representative of Soviet historical scholarship broadly speaking? Or should his influence rather be understood as the reassertion of certain aspects of a great tradition from an earlier day?[17]

According to Terence Emmons, Zaionchkovskii's method consisted in "the construction of straightforward empirical narratives based on the massive, systematic exploration of government documents and archives and the private papers of statesmen."[18] This, according to Emmons, was a new phenomenon in Soviet historiography, although surely not in European historiography more generally. Alfred J. Rieber noted how Zaionchkovskii put the Emancipation of the serfs in an "objective context" and stressed his emphasis on the role of the state.

In developing his interpretation of the reform, Zaionchkovskii, according to Rieber, "strongly emphasized the contradiction between the growing capitalist relationships in the countryside and the feudal structure of landholding." This is surely a plausible Marxist point of departure. As in other of his works, when Zaionchkovskii dealt with the Emancipation, he stressed the role of the state; the initiative "came from the top in the form of a reasoned response to profound socio-economic needs within the system, a response which, to be sure, reflected the rising though not yet dominant interests of capital."[19]

It is not clear how many of Zaionchkovskii's American students actually agreed with him about the importance of the "rising interests of capital," but his point of view seems to have provided a rubric sufficiently broad to have reduced disagreements between Marxists and non-Marxists to manageable proportions. Rieber usefully suggests that Zaionchkovskii's Marxist interpretation of the reform had the effect of reconciling the point of view of the "state school" toward reform with that of the "sociological school," particularly with its dominant Marxist form. Perhaps the relative success of this effort to reconcile points of view which are more usually strongly opposed to one another helps account for Zaionchkovskii's influence.

All of Zaionchkovskii's American students allude to the extraordinary command of sources which he possessed and insisted upon for those doing serious work on such a topic. Daniel Field goes so far as to say that "for [Zaionchkovskii] historical scholarship was virtually coextensive with *istochnikovedenie*. . . . This attitude links Petr Andreevich with the precepts, if not always the practice, of the nineteenth-century masters." From the standpoint of academic genealogy Zaionchkovskii's links with those "masters" is clear. He was the student of Iu. V. Got'e, himself a master of sources, who was in turn the student of V. O. Kliuchevskii.[20]

Zaionchkovskii's three major monographs are at the heart of his work on the reforms. These are his revised doctoral dissertation on the military reforms of the 1860s and 1870s and his two volumes on the abolition of serfdom.[21] In them collectively, Zaionchkovskii found an intellectual framework which could reconcile economic determinism with a renewed stress on the role of the state and a restored role for the principal agents of the autocracy, men like D. A. Miliutin and P. A. Valuev, whose diaries he published.[22] Impelled by economic change and frightened by the spector of peasant revolt, the government proceeded to transform the feudal monarchy into a bourgeois one. It had to begin by emancipating the serfs.

According to Zaionchkovskii, despite the government's anxiety there was little to fear from the amorphous and disorganized "peasant movement," which was years away from outgrowing its "tsarist character." But his was not the only nascent Soviet framework. Soon there was a rival, which took a substantially different attitude toward the importance of the "peasant movement" and on a number of other points.

The March–April number of *Istoriia SSSR* for 1958 informed its readers of the formation of a "Group for the Study of the Revolutionary Situation in Russia, 1850–1860." These eight scholars, publicly constituted as a group in December 1957, met for the first time on January 22, 1958, under the leadership of their organizer and leader, Militsa Vasil'evna Nechkina.[23] The meeting report was largely given over to the explication of their new paradigm: the "revolutionary situation." It was alleged that Marx and Engels had "already mentioned" the existence of a "revolutionary situation" in the journalism and correspondence of the late 1850s, but they do not seem to have actually used the term. But Lenin had. The term had occasionally been used by previous scholars, but now an enormous new importance was urged for it.

Several years later the first of a series of collective volumes by the group appeared, and in the opening article Academician Nechkina made her understanding of the revolutionary situation clearer. In several essays, she pointed out, Lenin had suggested that a decisive revolutionary moment is likely to come when the ruling class understands that it cannot rule as before and the masses are simply unwilling to go on living as before. But the crucial text that Nechkina chose was a polemical piece of 1915 entitled "The Collapse of the Second International."[24] No revolution, said Lenin, is possible without a "revolutionary situation," but not all revolutionary situations lead to revolutions. In order for there to be a revolutionary situation, he continued, three conditions must be met:

> 1. [it must be] impossible for the ruling classes to preserve their rule in an unchanged form; [there must be] some crisis or other "at the top," a political crisis of the ruling class creating a breach through which the discontent and the resentment of the oppressed classes can burst. For a revolution to take place, it has not usually been enough that "the lower classes don't want" to live in the same old way; it has usually also required that "the upper classes cannot";
> 2. the neediness and poverty of the oppressed classes [must have] reached a higher level than usual;
> 3. [there must be] a significant increase, for the reasons mentioned above, in the activity of the masses, who in "peaceful" times simply allow themselves to be plundered, but in turbulent ones are drawn by all the circumstances of the crisis, *even by the upper classes themselves,* into independent historical action.[25]

From these three conditions, Nechkina drew up a research agenda for herself and her colleagues as they came to grips with the Russian 1860s. They needed to study the maturation of capitalism, which created the economic crisis; the dissatisfaction of the lower classes, above all as it was expressed in the "peasant movement"; the development of the "revolutionaries of 1861," who attempted to "lead the mass movement"; and finally the "crisis of the upper classes" *(krizis verkhov),* comprising the government's overall response to the situation but focusing on the reforms that it was forced to grant. And all of these aspects needed to be understood and treated as a totality. Despite Nechkina's insistence on the centrality of the reforms to the *krizis verkhov,* no historical research on the reforms actually appeared in the first of the "revolutionary situation" collections.[26]

Two years later, the second of what were to be nine volumes in the Revolutionary Situation series appeared. In the first essay, Nechkina made her disagreements with Zaionchkovskii explicit; its title tells most of the story: "The Reforms of 1861 as a By-product of the Revolutionary Struggle."[27] In a historiographical essay, Nechkina observed that Lenin himself had coined her title phrase in a 1911 essay entitled "The Peasant Reform and the Prole-tarian-Peasant Revolution"; her essay suggested that no approach to the reform of 1861 was possible that was not grounded in the "revolutionary situation" concept.

After briefly criticizing pre-Soviet historiography and excoriating Pokrov-skii for neglect of the concept, she turned to Zaionchkovskii. After admitting that his *Abolition of Serfdom* had "deepened research on the question," especially with respect to the "realization of the Statutes of February 19" and his "scrupulous study" of thousands of land charters, she accused him of failing to understand that the reform was "wrested" from the government, as Lenin had understood. Radical intellectuals and rebellious peasants, in Zaionchkovskii's version, merely "helped the government realize the aboli-tion of serfdom by reformist means." Although the concept of the "revolu-tionary situation" was not absent from his work, it was mentioned only once and as an "abstract formula." Zaionchkovskii did not take the role of the masses seriously, she noted indignantly, nor the creation of "revolutionary organizations." Even Herzen and Chernyshevskii were not accorded much importance, merely a background role in the "preparation of the reform."[28]

Even scholars not disposed to base their understanding of the Emancipa-tion of the serfs on the idea of the "revolutionary situation" can accept some of what went into it—certainly the idea that in the second half of the 1850s the Imperial regime was frightened about its long-term future and felt obliged to make changes that would help ensure that future. The period was also characterized by peasant unrest and the development of revolutionary ideas among intellectuals. Almost all non-Soviet students of late Imperial Russia, moreover, would agree with Lenin about the importance of the Emancipation settlement for the Revolution of 1905. Most Western histori-ans, however, have not accepted the view that the crisis of the Old Regime was sufficiently severe or immediate to be called a "revolutionary situation" or that the reforms were "wrested" from the regime by either intelligentsiia or peasant pressure; some would even deny that Russia was undergoing a "major crisis."[29]

Perhaps an even more serious criticism of the "revolutionary situation" rubric, suggested by several American scholars, is that it produced little significant work on the reforms themselves, as opposed to continuing the previous focus on the revolutionary movement, the "peasant movement," social classes, and so on.[30] Several of the best of the articles in the series, while paying tribute to the "revolutionary situation" formula, do little to support it in the text.[31]

Serious efforts to understand the genesis of the reforms of the 1860s in American historiography began with the publication in 1966 of Alfred J.

Rieber's *Politics of Autocracy*.[32] While quite aware of the divergent views of Nechkina and Zaionchkovskii on the autocracy's decision to reform, Rieber rejected the notion of the reforms having been "wrested" from the tsar as unproven and implausible, and took still a different view. Perhaps influenced by his early interest in foreign policy, he attempted, through the publication of forty-two letters from Tsar Alexander II to Prince Bariatinskii, to deepen and make more specific what he called "the vague thesis that the Crimean defeat exposed Russia's weakness and something drastic had had to be done to correct it." In an influential if rather speculative essay, Rieber argued that Alexander came to the conclusion that Russia's very existence was threatened by the poor performance of the army in the Crimean War (and the inordinate expense of maintaining it) and that he further concluded that the army could only be reformed if the entire military establishment were reformed, which necessitated the abolition of serfdom.[33]

Two years later, Terence Emmons's *Russian Landed Gentry and the Peasant Emancipation* appeared. Emmons accepted the general thrust of Rieber's estimate of the central importance of military defeat, but his emphasis fell on long-term and cultural factors, such as the complex feelings of shame about serfdom created in the minds of educated Russians by the Westernization of the past half-century, the influence within the country of a variety of economic points of view about the need for capital to develop the country, with serfdom prominent as a factor retarding that development, and so on. Emmons, who unlike Rieber had studied with Zaionchkovskii in Moscow, laid greater stress on the fear of peasant revolt and on economic change, but he also refused to accept the idea that the government had been forced to grant reforms.[34] Above all, Emmons stressed the "concern for social and political stability" that animated the tsar and his advisers and their fear of a peasant uprising if serfdom were maintained. Emmons clearly took the government's official explanation that the Emancipation had been necessitated by the deterioration of relations between masters and serfs more seriously than Rieber had, but he too saw in it some element of "blackmail."

In the mid-1970s came Daniel Field's *End of Serfdom,* a volume essentially devoted to the question of why the Emancipation of the serfs came about, a question which Field took to be largely synonymous with how it came about.[35] Field gave short shrift to the "revolutionary situation," pointing out that the fear of peasant unrest became a factor in the government's policy only after the decision to emancipate had already been taken.[36] He seemed not much more interested in the nexus, stressed by Rieber and Emmons, between the Crimean defeat and the decision to emancipate, pointing out the almost totally circumstantial nature of the evidence. Nor was he willing to give Alexander II any real credit as an emancipator.[37] Rather, he concluded, by the 1850s serfdom in Russia had lost all "supporting political and ideological structures." When the state, confusedly and diffidently, withdrew its support, the institution collapsed. That withdrawal could not be understood as a single decision by the tsar, or by the tsar and his bureaucratic advisers, but only as the outcome of an intricate political process that lasted some seven years.

Over the past decade or so, the differences that existed among American and Soviet scholars as the eight-volume Revoliutsionnaia Situatsiia series drew to a close seem to have diminished. It is difficult to escape the conclusion that détente has been hard on Nechkina's militant revolutionism and tendency to see everything in sharply dialectical "two-camp" terms.[38] This narrowing of differences is quite apparent in Zakharova's articles and especially in her book on the autocracy and the abolition of serfdom, *Samoderzhavie i otmena krepostnogo prava v Rossii* 1856–1861, published in 1984. Like her mentor Zaionchkovskii, Zakharova formally accepts the "revolutionary situation" rubric and believes that the reform was "wrested" from the regime. But she declares that scholars ought to expend more effort studying the crisis of the upper class rather than radicalism and the revolutionary movement, which have been studied, as she tartly puts it, "rather fully." Zakharova regards the Emancipation as part of a much longer reforming process, extending from the Baltic emancipations before 1820 up to the obligatory redemption of the allotments in 1883, although the heart of her book is an examination of the creation of the legislation in the Editorial Commissions.[39] Her account is very much in the tradition of Zaionchkovskii, with a rather determinist Marxist framework, but the stress falls on the creation of a reformist mandate and a reformist vision within it. Miliutin is treated as a reformist hero within a Marxist framework. Whatever the importance of "crisis" and fear—and Zakharova has demonstrated the impact of peasant uprisings in Estonia on the government in 1858—the abolition of serfdom was a lengthy and intricate process that cannot be reduced to a response to the "revolutionary situation." V. G. Chernukha's book on government policy in relation to the press in the 1860s and 1870s also accepts the "revolutionary situation" rubric in general terms but avoids Nechkina's interpretation. Chernukha carefully examines the liberal and conservative press, not merely the progressive organs of the Left, and provides a sophisticated account of government policy.[40] These studies further diminish the differences between those Russians and Americans who have experienced Zaionchkovskii's influence more or less directly.

Despite these encouraging signs of convergence, it is important not to lose sight of how divergent the histories of the American and Soviet historical professions have been. These quite different histories will make it difficult to develop a unified scholarly approach to the reforms, even in the era of glasnost, unless Soviet and American scholars consciously create such an agenda. Any consideration of a study of the Great Reforms forces us to acknowledge that both communities of historians have been largely averse— for quite different reasons—to institutional history. The commanding figure of Petr Andreevich Zaionchkovskii did much to bridge the gap for a generation now middle-aged, but it is not clear how powerful his legacy will be in either culture.[41]

In the United States, we may expect the prevailing lack of interest in institutional history to continue. There seems little evidence that the dominant interest in social and cultural history will soon give way to renewed concern for the institutional history of the state, despite the belief of a few prominent social historians that the state should be "brought back in." Much of the best American work of the past decade that has touched on the reforms was part of a focus on the problem of Russian and Soviet bureaucracy, generally from the standpoint of something like interest-group politics. These American scholars were in conscious revolt against a decadent version of the State School, which suggested that the study of politics in Russia could focus on the tsar and a few influential members of the elite. They too felt the influence of Zaionchkovskii, but they were also affected by the general collapse of the "totalitarian paradigm" among Western students of the Russian/Soviet world.[42] Like other American scholars in the past decade, they sought to grasp the complex process of Russian politics rather than trying to understand everything from the nature of the commands issued at the top. The interest in bureaucratic studies seems largely spent, however, leaving social history in triumphant control of the field among American historians concerned with nineteenth-century Russia.[43]

In Russia, on the other hand, we may anticipate a greater volume of serious studies of the political history of the Old Regime. It is probable that the political changes of the present day will foster a greater sense of connectedness to Russia's imperial past and allow such a sense to be expressed. There is a relationship between the development of what is now generally known as a "civil society" in Russia in the half century after 1861 and what is widely viewed as the recreation of such a society at the present time. No doubt some Soviet scholars at least will examine the meaning of such a relationship.

The civil society of later Imperial Russia grew out of the reforms of the 1860s, whether they were "great" or not. What kind of society will ultimately result from the political changes currently taking place in the Soviet Union is hidden in the future, but our renewed sense of the impact of political change on our social world should help us all stay interested in the remarkable changes that occurred in Russia not only during the "revolutionary situation" of 1859–61 but also during the twenty years from 1855 to 1874. Russia and the Soviet Union need both outsiders and insiders to write their history.

NOTES

1. See "Sovremennaia nemarksistskaia istoriografiia i sovetskaia istoricheskaia nauka", *Istoriia SSSR* 1 (1988): 172–202. A. N. Sakharov's theses for the roundtable

read in part: "Experience shows that at times 'our truth' is not completely irreproachable and that often an unconditionally negative attitude toward honest, objectivist-minded, non-Marxist researchers is not justified, nor is the relegation of their works to the category of pseudo-scholarship" (174).

2. A recent book questioning the plausibility of an ideal of objectivity is Joan Wallach Scott, *Gender and the Politics of History* (New York, 1988). On the debate over "objectivity," see Peter Novick, *That Noble Dream: The "Objectivity Question" and the American Historical Profession* (Cambridge, England, 1988). For thoughtful critiques of Novick, see James T. Kloppenberg, "Objectivity and Historicism: A Century of American Historical Writing," *American Historical Review* 94, no. 4 (October 1989): 1011–30, and Thomas L. Haskell, "Objectivity Is Not Neutrality: Rhetoric vs. Practice in Peter Novick's *That Noble Dream*," *History and Theory* 29 (1990), no. 2: 129–57.

3. See the rather critical essay of Ronald Grigor Suny, "Rehabilitating Tsarism: The Imperial Russian State and Its Historians," *Comparative Studies in Society and History* 31, no. 1 (January 1989): 168–79.

4. Arthur Adams, *Imperial Russia after 1861: Peaceful Modernization or Revolution?* (Boston, 1965), vi. See also George Kennan, "The Breakdown of the Tsarist Autocracy," and the ensuing discussion in Richard Pipes, ed., *Revolutionary Russia: A Symposium* (Garden City, N.Y., 1969), 1–32, and Alfred J. Rieber, *The Politics of Autocracy* (Paris/The Hague, 1966), 15.

5. Terence Emmons, *The Russian Landed Gentry and the Peasant Emancipation of 1861* (Cambridge, England, 1968), 414.

6. For a sense of how recently Soviet historiography began to deal with the Emancipation, see P. A. Zaionchkovskii, "Sovetskaia istoriografiia reformy 1861 goda," *Voprosy istorii* 2 (February 1961): 85–104, esp. 91–102. See also B. G. Litvak, "Sovetskaia istoriografiia reformy 19 fevralia 1861 g.," *Istoriia SSSR* 6 (November–December 1960): 99–120.

7. "All of these fine books and articles," Daniel Field concluded his survey of Soviet historiography on the Great Reforms written more than a decade ago, "concentrated on the aspect of the great reforms that is most remote from institutional and legislative history and correspondingly close to the soil. They have fastened on the economic components of the reform—the size of allotments, the amount of dues, the pace and form of redemption—that were of immediate and vital significance for the millions of Russian peasants, and apparently care even less about the zemstvo, the new courts, the reformed censorship, and the universities than the peasants did." See Field, "The Reforms of the 1860s," in S. H. Baron and Nancy Heer, eds., *Windows on the Russian Past* (Columbus, Ohio, 1977), 101.

8. "The Emancipation as a historiographical problem," Terence Emmons observed, "has to some extent become a pawn in a neo-Scholastic concern with the proper interpretation and periodization of Russian history." Emmons, ed., *Emancipation of the Russian Serfs* (New York, 1970), 3. See also his remarks in the introduction to the English translation of Zaionchkovskii's *Otmena krepostnogo prava:* Zaionchkovskii, *The Abolition of Serfdom in Russia* (Gulf Breeze, Fla., 1978), viii–x.

9. See Konstantin Shteppa, *Russian Historians and the Soviet State* (New Brunswick, N.J., 1962), 121–206 and passim.

10. Field, "Reforms of the 1860s," 95.

11. See Abbott Gleason's brief "Glasnost' in Russian History," *Sovset News* 3, no. 1 (Jan. 27, 1987). Vladimir Shliapentokh, "Aleksandr II i Mikhail Gorbachev" (*Vremia i my* 97 [1987]: 104–22), is more ambitious but also more schematic and too much given to one-to-one comparisons.

12. N. Ia. Eidel'man, "'Revoliutsiia sverku' v Rossii," *Nauka i zhizn'* 10–12 (1988) and 1–3 (1989); Gavriil Popov, "Fasad i kukhnia 'velikoi reformy'," *Eko* 1 (1987):

144-74; L. G. Zakharova, "1861: Reformy i reformatory. Iz istorii otmeny krepostnogo prava v Rossii," *Nedelia* 5 (1989).

13. L. G. Zakharova, *Samoderzhavie i otmena krepostnogo prava v Rossii
1856–1861* (Moscow, 1984).

14. It is "revolutionary *perestroika*," according to Larissa Zakharova, "that has
again placed before society and historians the task of answering many 'difficult
questions' [about the past], among them those of alternatives in social development,
'revolution from above,' the question of the role of personality in history." Zakharova, "1861: Reforma i reformatory."

15. I use the term *Whig history* in the customary general sense, to mean a teleo-
logical kind of history writing, where one's own historical situation is more or less
consciously justified by the way in which one depicts historical development. The
reference was originally to English historians of a Whig persuasion, from Thomas
Babington Macaulay to George Trevelyan. See Herbert Butterfield, *The Whig Interpretation of History* (London, 1951). Of course, there were Whiggish elements in the
treatment of Soviet history by American historians during the Cold War as well.
Stephen Cohen makes that case in "Sovietology as a Vocation," *Rethinking the
Soviet Experience* (New York, 1985), 19–27.

16. *Istoriia SSSR* 4 (July–August 1963): 183. It is easier for an institutional historian than a social historian to admire the Great Reforms. Surely the fact that Druzhinin was a historian of rural Russia in the nineteenth century rather than of gentry
politics partially accounts for his attitude. Some non-Soviet social historians familiar
with the situation of the Russian village between 1861 and 1917 might agree. It may
be more difficult, in various ways, for Soviet historians really to feel that the reforms
were "great." "The Great Reforms did not . . . bring any perceptible improvement
in well-being to those who did not happen to be vigorous, venturesome and lucky.
It is the fate of this mass of the common people that provides the touchstone for
most Soviet historians." Field, "Reforms of the 1860s," 96.

17. See the informative obituaries by Alfred J. Rieber (*Jahrbücher für Geschichte
Osteuropas* 33 [1985]: 313–16, Daniel Field (*Russian Review* 42, no. 3 [July 1983]:
v–vii), and Terrence Emmons (*Slavic Review* 42, no. 4 [Winter 1983]: 742–43).

18. Emmons, *Slavic Review* 42, no. 4 (Winter 1983): 743.

19. Field agrees, noting that Zaionchkovskii's "favorite subject matter [was] high
politics, the doings of statesmen, generals and monarchs." *Russian Review* 42, no.
3 (July 1983): vi.

20. Terence Emmons, ed., *The Time of Troubles: The Diary of Iurii Vladimirovich
Got'e. Moscow July 8, 1917 to July 23, 1922* (Princeton, N.J., 1988), 12.

21. P. A. Zaionchkovskii, *Voennye reformy 1860–1870 godov v Rossii* (Moscow,
1952); *Provedenie v zhizn' krestianskoi reformy 1861 g.* (Moscow, 1958). *Otmena
krepostnogo prava v Rossii* (Moscow, 1954 [1960, 1968]) is essentially a high-level
popularization.

22. P. A. Zaionchkovskii, *Dnevnik D. A. Miliutina. 1873–1882*, vols. 1–4 (Moscow,
1947–50); *Dnevnik P. A. Valueva, ministra vnutrennykh del*, 2 vols. (Moscow, 1961).
For additional bibliographical information, see *Petr Andreevich Zaionchkovskii. K
semidesiatiletiiu so dnia rozhdeniia* (Moscow, 1974).

23. *Istoriia SSSR* 2 (March–April 1958): 225–29. The eight scholars were Nechkina, I. Ia. Linkov, A. F. Smirnov, S. V. Tokarev, I. I. Miller, V. A. Fedorov, I. S.
Kobetskii, I. N. Koblents.

24. "Krakh II Internatsionala," *Sobranie sochinenii* (Moscow, 1964), 213–14.

25. Quoted in M. V. Nechkina, "Revoliutsionnaia situatsiia v Rossii v iskhode
1850-kh—nachale 1860-kh godov," *Revoliutsionnaia situatsiia v Rossii v 1859–1861
gg.* (Moscow, 1960), 9.

26. In addition to the volumes themselves, see Charles C. Adler, Jr., "The 'Revolutionary Situation 1859–1961': The Uses of an Historical Conception," *Canadian*

Slavic Studies 3, no. 2 (Summer 1969): 383–89, and Alan Kimball, "Revolutionary Situation in Russia (1859–1862)," *Modern Encyclopedia of Russian and Soviet History*, vol. 31 (Gulf Breeze, Fla., 1983), 54–57. Field's "Reforms of the 1860s" contains a number of shrewd and trenchant observations on the "revolutionary situation" and the historiography it produced.

27. M. V. Nechkina, "Reforma 1861 goda kak pobochnyi produkt revoliutsionnoi bor'by," *Revoliutsionnaia situatsiia v Rossii v 1859–1861 gg.* (Moscow, 1962), 7–17. As B. G. Litvak and Alfred J. Rieber noted more than twenty years ago, Nechkina's most important predecessor in her insistence on the reforms as the result of pressure from below was E. A. Morokhovets, especially in his *Krestianskaia reforma 1861 g.* (Moscow, 1937), although he did not employ the Leninist formulae.

28. Ibid., 12–14. Adler, "The 'Revolutionary Situation,'" 389.

29. See, for example, Walter Pintner, "Reformability in the Age of Reform and Counterreform, 1855–1894," in Robert O. Crummey, ed., *Reform in Russia and the USSR: Past and Prospects,* Urbana, Ill., 1989, 86–103.

30. Not counting Nechkina's essay asserting that the reform of 1861 was merely a by-product, there were really only four articles on the reforms in the entire eight volumes: Iu. V. Gerasimova, "Krizis pravitel'stvennoi politiki v revoliutsionnoi situatsii i Aleksandr II," *Revoliutsionnaia situatsiia v Rossii 1859–1861 gg.* (1962), 93–106; E. D. Dneprov, "Proekt ustava morskogo suda i ego rol' v podgotovke sudebnoi reformy (aprel' 1860 g.)," ibid. (1970), 57–70; R. G. Eimontova, "Revoliutsionnaia situatsiia i podgotovka universitetskoi reformy v Rossii," ibid. (1974), 60–80; and V. I. Neupokoiev, "Podatnoi vopros v khode reformy 1861 goda," ibid. (1978), 212–29.

31. As was the case, for instance, with Dneprov, "Proekt ustava morskogo suda."

32. In his historiographical introduction to *The Politics of Autocracy,* Rieber takes note not only of the controversy between Zaionchkovskii and Nechkina but also of Theodore Von Laue's reassertion of the older idea, espoused by Engels, that the Russian autocracy abolished serfdom "as a conscious effort to overcome Russia's backwardness." See Von Laue, "The State and the Economy," in Cyril Black, ed., *The Tranformation of Russian Society* (Cambridge, Mass., 1967), 209–25.

33. Rieber, *Politics of Autocracy,* 15–58 and passim.

34. Emmons, *Russian Landed Gentry,* esp. 3–52.

35. Daniel Field, *The End of Serfdom: Nobility and Bureaucracy in Russia, 1855–1861* (Cambridge, Mass., 1976).

36. In his recent response to Larissa Zakharova, Field has conceded a somewhat greater role to fear of peasant uprising in the government's preparation of the Emancipation. He remains convinced, however, that the fear of a peasant uprising did not precipitate "the regime's public commitment to a reform of serfdom in 1857." *Russian Review* 44, no. 1 (January 1985): vi. His laudatory remarks about Zakharova's book were warmly received by Soviet scholars. See the remarks of N. G. Dumova in "Sovremennaia nemarksistskaia istoriografia," 181.

37. This assertion has caused concern to some of his reviewers. For a critique (in my view, not convincing), based on the proposition that Alexander's seeming obtuseness and indecision was a clever mask, see Norman Peirera, "Alexander II and the Decision to Emancipate the Russian Serfs, 1855–61," *Canadian Slavonic Papers* 22 (1980): 99–115.

38. For an interesting contrast between Nechkina and other Soviet scholars on a different set of issues—those centering on the Decembrists—see John Gooding, "The Decembrists in the Soviet Union," *Soviet Studies* 40, no. 2 (April 1988): 196–209.

39. Zakharova, *Samoderzhavie i otmena krepostnogo prava v Rossii 1856–1861.*

40. V. G. Chernukha, *Pravitel'stvennaia politika v otnoshenii pechati 60–70–e gody XIX veka* (Leningrad, 1989).

41. A number of scholars close to Zaionchkovskii, including B. V. Anan'ich and I. V. Orzhekhovskii, have concerned themselves with the political history of the

regime while not writing directly on the reforms. See the latter's *Iz istorii vnutrennei politiki samoderzhaviia v 60–70kh godakh XIX veka* (Gorkii, 1974).

42. Important works include Richard Wortman, *The Development of a Russian Legal Consciousness* (Chicago, 1976); Walter McKenzie Pintner and Don Karl Rowney, *Russian Officialdom: The Bureaucratization of Russian Society from the Seventeenth to the Twentieth Century* (Chapel Hill, N.C., 1980); Daniel T. Orlovsky, *The Limits of Reform: The Ministry of Internal Affairs in Imperial Russia, 1802–1881* (Cambridge, Mass., 1981); and W. Bruce Lincoln, *In the Vanguard of Reform: Russia's Enlightened Bureaucrats, 1826–1861* (DeKalb, Ill, 1982). W. Bruce Lincoln, *The Great Reforms: Autocracy, Bureaucracy and the Politics of Change in Imperial Russia* (DeKalb, Ill., 1990), readably summarizes this research as well as recent writings on the radicalism of the period. For a detailed survey of the first few years of this literature, see Daniel Orlovsky, "Recent Studies on the Russian Bureaucracy," *Russian Review* 35 (October 1976): 448–67.

43. One should not neglect the continuing interest of West German scholars in studies of the Russian bureaucracy. Erik Amburger, *Geschichte der Behördenorganisation Russlands von Peter dem Grossen bis 1917* (Leiden, 1966), is an impressive general study, as is Hans-Joachim Torke, "Das russische Beamtentum in der ersten Hälfte des 19. Jahrhunderts," *Forschungen zur osteuropäischen Geschichte,* 13 (1967): 7–345. Friedhelm Berthold Kaiser, *Die Russische Justizreform von 1864* (Leiden, 1972), is a comprehensive monograph.

Part I
State and Reform

II

AUTOCRACY AND THE REFORMS OF 1861–1874 IN RUSSIA
CHOOSING PATHS OF DEVELOPMENT

Larissa Zakharova
Translated by Daniel Field

The abolition of serfdom in Russia and the reforms associated with it—reforms that were called "great" before the revolution and "bourgeois" during the Soviet period—have attracted unremitting interest. At times this interest has acquired a special intensity, taken on a political coloration, and even found expression in polemical journalism. Now, when journalists and many of their readers in the former USSR are focusing on such questions as alternative paths of development, reform (or "revolution from above"), the role of the individual in the historical process, and Russia's place in the system of European powers, interest in the reforms of the mid–nineteenth century has reached its highest level since they were enacted. Economists, philosophers, writers, and political leaders have taken to writing about the most important of these reforms, the abolition of serfdom. Thus reforms are once again part of society's agenda.

The intensity of this interest obliges professional historians to turn again to the history of these reforms, to interpret them in the light of the problematic of current historical scholarship, and to illuminate aspects that have been neglected or ignored. We are obliged in particular to show the interconnections of the main reforms—the peasant reform of 1861, the establishment of the zemstvo in 1864, the reform of the courts in 1864, and the reform of city government in 1870—and the relationship of all these reforms to the issue of a constitution.

The abolition of serfdom was a watershed, a turning point in Russian history. Contemporaries ranging from the authors of the legislation to the novelists Tolstoi and Saltykov-Shchedrin understood the reform in that sense, and so have generations of scholars and the founders of Marxism-Leninism. Although this overturn was comparable in its consequences to the bourgeois revolutions of Europe, it was accomplished from above; state power took the initiative and played a determining role. Key issues, which historical scholarship has not fully elucidated, are the causes of the reform and the motives that prompted the autocracy (both the tsar himself and the bureaucracy) to act.

The Government's Initiative and Its Causes

There are certain textbook commonplaces that are acknowledged by all scholars, both those who consider Alexander II a liberator and those who deny him that distinction. It was Alexander II who, in a speech delivered in Moscow on March 30, 1856, to the marshals of the nobility, pronounced the fateful words, "it is much better that this [the emancipation of the peasants] come from above, than from below." It was with his consent that, at the time of the coronation in August, the new minister of internal affairs, S. S. Lanskoi, and his deputy, A. I. Levshin, negotiated with the marshals of the nobility in an attempt to get them to submit petitions to the tsar in favor of emancipation. It is beyond question that autocracy took the initiative, although timidly. What were the immediate motives that made the monarchy undertake the abolition of the institution that was its foundation?

Unlike his brother, the Grand Duke Konstantin Nikolaevich, Alexander II was not a man of liberal beliefs. In the fifteen years prior to his ascent to the throne, he had participated in both civil and military affairs without deviating from the reactionary political course Nicholas I had set. He chaired the most reactionary of the secret committees on the peasant question, those of 1846 and 1848, and participated in the establishment of the Buturlin Committee on the censorship. His initial speeches to the Council of State on the day of his accession and to the diplomatic corps four days later did not prefigure any changes. He did, however, have qualities that helped him to find his way amid the complex domestic and international political issues that confronted him. Among these qualities were his common sense, which his tutors and all his contemporaries appreciated; his capacity to size up a situation quickly and to grasp it as a whole; his lack of fanaticism; and the education he had received under the direction of the poet Zhukovskii, who had seen to it that humane and humanitarian values prevailed over the factitious precepts of ideology.

Defeat in the Crimean War prompted a perception of the flaws in the foreign-policy aspects of the Nicolaevan system and a desire to overcome Russia's isolation. Concern for European public opinion, which was at odds with the vainglorious ideology of "official nationality," was apparent in the first steps taken by the administration of Alexander II, even before it addressed the peasant question. In the middle of 1855, the government established a newspaper, *Le Nord,* in Belgium. Its purpose, as Lanskoi formulated it, was to "acquaint Europe with the real situation in Russia," "to attempt to eliminate false and groundless conceptions about our fatherland." There followed a circular to provincial governors with instructions to encourage the circulation of "so useful a publication." Significantly, the government's first declaration concerning reforms was contained in the Manifesto of March 19, 1856, on the occasion of the Peace of Paris. And when, in November 1857, the government adopted the rescript to Nazimov, which set the abolition of serfdom in motion, the rescript was published first in *Le Nord* and only subsequently in Russia.[1]

In the eyes of European public opinion, Russia's rapprochement with France—evidence of a break with the old traditions of the disintegrated Holy Alliance—was linked to a turn toward a more liberal course in the domestic policies of Alexander II. The same tendency is particularly apparent in a letter Alexander II sent in 1859 in response to an appeal from Pope Pius IX. Dismissing reproaches that he was too well-disposed to Napoleon III and put too much trust in him, Alexander wrote:

> As regards the baneful reforms which, according to Your Holiness, he prompted me to undertake, I can respond only as follows: I have been an adult for a good many years, and although I have no pretensions to genius, I do believe that I have too much common sense to follow anyone's promptings unless they correspond to my own convictions! What baneful reforms would I permit in my realm? If Your Holiness is hinting at my determination to abolish serfdom, can the supreme Christian pastor call that reform "baneful"? . . . If, on the occasion of the conclusion of the Peace of Paris, the emperor Napoleon did indeed encourage me to undertake that reform, perhaps a few months earlier than I had thought of doing, the edifice of my state did not suffer thereby in the least.[2]

The necessity of restoring the prestige Russia had lost in the international arena compelled Alexander II and his government to seek new paths and undertake new solutions.[3]

Another major stimulus to action for Alexander II and his administration was the realization that the domestic political course associated with the Nicolaevan system was in a state of crisis. The seal that Nicholas I had placed upon the printed word, and especially the "censorship terror" of the "dark seven years" (1848–55), was shattered by educated society's passionate and irrepressible need to speak out and produced an utterly contrary result, the circulation on a scale hitherto unknown of manuscript literature.[4] Glasnost emerged spontaneously, not "by disposition of the tsar" *(po maniiu tsaria).*[5] The government was trailing after events when it lifted extraordinary restrictions on the press. Only later would it take up glasnost as a weapon for its own political arsenal. Herzen appreciated the situation very well. Understanding how much his country needed the word of truth after an extended period of silence and dishonesty, he established the Free Russian Press in London in 1853 and there founded a series of journals: *Poliar-*

naia zvezda in 1855, *Golosa iz Rossii* in 1856, and *Kolokol* in 1857; all readers in Russia, including the tsar and tsaritsa, were familiar with these journals.

The word *glasnost,* like *thaw,* epitomizes the year 1856. Glasnost included exposé, but what was inspiring was its creative side, the constructive proposals and plans that it generated and that charged it with optimism and bright hopes. Thanks to glasnost, the gnawing fear that had been a characteristic trait of the Nicolaevan system began to disperse. The emancipation of the moral and intellectual forces of society preceded the turn to reform and was prerequisite to it.

Another powerful stimulus was economic. The government had long been aware that hired labor was more profitable than compulsory and that the servile structure retarded commodity production of grain and the development of agriculture in general. Now a symptom of the untenability of the existing servile structure of the economy made itself felt in an ominous way, and in a sphere to which the government was particularly sensitive—state finance. Between 1853 and 1858, the overall deficit increased from fifty-two million silver rubles to 307; the gold that backed paper money decreased by more than half, and the proportion of state revenues that came from the proceeds of liquor farming increased from one-third in 1845 to 43 percent in 1853–56. The celebrated economist Tengoborskii concluded in a memorandum of January 1857, "It is necessary at once to take the most radical measures to diminish expenditures . . . for otherwise bankruptcy is inevitable for the state."[6] The ever-growing budget deficit put the country on the brink of fiscal crisis and pushed the "top men" *(verkhi)* toward reform. On March 9 (March 20 NS), 1857, Alexander II wrote to his brother the Grand Duke Konstantin Nikolaevich, a member of the finance committee who was then traveling abroad, "I am extremely concerned now about our financial situation, it has reached the point where we must try to relieve it by any means possible." In his letter of reply and in his diary, Konstantin Nikolaevich in turn revealed that he was no less concerned by the "catastrophic financial situation." The situation of banks was no less catastrophic. In the two years between July 1857 and July 1859, the liquid assets of savings banks decreased from 150 million rubles to thirteen million; the government had to acknowledge that the condition and activities of banks also constituted a crisis.

The change of reigns corresponded with striking manifestations of the perception of the need for fundamental reforms, dictated by both external and domestic considerations, and thus with the crisis of the entire Nicolaevan system. Three months after the death of Nicholas I, M. P. Pogodin, who had been one of the ideologues of the old system, pronounced that "the old system has outlived its time." Renouncing the old system meant renouncing its ideological foundation, the theory of official nationality. Innovation in domestic policy found expression in the relaxation or elimination of a multitude of restrictions. Passports for travel abroad could now be freely issued; the number of persons departing abroad increased 4.5 times from 1856 through 1859, from six thousand to twenty-six thousand per year. The censorship was relaxed, as were various restrictions on the universities. Russian subjects were encouraged to "strengthen our commercial links with foreign nations and to adopt therefrom the advances in science that have been achieved in recent years in Europe." Relief also took such forms as the abolition of the military colonies,[7] a diminution in the size of the army, a suspension of conscription for three years, and amnesty for communities that had not met their quota of recruits. Most important, on the occasion of the coronation in August 1856, an amnesty was declared for political prisoners—surviving Decembrists, Petrashevtsy, and participants in the Polish insurrection of 1831; in all, nine thousand persons were freed from the control of the police and bureaucracy.[8]

Interesting information on the response of European society to the first measures of the administration of Alexander II can be found in a letter to D. A. Miliutin from A. V. Golovnin, who was accompanying the Grand Duke Konstantin Nikolaevich on his trip abroad in the summer of 1858:

> In Paris I saw some of the acquaintances I made last year, picking out the more intelligent among them, and we talked a great deal about events here and in Russia. Their view of our situation was especially interesting to me. They are overwhelmed by many of the measures that have been taken in our country. . . . They praise them exceedingly and predict that remarkable development lies in Russia's future. It is clear that at present it is internal development that gives Russia standing in European politics.[9]

No less interesting is the reaction of Dmitrii Miliutin himself to the new trends and new measures. Visiting St. Petersburg after a year's absence, he wrote on October 28, 1857, to Prince A. I. Bariatinskii, his commanding officer in the Caucasus: "What I found here, by and large, was an astonishing phenomenon: one and all are in the grip of an aspiration to reform and are trying to think up something new; they want to break down everything before they have thought out any replacement."[10]

A sense that large-scale transformations were impending, a feeling that a rare and extraordinary crisis was taking shape in the country, were characteristic of the era. It is significant that Lev Tolstoi compared this period of Russian history to the French Revolution of 1789.

Alternative Plans for Serfdom; the Disposition of Forces

When it took the initiative and addressed the peasant question, the government did not yet have either a definite plan of action or a program of reform. The preparation of the first and most important reform, the abolition of serfdom, had begun in a thoroughly traditional way in 1857 when yet another secret committee was convened in the Winter Palace. The committee, in turn, followed the traditions observed by the secret committees of the reign of Nicholas I: it tried to confine itself to expanding the application of such palliative measures as the decree of 1803 on free agriculturalists and that of 1842 on obligated peasants. In the new circumstances, however, given the advancing social and political thaw and in the face of a universal expectation of change, this reactionary reflex was soon overcome. The rescript of November 20, 1857, to V. I. Nazimov, governor-general at Vilnius—that is, the document that is generally held to mark the beginning of the abolition of serfdom—does not show any trace of the Secret Committee's initial plan. Its real underpinnings were two contrasting solutions of the peasant question that had already been approved and put into effect in delimited localities. These variants were the inventory reform launched in the Southwest (Kiev, Podolia, and Volynia Provinces) in 1848 and the emancipation of the peasants in the three Baltic provinces in 1816–19. The rescript reveals that at that moment the government had in mind some kind of variant intermediate between the two: the squires would retain a property right to all their land; peasants would gain the right to redeem only their household plots and the right to cultivate allotments of plowland in exchange for dues; the squire would retain his manorial authority. Moreover, while the legal position of the peasants was defined only by the vague phrase "amelioration of [their] way of life," the ultimate goal of the reform was not specified. Both the limited territorial scope of the rescript and its substantive elements demonstrate that initially the government intended to work from enacted and time-tested models and was not oriented toward a radically new solution of the peasant question.

What was new in the government's policy and signified a deliberate rupture with the practices of the past was glasnost. In rapid order the rescript was printed and distributed to governors and marshals of the nobility in all the provinces of European Russia. This action amounted to a declaration that the reform would be nationwide in scope and at the same time represented an appeal to the nobility for support of a kind that would look like "initiative" on its part. A week later the rescript appeared in the government's official newspaper, *Le Nord,* and on December 5 Alexander II sent a rescript to P. I. Ignat'ev, governor-general of St. Petersburg Province; then both rescripts appeared in the *Journal of the Ministry of Internal Affairs* and were also published in French and German. The fateful word had been spoken, the Rubicon lay behind. The preparation of the reform had passed outside the confines of the Secret Committee and government agencies. From this moment on, the government remained on top of events, but it would have to deal with the incalculable and unanticipated.

Although the nobility was hostile to the reform, government pressure compelled it to come forward with an "initiative" in favor of the application of the rescripts nationwide. In 1858 and the first half of 1859, forty-six provincial committees of the nobility (plus two interprovincial commissions) involving some fifteen hundred men convened across European Russia. These committees represented a new device in the history of reform. As they set to work, party divisions within the nobility came to light, and a liberal minority and a conservative or reactionary majority took shape in almost every committee. Representatives of various generations and various sociopolitical tendencies took part: amnestied Decembrists and Petrashevtsy, Slavophiles and Westernizers, and both partisans and opponents of the abolition of serfdom. Without seeking or awaiting instructions, the committees opened their sessions to the public, lithographed journals of their proceedings, indulged in party politics, and set up communications with one another (here A. I. Koshelev, Iu. F. Samarin, A. M. Unkovskii, V. A. Cherkasskii and other liberals took the lead). The committees were like a school, and the curriculum included how to discuss and resolve matters of state, how to carry on political struggle—in short, elementary constitutionalism. Glasnost took on unexpected forms with unexpected consequences. The press flexed its muscles, while the censorship lagged behind events.

The struggle within the nobility that unfolded in provincial capitals was, as Lenin put it, a struggle "solely over the extent and form of concessions." At issue were variants of the proposed reform. Some nobles held that the nobility should retain all its landed property and its manorial power—that is, that the peasants should be left landless—while others held that the peasants should be required to redeem some of their allotment land and that the squires' manorial power should be abolished; these latter saw the abolition of serfdom as part of a system of reforms that would lay the foundations of a *Rechtstaat*. The Main Committee, as the Secret Committee was now called, was drawn into a whirlpool of events, to which it had to react.

The government followed events closely, keeping an eye on the nobility, public opinion, and the press but paying special attention to the peasantry, which was tensely awaiting its fate. From the first rescript in 1857 through the abolition of serfdom in 1861, the minister of internal affairs was required by Alexander II to submit weekly reports on the mood of the nobility and the peasantry, on "rumors" and "gossip" in the provinces, on the activities of the provincial committees, and—this was a compulsory element—on all instances of peasant upheaval.[11]

In Soviet scholarship the role of the peasant movement in the abolition of serfdom has, of course, been exaggerated. This tradition goes back to the 1930s. It must be overcome without going to the opposite extreme. Although the peasants' protest was unorganized, spontaneous, and weak, the peasantry, as Saltykov-Shchedrin put it in 1863, "was able to put its indelible brand on the reform." As early as the end of the Crimean War, when the government's appeal to join infantry and marine militia units aroused the peasants' hopes for emancipation, there ensued a massive movement of the peasant population "posing a threat to tranquillity and order." And in June 1856, after the conclusion of peace, twelve thousand peasants set out for the Crimea, inspired by rumors that "circulated everywhere" about the emancipation of the peasants.[12]

The government's public commitment to reform did not at first evoke any dangerous response. The tense expectation of freedom was not disrupted by any major disturbance. Massive peasant protest did find expression later, in 1859, in the "sobriety movement."[13] But even earlier there was danger from an unexpected quarter. In Estonia, where serfdom had been abolished forty years earlier, peasant uprisings broke out in April 1858 in connection with the implementation of a new law that brought no relief to the landless peasantry. The uprisings lasted more than three months, took on massive proportions, and evolved into armed struggle (the "Makhtra War"). These uprisings were not so important in and of themselves as in the context of the sociopolitical situation in the nation at large. Although the uprisings were suppressed, the "Baltic variant" lost its luster in the eyes of Alexander II and the position of its many partisans within the government was weakened. Radical journals abetted this process. Herzen's *Kolokol* unmasked the "elder statesmen" who wanted to follow the Baltic example and deprive the peasants of land throughout Russia, while Chernyshevskii's *Sovremennik* defended the principle of emancipation with land for the peasants. Finally, although there was no immediate danger of an insurrection, memories of peasant wars of the past, especially the Pugachev Rebellion, and of the participation of the peasantry in European revolutions, magnified many times over the fear of "the lower depths" at "the top."

Against this background—the ongoing struggle between minorities and majorities in the provincial committees, the peasant uprisings in Estonia, the shaken authority of the "Baltic experience"—a new line of government policy began to emerge and quickly achieve dominance. According to this line, the ultimate objective of the reform should be the conversion of the peasants into the owners of their allotments, the abolition of the squires' manorial power, and the incorporation of the peasantry into the civil life of the nation. This line was put forth by a group of liberal bureaucrats headed by N. A. Miliutin, who from the middle of 1858 exercised decisive influence on the drafting of legislation abolishing serfdom and reforming local administration.

The liberal bureaucrats (some American historians prefer to call them "enlightened bureaucrats") began to emerge as early as the 1840s. They coalesced in the depths of ministries and agencies, not in isolation but rather in company with liberal scholars, writers, and other public figures. This collaboration culminated in 1845 in the founding of the Imperial Russian Geographical Society under the chairmanship of Grand Duke Konstantin Nikolaevich, who was a steady supporter of the liberal bureaucrats. By virtue of its status and personnel, the Geographical Society was subordinate to the Ministry of Internal Affairs, where the energetic activity of the liberal bureaucrats was particularly conspicuous. Nikolai Miliutin served there as director of the Economic Department and, between April 1859 and April 1861, as deputy minister (properly speaking, as "acting deputy minister").

In 1856, with the onset of the thaw, Miliutin was ready with a solution to the peasant question. He set forth his solution in a memorandum on the

emancipation of the serfs of Karlovka, an estate in Poltava Province belonging to the Grand Duchess Elena Pavlovna, who was Alexander II's aunt.
This memorandum would be the prototype for the reform of 1861, but in
1857, just before the establishment of the Secret Committee, Alexander II
emphatically rejected it. Miliutin was also in charge of the reform of local
administration, both urban (the reform of the city government of St. Petersburg in 1846) and rural (he worked out the zemstvo reform within the ministry in 1856, with the assistance of Saltykov-Shchedrin). Almost simultaneously, legal experts were working out the bases for a new system of
courts and court procedure. Even earlier, in 1854, the Naval Ministry underwent reform at the initiative of Konstantin Nikolaevich. No single document
set forth an overall program embracing all the impending reforms, but there
were links among the various drafts and plans. These consisted of the shared
principles and common points of departure that united the liberal bureaucrats. In the bureaucratic milieu, these men were a new breed, men of the
forties who stood ready, if circumstances should permit, to take up the task
of reform. The break in circumstances, the moment they had been waiting
for, came in the fall of 1858.

Looming over the liberalization of the government's policy concerning
the abolition of serfdom (and the other associated reforms) was the figure
of Adjutant-General Ia. I. Rostovtsev, a member of the Main Committee and
a close friend of Alexander II's. Amid the feverishly changing social and
political situation in Russia, Rostovtsev was able, because he enjoyed the
monarch's complete confidence, to facilitate the acceptance of the liberal
bureaucrats' programs and the consolidation of their positions. After much
effort, thought, and reflection, he renounced the landless variant of emancipation and adopted the liberal goals and ideas, which as late as April 1858
(when K. D. Kavelin was banished from the court for publishing in *Sovremennik* an article on the redemption of the peasants' allotments) were still
under ban and subject to persecution. The causes of Rostovtsev's conversion into a "zealous progressive and emancipator" are various and reasonably well known. Most important, I believe, was a personal motive, a wish to
clear himself of accusations of betraying the Decembrists and to rehabilitate
himself in the eyes of his son, the Decembrists (his sometime friends, now
returning from exile), and society at large.[14] Rostovtsev was deeply shaken
by the deathbed plea of his younger son in 1858 to "help the cause of emancipation" and restore honor to the family name, besmirched during the uprising of December 1825. The theme of "repentance" has a venerable tradition
in Russian history, although in various eras it takes on varying significance
in society and in the interactions of "fathers and sons." On the eve of the
reforms of the 1860s, at a time of rising social energies and bright hopes,
repentance brought father together with son, successful functionary together
with Decembrists who had been shunned by society for thirty years and
now returned thanks to the amnesty. Repentance flowed into the general
process that culminated in the abolition of serfdom. Through Rostovtsev,

through the Decembrists who served on provincial committees, De-
cembrism found one of its outlets, flowing into the history of the reforms of
Alexander II.

Rostovtsev set forth his new views on the peasant question in four "most
dutiful" letters that he sent from abroad to Alexander II in August–
September 1858. Alexander II turned these letters over to the Main Committee for discussion. Lanskoi had already smuggled in a petition from the
Tver' Provincial Committee favoring expanding redemption from household
plots to plowland. Now, on December 4, 1858, under pressure from Alexander II, who shared Rostovtsev's reviews, the committee and therefore the
government adopted a new program on the peasant question. The essence
of the program was the formation of a class of peasant proprietors, that is,
the redemption of allotment land from the squires and the emergence of a
two-tiered agrarian economy, consisting of a tier of large manorial units and
another of peasant household units. A majority of the Main Committee
opposed the program, but Alexander II cut off the debate and pronounced
the question resolved.[15]

The acceptance of the new program—which, incidentally, the government
could not bring itself to publicize as it had the rescript—necessarily
strengthened the position of the liberal bureaucrats, who exemplified the
creative potential of the existing political system. Alexander II's refusal in
October 1856 to approve the preliminary plan to set free the peasants of
Karlovka did not deter Nikolai Miliutin. Work continued for two years, with
the participation of Kavelin and Cherkasskii, among others. The plan was
ready by the end of 1858. It was discussed by the Main Committee and, on
February 1, 1859, approved by Alexander II.[16] Now the liberal bureaucrats
faced the challenge of converting a prototype intended for a particular private holding into statute law of general application. Meeting this challenge
entailed conquering new positions "on top." The upshot was another metamorphosis, analogous to the leaps from secrecy to glasnost and from the
rescript to the new program, a metamorphosis in the very structure of state
power at the highest level: the establishment of a new and unprecedented
institution, the Editorial Commissions.[17] The metamorphosis proved ephemeral, but it was decisive for the history of the abolition of serfdom and, in
the last analysis, for the history of the other reforms.

Liberal Bureaucrats, Autocracy, and Conceptions of Reform

The scale that the preparation of the peasant reform had assumed overwhelmed the capacity of the Main Committee and the traditional institutions
of the autocratic monarchy as a whole. It turned out that the minorities and
majorities of the provincial committees were compiling separate drafts, so
that the total was not forty-eight drafts, as expected, but about a hundred.
Matters were further complicated: the work of the committees had been

governed by the rescripts, while the government had adopted a new program on December 4, 1858, and, in the process, had given up the ideas of a separate local statute for each province and of proceeding gradually from west to east. It was necessary to legislate for all of Russia and to produce a new kind of law, distinct from the statutes issued in decades past. The elderly members of the Main Committee were not up to the work. What was needed was creative and constructive forces and an overall conception of the transformation; what was needed was new men. On February 17, 1859, Alexander II sanctioned the creation of the Editorial Commission, setting the sole condition that Rostovtsev, who was personally devoted to him, would serve as chairman. Soon public opinion in Russia and in Europe fixed upon the commission. Contemporaries saw the independent, autonomous commission as "without precedent in Russia."

The commission was untraditional first of all because a majority of its members were liberal activists who had, under the leadership of liberal bureaucrats, worked out a common platform and a common conception of reform. These were men of a single generation (most of them between thirty-five and forty-five), many of whom were notable statesmen or public figures: Iurii Samarin, P. P. Semenov-Tian-Shanskii, N. Kh. Bunge, and Prince Cherkasskii. By common consent their leader was N. A. Miliutin, who was endowed with the mind of a statesman, enormous dedication, and a passionate temperament combined with political selflessness. To be sure, adherents of serfdom and large landowners were represented on the commission, but they were in the minority. The formation of a liberal majority on the commission took on special significance in light of the overall balance of forces; liberals were in the minority on the provincial committees, among the nobility as a whole, and within the bureaucracy, both in its highest reaches and in local administration. The commission was no less at odds with tradition in the character of its activity. It used glasnost as a new kind of instrument of state policy. The proceedings of the commission were promptly sent to be printed and distributed in an edition of three thousand copies. Glasnost was also used to bolster the liberal forces in the country and to disseminate the liberal program of reform. When arguments broke out within the commission, Miliutin would tell his allies, "This is no time for disagreements. It will be well if we manage to sow some seeds." The commission worked at a rapid pace, without the usual delays and dilatoriness. No less characteristic was the way in which the commission's work was grounded in solid scholarly knowledge and the members' high level of accountability. They appreciated that they were involved in determining Russia's history and fate. They saw themselves as answerable to their fellow countrymen, to European public opinion, and to the judgment of posterity and history. They affixed their signatures to the published proceedings.

The Editorial Commission occupied a unique place in the political system. It was, through its chairman, directly subordinate to the emperor and constituted a "separate temporary institution of state," so to speak. It was "incorporated," as the saying went at the time, into the state structure of autocracy in a moment of "crisis at the top." Because the commission was by its very nature alien to the prevailing structure of the government, it was never given the kind of meeting place and office that were allotted to governmental institutions; for the same reason, it was abruptly shut down in October 1860. Never again in Russia would an institution like the Editorial Commission of 1859–60 be convened, but the conceptions it developed and the drafts it produced would form the basis for the statutes of February 19, 1861, and, in many respects, would determine the character and scale of the other reforms.

As the liberal majority of the Editorial Commission conceived it, the peasant reform, although embodied in a single legislative act, would be a process. The first stage would be eliminating the personal bondage of the serfs and the final stage would be their conversion into petty peasant proprietors, although noble landholdings and large-scale manorial agriculture would be retained to a significant extent. This goal was to be attained peacefully, avoiding the revolutionary upheavals that had been the lot of the nations of Western and Central Europe. An explanatory note to the final version of the commission's draft legislation pointed out: "In this respect, Russia is particularly fortunate. She has been granted the possibility of drawing upon the experience of other countries . . . [and] of grasping what lies ahead as a whole, from the beginning of this undertaking to the final termination of compulsory relations by means of redemption of land."[18] By availing themselves of the examples of France and Prussia, the members created a uniquely Russian resolution of the peasant question, a resolution based upon particular conditions, peculiarities, and traditions, such as the peasant commune.

This Russian variant of the new agrarian order entailed harmonizing the large-scale manorial economy and the small-scale household economy, and was intended to keep the peasants peasants—intended, that is, to avoid the emergence of a proletariat and the revolutionary upheavals associated with that process. In this conception practical and feasible goals were linked to utopian illusions of a kind that were characteristic of the era as a whole. The liberal members of the Editorial Commission believed they could direct the historical process, construct the future order, and influence the path of development of a country standing "on the threshold of a new life." In pursuit of these objectives the commission compiled legislation that regulated future development to an extent unknown elsewhere in Europe.[19]

This strict regulation was largely due to the fact that the liberal bureaucrats worked within the framework of a monarchy based on serfdom and were obliged to reckon with certain insurmountable obstacles—for example, Alexander II's refusal to permit the peasants to redeem their plowlands without the assent of the landowner, not to mention his unwavering attachment to his prerogatives as monarch. The Editorial Commission created a mechanism that would guarantee uninterrupted and undeviating progression from the first stage—the personal emancipation of the peasants—through the status of "temporary obligation" to the final goal, the transition to redemption. To this end, the peasants' right to use their allotments was pronounced "perpetual." Similarly, the dues they would have to render for these allotments would be established once and for all; they would be "permanent." With serfdom abolished, with land and grain subject to the fluctuations of the market, and given the squires' acute need for cash to reconstruct their mortgage-laden estates, "perpetual" usufruct and fixed dues were supposed to drive the squires to redemption, to make redemption their only escape from the net in which the state had so tightly enmeshed them. There was no more freedom of choice for the peasants. Fearful that the conditions under which land could be held or acquired as property would prove so onerous that many peasants would become landless, the legislators resorted to an artificial ban on peasants' giving up their land. In many respects, the retention of the commune and the restrictions on withdrawing from it (withdrawal was not absolutely forbidden) served the same objective. The redemption system, and especially the role of the state as creditor, imposed a heavy burden on the peasants. The expectations vested in "voluntary" redemption were well placed; by 1881, 85 percent of the peasants had undertaken redemption, at which time redemption was made compulsory for the rest.

The reform was conceived in a more systematic and decisive form in the sphere of civil and personal rights. The abolition of personal bondage combined, in the fullness of time, with the elimination of the squires' manorial power. Institutions of peasant self-administration with assemblies and elected peasant officials were created at the cantonal and village levels, with the latter based upon the commune. They opened the way for peasant participation in other institutions that emerged from the reform process, such as juries and the zemstvo. But while they defended the peasants' interests from yesterday's serfholders, the institutions were put under the supervision of local bureaucrats, which enhanced the role of state power in the village.

A premise of the Russian variant of the abolition of serfdom was one of the fundamental assumptions of the liberal bureaucrats: they counted on the monarchy to continue to take the initiative in the transformations to come. In their conception of the reform, the monarchy's initiative was a kind of guarantee that the abolition of serfdom would be realized and the reforms related to it would be implemented. The monarchy's initiative was a credo for them, a peculiar substitute for the constitution which, at that stage, was left off their agenda in order to make their program acceptable to the monarchy.

The criticism that met the Editorial Commission's program came from diverse quarters, but it was all scathing. The first assault came from the adherents of serfdom within the commission itself. Then deputies from the provincial committees went to St. Petersburg to discuss the commission's handiwork. Among them were liberals, conservatives, and reactionaries. Some opposed the redemption of plowland by the peasants, the abolition of manorial power, and the agencies of peasant self-administration. Others favored redemption (with allotments diminished by one-half) but also favored sweeping reforms of local administration, the courts, and the education system. And without exception all of them vigorously attacked the function state power would assume as mediator among the estates of the realm, and all opposed enhancing its role in social and economic affairs.

The commission's draft encountered further and stubborn opposition at the highest levels of the state, but Alexander II paid no attention, consistently endorsing the opinion of the minority of the Council of State that favored the draft statutes.[20] Although the Editorial Commission stood outside the autocratic system of state, its drafts were not, on the whole, subjected to review and revision. Even V. A. Dolgorukov, the chief of gendarmes, who at first tried to slow the reform down, was warning by 1860 that further delay was impossible, since "there is a limit to patience and expectation."[21]

Attempts to impede the reform did not bring it to a halt, but did introduce significant modifications in the commission's draft, especially concerning land: allotments were cut back by an amount corresponding to 20 percent of their total area, and dues were increased, which in turn made redemption more costly. The whole burden of redemption fell on the peasants, but the process proved profitable to the state. The prospect that a significant part of the peasantry would be brought to ruin, which the compilers of the legislation had taken such efforts to avert, loomed larger and became inevitable. The variant of agrarian development that the majority of the Editorial Commission had worked out was already laden with remnants of serfdom and its norms; the emendations made it even more of a contradictory half-measure, now even more onerous for the peasantry but also for the nobility. The monarchy, by contrast, emerged from the crisis renewed and strengthened.

So momentous an act as the statutes of February 19, 1861, which abolished serfdom, absolutely and inevitably required the transformation of various spheres of life that were organically connected to serfdom. First in line were the villages inhabited by state and appanage peasants. When the Editorial Commission began work, it was decided in principle that its program should provide the basis for all agrarian reforms; Rostovtsev announced as much in the early sessions. Furthermore, the reforms of the appanage peasants in 1863 and of the state peasants in 1866 and 1886 fully realized the commission's overall goal, the creation of a class of petty peasant proprietors who were not economically dependent on others, for these peasants were allotted substantially more land than the ex-serfs had been.

With the abolition of the nobility's manorial power and the grant of civil rights to the peasantry, the system of local administration and the courts could not remain unchanged. In March 1858, a commission, headed by N. A. Miliutin, was established under the Ministry of Internal Affairs to develop legislation on district and provincial self-administration, i.e., the zemstvo. Miliutin's commission also worked on a draft law concerning peace mediators, a new institution created to put the legislation of February 19, 1861, into effect; this activity shows the commission's organic link to the Editorial Commission and to the peasant reform. Although the mediators of the peace constituted a closed institution in that they were drawn entirely from the nobility,[22] the liberal bureaucrats did win certain of their principles that would later be incorporated into the reform of the courts: the mediators enjoyed secure tenure and independence, and glasnost prevailed in their work.

The introduction in 1861 of self-administration for the peasants opened the way to an elective zemstvo in which all estates of the realm could participate, and Miliutin's commission fully availed itself of these possibilities. Closed institutions paradoxically provided the basis for open institutions; village and cantonal self-administration, which involved only members of the peasant estate, helped yesterday's serf to enter an expansive and hitherto unfamiliar milieu in which all estates were involved. Once again, the new was not achieved by the revolutionary destruction of the old, but by reworking the old. The coherence and also the limitations of the idea of the peasant and zemstvo reforms that Miliutin and the other liberal bureaucrats had in mind were matched by the no less coherent program of P. A. Valuev. An ardent and tireless opponent of the Editorial Commission, he favored maintaining the nobility's landed property and the privileges that had gone with it; he would emancipate the peasants without land and erect a zemstvo system with the assemblies of the nobility as its foundation, in effect excluding the peasantry. The enactment of the zemstvo reform made inevitable the law of 1870, which inaugurated urban self-administration on the same principles.

Miliutin and the Editorial Commission had hoped that the mediators of the peace would evolve into justices of the peace, but this idea was frustrated by the efforts of Valuev, who, upon becoming minister of internal affairs in 1861, waged an open campaign against the first cohort of mediators of the peace, who had been appointed during the tenure of Lanskoi and Miliutin. The overall objective of linking the abolition of serfdom to a transformation of the administration of justice was to enjoy a better fate.

The Judicial Codes of November 20, 1864, which were the work of the best and most progressive of the nation's jurists and corresponded to the most advanced jurisprudential thinking of the progressive countries of Europe, gave Russia a new court system: it was public, adversarial, and open to all estates of the realm; the codes provided for a bar, elected justices of the peace, judges with secure tenure, and trial by jury. The juries were drawn from various estates and social groups, but a majority were peasants, which brings out the strong link between the court reform and the abolition of serfdom in 1861.[23] The codes represented the most consistent and radical of the reforms of the 1860s. They not only created a new, modern, bourgeois court but also, to some extent, limited the autocracy by establishing norms of legal order within the judiciary.

There were other reforms, involving, among other things, the censorship, the military, finance, statistics, education at all levels, and fiscal accountability (the state's income and expenditures were made public). Everything was set in motion. Only the supreme organs of state power, the central administration, the authority of the monarch and the all-powerful bureaucracy stood apart from this general process of reconstruction. As a consequence all the reforms, so resolutely undertaken, prepared, and enacted by the government in response to an aroused and excited public, were in peril.

The Monarchy and the Question of a Constitution

The abolition of serfdom was a watershed in Russian history. Serfdom as a structure, as a system of social relations, was gone. To be sure, many traits and remnants of serfdom were embodied in the reform legislation and still more in daily life, surviving even the Revolution of 1905 and up until the revolutions of 1917—and nowhere more prominently than in the structure and ideology of the state and in the political culture of the feudal autocracy, which proved remarkably tenacious and durable. Even in the period of public arousal and the onset of glasnost after the defeat in the Crimean War and the collapse of the Nicolaevan system, even amid the excitement surrounding the preparation of the abolition of serfdom and the other reforms, the autocratic monarchy imposed its unlimited and unaccountable authority. Even while the Secret Committee was being opened up by its transformation into the Main Committee, even while the provincial committees were beginning to work in open session, the Committee of Ministers was established. The committee, which was under the personal chairmanship of Alexander II, was a device not to promote a collegial and unitary administration but rather to enhance the unlimited power of the autocrat. For the first few years it did not even have its own charter but was simply convened each time by the personal disposition of the tsar; no record of the committee's deliberations was kept, it had no distinct procedure, and often its sessions broke off in midsentence if the august chairman got bored or weary.[24] Russia's distinctive traditions of statehood and statecraft found expression in this institution, and not in the Editorial Commission with its majority in solid support of the liberal plan of emancipation, with its involvement with society at large, with its new methods of statecraft (glasnost, publication of its proceedings, the professionalism and scholarship of its members); the commission illuminated the nature of the old-regime feudal state like a flare, but that state just grew stronger and underwent only minor and superficial modernization with the implementation of the abolition of serfdom. It is most appropriate that it was the Council of Ministers that on March 8, 1881, buried the so-called "Constitution" of Loris-Melikov; with this action the council, in effect, ceased to exist.

Alexander II, who had so firmly supported the abolition of serfdom, no less stubbornly and consistently denied the necessity and the possibility of a constitution for Russia. In his student years, the tsar had heard M. M. Speranskii's "Discourse on the Laws" *(Besedy o zakonakh),* a course of lectures lasting a year and a half, in which the man who had once been one of Russia's first constitutionalists now renounced his constitutionalist ideas and maintained that "pure monarchy" was essential for Russia; these arguments took root. Insofar as one can speak of Alexander II's convictions, one would have to begin with his belief that autocratic monarchy was the best and most natural form of rule for the Russian people. A good deal of evidence about his attitude to a constitution has survived. In the letter to Pius IX already cited, he wrote reproachfully and regretfully of his uncle, the king of Prussia: "He feared a constitution, granting one due to weakness." In the fall of the same year, 1859, he responded with anger and irritation to the addresses from the nobility insofar as they, whether in a liberal or reactionary spirit, hinted at a constitution. He expressed his view of a constitution with particular clarity in a conversation in St. Petersburg with the Prussian ambassador, Otto von Bismarck, on November 10, 1861. To a question about a constitution and liberal institutions, Alexander II responded:

> Throughout the land the common people sees the monarch as a paternal and all-powerful lord, the emissary of God. This feeling almost has the force of religious sentiment, it is inseparable from personal dependence on me, and I like to think that I am not mistaken. If the people should lose this feeling for the power that my crown imparts to me, the nimbus that the nation possesses would be ruptured. The deep respect which the Russian people from of old, by virtue of an innate feeling, has vested the throne of its tsar cannot be eliminated. I would reduce the authority of the government without any compensation if I undertook to include within it representatives from the nobility or the nation. God knows where we would have ended up on the matter of the squires and the peasants if the authority of the tsar had not been powerful enough to exert decisive influence.[25]

Alexander II expressed much the same view two years later in a conversation with Nikolai Miliutin just before dispatching him to Poland. The tsar said, in order to "restore the Sejm and the constitutional charter to the Poles, he would have to convene an Assembly of the Land in Moscow or St. Petersburg, and he did not suppose that the Russian people was sufficiently mature for such a change as that." Alexander II went on to say that he had in mind not only the "common people," whom he regarded as "the most reliable bastion of order in Russia," but also the upper classes of society, which "have not yet acquired the level of education that representative government requires."[26] Alexander II repeated the same arguments to a marshal of the nobility, D. P. Golokhvastov, in 1865. The pressure of social forces was not strong enough to compel concessions.

Finally Alexander II seemed to be disposed to concession and, on March 1, 1881, gave his consent to a session of the Council of Ministers to discuss the draft "Constitution" of Loris-Melikov; he was killed by terrorists the same day. The tragic end of the reformer was also the end of the era of reforms. Instead of a constitution, Russia got first a manifesto on the "irreplaceability of autocracy" and then the Statute on Measures to Preserve the Security of the State and Domestic Tranquillity of August 14, 1881. The statute provided that any locality could be declared subject to extraordinary rule, which meant that every inhabitant was subject to arrest and exile for five years without trial or could be brought before a court martial. Local administrators got the right to close institutions of learning and commercial and industrial enterprises, to stop the activities of zemstvos and city dumas, and to shut down organs of the press. As issued, the statute was "temporary," for three years. As each three-year term expired, it was renewed; it remained in effect right up to the February Revolution of 1917, becoming "Russia's real constitution."[27]

This statute hobbled the first steps toward the bourgeois legal order and judiciary system that the reforms of 1861–74 had inaugurated. The counterreforms of the 1880s and the early 1890s presented a further obstacle to the envisioned modernization of the structure of the state. Autocracy, the feudal structure and ideology of the state, and the associated political culture all received powerful legislative reinforcement. The era of glasnost and public participation in the discussion, and sometimes also in the resolution of matters of state proved short-lived. "Irreplaceable autocracy" stood outside the zone of permissible criticism. Glasnost, even in the period of reforms, was never part of a full-fledged bourgeois legal order; it was permitted out of necessity or even exploited by the autocracy, but it was alien to the nation's traditions of political culture and statehood. To take one example: even when official government policy was at the apogee of its liberal course concerning the abolition of serfdom, that is, when it adopted the program of December 4, 1858, it did not publicize that program. To take another: in February 1859, Alexander II wrote to Konstantin Nikolaevich, who was abroad, about "our unrestrained and imprudent literature, which long since has needed a bridle"[28]—and this was at the very moment when the Editorial Commission was established and began to publish and distribute its proceedings. There is no point in speaking of the later period. "Autocracy," Korolenko wrote in 1920, "having exhausted all its creative powers in the peasant reform and in the few reforms that followed upon it, became blindly reactionary and for many years repressed the nation's organic development."[29]

Therefore the sad and pathetic fate of the reforms is not in the least surprising. Overcautious and contradictory from the outset, as soon as they were enacted they were snatched from the hands of their creators and delivered over to their enemies for implementation. The conception of reform that the liberal bureaucrats had developed was under attack as soon as implementation began, and the devices to secure the reforms were loose and weak, while the traditions of Russian statehood stood firm. The peasant reform of 1861 did not solve the land question; instead it tied a new Gordian knot that even two bourgeois-democratic revolutions could not cut through.

Nonetheless, the abolition of serfdom and the other reforms were indeed a watershed in Russian history, an overturn, though not a revolution, from above. Describing in his diary for February 19, 1861, the ceremony at which Alexander II signed the manifesto and the associated statutes, Konstantin Nikolaevich observed, without any falsity of sentiment, "This means that from this day a new history, a new era begins for Russia. God grant that this be an era of indisputable greatness."[30] The Grand Duke's objective was achieved. The danger of Russia's losing its role as a great power in the family of civilized European nations had been overcome. The authority of Russia and of the Russian state, which had peacefully done away with bondage, rose high not only in Europe but also in America. Russia moved rapidly along the path of socioeconomic and cultural progress. This path, however, was onerous and even ruinous for the common people and held the promise of suffering and upheaval for the whole nation.

As a consequence of 1861, the power of the state over the economy increased, which meant an increase in its power over society. It was under these conditions that the masses of the population, the millions of peasants, were introduced to civic life. The emancipation of the peasants and the other reforms were a "most profitable deal" for the monarchy, but liberals saw the reforms as proof that the monarchy could take an initiative, as proof of autocracy's creative potential and capacity for progress. As the reforms came into effect, a clash between illusions and reality was inevitable. Consequently, liberalism lost its leading position right after the abolition of serfdom, and in the 1860s, still more in the 1870s and 1880s, it yielded its place to extreme tendencies. The failure of Loris-Melikov's "Constitution" meant the end of liberal illusions. Autocracy once and for all forsook the initiative, not only in day-to-day politics but also in the minds of those contemporaries who had believed in progress as a gift from the monarchy. The last liberals of the sixties, the authors of the "Great Reforms," passed from the scene with the onset of the era of counterreforms. In this era a new disposition of forces took shape, in which liberalism assumed new form and content. As we follow the line of development from 1861 to 1905, we must remember that the legacy of reform was burdened by the counterreforms and that serfdom, as Saltykov-Shchedrin observed at the time, found new ways to show its vitality. On the other hand, when we address, as we must, the question of the relationship between the reforms of the 1860s and the revolutions of 1917, we must follow all the twists and turns of the path from one to the other: not only the reforms and the counterreforms but also the

Revolution of 1905 and the legislation of the Stolypin era. Yet the goal of the reformers, to do better than Western Europe and avoid revolution (for five hundred years, as Kavelin would have it), proved to be utterly utopian.

NOTES

1. TsGIA, Leningrad, fond 1282, opis' 1, delo 1933, list 10b.
2. TsGIA, f. 1093, op. 1, d. 336, ll. 7–8 (one of several copies of the Russian translation). Pius IX's letter to Alexander II was first published in Italy in 1866.
3. In recent scholarship, Daniel Field has, more than any other historian, illuminated the significance of the West for the abolition of serfdom in Russia, but he touched upon only one aspect, cultural influence; I perceive the problem from a different perspectve and on the basis of different sources.
4. Notably the writings of P. A. Valuev, A. I. Koshelev, K. D. Kavelin, Iu F. Samarin, and B. N. Chicherin, among others.
5. "By the tsar's disposition," from Pushkin's "Derevnia."
6. TsGIA, f. 565 op. 14, d. 152, ll. 493–97; TsGAOR, Moscow, f. 722, op. 1, d. 928, ll. 266–71.
7. Peasant villages under administered military discipline; intended as a surrogate for military reserves, the colonies were notorious for maladministration and brutality.
8. TsGIA, f. 1284, op. 66, d. 11, ll. 1–10; f. 563, op. 2, d. 135.
9. ORGBL, Moscow, f. 169, karton 61, edinitsa khraneniia 25, l. 340b.
10. ORGBL, f. 169, karton 13, ed. 2, l. 188.
11. TsGIA, f. 1180, op. t. XV, d. 25.
12. TsGIA, f. 1284, op. 66, d. 8, l. 11a.
13. In 1859 many peasant communities passed resolutions to abstain from alcohol and imposed abstinence on their reluctant neighbors. Since liquor was a major source of government revenues, the movement had a political aspect even in those communities that did not go further and destroy neighborhood taverns.
14. When, on the eve of the uprising, Decembrists tried to recruit Rostovtsev, then a young officer, he reported their overtures to his superiors.
15. These dramatic pages of the history of the Main Committee are illuminated in the diary of Prince P. P. Gagarin. TsGAOR, f. 728, op. 1, d. 2197, chast' 6, ll. 16, 310b, 38, 41, 43, 58, 60, 67.
16. TsGIA, f. 1180, op. t. XV, d. 38, ll. 1–69; *Arkhiv Gosudarstvennogo soveta, Zhurnaly Sekretnogo i Glavnogo komiteta po krest'ianskomu delu,* 2 vols. in 3 (Petrograd, 1915), vol. 1, 333–36.
17. Formally plural, but singular in common speech and hereafter in this article.
18. Redaktsionnye kommissii, *Pervoe izdanie materialov Redaktsionnykh kommissii dlia sostavleniia polozhenii o krest'ianakh, vykhodiashchikh iz krepostnoi zavisimosti,* 18 vols. (St. Petersburg, 1859–60), vol. 18, 3–8.
19. Terry Emmons makes this point in his preface to P. A. Zaionchkovskii, *The Abolition of Serfdom in Russia* (Gulf Breeze, Fla., 1978).
20. L. G. Zakharova, *Samoderzhavie i otmena krepostnogo prava v Rossii, 1855–1861* (Moscow, 1984), 179–232, and the partial English translation: *Autocracy and the Abolition of Serfdom in Russia, 1855–1861* (*Soviet Studies in History,* vol. 25, no. 2 [1987]).
21. TsGAOR, f. 109, Sekretnyi arkhiv, op. 85, d. 23, l. 130.
22. The question of elective mediators of the peace and of peasant participation

in the elections had been raised, but could not be resolved prior to February 19, and so the issue was put off for three years.

23. In 1883, for example, in twenty provinces (excluding the provincial capitals), the composition of juries was: nobles and officials, 14.9 percent; merchants, 9.4 percent; *meshchane,* 18.3 percent; and peasants, 57.2 percent. A. K. Afanas'ev, "Sostav suda prisiazhnykh v Rossii," *Voprosy istorii,* 1978, no. 6.

24. TsGIA, f. 1275, op. 1, d. 4, ll. 40–46; d. 5, ll. 17–18; ORGBL, f. 169, karton 14, edinitsa 1, ll. 23–24; V. G. Chernukha, "Soviet Ministrov v 1857–61 gg.," *Vspomogatel'nye istoricheskie distsipliny,* fasc. V (Leningrad, 1973), 120–37.

25. *Die politischen Berichte des Fursten Bismarck aus Petersburg und Paris (1859–1862)* (Berlin, 1920), bd. 2, 130.

26. A. Leroy-Beaulieu, *Un homme d'Etat russe (Nicholas Miliutine)* (Paris, 1884), 163, 168–69.

27. V. I. Lenin, *Polnoe sobranie sochinenii,* 5th ed., 55 vols. (Moscow, 1967–70), vol. 21, 114.

28. TsGAOR, f. 722, op. 1, d. 851, l. 1030b.

29. B. G. Korolenko to A. V. Lunacharskii, in *Novyi mir,* 1988, no. 10, 217.

30. TsGAOR, f. 722, op. 1, d. 851, l. 103.

III

THE YEAR OF JUBILEE

Daniel Field

> Then shalt thou cause the trumpet of the
> jubile to sound . . . and proclaim liberty
> throughout all the land unto all the
> inhabitants thereof. . . . In the year of this
> jubile ye shall return every man unto his
> possession.
>
> Leviticus 25:9–13

> It must be now dat de kingdom am a comin'
> And de year of jubalo.
>
> "The Year of Jubalo"

In considering the implementation of the abolition of serfdom in Russia in 1861, we should begin with Luker'ia.

Since most local officials had shown no enthusiasm for the reform, the abolitionist governor of Kaluga Province feared that the good news would be conveyed to the peasants in distorted form. Accordingly, he dispatched 167 young subordinates as "heralds of liberty" to the districts of the province. They were to read and explain the most relevant sections of the statutes of February 19 to each peasant community. So it was that N. V. Sakharov set off from Kaluga city through the mud of the spring *rasputitsa*. He found that the peasants were polite but exhibited "astonishing restraint"; he wondered whether centuries of bondage had atrophied their capacity to express their feelings. The men were primarily concerned about the amount of land they would receive and the terms under which they would hold it, and some ventured to voice their concern to Sakharov. When he explained that allotments and dues fell within the jurisdiction of the mediators of the peace, who were not yet appointed, the men mumbled vaguely and wandered off.

The peasant women registered some pleasure, however. The statutes imposed a two-year transition period before the provisions concerning allotments, dues, and redemption would be put into effect, but the squires' rights to *stolovye zapasi* (exactions of fruit, mushrooms, fowl, cloth, and the like from the serfs) were abolished at once. The burden of *stolovye zapasi* fell primarily on women; they looked silently at one another, Sakharov observed, and smiled. One of them, Luker'ia, "no longer young and, apparently, a bit saucy," was so torn between doubt and joy that she ventured an inquiry of the herald of liberty.

"Tell me, does this mean that turning chickens over to the lords is now *shabash?*"[1]

"Now it's *shabash.*"

"And the eggs are *shabash?*"

"And the eggs, too. . . ."

"And gathering mushrooms and berries for the lords is *shabash?*"

"Yes, all *shabash.*"

"And when will it be *shabash?*"

"From this very moment, it's all *shabash.*"

"Does that mean that when summer comes, I don't have to go around getting mushrooms and berries for the squires?"

"You can do it for money or go for yourself, if that is your sweet will."

"You're not kidding?"

"No, it's the solemn truth. See, it's all written in this law book."

"Hey, gossips, see what's turned up for us!" Luker'ia joyfully cried, turning to the women. "Isn't that nice. All right, Aleksandra Sergeevna, here's for you." And she unceremoniously gave the finger (a greasy finger) in the direction of the manor house.

Sakharov reported that some men surrounded Luker'ia at once and took her to task, and one of them dismissed her as a mere *balalaika,* but Luker'ia was not fazed: "'Now I'm free!' You had to see the joyful radiance in her eyes, the way that feelings of self-satisfaction suffused her whole face, when she cried out, 'Now I'm free!'" Several peasants, shocked by Luker'ia's lack of restraint, said apologetically to Sakharov: "'Please don't be too hard on her, sir. You see what we have to put up with. You know, it's because she has lived in cities, among working women.'"[2]

Luker'ia's outburst reminds us that the while the "emancipation" legislation emancipated very imperfectly, it did deliver more than twenty million people from bondage. The statutes of February 19, the other reform legislation, and the administrative actions and amendment their implementation entailed, all discriminated against peasants, circumscribed their geographical and occupational mobility, and imposed fiscal and economic burdens upon them. Nonetheless, the very core of serfdom, the squires' unlimited and arbitrary power over their serfs, was abolished forever. Luker'ia was quick to appreciate this benefit; the menfolk were slow to do so.

The men fastened upon the main economic provisions of the reform, which concerned allotments of land and the obligations they entailed. Before considering those provisions, let us first reflect on the men's behavior in Sakharov's presence. Sakharov saw himself as a friend of the peasant, but from their perspective, he was one of *them*. He was a squire and an official; peasants found these categories hardly worth distinguishing, since a visit from either meant trouble for the village. Either should be treated with the reserve and show of deference that Luker'ia's neighbors hastened to display to Sakharov. Their behavior and that of their fellows in thousands of villages across Russia raise for us the issue of hegemony.

The promulgation of the manifesto and statutes of February 19 abolished bondage of peasants to squires, but the hegemony of the landed nobility, of officials, and, most generally, of nonpeasants over peasants emerged almost intact. One of the principal objectives of the reform (indeed, of the reforms) was achieved; one of the principal anxieties of the regime ought to have been allayed.

Maintaining hegemony had two aspects, short-term and long. The immediate task was preventing a firestorm in response to the news that serfdom was abolished. It might seem that the redress of centuries-old grievances would prevent, rather than provoke, upheaval, but the conventional wisdom held that the moment of maximum danger would come when the monarch formally renounced the only authority that obtained in much of the countryside. Nicholas I articulated this wisdom in a speech to the Council of State in 1842. It would be good to abolish serfdom in the remote future, he said, but

> at the *present* time any thought of such an undertaking would be neither more nor less than a criminal infringement on domestic tranquillity and the welfare of the state. The Pugachev rebellion showed what the turbulence of the mob can produce.[3]

Alexander II expressed the same anxiety in 1858 in setting the three standards that the reform legislation must satisfy, one of which was "that strong authority not waver for a minute in any locality, and hence that public order not be disrupted for a minute."[4]

To prevent a new Pugachev rebellion—a contingency that seems remote in retrospect, given the relative calm with which peasants assimilated the new legislation—the regime turned to two conventional and two unconventional agencies. The good offices of the church were implicitly invoked by a deliberate delay in the promulgation of the reform statutes. Alexander II signed them into law on the anniversary of his accession, February 19, but they were released to the public only at the beginning of Lent; during Lent, the Orthodox are supposed to abstain from that great fuel of civil disorder, alcohol. In addition, bishops were told to instruct their clergy to preach to peasants on the importance of meeting their obligations to squires and officials. One bishop duly told his subordinates to explain that freedom "is the equivalent of necessity and of complete submission to divine and civil laws, that it consists of carrying out the requirements of human nature and the social order, not the demands of the passions and the flesh."[5]

Military forces supplemented the religious. Elements of eighty regiments were dispersed around the country to assist the civil authorities.[6] Their primary function was not to use their arms, although peasant blood was shed in a few instances, but to overawe, to subdue, and in general to redress the imbalance of numbers that shaped the strategy of both sides when peasants confronted the authorities. In most districts of rural Russia, there were only two or three civilian officials and often only a handful of men who were not peasants.[7] Appreciating this circumstance, peasants avoided violence and the threat of violence, relying instead on the implicit menace of their massive numbers, perfect unanimity, and stubborn tenacity; they also appreciated the inconvenience of applying criminal penalties to hundreds or thousands of people from whom productive work is expected. Officials tried to break that unanimity by isolating and seizing a few peasants, classifying them as "initiators" or "inciters" (*zachinshchiki* or *podstrekateli*), and subjecting them to immediate punishment (to which criminal penalties might be added later). The way was open for the rest of the peasants to accept the official version that they had been the gullible dupes of persons fortuitously arrested and punished and then to disperse and to accede to what the officials wanted. Often they were helped along that way by summary punishment. It was difficult for a sheriff and a couple of subalterns to flog five hundred peasants without a squadron or so to back them up—a quiescent but menacing presence, mirroring the image that peasants presented to authorities. If these techniques did not procure compliance, the soldiers had a further use: they would be quartered upon the refractory village until it gave in. To have a soldier in every hut, availing himself of what little the household had, was a strain that scarcely any village could withstand for long. Each side, then, had an appropriate repertoire of techniques, but the government's repertoire required men in uniform and under discipline.

Because the circumstances of 1861 were so extraordinary, however, the regime went beyond these conventional weapons. It made one of its rare attempts to make practical use of the peasants' professed devotion to the tsar. To each province where there was a considerable number of serfs, the tsar dispatched one of his personal adjutants, a colonel or general attached to the monarch's suite, distinguished from all other officers by the tsar's monogram on his collar. The adjutants proved useless. In most cases they simply fell in with the regular authorities they were supposed to supervise; not one of them reported an instance where the parceled majesty he brought from St. Petersburg caused the scales to fall from peasant eyes.[8] They were recalled as soon as decently possible.[9]

The pretext for the recall of the adjutants was the institution of a new body of officials, the peace mediators (*mirovye posredniki*), specially charged with implementing the peasant reform. They constituted the lowest, and most important, level of a hierarchy of new agencies culminating in a Main Committee in St. Petersburg. The mediators were, in part, a response to the imbalance of numbers. Even if the local officials in place had been reasonably competent and sympathetic to the reform, they could not have overseen implementation on all the estates of the empire. This task entailed, along with knowledge of the statutes and direct inspection of each estate, a great deal of patient explanation of the new order to both squires and peasants. The task was hard because both parties tended to believe themselves despoiled by the statutes and often responded with stubborn incomprehension, feigned or genuine. For example, Lurker'ia's response to the immediate abolition of *stolovye zapasi* was perfectly complemented by that of a noblewoman of the neighborhood who wailed to Sakharov: "Oh my Lord, what's this? As it was, we received everything, everything, and all at once there is nothing. What kind of freedom is that? Now we are forbidden to order our slaves [sic] around. . . . You're making it all up yourself. Your Artsimovich made it up. I'm sure there's nothing like this in other provinces."[10]

As regards the purportedly more weighty matters of allotments and dues, the terms of the reform were infinitely more generous to the peasants, and far more prescriptive, than what the provincial nobility's elected representatives had grudgingly proposed a year or two earlier.[11]

The establishment of the mediators represented an attempt to draw on untapped reserves of humanitarianism and public spirit in rural Russia. They were to be men of irreproachable character who had given proof of their abolitionist sentiments.[12] Such men were hard to find in the Russian countryside, harder still because of the high property qualification. The mediators vaunted their objectivity and dispassion, particularly as they came under attack from their fellow nobles.

> In some districts there have been attempts by means of friendly persuasion and pressures from without to convert the mediators of the peace, if not de jure [then] de facto, into some kind of household institution of the nobility, before which the voice of the noble would count for everything and that of the peasant for nothing, but these attempts have been in vain. . . . As men of independent position, the mediators have preferred to remain independent in their spirit and disposition as well, to stand above the interests of the various estates of the realm . . . and to carry out the statute of February 19 in the spirit in which it was created.[13]

Many of the mediators may have fallen short of the ideal as regards dispassion and commitment to the reform, but the rancorous criticism that squires lavished upon them is indirect but telling evidence of their probity and efficiency. So is the testimony of provincial governors, who had reason to be suspicious of the mediators, who were not subordinate to them. The installation of the mediators, according to the governor of Smolensk Province, produced a striking change.

> Peasants' questions and uncertainties were no longer met with cries of "shut up!" or threats of rifle butts and bayonets; instead the law was read and explained to them, *the power of persuasion* was invoked. From that time there has been no occasion to call in military units, and summons of the rural police have been rare.[14]

A little later he reported that the peasants of the province, "having found the mediators to be patient and dispassionate interpreters of the new law, who do not burden them with paperwork and formalities or with constant summonses to court, have acquired deep respect and complete confidence in them."[15]

It does seem that, given the passions and interests involved, the reform of 1861 was implemented with astonishing calm and dispatch and that the mediators deserve major credit for this achievement.

From the vantage point of St. Petersburg, then, maintaining hegemony meant preventing a firestorm, whether of celebration or of outrage, and assuring that the crop of 1861 would be sown and harvested. Beleaguered squires and local officials shared these concerns but had an additional and more subtle task of long-term significance. They had quickly to convince the peasantry that times had not changed that much, and that they themselves were still entitled to the show and the substance of deference. Peasants who greeted the manifesto with some such expression as *Nyne ne prezhniaia pora!* (These are not the old times!)[16] were quickly made to understand that the old apparatus was still in place. Here is how the new times were brought home to a village near Minsk:

> as the peasants were brought into the office of this agency one by one, the main rules of the Imperial Statute [of February 19] were read to them by Constable Dvorakovskii, . . . after which each peasant was subjected to the appropriate punishment in the presence of the authorities. On this occasion a *zertsalo* [a prism emblazoned with a double-headed eagle] was displayed to them as a kind of simple reminder to obey the authorities, who act in the name of H[is] I[mperial] M[ajesty].[17]

Despite their reputation to the contrary, peasants can be quick on the uptake, and many displayed this gift in 1861. Consider the peasants of Molostovka, who

> refused to render dues according to the regulatory charter *(ustavnaia gramota)*, desiring to work as of old, without any change at all; they forbade the village elder to carry out the directives of the mediator of the peace concerning the implementation of the charter. Their stubbornness was based on the widely circulated rumor that in two years they will get complete freedom without having to pay for the land and on a misunderstanding of the imperial manifesto, where it says that during the two years designated for the implementation of the Statutes, the existing order should be maintained on estates.

The elder and six "selectmen" from Molostovka were favored with an invitation to the provincial capital to appear before the Provincial Tribunal on Peasant Affairs—for Molostovka was in Kazan' Province, a few miles from the newly celebrated village of Bezdna.[18] There, "after appropriate persuasions and explanations, they fully admitted their guilt, sincerely repented and signed [an undertaking] obligating them in the future to render all dues according to the regulatory charter and to carry out everything that the local authorities demand of them."[19]

This source is a bit cryptic. Judging from many similar documents, "appropriate persuasions and explanations" meant threats of punishment. What is remarkable is the alacrity with which these peasants responded to persuasion and repented.[20] Their adroit turnaround—and many others like it across Russia—is especially surprising because their resistance was grounded in the language of a law just issued by the tsar.[21]

Many other peasants fell, or jumped, into the same misinterpretation, which entailed fastening on one phrase in the manifesto of February 19 and ignoring all the appended statutes. An instance in Sumy District reported by the governor of Khar'kov Province is typical:

> on their knees the peasants asked the mediator of the peace and the squire to leave them on *barshchina* [serfs' labor dues] until the expiration of the two-year term, promising to do all their work and expressing the hope that when that term was over, they would pass over onto "the tsar's maintenance" *(na tsarskoe polozhenie)*. Although the peasants were completely submissive, no arguments or reasons could induce them to accept the regulatory charter.

The expectation of a new statute or "real *volia*"[22] at the end of the two-year transition period was, so to speak, the domesticated variety of a widespread myth. The governor went on to describe the wild variety.

> Other peasants, rejecting all the squire's proposals for the compilation of regulatory charters, profess their firm determination to remain under the existing state of things "until the hour that has been foretold" *(do sluchnogo chasa),* which some of them understand to coincide with the expiration of the two-year term and others explain with the mysterious word "awaited" *(zhdanoe).* They believe that when the awaited hour strikes, all compulsory relations with the squires will cease and the land will be given to the peasants without charge.
>
> Some squires, assisted by the mediators, have managed, with considerable sacrifice of their own advantage, to persuade the peasants to accept some kind of deal, but it very often happens that after an insignificant amount of time has passed the peasants renounce their adherence and the promises they have made, acting under the influence of some kind of absurd rumor which happens to reach them through passersby or which is even deliberately thought up by one of their fellows in order to dissuade the community from the agreement it has made.
>
> This almost general disposition of the peasants is the fruit of their backwardness and failure to understand the importance for themselves of the new statutes; it forces upon the mediators of the peace the painful necessity of implementing the regulatory charters by coercion. . . .[23]

The governor's report is clear and authoritative, and yet, given the distance from his study to the village, it is too pat. How could he get a sure hold on the mysterious, ecstatic, and myth-based hopes of the secretive peasantry?[24] Some part, at least, of his analysis derives not from observation but from the ideology that had sustained serfdom and would survive it. His implicit premise, that peasants can be stirred out of their natural and salutary inertia only by an outside ("passerby") or inside *(podstrekatel')* agitator, is clearly ideological in character; it is part of the myth of the peasant. This premise was widely shared, and held the more firmly the further one ascended from the village. It underlay the minister of internal affairs' circular of July 1, 1861, providing for the preemptory exile of *podstrekateli* against whom there was insufficient evidence for a criminal indictment. The circular explicitly covers nonpeasant members of the "taxpaying [nonnoble] orders," thus embracing passersby as well as homegrown agitators.[25]

While the governor may have slid over rough edges and areas of ambiguity, his account does find ample confirmation in other sources. More important than the accord among nonpeasants, however, is the consideration that expectation of some variant of the "hour that has been foretold" is one of the few instances in modern European history of an ecstatic and subversive belief, widespread among the populace, that left a clear statistical trail.

The peasants in Sumy District, like those in Spassk, refused to sign the regulatory charter or to participate in any way in its compilation. Now, the charter was not a contract. The law encouraged free agreements between squires and the former serfs, and some squires made concessions not required by law to encourage such agreements. If agreement was not forthcoming, however, statutory norms would be imposed on squire and peasant alike by the mediator of the peace. Representatives of both parties were obliged to sign the charter prior to its implementation, but the *assent* of the parties was not required.[26] When peasants refused to sign a charter or even to view the fields with the mediator, they were not withholding assent but seeking to avoid any involvement in a corrupt process that might impair their rights to the bounty the tsar had in store for his faithful peasants. It was as if the implementation of the statutes of February 19 was a test of their fidelity or a source of a contagion to be avoided at all costs. As a gendarme explained it, many peasants were inspired by "an unconscious [*bezsoznatel'noe*] fear of signing, supposing that a signature entails some kind of peonage [*kabala*] and obligation."[27]

As of January 1, 1862, only 2,796 charters had been approved and put into effect. This was about 3 percent of the total required for the empire and presumably involved the most amenable peasants and squires. More than one-third were not signed by the peasants.[28] A year later, a couple of months before the deadline, 73,185 had been implemented (about two-thirds of the total required), and slightly less than half of these had been signed by the peasants involved. The proportion of nonsigners (peasants covered by unsigned charters) ranged from a low of 20.4 percent in Poltava Province to a high of 99.8 percent in Minsk, with a nationwide average of 42.0 percent. There is no pattern in the range (in Chernigov Province, adjacent to Poltava, the ratio of signers to nonsigners was almost reversed), except that ethnic differences appeared to have enhanced peasants' misgivings.[29] The range is primarily a function of the varying zeal and talent of local officials; some mediators of the peace were able to persuade peasants that the statutes were authentic, whereas others yielded to the "painful necessity" of coercing peasants into signing[30] and the rest simply processed the charters without any peasant signatures.

Since the peasants had no valid reason under the law for refusing to sign and were under great pressure to do so, and since any peasant or a designated outsider could sign for the whole community, these figures are eloquent. They attest to an astonishingly wide spread of fabulous disillusionment and ecstatic hope—the latter pinned (to some degree) on the person of the far-off tsar.

The tsar himself responded with his own kind of eloquence. On August 15, 1861, he stated to a gathering of cantonal elders in Poltava: "Rumors have reached me that you are waiting for some other *volia*. There will not be any other *volia* than what I gave you. Do what the law and the statute [of February 19] require. Labor and toil. Be obedient to the authorities and the squires." Two weeks later, Minister of Internal Affairs Valuev sent a circular directing mediators of the peace to convey the substance of this and similar speeches to the cantonal elders in their jurisdiction.[31]

Insofar as peasants refused to sign the charters in hopes of obtaining a "new (and authentic) *volia*" in 1863, still more insofar as they were waiting for "the hour that has been foretold," their inspiration was utopian. Refusal was also grounded, however, in a more humdrum entity, the peasants' sense of justice.

Russians have a distinctive body of words and concepts to denote possession, for which true counterparts in West European languages are hard to find. Nonetheless, in the eighteenth century the Imperial regime firmly adopted concepts of property in land derived from Roman law and familiar to us. Nineteenth-century Russian statesmen, like their counterparts elsewhere in Europe, believed that property rights were the basis of a sound polity and economy and that upholding these rights was the first duty of the state. In tribute to this verity, the Manifesto of February 19 proclaimed the squires' "property right to all the land that belongs to them,"[32] even though the provisions of the reform for allotment and redemption violated that right.

Russian peasants, by all accounts, completely refused to adopt the regime's concept of property in land.[33] For them, to claim ownership of plowland in the sense that one owns a hat or an ax was as absurd as a claim to own sunshine or the Volga. Land *belonged* to the person who tilled it, but it was the *property* of God, the tsar, or (which came to the same thing) no one.[34] By this reasoning, plowland belonged to the serfs who tilled it even though they belonged to their master. The complete and growing incompatibility between two concepts of property was one aspect of the cultural gulf that divided the tiny cosmopolitan elite (*obshchestvo*) from the common people (*narod*, mostly peasants). This gulf derived in large part from status distinctions associated with the consolidation of serfdom in the Law Code of 1649.[35] It was mightily deepened and widened by the reforms of Peter I, not only because he imposed cosmopolitan cultural norms on the elite (while letting the peasants keep their beards) but because he simplified and reinforced the distinctions among estates of the realm. The more they were debased, the more firmly serfs clung to traditional concepts, partly for strategic reasons, partly to uphold their dignity. In the adage "we are yours but the land is ours" that serfs are supposed to have offered up to their masters,[36] an expression of submission came entwined in an assertion of right.

When peasants confronted squires and officials in 1861, the two sides proceded from utterly different value systems. From the peasant perspective, the requirement that they pay dues or redemption payments for *their* land was a greater outrage to justice than serfdom itself. Almost every encounter between ex-serfs and their betters in 1861 was informed by this sense of outrage.

Lenin observed that "1861 engendered 1905" and also that the Revolution of 1905 was a "dress rehearsal" for 1917.[37] There is indeed a causal chain linking the peasant reform of 1861 to the October Revolution. But we can also say that "1649 engendered 1861," that is, that the antagonism, mistrust, and noncomprehension that marked and shaped Russia's entry into a new era were products of serfdom.

The legacy of serfdom extended beyond social relations and competing cultural values, however, as we can see by reviewing the main elements of the reform legislation.

The terms of the legislation varied considerably from province to province. The authors of the reform wanted to accommodate the interests of the landed nobility. Hence in the North the allotments of land assigned to the ex-serfs were relatively large but very costly; since the land was of little value, the squires would rather have cash. To the south, as land became more valuable and the squires more eager to hold onto it, the allotments were smaller but (if still overpriced by the yardstick of market value) not so costly. Most peasant households could not make ends meet relying solely on the output of their household plots and allotments, either because the allotment was too small or because too much of its product had to go to dues or redemption payments.

The complexity of the reform settlement is compounded when one takes into account various special cases, some of them involving millions of peasants. The repartitional commune was unknown in most of the Ukraine and was not imposed there by the reform. State peasants, who had never been subject to a squire, would be more generously treated than serfs when the reform was extended to them in 1866, for the regime was more willing to sacrifice the interests of the treasury than those of the squires. Most household serfs *(dvorovye liudi)*, a category that included various kinds of craftspeople as well as domestic servants and constituted some 7 percent of the serf population, were not usually entitled to allotments of plowland and so were left less encumbered and less secure than their fellows.

If we set aside these and other special cases and focus on the experience of a majority of Great Russian peasants, a good understanding of the reform emerges from a comparison of the reform settlement and the system of serfdom on four counts: authority, ascription, status, and economics.

Authority. The essence of serfdom was the subjection of the serfs to the arbitrary power of their master or mistress, who could set them to any kind of work, settle them in a new place, break up their families, impose criminal penalties on them, and have males drafted into the army. Squires could buy and sell serfs, mortgage them, or give or gamble them away. Many serfs suffered physical or sexual abuse. The laws delimiting the squires' powers were few, vague, and rarely enforced, although custom may have restrained the squires in ways the government did not.

The arbitrary power of the serfholding noble was utterly abolished by the legislation of 1861. The emancipated serfs found themselves subject in a new way, however, to the squires as a class. The government arranged that the landed nobility would utterly dominate the local administration, including the agencies charged with implementing the abolition of serfdom.[38] And most ex-serfs had to turn, as renters or wage laborers or sharecroppers, to a landowner in the neighborhood, though not necessarily to the one who had been their master under serfdom.

Ascription. A second element of serfdom was *prikreplenie,* "fastening" or ascription.[39] A serf could travel away from his home village only with his master's written permission. He might spend months away from the village as a barge hauler or years as a factory worker, but was still regarded by law as a member of his home community and required to bear his share of the taxes and dues imposed on that community.

With the abolition of serfdom, serfs were still ascribed, but the power to regulate their comings and goings passed from the squire to the village commune. Now the commune issued the passports that enabled peasants to seek wage work. Passport-holding peasants, obliged to send part of their earnings back to the commune to which they were ascribed, made up the bulk of the labor force in industry, transport, and the building trades. Passports were not hard to obtain, since many communities could not meet their obligations on the basis of village agriculture alone, so ascription did not much impede the flow of labor into industry.[40]

The government saw ascription as a safety net: a laid-off worker was supposed to go back to the village and hunker down until an employer needed him again. Many peasants who were essentially full-time workers chose to return to their villages for holidays or to help with the harvest. The safety net was not simply a matter of wishful thinking, but it was not strong enough to support labor peace. Johnson has shown that in the city of Moscow, workers with strong ties to their native villages and to village agriculture were more disposed to strike and otherwise stand up to their employers than full-fledged proletarians were.[41]

Status. The reform legislation elevated the status of ex-serfs but did not eliminate status differences. The statutes of February 19 declared ex-serfs to be "free rural inhabitants." However, the hierarchy of estates of the realm *(sosloviia)* endured. Furthermore, in all but a few areas, such as felonies and civil litigation involving nonpeasants, a peasant was subject to local customary law rather than the general laws of the empire. In other respects, distinctions that had once followed from the *soslovie* system were retained by other means. For example, peasants were eligible to serve on the juries established by the judicial reform of 1864, but the property qualifications for jury service excluded all but a few rich peasants.

Economics. It was the economic elements of the reform legislation, not formal status distinctions, that most severely restricted the freedom of ex-serfs. Most peasants received (through the commune) an allotment of land and were compelled to meet the obligations that went with the allotment. In practice, it was almost impossible to dispose of the allotment and so disencumber oneself of the obligations.[42] Even in Vladimir Province, where manufactures were relatively well developed and serf capitalists relatively numerous, only half of one percent of the ex-serfs had detached themselves from the commune by 1880.[43] Most peasants did not want to break with the commune or get rid of their land. The point is that very few of those peasants who, like pioneers in America, wanted or were obliged to pull up stakes and make a fresh start could do so.

Servile agriculture had four main characteristics. One of these was the sway of large estates. The *average* estate had more serfs (about one hundred males) than there were slaves on all but the biggest plantations in the United States. These estates rarely attained their potential for efficient and productive agrobusiness, since, large as they were, most were simply agglomerations of peasant villages. The simple tools and puny draft animals that worked the squires' lands belonged to the peasants and were employed there as they were on the peasants' allotments. It was not the dictates of agronomy and the demands of the market that determined techniques of cultivation and the choice of crops but, at least primarily, peasant custom.[44]

A second characteristic was the repartitional commune. A peasant household held its house lot and kitchen garden from generation to generation, but plowland was held by the commune and subject to periodic repartition. The objective of repartition was to equalize landholding to match consumption needs so that no household would go hungry, but especially to match the labor power of each household. For the commune allocated and reallocated burdens (taxes and other obligations to the government and the squire) as well as assets (plowland). Squires and officials alike insisted on a system of mutual responsibility *(krugovaia poruka)*. If one household did not meet its obligations, the others were supposed to make up the difference. Hence it was in the interests of all households and of the commune that each household have plowland proportional to its productive capacity, and the major ingredient of that capacity was human labor. While land was held collectively, cultivation was not collective. As on a U.S. farm, the household was the basic unit of production. Under serfdom, the household was understood to own its draft animals and tools, and these passed into its ownership under the reform legislation. A serfholder with thousands of acres who retained most of this acreage after the abolition of serfdom was not likely to possess the draft power and equipment necessary to cultivate his land.

A third characteristic of the servile economy was "extraeconomic compulsion." Economic relations between master and serf were not determined by the market—by the supply of land, labor, and agricultural products and the demand for them. Under serfdom, it was the serfholders' arbitrary authority, or in practice their sense of what they could or should get away with, that fixed the size of the serfs' allotments and the amount of labor or cash they had to render. The government would try to enforce the master's demands, even using the army if a village mounted a concerted resistance to its squire's demands.

Finally, under serfdom, squires exacted dues from their serfs in two primary forms: *obrok,* or dues in cash, and *barshchina,* or dues in labor.

By and large, the characteristics of the servile economy survived the abolition of serfdom, often in altered form, and broke down only slowly. One reason was the timidity and inertia of the squires, yesterday's serfholders. They *could* buy horses and equipment, hire laborers to cultivate the land they retained, and play a vigorous entrepreneurial role. Most of them preferred to avoid investment, minimize risk, and exploit the economic plight of the ex-serfs, whose allotments were so small and whose obligations were so high that they could not make ends meet out of their own resources. Many squires resorted to the Russian equivalent of sharecropping, called *otrabotka:* a peasant household, using its horses and tools, would cultivate a specified portion of the squire's plowland in return for which it could cultivate another, smaller portion for its own use. This was very like *barshchina*.

The main reason for the slowness of change in Russian agriculture, however, was deliberate choices made by the regime and embodied in the reform legislation. To minimize disruption, the reformers took the economic characteristics of serfdom as their point of departure. For example, the size of the allotments set by statute derived from the size of the allotments under serfdom. The reformers retained the commune, although they supposed it to be a barrier to agricultural progress;[45] they preferred, as the serfholders had, to rely on it as an intermediary, sparing the regime the necessity of dealing directly with twenty-two million ex-serfs. The statutes did seek, although equivocally, to minimize the economic dependence of ex-serfs on their former masters. To this end, the legislation of February 19 provided that peasants could redeem their allotments over a forty-nine-year period. Redemption usually entailed an agreement between the squire and his ex-serfs, and this was hard to achieve. Until the redemption process began in a particular village (and it became compulsory only in 1881), the ex-serfs were in a state of so-called "temporary obligation," a term that underlined their continued subjection to their former master or mistress. Within limits set by the reform statutes, they had to render dues (*obrok* or *barshchina*) as the equivalent of rent for their allotments. The slow rate at which peasant communities passed from temporary obligation to redemption further diminished the sharpness of the transition from serfdom.

The abolition of serfdom regulated and systematized more than it changed. Regulation was in itself an enormous change, since the arbitrary power *(proizvol)* of the serfholder (and the state's support of this authority) had been the very essence of serfdom. Because the reform deliberately perpetuated so many of the social and economic characteristics of serfdom, it may be that the regime was indulging in wishful thinking or placing hopes in the power of words, supposing that great benefits must accrue simply because it had found the courage to declare that serfdom, the basic institution of Russian life, was abolished. From such a *podvig*,[46] surely great benefits must flow. . . .

The ambivalent nature of the reform also reveals the regime's mixed motives. The statutes of February 19 could not and did not provide a great, immediate stimulus to economic development. Nineteenth-century tsarism, however, set a higher value on social and economic stability, on the prosperity of the landed nobility, and on the welfare of the peasantry than on economic development. The tsar and his advisers feared chaos more than they wanted progress. So the reform produced an imposed stability, reimposed the hegemony of nonpeasants over peasants, and opened the way for a slow passage out of the social and economic forms of serfdom.

NOTES

I would like to thank Peter Kolchin, L. G. Zakharova, and the members of Syracuse University's European History seminar for their comments on an earlier draft of this essay. I should emphasize that they objected forcefully to many points that I made, and I doubt that my revisions fully meet those objections. I am also grateful to Joan Neuberger and other participants in the Philadelphia conference for their observations and suggestions.

1. *Shabash,* derived from the Hebrew word for Sabbath, means "it's all over," and is usually said at the end of a great task.

2. N. V. Sakharov, "Iz vospominanii o V. A. Artsimoviche," in *V. A. Artsimovich. Vospominaniia—kharakteristiki* (St. Petersburg, 1904), 438–39; on the number of heralds, A. A. Kornilov, "Krest'ianskaia reforma v Kaluzhskoi gubernii pri V. A. Artsimoviche," in ibid., 265.

3. In M. A. Korf, "Imperator Nikolai v soveshchatel'nykh sobraniiakh," *SbIRIO* 98 (1896): 115.

4. Imperial Order of Oct. 26, 1858, quoted in Daniel Field, *The End of Serfdom* (Cambridge, Mass., 1976), 159. The minister of internal affairs responded to this

anxiety by beginning his first report on the implementation of the reform, "Complete peace and quiet greeted the manifesto. . . ." S. S. Lanskoi to Alexander II, Mar. 31, 1861, in S. N. Valk, ed., *Otmena krepostnogo prava. Doklady ministrov vuntrennikh del o provedenii krest'ianskoi reformy 1861–1862* (Moscow–Leningrad, 1950), 7.

5. P. A. Zaionchkovskii, *Provedenie v zhizn' krest'ianskoi reformy 1861 g.* (Moscow, 1960), 47–49.

6. See P. A. Zaionchkovskii, ed., "O pravitel'stvennykh merakh dlia podavleniia narodnykh volnenii v period otmeny krepostnogo prava," *Istoricheskii arkhiv,* 1957, no. 1, 151–93.

7. Nineteenth-century Russians supposed that they were beset by a plague of bureaucracy, but S. F. Starr has shown that the problem was rather "undergovernment": the proportion of civil servants per capita (to say nothing of per square kilometer) was about a quarter the rate in France or England at midcentury. Starr, *Decentralization and Self-Government in Russia, 1830–1870* (Princeton, N.J., 1972), 48–49.

8. The adjutants' reports have been published by E. A. Morokhovets as *Krest'ianskoe dvizhenie v Rossii posle otmeny krepostnogo prava* (Moscow–Leningrad, 1949). Judging by these reports, the adjutants had degenerated since the time when, according to Okudzhava,

> Behind the emperor ride the generals of his suite,
> Full of glory, covered with wounds, but not killed.
> Then come the duelists, the fligel-adjutants, with epaulettes shining.
> They are all handsome, all talented, all poets.

9. See the decree of May 20 in *Sbornik pravitel'stvennykh rasporiazhenii po ustroistvu byta krest'ian, vysshedshikh iz krepostnoi zavisimosti,* vol. 2, pt. 1 (St. Petersburg, 1867), 49.

10. Sakharov was quick to remonstrate with this woman, who presumably was not Luker'ia's mistress, for referring to serfs as "slaves" *(raby).* Sakharov, "Iz vospominanii," 441.

11. Judging by the positions taken by the second convocation of deputies from the provincial committees, the last forum provided to the nobility at large for commenting on the emerging reform legislation, the squires became less disposed to compromise as they came to understand that the position most of them had held in 1856–57—that serfdom be preserved intact—was untenable. See Field, *The End of Serfdom,* 339–43.

12. Circular of the Minister of Internal Affairs to provincial governors, Mar. 23, 1861, in *Sbornik pravitel'stvennykh rasporiazhenii,* vol. 2, pt. 1, 99–102.

13. Their "position" was "independent" because they could not be removed by a provincial governor or even the minister of internal affairs, to say nothing of their brother nobles, but only by a solemn act of the Senate. *Mirovoi posrednik,* no. 25, quoted in N. F. Ust'iantseva, "Institut mirovykh posrednikov v otsenke sovremennikov (po materialam gazety 'Mirovoi posrednik')," *Vestnik Moskovskogo gos. universiteta,* ser. 8 (1984), no. 1, 72; see also Ust'iantseva's *Institut mirovykh posrednikov v sisteme gosudarstvennogo stroia Rossii (1861–1863 gg.)* (Avtoreferat dissertatsii na soiskanie uchenoi stepeni kandidata istoricheskikh nauk) (Moscow, 1984). Much less useful is Jerman W. Rose, "The Russian Peasant Emancipation and the Problem of Rural Administration: The Institution of the *Mirovoi posrednik*" (Ph.D. diss., University of Kansas, 1976).

14. Quoted in D. I. Budaev, *Krest'ianskaia reforma 1861 goda v Smolenskoi gubernii* (Smolensk, 1967), 116; emphasis in the original.

15. Valuev's paraphrase, dated Aug. 11, 1861, in Valk, ed., *Otmena krepostnogo prava,* 59. In his weekly reports to the tsar in May, June, and July, Valuev scarcely

registered the existence of the mediators except as it was reflected in his tallies of the establishment of peasant institutions of self-administration, which was the mediators' first duty; apparently reports like the one cited obliged him to be more generous.

16. For an example, see S. B. Okun' and K. V. Sivkov, eds., *Krest'ianskoe dvizhenie v Rossii v 1857–mae 1861 gg. Sbornik dokumentov* (Moscow, 1963), 327.

17. Marshal of the nobility of Rechitsa District to the Governor of Minsk, Apr. 13, 1861, in Okun' and Sivkov, eds., *Krest'ianskoe dvizhenie v Rossii v 1857–mae 1861 gg.*, 399.

18. The owners of Molostovka were the Messrs. Molostov, one of them presumably V. V. Molostov, the marshal of the nobility who had conferred with General Apraksin prior to his assault on Bezdna and then fled in panic to Kazan' city. See Daniel Field, *Rebels in the Name of the Tsar* (Boston, 1989), 77, 70.

19. Despite their penitence, the elder and many of his fellow villagers were punished on their return home. The acting governor of Kazan' Province to the Minister of Internal Affairs, Nov. 30, 1861, in L. M. Ivanov, ed., *Krest'ianskoe dvizhenie v Rossii v 1861–1869 gg. Sbornik dokumentov* (Moscow, 1964), 51.

20. Occasionally a Russian police official informed his superiors that a peasant in his custody remained stubborn, but I have never seen a report of *feigned* repentence, and usually the repentence is characterized as "sincere" (*iskrennee* or, as here, *chistoserdechnoe,* literally meaning "purehearted").

21. Of course, the peasants' invocation of the law may have been a manifestation of their ability to put a seemly face on resistance to authority; they "cover their disobedience in a mask of modesty and simplicity, knowing that thereby they will escape punishment," as the governor of Vladimir Province observed of some intransigent peasants in Aleksandrov District. P. V. Safronov to Minister of Internal Affairs Valuev, Dec. 13, 1862, in Ivanov, ed., *Krest'ianskoe dvizhenie v Rossii v 1861–1869 gg.,* 132.

22. *Volia* means "freedom" in its broadest and most promising sense; nonpeasants supposed that peasants understood *volia* as license to idleness and, in particular, as freedom from taxes, dues, and all other obligations to outsiders.

23. Governor of Khar'kov Province to the Minister of Internal Affairs, Dec. 7, 1861, in Ivanov, ed. *Krest'ianskoe dvizhenie v Rossii v 1861–1869 gg.,* 112–13. In his annual report to the tsar, the head of the Third Section reported that rumors of "new, complete *volia*" after two years were "circulating everywhere." But, he added reassuringly, refractory peasants "consistently expressed their unshakable faith in the tsar's will. It is only the fear of deviating from it and becoming subject to servile dependency once again that provoked their disobedience. . . ." E. A. Morokhovets, ed., *Krestian'skoe dvizhenie 1827–1869* (Moscow, 1931), fasc. 2, 21–22.

24. We cannot, however, characterize these hopes as "millenarian." The title of this essay provides an ironic contrast between the serfs' expectations and the legislation of February 19, but also a contrast, by no means ironic, between the serfs in Russia and slaves in the United States. The earthy and worldly character of the serfs' hopes for "the hour that has been foretold" stands out when compared to the millenarian vision of many U.S. slaves. On the latter, see J. Scott Strickland, *Across Space and Time* (Chapel Hill, N.C. 1993).

25. *Sbornik pravitel'stvennykh rasporiazhenii,* vol. 2, pt. 1, 53–54. In the event, 913 persons were pronounced guilty of inciting peasant disorders in 1861 and 1862, almost as many as the 990 peasants taken into custody for participating in disorders. Morokhovets, ed., *Krestian'skoe dvizhenie 1827–1869,* fasc. 2, 17, 19, 40, 44.

26. See articles 36, 49, and 69 of the Great Russian Statute, in K. A. Sofronenko, ed., *Krest'ianskaia reforma v Rossii 1861 goda: Sbornik zakonodatel'nykh aktov* (Moscow, 1954), 169–75.

27. Lt.-Col. A. P. Koptev writing from Ardatov District, Nizhnii Novgorod Prov-

ince, to the Chief of Gendarmes, in Ivanov, ed., *Krest'ianskoe dvizhenie v Rossii v 1861–1869 gg.*, 78.

28. Zaionchkovskii, *Provedenie v zhizn'*, 103. A related problem was the refusal of peasants to serve as witnesses *(dobrosovestnye)* for charters in neighboring villages. Arkhiv zakonodatel'nykh del, *Zhurnaly Glavnogo komiteta ob ustroistve sel'skogo sostoianiia*, Vol. 1, *S 5 marta 1861 goda po 28 dekabria 1862 goda* (Petrograd, 1918), 438–42.

29. The rate of signing was lowest of all in three provinces (Kovno, Grodno, and Minsk) where most squires were Poles and Catholics and most peasants were East Slavs and Orthodox. Table in Valk, ed., *Otmena krepostnogo prava*, 287. For thirty-one Great Russian and left-bank provinces, there is no statistically significant correlation between the percentage of signers and *any* of the variables concerning serfdom that we have at the corresponding level of aggregation: mean serf allotment, serfs as a percentage of the province's population, mean male serfs per estate, and the proportion of serfs on *obrok*.

30. An entire village of peasants who refused to sign was taken under military guard to the provincial capital, Novgorod, and flogged on the public square. N. M. Druzhinin, *Russkaia derevenia na perelome 1861–1880 gg.* (Moscow, 1978), 48; see also *Otmena krepostnogo prava*, 76.

31. Fifteen months later the tsar delivered a similar speech to a gathering of peasant officials; it was read aloud in all cantons and, according to the head of the Third Section, "brought false expectations to an end." *Sbornik pravitel'stvennykh rasporiazhenii*, vol. 2, pt. 2 (St. Petersburg, 1868), 46–47; Ivanov, ed. *Krest'ianskoe dvizhenie v Rossii v 1861–1869 gg.*, 553, n. 42; S. S. Tatishchev, *Imperator Aleksandr II. Ego zhizn' i tsarstvovanie* (St. Petersburg, 1903), vol. 2, 407; Morokhovets, ed., *Krestian'skoe dvizhenie 1827–1869*, fasc. 2, 27.

32. Sofronenko, ed., *Krest'ianskaia reforma*, 32.

33. Despite various kinds of attempts to make them do so, of which the most formidable, of course, was the Stolypin reforms of 1906–11. The terminology of the legislation of 1861, however, represented another such attempt. The laws classified peasants who had begun the redemption process as "peasant proprietors" *(krest'iane sobstvenniki)*, even though their property rights in allotments were extremely constrained, presumably in hopes that they would begin to think of themselves as property owners.

34. One squire tried in 1861 to disabuse his peasants of the "completely communist conception of property they all professed" by emphasizing the analogy between the ownership of clothes and livestock and the ownership of land. S. I. Nosovich, *Krest'ianskaia reforma v Novgorodskoi gubernii. Zapiski S. I. Nosovicha. 1861–1863 gg.* (St. Petersburg, 1899 [reprint from *Istoricheskoe obozrenie*, vols. 10–11]), 19.

35. Richard Hellie, *Enserfment and Military Change in Muscovy* (Chicago, 1971), 247. Keenan finds that in sixteenth-century Muscovy the court, the bureaucracy, and the village each had its own political culture. If we conflate Hellie's interpretation with Keenan's (which neither would welcome), we can say that by the beginning of the eighteenth century, the cultures of the court and bureaucracy had coalesced into one, which became ever more remote from the culture of the village as the century unfolded. E. L. Keenan, "Muscovite Political Folkways," *Russian Review* 46 (1986), no. 4: 123–45; cf. Richard Hellie, "Edward Keenan's Scholarly Ways," *Russian Review* 47 (1987), no. 2: 177–90.

36. As attested, for example, by Dmitrii Samarin, in "Ustavnaia gramota," *Den'*, 1861, no. 7, quoted in A. A. Kornilov, "Deiatel'nost' mirovykh posrednikov," in A. K. Dzhivelegov et al., eds., *Velikaia reforma. Russkoe obshchestvo i krest'ianskii vopros v proshlom i nastoiashchem* (Moscow, 1911), vol. 5, 243.

37. V. I. Lenin, *Polnoe sobranie sochinenii*, 5th ed. (Moscow, 1967–70), vol. 20, 177.

38. The authors of the reform legislation had specified that the mediators of the peace would be elected by the peasantry from among the local nobility; in the event, they were nominated by provincial governors on the advice of marshals of the nobility and confirmed in office by the Senate. L. G. Zakharova, "Krest'ianstvo Rossii v burzhuaznykh reformakh 60-kh godov XIX v.," in V. T. Pashuto et al., eds., *Sotsial'no-politicheskoe i pravovoe polozhenie krest'ianstva v dorevoliutsionnoi Rossii* (Voronezh, 1983), 203; "Polozhenie o gubernskikh i uezdnykh po krest'ianskomu delu uchrezhdeniiakh," chap. 1, art. 13, in Sofronenko, ed., *Krest'ianskaia reforma,* 137, but also see Ust'iantseva, *Institut mirovykh posrednikov v sisteme gosudarstvennogo stroia,* 16.

39. The etymology of the Russian word for serfdom, *krepostnoe pravo,* reflects the origins of the institution in ascription imposed by the ban on peasant movement in the "forbidden years" of the 1590s. The first element of serfdom to take shape was the last to disappear.

40. If we accept the provisional premise that, in the first stage of industrialization, factory wages will fluctuate close to subsistence levels, then ascription was, among other things, a tax on Russia's emerging industries: wages had to cover workers' subsistence plus their fiscal obligations to the communities to which they were ascribed. Industrialists managed to pass some of this tax along to their workers by providing housing that was, to judge from narrative sources, even worse than what their counterparts in other industrializing economies had to put up with.

41. R. E. Johnson, *Peasant and Proletarian: The Working Class of Moscow at the End of the Nineteenth Century* (New Brunswick, N.J., 1979), 158.

42. The relevant articles are 140–43 of the Great Russian Statute, in Sofronenko, ed., *Krest'ianskaia reforma,* 212.

43. Druzhinin, *Russkaia derevenia na perelome,* 226.

44. Russian peasants represented their customs as ancient and immutable, but they could modify their practices rapidly in response to economic opportunity. Much of what passed for venerable peasant custom was attempts to minimize exploitation by outsiders coupled with the risk-aversive strategies common to peasant economies around the world.

45. Field, *The End of Serfdom,* 444n.

46. A deed of exemplary courage and piety.

IV

INTEREST-GROUP POLITICS IN THE ERA OF THE GREAT REFORMS

Alfred J. Rieber

The Great Reforms were the seedbed of modern Russian politics. There had always been some kind of court politics in autocratic Russia. Factions formed around powerful personalities or influential families and their clients. Issues and ideologies were secondary to the struggle for place, honor, and influence over the autocrat. In pre-Petrine Muscovy the main foci of internal politics had been cultural and religious questions. Thereafter foreign policy became the favorite field for factional strife. It offered the greatest immediate rewards for ambitious men who sought to carve out careers as proconsuls of the Empire. Only occasionally during succession crises, as in 1730 and 1825, did an interest group representing part of the nobility coalesce briefly to defend privilege or rights. By the early nineteenth century there were already harbingers of new organizational forms and new patterns of communication that enlarged the institutional setting of politics and increased the number of participants in political life. The creation of ministries, the evolution of a bureaucracy of merit, and the opening of institutions of higher learning marked the beginning of the slow process of depersonalizing factional politics and enlivening its ideological content.

In the reforming decades we are still dealing with a relatively small ruling elite. But its internal structure and relations with the rest of the population have become more complex. The autocrat remains at the center of political life. His family, by virtue of its fecundity, begins to clutter up the corridors of power; the phenomenon of the grand dukes makes its appearance. The policymakers at the highest level become increasingly penetrated by professional bureaucrats. The court continues to enjoy high social prestige and access to the tsar. But it no longer commands the skills and knowledge necessary to administer a complex economy and society. A commission in the guards leading to a military career is no longer the sole or even the main prerequisite for advancement to the highest rank. Factions and clientele networks do not fade from the scene, but the focus of the networks shifts from the court to the ministries. The creation of ministerial government, which ends the collegial restraints on top administrators, and the absence of a cabinet system give great autonomy to the individual minister. He becomes an autocrat in his own right with a vast network of clients who are professionally trained and loyal to their department. Potentially every minister is the center of a faction.

The Shape of Interest Groups

For the first time in the history of the autocracy, political interest groups emerged under the reign of Alexander II. Still part of the ruling class, interest groups were associations of individuals from the upper and middle strata of society who acted in concert to defend and advance public policies that met their ideological aspirations and material needs. They were either occupational or opinion groups, formally or informally organized. The occupational groups clustered around specific ministries; indeed, at times it was difficult to distinguish between the traditional type of faction with a powerful minister as patron and his ministerial subordinates as clients and the newer form of an interest group. The difference lay in the attachment of the members of the group to a set of aims and objectives, a policy that transcended the personality and the tenure of a single minister. The group took on an ethos of its own, impersonal and bureaucratic, deeply attached to the values of professional pride and service. But traditional political loyalties and forms died slowly; the factional leader and his clientele network were no exception. So the distinction between factions and interest groups was not clear at all times.

Opinion groups cut across professional and occupational lines. They were composed of individuals who shared a common view on some public policies usually in conflict with that held by other members of the same occupation; at the very least these groups represented a variety of occupations, recruiting individuals inside and outside the government and developing their own policy programs on single or multiple issues. These issues normally were sufficiently broad in scope to exceed the functional competence of any single ministry to deal with them. Or else, as in the case of the Slavic Benevolent Society, they sought to act in areas that were outside the sphere of government as traditionally defined in Russia.

The interest groups in the era of reforms were by and large informal principally because the autocracy nourished a profound suspicion of organizations that might have the slightest interest in politics. In the eighteenth century there were only a handful of societies officially recognized by the government, of which the two most important were the Free Economic and the Free Russian assemblies. The law of April 8, 1792, lay down strict rules on their organization and on state surveillance over them. A brief boom in societies in the reign of Alexander I roused fears that prompted a law against secret societies in 1822 and, after the December Uprising, brought down the heavy hand of repression. Under Nicholas about two dozen societies were founded, but all of them were concerned with scholarly, charitable, or economic, mainly agricultural, issues. Only the Russian Geographical Society had any real potential for political activism. When it timidly explored this avenue it ran into trouble even in the reforming sixties. The Ministry of Interior closed its political economy section for having arranged debates on current questions. Even joint stock companies had to be approved by the government on an ad hoc basis, all attempts to create a general law of incorporation having failed.[1]

The first formal opinion interest groups to appear in the sixties were the Russian Technological Society and the Society for the Aid of Russian Industry and Trade. The Technological Society was the principal advocate of technical education in Russia, while Aid to Industry lobbied intensively for protective tariffs and an end to monopolies and government interference in domestic industry. Despite criticism by both groups of government policies, they exhibited a quasi-official character by virtue of their restrictive statutes and overlapping membership with government ministries.

The most influential interest group in the reform period, which I have analyzed elsewhere as the Moscow Entrepreneurial Group, was completely informal and had to be brought to light from private correspondence, common membership in joint stock companies, and sponsorship of press organs and cultural activities.[2] More short-lived and narrowly focused were the regional interest groups. Normally they were composed of local notables, including government officials, big landowners, and a few commercial or industrial entrepreneurs, gathered together to promote a regional economic interest, which was, in the reform period, mainly the construction of railroads. The local zemstvos were too unwieldy and untested in the competition for economic favors to serve effectively in that role.

It is difficult to know just how to define the role of the *soslovie* organizations. In the reform era they usurped functions that the government had no intention of granting them, to judge by the legislative acts that established them. The corporations of the nobility and of the merchants became organs of opinion, one is tempted to say pressure groups, in relation to the government. Of all the public organizations they were most representative of large social groupings, but their status was highly ambiguous. They were self-regulating associations that carried out state functions, but they also had the potential to become political organizations in their own right. The noble corporations were especially active in the debate over emancipation, where their role became openly political. The merchant corporations, including the Stock Exchange Society, played an active part in the trade and tariff discussions of the sixties and seventies.

The great mass of urban and rural population took no part in national politics. Even after the creation of the zemstvos and town dumas the electors from the *meshchanstvo* and peasantry did not organize themselves into factions or parties at the local or provincial level. Only occasionally was there any sign of concerted political action, as in the rare case of the revolt of the meshchanstvo against the intelligentsia in the Moscow duma elections of 1879–80. The illegal political groups that claimed to represent the masses played no direct role in political life. Their importance for a history of interest groups lies in the uses made of their threat to established order by certain factions in the government. The manipulation of the "red scare," for example, should not be underestimated as a factor in factional and interest-group politics.

The institutional setting for politics in the reform era underwent a slow but significant evolution, while the patterns of communication about politics changed dramatically. From the very beginning of Alexander II's reign the legislative process became more complex if not more systematic. The creation of the Council of Ministers was intended to provide a greater degree of coordination among the individual ministers than the old Committee of Ministers; yet the committee was not abolished. A proliferation of special ad hoc conferences and investigative commissions continued deliberations for years and produced mountainous documentation. It began with the creation of the Secret and the Main Commissions for drafting legislation to emancipate the serfs and continued through the Shtakel'berg Commission on labor and the Baranov commission investigating the railroads, which deliberated for eight years. The State Council evolved into something resembling a proto-parliament. Attached to it, the State Chancery, with specialized departments staffed by experts, became another important agency for facilitating administrative and legislative action.[3] Possessing overlapping and ill-defined functions, all these bodies nevertheless broadened the range of political action and gave greater scope for building alliances and coalitions.

The really startling innovation in enlarging the field of politics came with the emergence of a mass press at the national level. A combination of political and technical factors created the possibilities for mass-circulation dailies in the 1860s. For ten years after relaxation of the censorship terror, Russian press laws were in a state of complete anarchy, marked by the absence of any guiding principles or unity of administration. Repression was a hit-or-miss affair that encouraged the bold and the enterprising. Improvements in mechanical printing techniques allowed large runs of papers. Government permission for commercial advertising enabled papers to lower subscription rates. The expanding railroad network created new communities of readers outside a single locality. Together with the telegraph, the railroads facilitated the rapid—indeed, instantaneous—transmittal of news and information from Europe. Government ministers quickly grasped the political uses to which the mass-circulation press could be put. Departmental organs, drab and dull sources of official announcements and information, were transformed into opinion papers engaged in sharp polemics with rival papers of other ministries or the private press. The print war became part of factional bureaucratic politics. But the truly phenomenal change took place among private papers, such as *Moskovskie vedomosti, Golos, Syn otechestva,* and *St. Peterburgskie vedomosti.* Under independent press lords such as Mikhail Katkov, A. A. Kraevskii, A. V. Starchevskii, and A. S. Suvorin, these papers reached a mass market. Before 1855 the largest circulation of a daily was about 3,500; by the mid-sixties Katkov's *Moskovskie vedomosti* was printing 12,000 and *Syn otechestva* 20,000 copies. Political factions in the government tried to influence their opinion by cajoling, subsidizing, or threatening, but this did not always work. The press became a wild card in political life. Interest groups attempted to create their own organs of opinion or to gain the support of one already established. Government policies, particularly on economic questions, were heatedly debated in the press. Information and argument provided in the dailies had pronounced effects on decisions over such wide-ranging questions as nationalities, particularly in the Polish and Baltic provinces; education; and railroad construction. The tsar himself was not immune to the currents of opinion. On several occasions press exposés of his ministers, whether inspired by enemies or instigated by journalistic muckrakers, provoked him to insist on an end to intradepartmental polemics and even the resignation of a minister.[4]

Despite the increase in publicity (the term *glasnost'* was widely used), the political game was largely hidden from public view. It was a game played without rules. In the absence of a legislature there were no established norms for drafting or passing laws. In the absence of a cabinet there was no mechanism for forming a governmental consensus. Within the narrow confines of the ruling class there was a freewheeling atmosphere; shifting coalitions and alliances, intrigues, and personal vendettas immensely complicated the process of introducing unprecedented changes in a highly stratified society. The central object of the game was to capture the autocrat. There were two main approaches to the inner citadel of power. One was to build up a unified government. The object here was to secure a strong factional base in the bureaucracy, to gain support in the press, and to penetrate and colonize other government departments with the aim of replacing rival ministers with trustworthy allies or clients. This tactic was favored, for example, by Grand Duke Konstantin Nikolaevich in the early years of his brother Alexander's reign and by Count Shuvalov in the late sixties and early seventies. Another approach was to become the tsar's éminence grise, to persuade him to place his complete trust in a single minister who would set the tone and establish general lines of policy for the whole government. Valuev and to a lesser extent Miliutin aspired to such a position, and they were disappointed that the tsar refused to accept their leadership.[5] The tsar alertly maneuvered to elude these snares and nets. He refused to give up his autocratic prerogatives; it was his God-given responsibility to possess it and use it according to his own will even though he did not know much of the time precisely what course of action to take. He was clearly open to influence and even manipulation on such issues as financial stability, national defense, and threats to public order. But there were times when one of these imperatives came into conflict with another and he was forced to chose. These were painful moments for him.

The complex interaction of the factions and interest groups cannot be simplified by attaching to them traditional ideological labels. There are two problems here, one structural and the other linguistic. The language of politics spoken in nineteenth-century Russia and subsequently adopted by most historians is borrowed from the West European experience. In the Russian context the terminology is confusing, misleading, and politically highly charged. Most often such descriptive terms as *liberal* or *conservative, red* or *reactionary,* and *bourgeois* or *feudal* are used to identify enemies rather than friends or supporters. Hostile labels do not advance historical analysis. The question must be asked: what are the defining attributes of these dualist concepts? Because of Russia's peculiar social structure and political institutions, answers do not come easily. Is the definition of *liberal* to hinge on the support of representative government and defense of private property? Then the *dvorianstvo* qualify as liberal. Is it to hinge on support of freedom of the press and speech and educational reform, which stresses humanistic values? Then Katkov qualifies as liberal. On the other hand, is bureaucratic centralization and Great Russian chauvinism a sure sign of reaction? Then the Miliutin brothers must be placed in that camp. And what is one to do with a free floater like Valuev, a champion of military reform, autonomy for nationalities, economic development, and creation of a representative-consultative assembly but also an advocate of patrimonial control over the peasantry, defense of noble privilege, and restrictions on the press and universities? It will not do to call such people liberal-conservatives, or vice versa. Nor can these judgments be made on the basis of abstract objective criteria, for this assumes a uniform process of social change that is belied by historical reality. Linguistically and structurally, the Russian political scene requires a different vocabulary.

Autocratic politics in nineteenth-century Russia owed its peculiar form to an incomplete and distorted implementation of Speransky's reform program. The failure to create a legislative branch, if only of a consultative variety, fatefully postponed the creation of a national forum for discussion as a means of educating the ruling elite and literate public about the nature of politics. Repeated attempts in the 1860s and 1870s to bridge the gap between state and society, culminating in Loris Melikov's scheme, encountered repeated resistance from the autocrat. The long-delayed promise of a consultative assembly (the Bulygin Duma), squeezed out of a reluctant autocrat in 1905 by an armed rebellion, came too late. All classes demanded a genuine parliamentary system. The autocracy yielded temporarily. Then it quickly repudiated its own handiwork when the democratically elected First Duma threatened to destroy the social base of monarchy by passing a radical land settlement. The coup of June 3, 1907, did not crown the reforms of the 1860s; it decapitated them.

In the executive branch Speransky's view of a civil service based on high entrance standards and promotion by merit was adulterated under pressure of the *dvorianstvo*. What survived was a ministerial form of administration and a series of new institutions of higher learning, but the close relationship between the two was only gradually and incompletely established. Consequently, the Russian state lagged far behind Western and Central Europe in moving toward the Weberian ideal of a rational, hierarchical bureaucracy operating under the rule of law. The traditional patron-client relationship did not disappear in Russian governing circles. The two political styles— patronage and professionalism—coexisted, sometimes merging, as when a high-ranking official or even a court figure took a group of professional bureaucrats under his protection.

There were four major bureaucratic factions, or interest groups, that took the field by the mid 1860s: the economists, the engineers, and the military and Shuvalov factions. The first on the scene and the most influential during the first decade of Alexander II's region began as a clientele network and evolved into an occupational interest group. Initially it coalesced around the tsar's younger brother, Grand Duke Konstantin Nikolaevich, and was generally called by contemporary accounts the Konstantinovtsy or "the eagles of Konstantin Nikolaevich." Many of them also benefited from the patronage of the tsar's enlightened aunt, Grand Duchess Elena Pavlovna. Konstantin Nikolaevich enjoyed great influence over his brother up to the Polish revolt and was able to obtain the appointment of a number of his protégés to ministerial positions, including at one time or another the ministers of education (A. V. Golovnin), justice (D. N. Zamiatin), navy (Admiral N. K. Krabbe), and finance (M. Kh. Reitern), as well as a large number of middle-range bureaucrats who were instrumental in designing and carrying out the emancipation of the serfs; the judicial, university, press, and fiscal reforms; and the great program of railroad construction under mixed private and public control.[6] His influence declined precipitously in the midsixties. He lost much prestige when, as viceroy of Poland, his policy of reconciliation with the Poles collapsed in the violence of a full-scale rebellion. Then the attempted assassination of the tsar in 1866 discredited his domestic policy of greater openness and legality in favor of more repressive police measures. Most of his eagles fell from their perches; only Reitern survived. Although Konstantin Nikolaevich returned from a two-year self-imposed exile to take up his duties as the president of the State Council, he never fully recovered his influence or his leadership role. By this time, however, his eagles were ready to soar on their own.

The Economists

The economists' interest group was composed of a hard core of financial specialists, statisticians, and economic theorists and journalists gathered around the finance minister, Reitern. That they managed to survive the eclipse of Konstantin Nikolaevich was a sure sign that they represented something more than the traditional clientele network, which normally folded up at the decline or demise of its patron. Relying on their professional expertise and skills in bureaucratic infighting, they consolidated their position in the bureaucracy and even survived the resignation of their leader in the late 1870s. They forged alliances with regional entrepreneurial groups. They developed their own long-range plans for Russia's economic growth based on the principle of a mixed economy in which the state and private interests cooperated under the tutelage of the Ministry of Finance and the State Bank in order to manage the economy through the dangerous shoals of capitalist expansion and industrialization. After a period of trial and error, their views on taxation, monetary policy, banking, tariffs, railroads, and foreign trade gradually were integrated into official state policy. When forced to defend their policies in public, they could rely on several domestic house organs, *St. Peterburgskie vedomosti,* and *Birzhevye vedomosti.* Abroad, where Russia's credit standing was vital for the success of their economic development plans, they enjoyed the support of government-subsidized organs such as *Le Nord.* Initially Katkov was one of their allies, and he opened the pages of the thick journal *Russkii vestnik* to their economic projects. But he broke with them over the Polish and Baltic questions. The economists' policy of internal development required stable relations with Western Europe, especially France and Britain, to preserve a ready money market for the placement of Russian railroad loans and other government securities. They favored, therefore, a policy of conciliation in the Kingdom of Poland and the preservation of local rights in the Baltic Provinces in order to placate the regional commercial interests that were closely tied to European markets. They also sought to avoid offending the influential Polish émigré community in Paris and London. This earned them the hostility of those in the government, particularly the military faction, who perceived autonomy in the western borderlands as a security risk.[7] Their greatest test of strength came, however, over attempts to wrest control over provincial fiscal policy out of their hands. It stimulated Reitern to draft his famous memorandum of 1866, which won the approval of the tsar, confounded Reitern's opponents, and became the touchstone for Russian economic policy down to Witte's time.

Reitern's memorandum reflected his own cautious approach to economic questions but also appealed to Alexander II's stoic view of the world. There were no quick or complete remedies for Russia's economic ills, Reitern lamented, but a sober and sound policy of savings and investment requiring heavy sacrifices would produce steady if slow economic growth. Russia was still passing through a transitional period when new institutions had not yet matured to the point where they could meet unaided the demands of the new society. The growing need for investment in capital goods demanded forced savings. He defined the two major sources as credit restrictions on unproductive borrowing and heavier taxation. The first struck at the nobles' privileges, the second at peasant subsistence.

It was politically impossible for Reitern to place the entire burden on the nobles, but it was economically unsound to make the peasants carry the whole weight. Reitern had already alienated the landed nobility and antagonized their chief spokesman in the government, Count Shuvalov. He had generally supported the majority of the Main Committee chaired by Konstantin Nikolaevich in defending peasant interests against landlord claims in the early postemancipation period. He had opposed Valuev's proposals to create a noble land bank and attempted to reduce the sale of alcoholic beverages, which would have further reduced the income of many big landowners. It was partly for these reasons that he was engaged in 1866 in a fight for his political life against the Shuvalov faction. His memo preached a compromise, but as usual the politically helpless peasants were obliged to shoulder the major burden. Reitern estimated that between 1831 and 1865 the government and landlords had borrowed two billion rubles, only a small part of which had been invested productively. The rest had been spent on wasteful wars and the high living of an irresponsible noble class. "If only half the sum had been invested productively," he charged, "then Russia would be covered with a network of railroads, would possess heavy industry, active commerce, a rich population and flourishing finances." There would be no further consumption loans for the nobility, but neither would he consider levying a land tax. Regretfully, he proposed a fifty-kopek increase in the head tax, which fell on the most indigent part of population, a fact that Reitern did not deny.[8]

Reitern's main recommendations constituted a three-point plan that was in essence highly political: (1) to stop the flight of capital abroad by increasing confidence in the government "through the constant and rapid application in civil relations of the main principles of reform and through assurances that we have no intention of interfering in the political troubles of other powers"; (2) to reduce government spending so that free capital could find the most profitable investments; (3) to borrow only for productive investments "of which railroads occupy first place." For Reitern railroads were the major instrument of increasing exports, reestablishing Russia's favorable balance of trade, and earning hard currency for further investment. They became the cornerstone of his economic policy and the center of political storms over the next decade. The tsar approved the general lines of the memo and reconfirmed Reitern's full authority in all financial matters. Valuev's sensitive antennae told him that it was time to make peace in order "to smooth the way for future relations with the Minister of Finance."[9]

The battles over railroad construction pitted the economists against the engineers and the military and Shuvalov factions on the occasion of every concession granted by the government to private builders. Reitern's plan was to create a kind of partnership between the state and private entrepreneurs. The state would identify a network of lines it desired to construct, request bids, advance a third of the capital, and guarantee bonds for the remaining two-thirds. The private company would market the bonds, that is, raise two-thirds of the capital, and actually construct and run the lines. To strengthen the government's financial position and thus its ability to bargain on equal terms with the entrepreneurs, Reitern proposed the creation of a railroad fund to finance successive lines. His first initiative was to organize the sale of Alaska and the second was to sell the state-owned Nikolaevskii railroad to a private company. Negotiations for the sale of Alaska were carried on in great secrecy. With the exception of Reitern, Gorchakov, and the navy minister, Admiral Krabbe—another eagle from the nest of Konstantin Nikolaevich—none of the ministers even knew about the plan until they received the news several days after the convention had been signed with Washington. Shuvalov and Valuev were stunned when they learned about it.[10]

The sale of the Nikolaevskii line could not be settled out of court and was bound to arouse partisan feelings. In defending his recommendation to the tsar, Reitern argued that the completion of a network was imperative, not only to lighten the financial burden but "because the political strength of the state itself is directly dependent upon rapid completion of railroad lines." By giving equal weight to economic and security issues, Reitern touched two of his master's most sensitive chords. The treasury still lacked the necessary resources even to fulfill its past commitments. Pledged to construct two state lines, the Moscow-Kursk-Kiev and the Odessa-Kharkov, it needed thirty million rubles a year over the next three years in addition to thirty million rubles budgeted for 1867 to help finance the construction of private lines. Neither foreign nor domestic credit could supply such huge sums. Only one source of capital remained, the alienation of state lines. Forestalling criticism that a vital artery should not fall into private, to say nothing of foreign, hands, Reitern flatly declared, "It may be taken as an axiom that every railroad belonging to a private company serves in every capacity as effective an instrument of government as does a state railroad."[11] Implicit in his argument was the conviction that as long as the Russian state remained strong and stable, there was no reason to fear that major national assets owned by foreigners might become an instrument of political influence or control, an assumption that was consistently maintained by his successors down to the revolution of 1917.

The main opposition to Reitern's plan came from the engineers. The minister of transportation, P. P. Mel'nikov, regarded the Nikolaevskii as setting a kind of moral standard by which to measure the performance of all lines. It bore the social costs which private lines avoided: cheap movement of building materials for other railroads and the lowest third-class rates in the country. Mel'nikov set "high hopes for the influence of its future development upon an improved standard of living for (all) society." Private owners would simply milk the line for all it was worth and raise freight prices to the detriment of the general welfare, whereas "by its own management (the state) can promote trade by reducing rates to the lowest level and even sacrificing if need be income to circulation of traffic when this can lead to an increase in the power of the state or its income in other sectors."[12]

The proposed sale rapidly escalated into a public controversy involving other interest groups and the press. The engineers joined forces with the Moscow entrepreneurs and leaked information to the Slavophile press of F. V. Chizhov and Ivan Aksakov. Within the government the War Ministry mounted a campaign to defend the state lines in the name of military security. Reitern lost his first skirmish when an overwhelming majority of the Council of Ministers voted against his plan. But then he deftly shifted further discussion to a more congenial milieu, the Finance Committee under his control. A strong endorsement from that body of specialists enabled the tsar to satisfy his conscience, and he approved the sale.[13] This set the stage for a more intense conflict over who would buy the line, a Russian or a foreign group.

The two main contenders for the purchase of the Nikolaevskii were the Grande Société des chemins de fer russes, backed by the economist faction, and the Moscow entrepreneurial group, backed by just about everyone else. The Moscow entrepreneurs mounted a three-pronged campaign to win government approval of their bid: within the duma and zemstvo organizations in the provinces most affected by the railroad, Nizhnii Novgorod, Moscow, Tver, and St. Petersburg; in the press, primarily Aksakov's newspapers *Moskva* and *Moskvich;* and through personal lobbying of individual ministers by merchants whose activities in state-licensed businesses such as the liquor monopoly brought them into contact with high officials. To the surprise and dismay of Reitern and his associates, the entrepreneurs won over not only a majority of the Council of Ministers but also the heir to the throne, Alexander Alexandrovich. In the end their own inexperience in railroad affairs, ignorance of technical questions, and naive exaggeration of their importance in the European money markets doomed their project. Reitern managed to squeeze out a narrow majority from a joint session of the Finance Committee and an ad hoc committee established to examine the specific terms of the sale, but his proposal was badly defeated in both the committee and the Council of Ministers. Nevertheless, Alexander II once again confirmed the minority. Reitern's hard-won victory was sweetened by the addition of over 100 million rubles to the railroad fund.[14]

To crown his success Reitern needed to replace Mel'nikov as minister of transportation. For, despite his control over general policy, each concession still resembled a tug of war between the economists on one side and the engineers and military on the other over the trace that would best conform to their respective interests. Miliutin was impregnable. So an intrigue was set in motion to discredit Mel'nikov. Rumors spread of spiritual séances held in his house; scandals growing out of mismanagement on state lines received unusual publicity in the press organs of the economists. The tsar, convinced that Mel'nikov had become a liability to the financial respectability of the government, asked him to resign. Reitern succeeded in getting one of his friends, Count V. A. Bobrinskoi, who also enjoyed the patronage of Grand Duchess Elena Pavlovna, was appointed acting minister of transportation.[15]

Together Reitern and his ally Bobrinskoi designed a new network of eighteen lines that offered entrepreneurs so many potentially profitable outlets for their investments that the political and strategic lines favored by the engineers and the military were left without any bidders. The economists manipulated the flaccid rules on concessions to award contracts to their favorite entrepreneurs, mainly Baltic Germans and Jews who had good connections with the European money markets, men such as Von Derviz, von Meck, and Poliakov. The economists persuaded the tsar to sell off the remaining state lines to private companies. The engineers fought a rear-guard action to delay the dismantling of their life's work. Even the fates seem to have smiled on Reitern's ambitions. In 1871 the last check on his financial operations was removed: the controller general, V. A. Tatarinov, died. Reitern easily managed his replacement by another member of his own faction, also a big landowner in the southwest and another client of Elena Pavlovna, A. A. Abaza. Despite a surge of speculation and scandals, Reitern remained the unchallenged master of the government's economic policies.[16]

The Engineers

The professional training, sphere of activity, and task-oriented role of the engineers tended to restrict the political outlook of this occupational interest group compared to the economists. But unlike most engineers in Anglo-American societies, they were imbued with a broad philosophical and moral outlook. It would not be too much to say that they cultivated their own version of a moral economy. This was due in general to the Petrine ethos of the engineer as the servant of the state and more specifically to the influence of the French model of the engineering profession.[17] Consequently, they envisaged public works as a powerful instrument of social as well as economic change. Their main inspiration came from a small band of French polytechnicians—Lame, Clayperon, Raucourt—who had lived, taught, and worked in Russia in the formative years of the Institute of Transportation Engineers and whose portraits still grace the institute's corridors in Leningrad. The French engineers and their Russian students were advocates of the original version of Saint-Simon's political economy, which stressed the creative role of the state. In the hands of French epigones of Saint-Simon such as Michel Chevalier and the Pereire brothers, the emphasis had shifted away from an exclusive statist to a mixed or guided capitalist position; and it was this second strand of Saint-Simonian thought, which penetrated Russia in the 1840s and 1850s, that influenced the economists, whereas the Russian engineers remained by and large more faithful to the older tradition.

In the 1840s the Russian engineers had been in the forefront in constructing the great public works launched by the engineer in the Winter Palace, Nicholas I. But the tsar missed the chance to become Russia's Saint-Simon on horseback. Nicholas felt uneasy about the presence of the French engineers and harassed them for their sympathies with the Poles in the revolt of 1830. Despite his general enthusiasm for technological progress, he regarded the Institute of Transportation Engineers as a "cradle of free-thinkers." It was one of the many institutions of higher learning in Russia which he subjugated to strict military discipline after 1848. The police terror tempered but did not break the Saint-Simonian spirit of the Russian engineers.[18]

A generation before the Crimean War the Russian engineers had advocated both the introduction of railroad construction into the curriculum of the institute and the construction of state-built railroads. Their opinions had consistently been informed by strategic and developmental concerns. But, restricted to the pages of their professional *Zhurnal Putei Soobshcheniia* and confidential reports to the tsar, they had not reached a larger public. They nurtured a strong sense of professional pride and accomplishment by having built the first trunk line in Russia, the Moscow–St. Petersburg (Nikolaevskii) railroad. Although the American Major Whistler was the chief consulting engineer, the Russian transportation officers Mel'nikov and N. O. Kraft were the operating engineers on the ground. Subsequent criticism of the line had nothing to do with its technical aspects; on the contrary, it was the most solidly built and safest of Russian railroads. Its only problem was a high cost per mile.

If the French engineering profession provided the theoretical underpinning of the Russians, the American experience in building railroads provided the practical model. Mel'nikov had made an extensive tour of the United States in preparation for planning and building the Nikolaevskii. The deep impression left by the trip lasted all his life. "The Americans were primarily an industrial people," he noted, and they quickly grasped "the enormous future of the application of steam power to locomotion of railroads." Railroads had enabled the United States to overcome the great sparsely populated spaces that threatened to slow its economic growth. The rapid expansion of its network converted the nation into a dangerous rival of Russia as a supplier of grain to Europe. Given the startling transformation railroads had brought about in American life, he declared, "we will find the very same reason to an even greater degree exists for the extension of railroads in Russia."

Mel'nikov and his colleagues envisioned a planned national railroad network that would balance the economic development of different regions and assure the rapid movement of troops from the interior to concentration points on the exposed frontiers. The iron framework of the major trunk lines assumed the shape of a great cross: a vertical line from Moscow to Sevastopol and a horizontal line from Saratov to Dunaburg. The scheme facilitated, in Mel'nikov's words, the exchange of grain from the south and east; coal from the Donets Basin; salt from the Crimea; flax and hemp from the Baltic and Central Agricultural Region; cattle, tallow, wool, and tobacco from the shores of the Black and Caspian seas; and manufactured goods from the center.[19]

The engineers did not always agree on the specific direction of the lines; some paid greater attention to strategic than to economic considerations. For example, the veteran railroad engineer and instructor at the institute, M. S. Volkov, favored a Petersburg to Sevastopol line that would pass through the western regions "where the loyalty of the people is in any case doubtful" and intersect the main east-west traffic, thus "making it possible to dispatch troops by rail lines perpendicular to the frontiers."[20] But whatever the differences, they agreed that the state, by planning and constructing railroads, should become the main engine of economic development, political integration, and military security.

Until 1862 the voice of the engineers had been filtered through the bureaucracy by intermediaries who occupied the top policymaking positions dealing with railroads. With the appointment of Mel'nikov as minister of transportation the engineers advanced to the forefront of planning. Mel'nikov moved rapidly to transform the ministry and the Corps of Engineers into professional organizations. On his recommendation the institute shed its military character and became a special institution of higher education, which gave it the prestige and privileges necessary to attract the well-born and ambitious. He converted the Corps of Engineers from a military to a civilian agency. His administrative reorganization of the ministry eliminated the rigid compartmentalization of the various departments and permitted each to deal with the whole range of collateral problems connected with its work.[21] Out of this professional structure the engineers drafted the first really comprehensive railroad network for European Russia. The product of more than twenty years of internal planning, the network consisted of five trunk lines that fulfilled the engineers' vision of linking the major productive regions of the empire and satisfying at the same time the country's strategic needs. For the next generation they sought to implement and expand their original design.

Although Mel'nikov was forced out of office in 1871 and Reitern's system won all along the line, the engineers were not beaten. Their alliance with the military faction salvaged some developmental and strategic lines, though it was difficult to find the funding to build them. A few of the more politically astute engineers recognized the necessity of breaking out of their narrow occupational mold and forming a broadly based opinion group. They were instrumental in founding the Russian Technological Society. At the same time, the technicians in the ministry never gave up their campaign to restore state construction to a central place in government policy.

In the early seventies they took charge of a special commission established to trace a trans-Siberian railroad and began the planning that ultimately culminated in the state-built line under Witte. With the appointment of Admiral Pos'et as minister of transportation the engineers gained a new leader who opened a drumfire of criticism against the Reitern system and succeeded in having an investigative commission appointed. The Baranov Commission was controlled mainly by the economists, including Baranov himself, and labored for eight years with little concrete result. But the criticisms that created it had a more telling effect. Following the Russo-Turkish War the military faction increased its demands for strategic state-built lines. The Lieven report on the condition of state mines and state metallurgical plants recommended a more systematic state program for railroad construction linked to the development of the Donets basin. Under these pressures the Ministry of Transportation, although led by one of the economists, finally conceded that a new state program of state-built lines was necessary to meet pressing strategic and industrial needs.[22] A new era of state construction was launched.

The Military

The military faction, often in close alliance with the engineers on railroad policy, had a much more ambitious political agenda. Like the engineers, the military faction was essentially an occupational interest group. It crystallized around a small group of officers who were graduates or teachers at the Nikolaevskii Academy of the General Staff and Engineering Academy. Together with the third military academy, Artillery, these institutions attracted members of the lesser, often landless, gentry rather than the aristocratic families whose sons completed their formal education in the Page Corps and enrolled in the glamorous elite guards regiments. Although the military, like the engineering schools, had suffered from the deadening routine of the Nikolaevan period, they produced a number of thoughtful officers who subsequently became both the architects of the military reforms and the leading strategists of the sixties and seventies, occupying the top military-administrative posts in the empire to the end of Alexander II's reign. The graduating class of the Nikolaevskii Academy was small, ranging between twenty-five and twenty-eight a year. But the talent was deep. The leader of the military faction was Dmitrii Miliutin, minister of war from 1862 to 1881, who graduated in the midthirties and later taught at the academy, where he became one of the severest critics of the overly schematic, theoretical, and pedantic course of instruction.[23]

During the early years of Miliutin's ministry the thoughts and energies of the reformers were almost completely absorbed by problems related to the restitution of Russia as a first-class military power: reorganizing the central and local military administrations along territorial lines, creating a standing reserve, rearmament and retraining troops for greater combat effectiveness. They were slower to realize the importance of technological backwardness and its effect upon the army. Devoted to the Suvorov school of thinking, they emphasized moral factors.

By the midsixties the military group realized that the reconstruction of the army required new perspectives on the broader questions of economic development and social reform. Their demands for the improvement of artillery and the construction of strategic railroads plunged them into debates over the financial and industrial policies of the government. At the same time they were drawn into deeper political controversies swirling around the Polish and Baltic provinces, where they feared the effect of centrifugal forces on imperial defense. To provide a strategic counterweight to European pressures on the western borderlands, they advocated a forward policy in Central Asia. Educational reforms in the army's academies and secondary schools involved the military group in disputes over general educational reform.

To represent, defend, and advance their views the military factions turned the unofficial section of the ministry's official daily *Russkii invalid* into a special organ, *Sovremennoe slovo,* which was subsequently published separately. Its profession de foi was a litany of reformist causes: "the full, free development of the individual to the limits of its reasonable expression," "the free association of labor and property owners," "broadening women's rights," "free education," "equality before the law," broadening of local self-government."[24] Both papers took strong and independent stands on most foreign and domestic policies, engaging in fierce polemics with other ministerial organs and the public press. Occasionally the tsar felt compelled to intervene when he concluded that passions were running too high and threatened a vital interest. On at least one occasion, Miliutin's chauvinistic criticisms of the Baltic German newspapers brought down the wrath of the tsar. He "expressed the wish that the polemic newspaper not be so intemperate that instead of (encouraging) the joining together of Russia in a unified whole it entails its disintegration."[25] Throughout the sixties and seventies the military group, with Miliutin as its head, found itself at odds with the economic group over fiscal and foreign policy and with the Shuvalov group over education, the peasant question, and the role of the nobility in consultative organs of government. At first the clash with the economists came over fiscal policy. After 1862 the Finance Ministry's new budgetary procedures and Reitern's determination to slash expenditures pitted them against the military group. The most critical moment came in 1866 when Reitern's demand to reduce the military budget by fifteen to twenty million rubles infuriated Miliutin. Alexander, caught between his two reforming ministers on the issues of greatest moment to him, fiscal stability and military security, resorted to his characteristic response. He urged the ministers to make every effort to comply with Reitern's budget reductions and then privately assured Miliutin that the only cuts he would permit would be those that "in no way affected the existing organization of the army and did not weaken its combat effectiveness."[26]

A similar clash took place over Reitern's reforms in granting railroad concessions. Miliutin regarded the capitalist entrepreneurs as scoundrels and cheats who filled their pockets with hundreds of thousands of rubles stolen from the treasury. He accused them of having saddled Russia with poorly built, unprofitable lines that lacked adequate carrying capacity, swallowed up additional capital for immediate repairs, and burdened the treasury with heavy debt from a state-guaranteed return on private investment. On this issue, however, Alexander gave the form of satisfaction to Miliutin by agreeing to include strategic lines in the planned networks and the substance to Reitern by leaving their construction up to private investors, who preferred to bid on the more profitable commercial lines.

In foreign policy the military group clashed repeatedly with its bureaucratic rivals over its hard line in the Polish provinces and its forward policy in Central Asia. In both cases the economists and their supporter in the Foreign Ministry, the minister himself, Prince A. M. Gorchakov, were advocates of caution and compromise. They sought to reach an accommodation with Polish nationalists in order to placate western financial interests necessary for Russia's economic development and to avoid costly diplomatic crises that threatened war. They feared antagonizing Britain by penetrating Central Asia too close to the sensitive Afghan frontier and the approaches to India. Nikolai Miliutin, the radical reformer in peasant affairs and local government, took a different view of the Polish aspirations for freedom; and the war minister was a vigorous supporter of his brother's nationalist policy in Poland. "I cannot tell you," Nikolai wrote his brother in the spring of 1863, "what a pitiful impression is produced here [in Warsaw] by our failure to act against a half-armed mob of priests, kids, and every kind of bastard (svoloch)."[27] Dmitrii Miliutin skillfully maneuvered to obtain appointments of key officials in the western provinces. His aim was to unify military and civil administration in all areas where Polish influence threatened to become dominant. Against Valuev and Dolgorukov, he won over the tsar to appoint two of his military leaders, General K. P. fon Kaufman and General A. P. Bezak, as governors-general and commanders of the northwest and southwest provinces respectively. Together with Nikolai Miliutin in Warsaw they conducted a vigorous campaign against the Catholic Church and Polish landlords.[28] As the danger of Polish opposition diminished, the Shuvalov faction reasserted its influence in the western provinces. Following the death of Bezak in 1868, the unity of command was dismantled and "their man," Prince Dondukov-Korsakov, was appointed the new civil governor-general.[29]

In the great battle over educational reform the War Ministry built up what virtually amounted to an alternative school system of *voennye uchilische* and *gymnazii* running parallel to the civilian schools under the Ministry of Education. The military gymnasia, for example, quickly gained a reputation for innovative teaching inspired by the reformer pedagogues Nikolai Pirogov and Konstantin Ushinskii. The most serious challenge to Miliutin's educational reforms came from the Shuvalov group. The minister of education,

Count Dmitrii Tolstoi, a Shuvalov client, opposed the dual educational structure created by the military schools and feared Miliutin's so-called democratization of education and the army. The military reformers were vulnerable on the issue of radical agitation in their secondary schools and academies. When disorders broke out in 1867 at the Petersburg Medical-Surgical Academy, Tolstoi and Shuvalov launched a campaign to link the agitators and some professors with the attempted assassination of the tsar by Karakozov, discredit Miliutin, and transfer the academy to the jurisdiction of the Ministry of Education. Broadening their attack, they blamed the press for the incident and accused army officers in Poland of leaking information to Katkov's paper, *Moskovskie vedomosti,* which defended Miliutin's position.[30]

Dragging on for seven years, the controversy over the Medical-Surgical Academy became intertwined with the larger dispute over educational counterreforms, the battle of classical against real curricula. By this time Miliutin had lost Katkov's support, for with Poland subdued the fiery editor had taken up the cause of classical education. Miliutin turned the dispute over the academy into a "personal question," that is, one involving his resignation if he lost.[31] Here he was clearly within his jurisdictional right as war minister, and Alexander II finally recognized this. But on the larger issue of classical education, where the military group was just as clearly acting outside its officially recognized field of bureaucratic competence, they lost.

The Shuvalov Faction

The Shuvalov group is the most difficult and elusive to categorize. It shared attributes of both the traditional clientele network and the emerging opinion-interest group. Composed mainly of high nobility gathered around Count Peter Shuvalov, a grandee who dabbled in bureaucratic politics, it came closer than any of the other groups to building a unified government. To that extent it resembled the original group of Konstantinovtsy, which also had a highborn patron and aspired to a unified government at the beginning of Alexander's reign. The Shuvalov group emerged from the so-called planters' party, which opposed the terms of the emancipation. It originally included such aristocrats as Shuvalov's father; the Court Marshal Count Andrei Petrovich; another relative, the marshal of the St. Petersburg nobility, Count Peter Pavlovich Shuvalov; Prince V. V. Dolgorukov, Prince F. I. Paskevich; and Prince A. S. Menshikov. But the younger Shuvalov was more astute than his hidebound elders. He sensed that he could not openly oppose the spirit of the times. His efforts to involve the nobility in the central organs of power without appearing to diminish the autocratic authority earned him a reputation for "phony liberalism." But it also enabled him by the end of the decade to become one of the two or three most powerful men in Russia below the tsar.

Shuvalov was only thirty-three when Alexander II, shaken by the Karako-zov attempt, recalled him to the capital from Riga to succeed Prince Dolgor-ukov as chief of gendarmes and head of the Third Section. In the overheated atmosphere of the times it was easy for an ambitious man to turn the security services into a springboard to power. For the next seven years Shuvalov used his position to manipulate the tsar and extend his influence throughout the administration, gradually gathering around himself a group of like-minded security men, dubbed by Valuev "the Committee of Public Safety." From the very beginning of his tenure in office Shuvalov spread before the tsar a witches' sabbath of conspiracies, real and imagined, that his agents had uncovered. He claimed that secret criminal activities were actually in-creasing after the attempt on the tsar's life; that "harmful tendencies had even infected many servitors in various government departments, especially the Ministries of Justice, Education and Finance," that is, ministries headed by former Konstantinovtsy, leaders of the economist group. Launching a direct attack on the judicial reforms, Shuvalov reported that the new laws permitted "insolent and insulting" remarks against the emperor and the im-perial family to be made freely within the walls of the courts.[32]

Playing on Alexander's fears of subversion, Shuvalov gradually gained control over all the ministries directly concerned with public order. Within two years he replaced the Konstantinovtsy Golovnin and Zamiatin with Dmi-trii Tolstoi and Count K. I. Pahlen at Education and Justice. When Valuev left Interior, Shuvalov had one of his former deputies, A. E. Timashev, appointed to succeed him. He added a fourth, Count A. P. Bobrinskoi, as minister of transportation to replace Mel'nikov and keep a thorn pressed in Reitern's side.

Unlike his aristocratic forebears Shuvalov understood the importance of the press as an organ of political persuasion. The aristocratic journal *Vest'* was his staunchest supporter. In general its program was his program. The credo of *Vest'* had at its center the revitalization of the landed nobility in the political and economic life of the countryside and the renewal of the clergy as its staunchest bulwark in the social sphere. The foundations of the new politics of the nobility would be respect for law (that is, noble property), freedom of the press as a weapon against arbitrariness (that is, the bureauc-racy), and vigorous participation in the zemstvo movement. Firmly opposed to any social or political equality, *Vest'* reaffirmed the noble ideal of mentor to the peasantry. It opposed obligatory elementary education and obligatory redemption of peasant allotments, which were favored by the economists; insisted that the peasantry needed the paternalistic supervision of the nobil-ity; and denounced overly zealous justices of the peace who intervened in this natural relationship. It extolled the Orthodox Church and demanded new social privileges for the clergy. It overtly preached anti-Semitism. At times its class position overrode its patriotic sentiments. In the case of the Polish uprising it absolved the Polish *szlachta* from accusations by the mili-tary group that it was the chief culprit and argued for reconciliation based on class solidarity of the imperial nobility.[33] Occasionally, however, even Shuvalov found its tone lofty and its polemics against the bureaucracy too embarrassing. For this reason he cultivated Katkov, affected to protect him, and insinuated himself into the role of intermediary between the editor and the tsar, with mixed success.[34]

Shuvalov nourished the ambitions of a Disraeli or Bismarck but was always too much of an intriguer and too little of a statesman to measure up to their standard. He lacked a clear-cut political philosophy yet was conscious of the need to protect the aristocracy without challenging the autocracy. He perceived threats to his class on two fronts: democracy, socialism, and nihilism on the left and bureaucratic absolutism on the right. In his search for an alternative he cultivated the fertile mind of P. A. Valuev, "notre doyen," as he affectionately called him. Valuev's personal political philosophy, modified and occasionally distorted by Shuvalov, combined two contradictory principles of government: ministerial centralization and provincial devolution. But the contradiction was only apparent. Both men intended to reserve the levers of political power to the highest appointed officials of the tsar, presumably aristocrats like themselves, and to permit only a consultative role for elected representatives from the provincial notables. Their aim was to revive the nobility as a political class, to disarm the revolutionaries by winning over public opinion, and to bind the restless borderlands to the Russian core; that is, in Valuev's words, "to give Russia an extra step over Poland on the road to the development of state institutions and force the western region to turn its face to Moscow and its back to Poland."[35]

The Shuvalov group exercised a powerful influence on the evolution of the Great Reforms from 1866 to 1874. At Education, Tolstoi imposed administrative centralization and a classical curriculum as the dominant features of the secondary schools until the revolution of 1905. Pahlen at Justice was also a staunch supporter of administrative hegemony and supported the governors and police in their running battles with the independent judiciary. Timashev, less capable than his colleagues, was obsessed by the need to stiffen censorship and to incorporate the principle of state intervention into the Municipal Reform of 1870. Yet none of them succeeded in reversing the major reforms of their predecessors. On important issues they were forced either to compromise, as in the case of municipal reform, or to give up altogether their plans for new legislation, as with elementary education and censorship.[36] In part they were victims of the new-era politics. The cumbersome process of legislation permitted all kinds of tactical maneuvers to delay and water down draft laws. Political opposition within the ministries and factional strife within the Council of Ministers and the State Council not only had the effect of frustrating the reforms but also of hampering the counterreforms. But they also failed to free themselves of traditional politics with its overreliance on patron-client relationships and the internal contradictions this bred within an increasingly centralized bureaucratic system.

The most sustained and effective opposition to a unified government under Shuvalov's lordly aegis came from the economists and the military group. Reitern and his colleagues beat back an attempt to restore full powers over local justice and finances to the governors-general. It would, wrote Reitern to the tsar, plunge the provinces into administrative chaos, spawn "endless wrangling and a fall in state revenues," and reverse a ten-year trend of "giving power to the person responsible for getting things done." Like Shuvalov, Reitern knew his master's weaknesses. He invoked threats of economic chaos to counterbalance fears of revolutionary anarchy.[37] The economists also outmaneuvered Shuvalov on the issue of the proposed income tax. If they were forced to make concessions over railroad policy and accept more state-built lines, they exacted their revenge by forcing Shuvalov's creature, Minister of Transportation Bobrinskoi, out of office.[38] When Shuvalov left the scene in 1874, Reitern's system was intact. The attempt of Shuvalov to break Miliutin's power was also largely unsuccessful. His one victory was to clip the wings of *Russkii invalid*. But his major assault on Miliutin's great army reform of 1874 fell short despite support from aristocrats like Field Marshal Prince A. I. Bariatinskii, a close personal friend of the tsar. At the same time Shuvalov was engaged in his last campaign to introduce a major change in the institutions of government. In the early seventies he returned to his cherished project of bringing representatives of the landed nobility into the central organs through the guise of electing zemstvo members to serve on two special commissions established to investigate the chronically depressed conditions of agriculture and the equally persistent labor question. In the ensuing bureaucratic infighting Shuvalov as a political manager displayed the weaknesses characteristic of his social class. Opposed by Reitern and Miliutin, the bureaucratic centralists par excellence, and drowned out by cries of "zemskii sobor" and "constitution," Shuvalov's plan collapsed.[39] His political career went down with it.

The Managerial Tsar

There are instructive lessons in these struggles. For all his apparent hesitations and uncertainties, Alexander II remained remarkably consistent and loyal in his attachment to the leaders of the economists and the military group. They represented for him the most effective defenders of the two bulwarks of the autocracy: fiscal stability and economic growth on one side and a modern army and defense of imperial interests on the other. These aims could not be achieved, it was clear, without a transformation of the rest of society. But there were fewer clear guidelines in that broad and uneven terrain. In crossing it there was always the danger, however exaggerated, of disturbing public order. It was there that Shuvalov and his Committee of Public Safety, though not unchallenged, could range most freely. Whenever the economists or, more frequently, the military group attempted to move beyond their professional competence strictly defined, they could be burned and forced back. But whenever the security services attempted to penetrate their turf the same rebuff could be expected. Of course, in the final analysis it was the autocrat who drew the lines. And often, too often for his subordinates' peace of mind, he hesitated for years to draw the line while the bureaucratic infighting raged. As the economy developed, the social structure evolved, and political questions multiplied, Alexander II increasingly adopted the role of mediator among the interests. He became a managerial tsar. His style of governing merely encouraged the proliferation of interest groups that had their roots in other causes. In the end the tsar's arbitrary authority confronted a welter of uncoordinated, even competing, groups. The autocrat was losing control over the governing process; the groups were too divided to take it over.

This new style of governing represented a significant shift in the evolution of autocratic politics. Gone were the days when ministers and governors-general served as unthinking instruments of the tsar's will. As Count Stroganov stated, "the late tsar (Nicholas I) wished to do everything himself but it is already impossible to do everything by oneself." The Great Reforms had created new institutions, defined interest groups, and set in motion socioeconomic processes that the autocrat could no longer eliminate, repress, or, in some cases, even control. In his characteristically blunt fashion Valuev reminded the tsar of the limitations which were beginning to hedge in his absolute power: "One stroke of Your Majesty's pen is sufficient to abolish the entire Code of Laws of the Russian Empire, but no imperial command can raise or lower the level of state bonds on the St. Petersburg Stock Market."[40] Again and again over the next two reigns the tsar learned by bitter experience that there were other matters which he could not resolve with a stroke of the pen.

In short, the Great Reforms accelerated the evolution of a complex society. In this sense they were irreversible. The tsar could not, practically speaking, reenserf the peasantry, level the industrial base, tear up the railroads. Even the counterreforms of the eighties were not successful in dismantling the major accomplishments of the Great Reforms. It was possible to replace the reformers in the top administrative bureaucratic posts. But to have purged them from the middle ranks of the bureaucracy would have been to paralyze the state machine. They were too entrenched in the State Council, the ministries, universities, zemstvos, and editorial rooms of the mass press. From these positions they resisted, evaded, and blunted the counterreforms as their opponents had attempted twenty years earlier to disrupt and delay the reforming process. The political struggle continued, with the tsar favoring one or another interest at different times. But he found himself in the position of regulating rather than eliminating the bureaucratic conflicts.

With the growth of industrialization and urbanization, the increase in social mobility and literacy, and the greater involvement in overseas trade and foreign investment, there was simultaneously a proliferation of interests, social, ethnic, and regional. The tsar was helpless to unify and coordinate them. But there was no institutional framework in which the tsar could resolve the conflicts among them. There was no shared national political culture and no effective means to create it. Consequently, following the Great Reforms the autocrat steadily lost control over the governing process, but the competing interest groups were too fragmented to take it over. When the final test came in 1917, neither the tsar nor the interest groups that constituted the ruling elites were able to hold on to state power.

NOTES

1. No study exists of private organizations before the Great Reforms, but a useful starting point is the article "Obshchestvo," in Brokgauz i Efron, *Entsiklopedicheskii slovar'* (St. Petersburg, 1897), vol. 42, 607–28. PSZ, Series I, Apr. 8, 1872, no. 15356; *Bulletin de la Société imperiale des naturalistes de Moscou. Séance extraordinaire solonelle du 28 décembre 1855 à l'occasion du jubilé sémiséculaire, supplément,* vol. 29, 1856, includes a set of testimonials from the major scientific and scholarly societies in the empire; for the law of December 1836 on joint stock companies, see L. E. Shepelev, *Aktsionernye kompanii v Rossii* (Leningrad, 1973), 46–54; for the Geographical Society, see L. S. Berg, *Vsesoiuznoe geograficheskoe obshchestvo za sto let* (Moscow, 1946), 180–82; for charitable societies, see Adele Lindenmeyr, "Voluntary Associations and the Russian Autocracy: The Case of Private Charity," *Carl Beck Papers,* no. 807, Pittsburgh, June 1990.

2. Based on an extensive reading of the *Zapiski* of the Russkoe teknologicheskoe obshchestvo and the *Trudy* of the Obshchestvo dlia sodeistviia russkoi promyshlennosti. For the Moscow entrepreneurial group, see my *Merchants and Entrepreneurs in Imperial Russia* (Chapel Hill, N.C., 1983), esp. chaps. 4 and 5, and Thomas Owen, *Capitalism and Politics in Russia* (Cambridge, Mass., 1981), esp. chaps. 2 and 3.

3. George Yaney, *The Systematization of Russian Society* (Urbana, Ill., 1973); Heidi W. Whelan, *Alexander III and the State Council* (New Brunswick, N.J., 1982); on the Shtalkel'berg commission, see Reginald Zelnik, *Labor and Society in Tsarist Russia* (Stanford, Calif., 1971), chap. 4; on Baranov, no monographic treatment exists. See ORGBL, f. 169 (Miliutin), karton 37, no. 18, Kommissiia dlia issledovaniia zheleznykh dorogov v Rossii (red. E. T. Baranov), August 1882, "Obshchii doklad kommissii."

4. A. M. Skabichevskii, *Ocherki istorii russkoi tsenzury (1700–1863)* (St. Petersburg, 1892), 398–407, 421–43, 490; Mikhail Lemke, *Epokha tsenzurnykh reform, 1859–1865 godov* (St. Petersburg, 1904), 202; Ministerstvo vnutrennikh del, *Sobranie materialov o napravlenii razlichnykh otraslei russkoi slovestnosti za poslednee desiatiletie i otechestvennoi zhurnalistiki za 1863 i 1864 g.* (St. Petersburg, 1865), 216–17, 244–45; Charles A. Ruud, *Fighting Words: Imperial Censorship and the Russian Press, 1894–1906* (Toronto, 1982), chaps. 7 and 8; V. A. Tvardovskaia, *Ideologiia poreformennogo samoderzhaviia (M.N. Katkov i ego izdaniia)* (Moscow, 1978).

5. ORGBL, f. 169 (Miliutin), karton 14, no. 2, l.. 111; P. A. Valuev, *Dnevnik* (Moscow, 1961), vol. 1, 301, 358 n. 93; Prince V. A. Dolgorukii expressed similar sentiments, ibid., 292.

6. For the career lines and biographies of the Konstantinovtsy, see W. Bruce Lincoln, *In the Vanguard of Reform: Russia's Enlightened Bureaucrats, 1825–1861* (DeKalb, Ill., 1982); for their participation in the emancipation, Daniel Field, *The*

End of Serfdom (Cambridge, Mass., 1976); for the judicial reform, Richard Wortman, *The Development of a Russian Legal Consciousness* (Chicago, 1976), 215, 246–52; for the Navy Reform, Jacob Kipp, "Consequences of Defeat: Modernizing the Russian Navy, 1855–1863," *Jahrbücher für Geschichte Osteuropas* 20, no. 2 (June 1972), 210–25; and for censorship, Charles Ruud, "A. V. Golovnin and the Liberal Russian Censorship, January–June 1862," *Slavonic and East European Review* 50, no. 119 (April 1972): 199–219, and "The Russian Empire's New Censorship Law of 1865," *Canadian Slavic Studies* 3 (1969), no. 2: 369–88.

7. For careers and biographies, see L. E. Shepelev, *Tsarizm i burzhuaziia vo vtoroi polovine XIX veka* (Leningrad, 1981), 44–52; a sample of articles in *Russkii vestnik* includes Gagemeister, "Vzgliad na promyshlennost' i torgovliu Rossii," *Russkii vestnik*, 1857, no. 7, 5–52, perhaps the most important of these, stressing the peculiar nature of Russia's path to industrialization and implying the need to free the serfs; but see also N. Bunge, "O meste, zanymaemom politicheskoiu ekonomiiu v sisteme narodnogo obrazovaniia i ob otnoshenii ego k prakticheskoi deiatel'nosti," ibid., 1856 no. 3, 417–57; I. Vernadskii, "O vneshnei torgovle," ibid., 1856, no. 2, 603–24; E. I. Lamanskii, "Vklady v bankakh ili bilety nepreryvnogo dokhoda?," ibid., 1859, no. 2, 221–40. For the subsidy to *Le Nord*, TsGAOR, f. 722 (Mramornyi dvorets), op. 1, ed. kh. 459, "Otnoshenie Konstantina Nikolaevicha k A. N. Gorchakovu," Jan. 13, 1858.

8. A. N. Kulomzin, V. G. Reitern-Nol'ken, *M. Kh. Reitern. Biograficheskii ocherk* (St. Petersburg, 1910), 64, 71, 76.

9. Ibid., 82, 98, 100; Valuev, *Dnevnik*, vol. 2, 149, 153, 154.

10. Valuev, *Dnevnik*, vol. 2, 195; ORGBL, f. 120 (Katkov), karton 25, no. 32, Markevich to Katkov, Mar. 23, 1869.

11. ORGBL, f. 169 (Miliutin), karton 37, no. 12, M. Kh. Reitern, "O sredstvakh k obrazovaniiu fonda sooruzheniia zheleznykh dorog," Feb. 3, 1867, stamped "secret," ll. 1–5, 7, 8.

12. Ibid., karton 37, no. 13, P. P. Mel'nikov, untitled memorandum, dated Feb. 17, 1867, ll. 1–6.

13. ORGBL, f. 332 (Chizhov), karton 25, no. 4, letters 186, 187, Del'vig to Chizhov, Mar. 2 and 9, 1867; *Moskva*, Mar. 15, 1867; Valuev, *Dnevnik*, vol. 2, 191, supplementary n. 266, 484–85; ORGBL, f. 169 (Miliutin), karton 16, no. 1, ll. 32–34.

14. ORGBL, f. 332 (Chizhov), karton 25, no. 5, Del'vig to Chizhov, Dec. 14, 27, 1868; karton 73, no. 8, "Zapiska Del'vigu"; no. 10 "Tovarishchestvo po preobretenii Nikolaevskoi zheleznoi dorogi. Zapiska na imia ministerstva M.Kh. Reiterna. (Otvet po voprosu)," January 1868; Valuev, *Dnevnik*, vol. 2, 228, 264; N. A. Kislinskii, *Nasha zheleznodorozhnaia politika, po dokumentam arkhiva Komiteta ministrov* (St. Petersburg, 1899), vol. 1, 305, 312–15, 320–21.

15. ORGBL, f. 169 (Miliutin), karton 16, no. 2, ll. 223–4; Valuev, *Dnevnik*, vol. 1, 198; S.Iu. Vitte, *Vospominaniia*, vol. 1, 216–17.

16. Kislinskii, *Nasha zheleznodorozhnaia politika*, vol. 2, 39–42, 64–69, 54, 58, 79–80; ORGBL, f. 169 (Miliutin), karton 10, no. 13; Vitte, *Vospominaniia*, vol. 1, 216–17.

17. This section draws heavily on my article "The Rise of Engineers in Russia," *Cahiers du monde russe et sovietique*, October–December 1990, 539–68.

18. A. J. Rieber, "The Formation of la Grande Société des chemins de fer russes," *Jahrbücher für Geschichte Osteuropas*, June 1973.

19. Biblioteka Instituta inzhenerov putei soobshchenii, rukopisnyi otdel (BIIPS-RO), P. P. Mel'nikov, "O zheleznikh dorogakh", 1856, ll. 4–5. For Mel'nikov's formal report on his American trip, *Krasnyi arkhiv*, 1936 no. 3, pp. 127–44.

20. BIIPS-RO, M. S. Volkhov, "Peterburgsko-Sevastopol'skaia zheleznaia doroga," n.d. [1857], sent to Baron Del'vig, ll. 1–2.

21. Ministerstvo putei soobshcheniia, *Kratkii istoricheskii ocherk razvitiia i deia-*

tel'nosti Vedomstva putei soobshcheniia za sto let ego sushchestvovaniia, 1789–1898 (St. Petersburg, 1898), 121–28; Kislinskii, *Nasha zheleznodorozhnaia politika,* report of Mel'nikov to Alexander II, July 7, 1863, appendix to the Council of Ministers, no. 51.

22. TsGIA, f. 678, op. 1, ed. kh. 683, "Vsepoddaneishyi otchet stats-sekretaria Livena o sostoianii gosudarstvennykh kankakh i kazennykh gornykh zavodov" (1880), ll. 27–90; *Kratkii istoricheskii ocherk Vedomstva putei soobshcheniia,* 168ff.; A. P. Pogrebinskii, "Stroitel'stvo zheleznykh dorog v poreformennoi Rossii i finansovaia politika tsarizma (60–90 gody XIX v.)," *Istoricheskie zapiski,* vol. 47, 1954, 167–70; A. M. Solov'eva, *Zheleznodorozhnyi transport Rossii vo vtoroi polovine XIX v.* (Moscow, 1975).

23. P. A. Zaionchkovskii, *Voennye reformy 1860–1870 godov v Rossii* (Moscow, 1952), 213–36; P. K. Men'kov, *Zapiski,* 3 vols. (St. Petersburg, 1898).

24. *Severnaia pchela,* Oct. 12, 1862, carried the subscription announcement for *Sovremennoe slovo.* See also the memoirs of one of the editors of *Russkii invalid,* S. P. Zykov, "Nabroski iz moei zhizni," *Russkaia starina,* 1910, no. 6, 502–8; no. 7, 21–22, 34–35.

25. ORGBL, f. 169 (Miliutin), karton 15, no. 2, l. 192.

26. ORGBL, f. 169 (Miliutin), karton 15, no. 2, ll. 260–62; no. 3, ll. 269–73; N. N. Obruchev, "Obzor deiatel'nosti Voennogo ministerstva v poslednee piatiletie (1861–1865), finansovykh ego sredstv i nuzhd armii," *Voennyi sbornik,* 1865, nos. 10, 11; Valuev, *Dnevnik,* vol. 1, 155–56.

27. ORGBL, f. 169 (Miliutin), karton 14, no. 3, ll. 180–81, letter of Nikolai Miliutin to Dmitrii Miliutin, Apr. 23/May 5, 1863.

28. Ibid., karton 15, no. 2, ll. 18–19, 21–22, 116–17, 121–23; TsGAOR, f. 728 (Zimnyi dvorets), op. 1, ed. kh. 2812, Doneseniia Alekseia Pavlovicha Bezaka k Imperatoru Aleksandru II-omu, 1865, 1866, 1868.

29. ORGBL, f. 169 (Miliutin), karton 16, no. 2, ll. 177–78.

30. Zaionchkovskii, *Voennye reformy,* chap. 6; Forrestt Miller, *Dmitrii Miliutin and the Reform Era in Russia* (Nashville, Tenn., 1968), chap. 4; ORGBL, f. 120 (Katkov), karton 36, nos. 30–32, ll. 31–34.

31. *Dnevnik D. A. Miliutin,* vol. 1 (Moscow, 1947), 197–203.

32. TsGAOR, f. 109 (Otchety III otdeleniia i korpusa zhandarmov), op. 223, ed. kh. 31, ll. 3–4, 6.

33. *Vest',* Sept. 14, 1863, contains the fullest statement of the credo, but see also Aug. 11 (on Orthodoxy and Poland), Aug. 25 (on the peasantry and anti-Semitism), Sept. 1 (on the press), and Sept. 8 (again on the peasantry). The quality and depth of its coverage declined after 1865 and especially after 1869, when it attempted to become a daily. Its large printing, 3,700 in 1868, was misleading. Most of its copies were distributed without payment, in particular to all marshals of the nobility; *Russkaia periodicheskaia pechat' (1702–1894). Spravochnik* (Moscow, 1959), 435.

34. ORGBL, f. 120 (Katkov), karton 19, kn. 1, letters of Shuvalov to Katkov, Oct. 1, 1866; Feb. 3, 1872; March 14 (1867?); Dec. 13 (no year given); karton 46, letter of Katkov to Shuvalov, October 1866, ll. 105a–7.

35. *Dnevnik Valueva,* vol. 1, 123, 329 n. 32; vol. 2, 132. For additional commentary on Valuev's role, see P. A. Zaionchkovskii's introduction to ibid.; the new material uncovered by V. G. Chernukha, "Problema politicheskoi reformy v pravitel'stvennykh krugakh Rossii v nachale 70-kh godov XIX v.," *Problemy krest'ianskogo zemlevladeniia i vnutrennei politiki Rossii. Dooktiabr'skii period* (Leningrad, 1972), 130–39; and Daniel Orlovsky, *The Limits of Reform* (Cambridge, Mass., 1981), 63–84.

36. For recent treatments of the educational, judicial, and administrative counterreforms, see Allen Sinel, *The Classroom and the Chancellery: State Educational Reform under Count Dmitrii Tolstoi* (Cambridge, Mass., 1973); Wortman, *Development,* esp. 276–83; and Orlovsky, *Limits,* esp. 84–93, 154–57, 163–64.

37. S. M. Seredonin, *Istoricheskii obzor deiatel'nosti Komiteta Ministrov,* vol. 3, pt. 1 (St. Petersburg, 1902), 138–39; *Dnevnik Valueva,* vol. 2, 467–69; ORGBL, f. 169 (Miliutin), no. 3, ll. 205–6.

38. V. G. Chernukha, *Vnutrenniaia politika tsarizma s serediny 50-kh do nachala 80-kh gg. XIX v.* (Leningrad, 1978), 233–35; Kislinskii, *Nasha zheleznodorozhnaia politika,* vol. 2, 117–18, 127, 131–35, 139–59.

39. Chernukha, *Vnutrenniaia politika,* 67–69; *Dnevnik Miliutina,* vol. 1, 140–41; Valuev, *Dnevnik,* vol. 2, 299–300; TsGIA, f. 722 (Mramornyi dvorets), op. 1, d. 106, ll. 22, 24–25.

40. Valuev, *Dnevnik,* vol. 1, 99, 115.

V

THE MEANING OF THE GREAT REFORMS IN RUSSIAN ECONOMIC HISTORY

Peter Gatrell

Historians have followed contemporary observers of the Russian scene in adhering to the belief that the "long" nineteenth century (1800–1914) was marked by several discontinuities, of which the decade of reforms (the 1860s) and the revolution of 1905 are the most dramatic. To what extent can the economic historian share in the portrayal of the 1860s as a rupture with the past? It cannot be taken for granted that the changes then taking place were associated with discontinuities in the pattern of economic development. Indeed, the concept of temporal discontinuity is itself increasingly being called into question by historians of European economic development.

The idea of a clear discontinuity in the historical record of economic growth became widespread during the 1950s and 1960s, finding expression in W. W. Rostow's influential theory of the "take-off into self-sustained growth." This approach has lost much of its credibility, because there is now overwhelming evidence of economic growth and structural change in the period prior to "take-off." It is striking that even economic historians sympathetic to the concept frequently disagree about the chronology of "take-off" in any given country. The more evidence accumulates of significant increases in productivity in the "prespurt" period and of important initiatives in economic policy or entrepreneurship, the more difficult it is to accept the idea of a revolutionary break with the past.[1]

An alternative approach admits to the possibility of an acceleration in the trend rate of economic growth but denies that the spurt can be located in one or two decades. In this scheme there is no sudden leap forward to a higher plateau; rather the growth trend is best described as a curve whose slope gradually becomes steeper. The historiography of European economic development has lately begun to shift in favor of this concept of an acceleration in growth. There is now much less sympathy for the idea that a brief moment in time was associated with a decisive break in the growth trend.

Instead, economic historians are impressed by the continuity of economic growth over the long term, in a range of European economies.[2]

Does Tsarist Russia fit the pattern of discontinuity or the pattern of trend acceleration? Anyone familiar with the historiography will recognize the importance of discontinuity in Alexander Gerschenkron's interpretation of the pattern of Russian economic development. According to Gerschenkron, the failure of the agrarian reforms to create the conditions for economic growth intensified the need for decisive institutional measures to overcome accumulated backwardness; such measures produced the "growth spurt" of the 1890s. Recent research suggests, however, that the spurt has been exaggerated. Instead, as we shall see, the evidence indicates that growth accelerated during the final third of the nineteenth century on foundations already laid in the prereform era.[3]

The economic historian must begin by establishing the quantitative evidence on economic change, without which any connection between reform and development will remain purely speculative. The emphasis in the first part of this essay is accordingly on economic trends during the nineteenth century. Brief attention is also given to the behavior of the major economic variables during the reform era, which is here taken to cover the years between 1855 and 1875. The second part is devoted to the economic significance of reform. The purpose here is to ask to what extent the era of great reforms was associated with fundamental changes in economic organization and behavior.

Economic Growth during the Nineteenth Century

The first requirement for an analysis of trends in economic growth during the nineteenth century is the construction of adequate series of data. Unfortunately, series do not exist for such basic variables as gross agricultural production, gross industrial production, employment, and investment. Demographic data are similarly skimpy. The only readily available and reasonably reliable series at our disposal are the statistics of foreign trade. For the other economic aggregates no reliable series exist prior to about 1885. Our knowledge is woefully inadequate where three important variables are concerned: labor, investment, and small-scale industrial production. Nonetheless, it would be wrong to become too lachrymose about this state of affairs. We can derive reasonable approximations of the behavior of large-scale industrial production. The construction of a series for agricultural production poses more serious problems. However, consistent information about grain output becomes available from 1850 onward. Foreign trade statistics, as already indicated, also allow comparisons to be made between the pre- and postreform eras.[4]

For the purpose of measuring the growth of industrial production, economic historians have at their disposal two distinct series. One series, prepared by N. D. Kondrat'ev in 1926 and reworked by Raymond Goldsmith thirty years later, is based on the physical output of twenty-one commodities. Kondrat'ev's original series covered the period 1885 to 1913, but Goldsmith took this series back to 1860, using similar sources. He also constructed an original index of industrial production, based on quite different procedures from those adopted by Kondrat'ev. Analyzing these different indices, Goldsmith concluded that large-scale industry grew on average by just over 5 percent per annum between 1860 and 1900.

The second index of industrial output derives from data on the gross value of large-scale production. These data imply that industrial production increased on average by 4.6 percent per annum between 1860 and 1900, in current prices. Since industrial wholesale prices appear to have fallen throughout the 1870s, it is likely that the rate of growth of industrial production in constant prices was slightly higher than this. A figure of around 5 percent thus seems reasonable for the rate of growth of industrial production between 1860 and 1900, by whichever means it is derived.[5]

The trend in industrial growth accelerated after 1875 and again after 1888. To this extent the statistics confirm the commonly accepted view that Russian industrialization gathered pace toward the end of the century. But the evidence is hardly overwhelming that there was a "big spurt" around 1885. Goldsmith himself was cautious about the idea of a sharp break in the trend around that time.

The notion of a major discontinuity has also more recently been called into question by the authors of an econometric analysis of European industrial growth in the nineteenth century. Steady rather than spectacular growth seems a more appropriate characterization of Russian industrialization. This image is strengthened if one bears in mind the rapid growth in population toward the latter part of the nineteenth century. Expressed in per capita terms, the rate of growth of industrial production becomes less impressive. Skeptics may respond that Witte and his contemporaries believed that they were living through industrialization at breakneck speed. But contemporaries are always prone to magnify the extent of the changes they experience and are not well placed to detect long-term trends.[6]

Industrial production increased during the preemancipation period, although the rate of growth cannot be measured very accurately. Data on industrial wholesale prices imply that growth was not especially rapid between 1823 and 1843. To judge from the price data, growth accelerated in the two decades after 1845. M. I. Tugan-Baranovskii attributed this growth to the expansion of small-scale production, arguing (not entirely convincingly) that factory production entered a prolonged stagnation after 1845. By contrast, S. G. Strumilin maintained that large-scale production was dynamic. Expressed in silver rubles, output per person in large-scale industry increased by 25 percent between 1845 and 1855; between 1855 and 1863 the increase amounted to an impressive 85 percent. However, as we shall see, not all large-scale enterprises shared in this growth.[7]

The performance of Russian agriculture is not synonymous with the behavior of the grain harvest. At the end of the nineteenth century, grain accounted for only one-half of total agricultural production. Unfortunately, we lack adequate data for other components of agricultural production. The following remarks are therefore confined to grain output. The failure of grain production to keep pace with the growth of rural population during the first half of the nineteenth century has been well documented by I. D. Kovalchenko, A. S. Nifontov, and S. G. Wheatcroft. Output per capita fell by roughly 8 percent between 1802–11 and 1841–50, and remained approximately at that level for the ensuing two decades. During the 1870s and 1880s we can speak of only a modest improvement, and during the final decade of the nineteenth century the output of grain per person remained below the level it had reached a century before.[8]

The disaggregation of the national picture into constituent regions reveals significant disparities in regional performance. In the Northern Consumer Region the long-term decline in output per capita was interrupted by a brief recovery during the 1880s.[9] In 1802–11 this region accounted for 37 percent of total grain production; by 1851–60 its share had fallen to 28 percent. But we should not interpret this to mean that the region was in a state of crisis. Economic activity was increasingly concentrated upon nonagricultural production, and this region could draw upon imports of grain from elsewhere. A process of regional specialization was under way. Much more disturbing was the decline during the first half of the century in per capita production of grain in the Central Producer Region, where the decline during the 1850s was not halted until the 1870s.[10] But with the rapid growth of population the situation deteriorated further during the 1880s and 1890s, by which time the "crisis of the center" had become acute.

In contrast to this poor performance, output per capita improved in the Eastern Producer Region.[11] However, the overall contribution of this region to total grain output remained modest: 12 percent in the 1850s and 15 percent in the 1890s. More significant was the subsequent improvement in the performance of the Southern Producer Region, whose grain output per capita by the 1880s was 20 percent above the level recorded at the beginning of the century and 30 percent higher than that reached in the 1850s. In 1802–11 this region accounted for less than one-fifth of total output. The figure had not changed by midcentury, but by the 1890s the proportion of grain contributed by this region had increased to one-third.[12]

A more nuanced picture of pre- and postemancipation agriculture is therefore required to take proper account not only of the failure of output per person to grow in the densely populated Central Black-Earth provinces and Lower Volga but also of the more dynamic development elsewhere and the onset of regional specialization, well before emancipation. This process gathered pace after 1860, with the spectacular growth of agricultural production in Ukraine and the expansion of interregional grain shipments during the second half of the nineteenth century.

The main problem in cereal agriculture was that yields failed to improve much during the first half of the century. According to Kovalchenko, average yields were only 5 percent higher in the 1850s than they had been a half-century before. This virtual stagnation in the productivity of land was offset by the growth in the sown area. Nonetheless, the extension of the land under cereal cultivation failed to ensure an increase in grain output per head of population.

During the second half of the century, grain output increased by 65 percent. Yields improved by just under 50 percent and the area sown to cereals expanded by 12 percent. Most of the growth in yields took place during the 1870s, 1880s and 1890s; the reform decade was one in which yields improved only slightly. The national picture again conceals interesting regional differences. In the north, yields improved steadily during the second half of the century. In the south, yields showed a dramatic improvement, but this was entirely a consequence of changes at the end of the period. During the 1860s and 1870s yields stagnated, and the expansion of output prior to 1880 was very largely a function of the growth of the sown area. In the center the area sown to crops hardly altered. But contrary to received opinion, yields steadily improved in this region. Finally, cereal cultivation expanded in the east. This region, like the southern region, included areas that were being newly opened up to colonization and agricultural production.

The steady progress of Russian agriculture during the nineteenth century was marked by regional differences in performance, by the extension of the area under crops, and by modest improvements in the productivity of land. The cultivation of new land, the application of new techniques, and the diversification of agricultural production formed part of a secular process, which did not depend directly on serfdom or its abolition. The increase in population, the growth of the market, and the opening up of new land by the railways played the major role.[13]

Foreign trade statistics provide a further indicator of economic trends in nineteenth-century Russia. Between 1850–52 and 1870–72 exports increased at an average annual rate of 6.3 percent. During the 1860s and 1870s the growth rate leaped to 11.6 percent, nearly three times greater than the rate at midcentury (1840–42 to 1860–62). Subsequently the rate of growth fell sharply. During the last two decades of the century, the rate declined to around 2 percent per annum. The trend of imports was somewhat different. Certainly there appears to have been an increase in the rate of growth after 1850, although the surge that is apparent in export values is missing in the case of imports. Imports similarly registered a sharply falling rate of growth after 1870–72, suggesting once again that the final quarter of the century was not associated with rapid growth in foreign trade. The acceleration in the trend growth of foreign trade thus occurred during the third quarter of the nineteenth century.[14]

These figures reinforce the point that sustained growth was registered prior to the reform era. They also indicate that the rapid growth of exports during the third quarter of the century was associated with burgeoning continental demand for Russian cereals. The construction of railways linking Russian ports with the country's grain-producing regions facilitated the huge expansion of exports. During the early 1860s grain accounted for around one-third of total exports; a decade later its share had risen to one-half. However, the increase in export volumes did not entail a parallel growth in invisible earnings, because the goods were carried in foreign merchant vessels.[15]

Although imports grew less rapidly than exports between 1860–62 and 1880–82, important changes took place in their composition during that period. In particular, Russia began to import rails, locomotives, and other capital goods on a larger scale than hitherto, a practice that contributed toward a sustained trade deficit during the late 1860s and early 1870s. In the early 1860s imports of metals, metal products, and machinery represented 10 percent of total imports; by the late 1870s their share had doubled. This proportion was not maintained during the 1880s, when imports of raw cotton began to accelerate once more. Only when investment in industry and rail transport reached a higher level during the later 1890s did a second upsurge take place in imports of semimanufactured and capital goods.

Exogenous factors, notably the increase in European demand for Russian grain, played a vital part in the growth of Russian exports. The government contributed indirectly toward the expansion in grain exports and capital goods imports by supporting the construction of railways. The government influenced imports through its tariff policy. Between 1822 and 1850 high duties were maintained. The reform era was associated with lower duties (reductions were enforced in 1850, 1857, and 1868) and the liberalization of trade on the continent of Europe. A series of increases between 1877 and 1891 reversed this trend. It is not difficult to spot the reaction of the tsarist government to the adverse trade balance during the 1870s. By 1891 duties on cotton cloth were twice as high as they had been in 1868; duties on kerosene had trebled; duties on rails and locomotives had quadrupled; and duties on pig iron were ten times higher.[16]

Government intervention and exogenous factors therefore combined to produce an increase in trade volume during the third quarter of the nineteenth century. In this period, the government adhered to a policy of trade liberalization, enabling Russia to take advantage of the concurrent expansion in European trade, and promoted railway construction, thereby facilitating the shipment of grain. Subsequently, and by contrast, the tsarist government imposed stringent tariff barriers, largely for fiscal reasons, a decision that hastened the decline in the rate of growth of imports. At the same time, the government sought to promote grain exports, although the rate of growth of export values continued to fall, because of the decline in the world price of agricultural products.[17]

It seems unlikely that the institutional changes engendered by the Great Reforms in themselves induced an acceleration in economic growth, although they may have played a part. Greater account should be taken of other factors in explaining the acceleration that occurred: exogenous factors such as the demand for Russian grain on the international market, the prevalence of free trade, population growth and urbanization which swelled consumption, and the first wave of railway construction. It is true that the liberalization of trade and the construction of railways reflected a change of attitude in some quarters of government. To that extent, the spirit of reform should not be overlooked by the economic historian.

The study of economic fluctuations provides an indication of the economic impact of the government's reform program in the short term. Unfortunately, economic historians have devoted little attention to fluctuations in economic activity, except in regard to grain yields. What can be stated with some confidence is that the years between 1860 and 1865 present a rather disturbed picture, especially when contrasted with the more propitious conditions that characterized the second half of the decade. In industry, a period of rapid growth between 1858 and 1861 came to an abrupt end, and manufacturing output subsequently slumped until 1866. Industry was thrown into confusion by the emancipation of unfree labor. The sharp (though short-lived) decline in wages may have depressed mass consumption of manufactured goods during the first half of the 1860s. Industry recovered toward the end of the decade, and employers were subsequently helped by government subsidies and orders. Capital investment and exports also behaved disappointingly in the four years after 1861, reflecting market uncertainties. By contrast, and fortuitously, these were favorable years for grain production. The reform process in rural Russia definitely disrupted grain sowings between 1861 and 1863. But favorable yields compensated for the depressed level of sowings. The main factor at work here was probably the weather. It was fortunate for the perestroika of rural Russia that yields remained buoyant: only in 1865 did grain yields give serious cause for concern.[18]

These brief observations suggest that rapid economic growth and economic restructuring were incompatible in the short term. Only toward the end of the 1860s did the economy assume a more stable character. This is clearly an area where further research is required.

Economic Organization and the Great Reforms

The economic significance of reform is not to be judged solely in terms of economic growth, whether in the short or the long term. We must also take account of changes in economic organization and behavior, and ask to what extent these changes reflected institutional reform. The obvious place to begin is with serfdom and its abolition.

Peasant emancipation was a complex process, not just a straightforward act of legislation. The process of enactment was complicated by the character of the landlord-serf relationship that prevailed prior to 1861. This relationship entailed a much greater degree of flexibility than had been the case in Western Europe. In the west, a pattern evolved over generations whereby the obligations of corvée and quitrent tended to become fixed, either by custom or by law. In Russia, by contrast, there were few exceptions to the principle that the lord had an unfettered right to determine the quantity of *barshchina* and *obrok*. He could vary feudal dues virtually at will, in accordance with changing economic circumstances. In practice, the lord's ability to enforce his will was circumscribed, notably by the difficulty of supervising peasants even when they performed labor service on the demesne. Arrears in the payment of obrok also suggest that Russian lords, like their Prussian counterparts, did not always succeed in collecting increased dues from their serfs.[19]

It is commonly believed that the majority of Russian landlords neither managed their estates well under serfdom nor derived lasting economic benefit from its abolition. There is a large measure of truth in these views of gentry entrepreneurship. However, the extent and burden of gentry indebtedness prior to 1861 has been exaggerated. Landlords deposited substantial savings with the state banks before emancipation, and these funds were recycled in the form of loans to serfowners, as well as to the state. Russian serfowners failed to take up their full entitlement to loans. B. G. Litvak found that the *pomeshchiki* in six black-earth provinces could borrow up to seventy silver rubles per soul, but that they borrowed on average no more than half this amount. A recent estimate puts the combined value of the lords' fixed assets at 2,100 million rubles on the eve of emancipation; given that they owed a total of 425 million rubles in 1859, this ratio of debt to assets does not seem outrageously large. It cannot be the case that the debts represented outright profligacy on the part of landowners. Interestingly, it was the estate owners whose serfs were on obrok who tended to borrow, suggesting that they used these funds in part to finance nonagricultural activities. We should perhaps give the landlord credit for being rather more discriminating than has hitherto been thought.[20]

Serfdom obviously constrained the entrepreneurial potential of peasants, but its deleterious features should not obscure the fact that serf entrepreneurs managed to accumulate substantial fortunes. This wealth was vulnerable to a rapacious master, but it was in his interest to sustain rather than jeopardize the source of revenue. Did the wealthier serfs succeed in retaining increments in their income? The evidence here is ambiguous. I. D. Kovalchenko has shown that obrok was not a progressive tax on income and that the incomes of the more dynamic peasants did forge ahead. On the other hand, he also describes the tactics whereby the lord could attempt to claw back part or all of the gain, for example, by accepting a bribe from the household in order to release able-bodied young males from the recruit levy. Serfdom thus provided the peasantry with some scope for saving, but also provided the lord with the capacity to undermine capital accumulation in the village.[21]

To the extent that serfowners transferred peasants to obrok during the second quarter of the nineteenth century, Soviet scholars have argued that serfdom was being transformed. The coercive measures traditionally associated with feudalism were giving way to an economic system in which monetary transactions played a greater part, in which the household allotment *(nadel)* assumed a reduced significance as a means of subsistence, and in which peasants themselves could become more autonomous economic agents. Some Western historians agree with this assessment, associating the spread of obrok with "proto-industrialization."[22]

It should not be assumed that emancipation automatically conferred greater autonomy and economic opportunity on Russian peasants than they hitherto enjoyed. The provisions of the emancipation legislation had the practical consequence of reintroducing some of the features of serfdom that were least conducive to economic progress while creating financial pressures that limited the scope for peasant savings.

Seen from the angle of the pomeshchiki, emancipation required that arrangements be made for the conversion of serfs into free peasants without jeopardizing their income and the productive potential of their demesnes. The lord had somehow to substitute for the equipment and draught animals that the peasants had hitherto brought to bear upon the demesne lands. But his priority was to safeguard his income.

In the Black-Earth provinces, where barshchina prevailed, the emancipation edict posed difficulties for the former serfowners, who wished to exploit the buoyant grain market. They were unable to adjust the temporary obligations they were now owed by the serfs, as they had adjusted labor dues in the past. Under these circumstances, and given the conversion to obrok stipulated in 1862, it suited them to begin the process of redemption with all possible speed, so that they could obtain sufficient working capital for wages, livestock, and equipment. A further consideration was their fear that peasants would find it difficult to pay the new obrok: far better, in that case, that the government, not the gentry, shoulder the burden of peasant arrears. It does indeed seem to have been the case that peasants in some Black-Earth provinces, in the Middle and Lower Volga, had difficulty in meeting their new monetized dues.[23]

By contrast, in those regions where obrok prevailed, the gentry preferred to receive obrok as before, rather than rush into the redemption procedures. The obrok rates had already been inflated there, because the lords wished to improve the level of compensation to which they were entitled. Peasants could continue to meet their dues by working beyond the village. Only later, during the early 1870s, did the accumulation of arrears persuade these lords too that it was in their interests to conclude redemption agreements and let the government deal with the burden of peasant arrears.[24]

Emancipation offered fresh scope to the Russian gentry. In the six Black-Earth provinces studied by Litvak, serfowners were entitled to just under two-thirds of the proceeds from redemption, the residue being absorbed in settling their liabilities to state financial institutions (the outstanding debt amounted to around 320 million rubles in 1861). Contemporaries believed that these sums were more than sufficient to reconstruct the estates on modern lines. Some reconstruction undoubtedly took place. Nor is it true that the proceeds of emancipation represented a windfall gain that the lords immediately proceeded to squander. The Russian gentry invested in railway shares. They bought and sold urban real estate. Some of the more substantial landowners exploited new opportunities in industrial production.[25]

The formal abolition of extraeconomic coercion clearly represented a major step forward for the peasants as a whole. But from their point of view, the process of adjustment was more painful than it was for the landlord. The provisions of the 1861 legislation disadvantaged the peasants in a number of important respects. First, emancipation saddled them with the inescapable need to compensate the former serfowners for the allotments. The ex-serfs were burdened with redemption dues, in addition to the taxes imposed by central and local government. Second, the need to offset the decline in the land-to-population ratio (a decline partly attributable to the emancipation edict) obliged peasants to rent additional amounts of land. The inflated rents ate further into their receipts from agriculture or other pursuits. The financial burden that peasants had to shoulder placed limits on their capacity to save. Finally, the more dynamic peasants may have been constrained by the redistributional commune, whose powers were considerably enhanced, and by mutual responsibility *(krugovaia poruka),* which encumbered them with the debts of the economically inefficient.

The "temporary obligations" and redemption payments constituted a burden for the former serfs, of that there can be little doubt. But did these payments render peasants worse off than they had been before? The obrok to which peasants were temporarily liable remained at the preemancipation level, although the reduction of allotments raised it in real terms. On the other hand, in some instances, mostly in the non-Black Earth provinces, peasants who remained "temporarily obligated" managed to evade claims upon them for obrok. It was much more difficult to evade redemption payments. These were calculated according to an inflated value of the land and bore no relation to current market values. Redemption payments exceeded receipts from agriculture, leading to the accumulation of substantial arrears. But it should be remembered that the situation varied from region to region and changed over time; a reduction in annual assessments took effect from 1883. Peasants in the fertile provinces of the Mid and Lower Volga took the so-called beggars' allotment and paid no redemption dues. The better-off among them subsequently rented additional land. Peasants with other sources of income were probably more fortunate (as were the former state and *udel* peasants). Some were able to accumulate profits from craft production and from trade, although incomes from *otkhod* (nonagricultural wage labor away from the village) may have declined after 1880, because competition for work drove down wage rates.[26]

The most important point about redemption payments on allotment land, however, is that the peasants collectively had security of tenure, notwithstanding the arrears they accumulated. The allotment land may have been poor in quality and smaller in quantity than the land they farmed before emancipation, but it could not be alienated from the peasantry.[27]

The multiple opportunities that were built into the emancipation decree for former serfowners to cut off allotment land, to assign allotments in inappropriate shapes, and to curtail access to nonarable resources all led to a demand from the peasantry for additional land. Rapid population increased the demand for land still further. Peasants were obliged to conclude short-term agreements, at considerable disadvantage to themselves, in order to restore the size and shape of their holdings. Various forms of sharecropping emerged to offset the effects of cutoffs *(otrezki)*. Peasants grazed their cattle on the lord's land, fished in his rivers, and hunted in his woods, often without permission. The fines that were levied for trespass and the labor contracts that were drawn up in return for the legal right of access to the lord's land seemed to peasants to imply the restoration of servile relations. This reinforces the point that there were profound elements of continuity across the divide of "reform."[28]

The emancipation settlement strengthened the economic and administrative role of the traditional land commune. The commune controlled the allocation of allotment land among its members, determined cropping routines, and organized work teams for a wide range of village tasks. It assumed administrative responsibilities, such as the movement of its members, that had previously been handled by the serfowner. Fiscal functions also devolved upon the commune. The commune offered its members a degree of security against the recurrent risks to which the Russian peasants were subject, notably fluctuations in weather and crop yields. Emancipation terminated the protection that the lord had customarily provided his serfs; the community now assumed the responsibility for protecting the destitute. In this sense, the enhanced power of the commune concealed a major flaw in the postemancipation settlement. The depletion of the resources of the village in times of dearth or other misfortune restricted opportunities for capital investment in agriculture.[29]

B. N. Mironov has expressed admirably the conflicting forces in the post-emancipation rural community that both favored and hindered capital accumulation. Emancipation did not unleash capitalist forces in the countryside. The actions of the redistributional land commune, in conjunction with the provisions of the 1861 legislation, hindered the accumulation of capital. At the same time, it is worth remembering that entrepreneurial forces struggled to break free of their shackles, just as ambitious serf entrepreneurs had earlier succeeded despite the obstacles imposed by serfdom. Peasants acquired assets, including land, that did not come under the control and jurisdiction of the commune.[30]

Peasants who purchased nonallotment land were not hampered by communal constraints but by the lack of rural credit. For all its reforming zeal, the tsarist government failed to improve the supply of credit to farmers, which would have encouraged the acquisition of seed, agricultural equipment, and livestock. The formation of the Peasant Land Bank in 1883 and of credit cooperatives a decade later allowed peasants to purchase land, but the new institutions did nothing to stimulate the purchase of much-needed complementary inputs. The failure to create an adequate supply of rural credit was a missed opportunity, a reform *manqué*.[31]

The abolition of noneconomic coercion also implied important changes in industrial organization and activity. However, a brief glance at industrial development suggests that no sharp distinction can be sustained between the prereform and postreform era. It is true that the reform of possessional enterprises was associated with profound changes in the character of metallurgy and metalworking. It is also true that the government abolished indentured labor at state armories. But the reforms of the 1860s do not appear to have induced fundamental changes in the organization and administration of votchinal enterprise. Wage labor had already become more widespread, and the traditional relationship between master and serf had already been subverted before 1861. Votchinal enterprise may even have had a head start over other forms of enterprise. The most advanced industrial enterprise in late-nineteenth-century Europe rested upon a bureaucratic system of management. Perhaps arrangements in the Russian votchinal enterprise were tailor-made for the new conditions.[32]

The extent of change induced by reform must not therefore be exaggerated. Some branches of industry felt the effects of reform more than others. The nobility lost its monopoly of distilling in 1863. Noble enterprises in other sectors, such as cloth, candle, and carpet making, experienced difficulties. Sugar producers fared better, thanks largely to government assistance. In general, the tenacity of gentry industrial enterprise is suggested by a study of the two thousand noble-owned enterprises that operated in 1903. One-fifth of them had been established before 1861.[33]

In small-scale production, greater numbers of craftsmen had already become involved before 1861 in a wide variety of tasks. The growth in numbers reflected the diffusion of obrok, notably in the non-Black Earth region. Activity increased especially rapidly during a depression in trade, because owners of votchinal enterprises ran down their operations and transferred their workers to obrok. Tengoborskii reckoned that the gross output of small-scale industry amounted to 23 percent of total industrial production during the 1850s. It goes without saying that this proportion conceals wide regional variations. Cottage industry was widespread in the central industrial region and elsewhere in the non-Black Earth provinces. In Ukraine, by contrast, small-scale production contributed no more than 10 percent of the total, reflecting in large part the success with which the votchinal factories—especially those producing sugar and spirits—managed to retain their share of the market.[34]

Small-scale production for the growing peasant and urban markets satisfied the needs of peasants for side earnings or for year-round employment.
The income of cottage producers satisfied the demands of serfowners and
state tax collectors alike. But its long-term dynamic existed independently
of the pomeshchiki and the state. *Kustari* depended upon the growth of the
market, upon the development of interregional trade in raw materials and
semifinished goods, and upon the availability of credit, none of which turned
directly upon serfdom or its abolition.

Cottage industry survived emancipation. It also survived the spread of
large-scale enterprise. Small-scale industry was still growing rapidly during
the early twentieth century. The factory actually conferred advantages on
the cottage producer by making available cheaper and better semifinished
goods, such as cloth, iron, and timber. The ebb and flow of small-scale
production in any given region was likely to depend on the strength of
competition from small-scale producers in other regions. This fact can be
established for the 1870s and beyond; only then did improved transportation
bring hitherto isolated regions within the orbit of those areas that had a
comparative advantage in the given product. To take one example, the producers of ribbons and belts in Kursk Province were destroyed not by the
factory but by competition from kustari farther north.[35]

There was thus a well-established pattern of "proto-industrial" development in prereform Russia which survived unscathed into the twentieth century. Russian industrial development reflected the active participation of
villagers—sometimes making use of odd hours in the day, sometimes working full time—in small-scale production. The implications of this observation
are important. In the words of Eric Jones, "the lingering notion of 'take-
off' can hardly survive recognition of how widespread rural industry was
and how long and gradually it grew." The fortunes of cottage industry in
nineteenth-century Russia may have ebbed and flowed, but the reform era
did not mark a fundamental discontinuity in its evolution.[36]

To what extent was the reform era associated with significant changes in
public finance, the banking system, and company law? Reform and public
finance were inextricably linked, partly because reforms cost money and
partly because changes in budgetary practice themselves became a touchstone of reform. Commercial banking received a fillip during the reform era,
but modern banking practices did not take root for several decades. Company law retained several archaic features, but these did not prevent the
spread of the principle of corporate enterprise.

Reform had its price. The government took over the costs of liquidating
the liabilities of the old financial institutions. The government also shoul-
dered the short-term cost of emancipation. By 1881 the government had
committed 750 million rubles to the redemption process, of which 300 million represented the obligations of landlords to their former creditors and
350 million represented the issue of redemption certificates (*svidetel'stva*)
and bank *bilety* to the former serfowners. As a result of these various com-

mitments, the size of the state debt increased by 3,000 million rubles during Reutern's tenure of the Ministry of Finances (1862–78). The government reluctantly entered the domestic and international money markets in a much more purposive manner than hitherto.[37]

The need to borrow, engendered in part by reform, led in turn to the consideration of further reforms. The most important initiative related to the reform of budgetary practice. A report prepared by V. A. Tatarinov in 1858 called for the systematic and speedy compilation of accurate departmental budgets, the simultaneous approval of the new estimates and scrutiny of the previous year's budget, and a veto of any attempt to transfer funds from one account to another without prior approval. The standardization of departmental practice was eventually agreed to by the State Council. Tatarinov himself became state comptroller in 1863, with responsibility for checking departmental submissions and assessing their consistency. With the formation of this new government department, the spotlight allowed by glasnost was directed at the state budget. Greater public access to the budget and confidence in its integrity epitomized the progress of reform.[38]

Some reform initiatives never reached fruition. The decade of reforms witnessed no significant change in fiscal policy. The poll tax survived until 1883, although its fiscal significance had declined long before 1860. Proposals for an income tax were aborted. The government instead relied heavily upon indirect taxation. Significant changes in fiscal measures date not from the 1860s but from the 1880s. The other "missing reform" concerned monetary policy. Plans were afoot during 1862–63 to take Russia on to the gold standard, but they were shelved amid the crisis induced by the Polish insurrection. It took three decades before the government approved the introduction of the gold standard, thereby setting the seal on Russia's acceptability to international money markets.[39]

Prerevolutionary specialists contended that the creation of joint-stock banks during the 1860s represented a major turning point in the financial structure of Russia. There is little doubt about the significance of this example of institutional change. The first commercial bank in Russia was established in 1864. As a joint-stock venture, its statutes had to be approved by the government. The involvement of the government extended much further than this. The state provided up to half of the foundation capital but renounced its right to dividends below 5 percent in order to stimulate private investment. Other ventures quickly followed: between 1864 and 1873, sixty commercial banks came into existence. In the competitive environment that emerged, the new institutions offered high dividends to attract and retain the interest of shareholders. It has been argued that the banks thereby diverted funds away from investment in the manufacturing sector. However, this line of argument carries little conviction, because manufacturing industry did not at this stage require substantial amounts of capital for fixed investment. Instead the banks provided much-needed working capital to industry.[40]

However, the role of commercial banks in the immediate postreform economy (1864–81) should not be exaggerated. Other institutions, in particular
the State Bank, attracted at least as much interest from depositors. By
1875—admittedly a poor time for the commercial sector—the State Bank
held 30 percent of current and deposit accounts, compared to 40 percent
held with commercial banks. In 1881 the State Bank maintained its share,
but the commercial banks' share had fallen to 28 percent. Similar tendencies
may be identified in the loan and discounting activity of the Russian financial
sector, where other institutions, such as the municipal banks, were gaining
in importance. Only after 1880 did the commercial banks begin to forge
ahead and gain a higher profile, as a result of their increasing willingness to
lend against shares and other secured paper, and of the growing public interest in such securities.[41]

The systematization of Russian company law properly dates from 1836,
when the principles of company registration and limited liability were written into the statute book. The act of 1836 was remarkable, less for its evident
intention to concentrate powers of veto in the hands of the central government than for the fact that the principle of limited liability was firmly en-
shrined in law. It is worth remembering that limited liability was not
introduced in Britain for another two decades, and in Germany only during
the so-called *Gründerjahre* in the 1860s. Throughout the rest of the century,
the basic elements of the 1836 legislation remained in force. Subsequent
attempts to simplify the law, such as those made in 1867 and 1874, foundered
on the rock of bureaucratic intransigence, which was strengthened by the
European stock market crashes in those years. More liberal legislation had
little prospect of success. Nevertheless, despite the obstacles to company
formation, many successful ventures were floated during the late 1850s and
early 1870s. The tax system afforded considerable protection to these fledgling companies.[42]

The changes already mentioned were accompanied by changing attitudes
toward the private sector. In the postreform period, government assistance
enabled private enterprise to expand in iron and steel and in engineering.
The measures included "nonstatutory loans" to specific firms including railway companies, larger orders than hitherto (on similarly advantageous
terms), and even the acquisition of shares. It is likely that the pragmatic
need to support private firms, when railways were being built at breakneck
speed, prompted this more widespread willingness of the tsarist government
to take such initiatives.[43]

The abolition of noneconomic coercion, which was the essence of peasant
emancipation, was a major step forward and offered new opportunities for
two-fifths of the population. But the economic historian should be more
impressed by the subversion of serfdom that was already taking place before
1861—the growth of wage labor, the opportunities which obrok afforded the
peasant—as well as by the preservation of coercive elements after 1861. In

the sphere of industrial organization, the evidence suggests that the reform decade did not mark a sharp discontinuity: possessional factories were already in decline, the votchinal enterprise drew upon reserves of free labor, and the petty craftsman continued to function in much the same way as before 1861. The relations of production in Russia were not fundamentally transformed.

On the other hand, there does seem to have been a change in attitudes and in policy on the part of the tsarist government, to the extent that it cleared the ground for more modern financial institutions. This shift in policy was linked to the critical need for funds, in the light of government commitment to agrarian reform and railway construction. The significance of railway construction should not be overlooked. From the point of view of long-term economic development, it was more important to emancipate Russia from the limitations imposed by her geography than it was to emancipate serfs from their masters.

Conventional wisdom in Russian economic history attaches great significance to the reforms of the 1860s. For Soviet historians, the reform era is a watershed, marking the transition from feudalism to capitalism. For many non-Soviet historians, the reform era ushered in the transition from traditional to modern society. This survey of the problems offers a different interpretation. It concludes that the reforms coincided with, but did not initiate, an acceleration in economic growth. Growth in the prereform era was associated in part with noncapitalist forms of production, of which unfree labor was the most obvious manifestation. But the prereform period also witnessed the emergence of modern production relations and institutions: wage labor and corporate business activity. The prereform era manifested signs of economic progress, such as technical change in industry, the expansion of small-scale industry, and the onset of regional economic specialization.

There is no suggestion here that the reforms were politically or socially insignificant. But their economic effects must be judged cautiously. The significance of reform begins to pale when set against the background of long-run economic development. The influence of geographic and other non-institutional constraints upon economic development assumes greater importance than institutional constraints, such as serfdom, that could be circumvented by human agency. In this interpretation, exogenous developments, such as the peace in Europe during the "long" nineteenth century and the growth of the international economy with its accompanying diffusion of products, capital, skills, and technology, occupy center stage.

NOTES

1. W. W. Rostow, *The Stages of Economic Growth: A Non-Communist Manifesto* (Cambridge, England, 1960); P. K. O'Brien, "Do We Have a Typology for the Study

of European Industrialization in the Nineteenth Century?" *Journal of European Economic History* 15 (1986): 291–333.

2. N. F. R. Crafts, *British Economic Growth during the Industrial Revolution* (Oxford, England, 1985); D. F. Good, *The Economic Rise of the Habsburg Empire, 1750–1914* (Berkeley, Calif., 1984).

3. A. Gerschenkron, *Economic Backwardness in Historical Perspective* (Cambridge, Mass., 1960). See also Olga Crisp, *Studies in the Russian Economy before 1914* (London, 1976), chap. 1, and R. L. Rudolph, "Agricultural Structure and Proto-industrialization: Economic Development with Unfree Labor," *Journal of Economic History* 45 (1985): 47–69.

4. For a survey of data sources, see *Massovye istochniki po sotsial'no-ekonomicheskoi istorii Rossii perioda kapitalizma* (Moscow, 1979).

5. R. W. Goldsmith, "The Economic Growth of Tsarist Russia, 1860–1913," *Economic Development and Cultural Change* 9 (1961): 441–75. S. G. Strumilin, *Ocherki ekonomicheskoi istorii Rossii i SSSR* (Moscow, 1966), 380, 423, 428–29, 434–38, 442, 445.

6. N. F. R. Crafts, S. J. Leybourne, and T. C. Mills, "Britain," in R. Sylla and G. Toniolo, eds., *Patterns of European Industrialization: The Nineteenth Century* (London, 1991), 109–52.

7. Strumilin, *Ocherki,* 380, 387; M. I. Tugan-Baranovsky, *The Russian Factory in the Nineteenth Century* (Homewood, Ill., 1970), chaps. 1 and 7.

8. I. D. Koval'chenko, *Russkoe krepostnoe krest'ianstvo v pervoi polovine XIX veka* (Moscow, 1967); A. S. Nifontov, *Zernovoe proizvodstvo Rossii vo vtoroi polovine XIX veka* (Moscow, 1974); S. G. Wheatcroft, "Grain Production and Utilization in Russia and the USSR before Collectivization" (Ph.D. diss., University of Birmingham, 1980).

9. The Northern Consumer Region corresponds to the Central Industrial Region, North, North-West, and Belorussia.

10. The Central Producer Region includes the Central Black-Earth, Lower and Middle Volga.

11. The Eastern Producer Region corresponds to the Urals and western Siberia.

12. The Southern Producer Region includes the South-West, Little Russia, and New Russia.

13. See P. W. Gatrell, *The Tsarist Economy, 1850–1917* (London, 1986), chap. 4; H.-D. Löwe, *Die Lage der Bauern in Russland, 1880–1905: Wirtschaftliche und soziale Veränderungen in der ländlichen Gesellschaft des Zarenreiches* (St. Katharinen, 1987).

14. The percentage growth rates are derived from the data in P. A. Khromov, *Ekonomicheskoe razvitie Rossii v XIX–XX vekakh* (Moscow, 1950), 437, 439, 453, 455.

15. Khromov, *Ekonomicheskoe razvitie,* 252, referring to data for 1900.

16. Crisp, *Studies,* 98.

17. T. M. Kitanina, *Khlebnaia torgovlia Rossii v 1875–1914 gg.* (Leningrad, 1978).

18. L. A. Mendel'son, *Teoriia i istoriia ekonomicheskikh krizisov i tsiklov* (Moscow, 1959), vol. 2, 398.

19. The exceptions noted in the text were the 1832 legislation and the introduction of inventories in the South-West during the 1840s. See N. N. Ulashchik, *Predposylki krest'ianskoi reformy 1861 g. v Litve i zapadnoi Belorussii* (Moscow, 1965), 453, and G. L. Yaney, *The Systematization of Russian Government: Social Evolution in the Domestic Administration of Imperial Russia, 1711–1905* (Urbana, Ill., 1973), 169–75. For further discussion of other points raised in this paragraph, consult Koval'chenko, *Russkoe krepostnoe krest'ianstvo,* 106–8, 154, and E. Domar and M. Machina, "On the Profitability of Serfdom," *Journal of Economic History* 44 (1984): 919–55.

20. V. G. Litvak, *Russkaia derevnia v reforme 1861 g.: chernozemnyi tsentr, 1861–*

1892 gg. (Moscow, 1972), 380, 384; Domar and Machina, "On the Profitability," 948–49.

21. Koval'chenko, *Russkoe krepostnoe krest'ianstvo,* 285; H. Rosovsky, "The Serf Entrepreneur in Russia," *Explorations in Entrepreneurial History,* vol. 6, 1953–54, 207–29.

22. P. G. Ryndziunskii, *Utverzhdenie kapitalizma v Rossii, 1850–1880* (Moscow, 1978); but see the remarks of Yaney, *Systematization,* 152–53.

23. N. M. Druzhinin, *Russkaia derevnia na perelome, 1861–1880 gg.* (Moscow, 1978), 64–67.

24. Druzhinin, *Russkaia derevnia,* 253–54; Litvak, *Russkaia derevnia,* 399–400.

25. Litvak, *Russkaia derevnia,* 385–87; A. P. Korelin, *Dvorianstvo v poreformennoi Rossii, 1861–1904 gg.* (Moscow, 1979), 106–22; P. A. Zaionchkovskii, *Otmena krepostnogo prava v Rossii* (Moscow, 1968), 296–98; A. E. Lositskii, *Vykupnaia operatsiia* (St. Petersburg, 1906), 13, 44, 54–55.

26. Druzhinin, *Russkaia derevnia,* 255–56; Zaionchkovskii, *Otmena,* 233–36, 301–5.

27. O. Crisp, "Peasant Land Tenure and Civil Rights Implications before 1906," in O. Crisp and L. H. Edmondson, eds., *Civil Rights in Imperial Russia* (Oxford, England, 1989), 33–64.

28. Koval'chenko, *Russkoe krepostnoe krest'ianstvo,* 156, 160–61, 219; B. Kerblay, "La réforme de 1861 et ses effets sur la vie rurale dans la province de Smolensk," in R. Portal, ed., *Le Statut des paysans libérés du servage, 1861–1961* (Paris, 1963), 267–310.

29. B. N. Mironov, "The Russian Peasant Commune after the Reforms of the 1860s," *Slavic Review* 44 (1985): 438–67.

30. Mironov, "Peasant Commune"; T. Shanin, *The Awkward Class: Political Sociology of Peasantry in a Developing Society, Russia 1910–1925* (Oxford, England, 1972). Lenin's approach was wholly different; see V. I. Lenin, *The Development of Capitalism in Russia* (Moscow, 1977).

31. A. P. Korelin, *Sel'skokhoziaistvennyi kredit v Rossii v kontse XIX-nachale XX v.* (Moscow, 1988).

32. Tugan-Baranovsky, *Russian Factory,* 249–51; J. Bradley, *Guns for the Tsar: Technology Transfer and the Small Arms Industry in Nineteenth-Century Russia* (DeKalb, Ill., 1990).

33. Korelin, *Dvorianstvo,* 107–8, 390.

34. L. G. Mel'nik, "K voprosu o nachale promyshlennogo perevorota v Rossii," *Problemy genezisa kapitalizma* (Moscow, 1979), 104–36; V. K. Iatsunskii, *Sotsial'no-ekonomicheskaia istoriia Rossii, XVIII-XIX vv.* (Moscow, 1973), 97.

35. Druzhinin, *Russkaia derevnia,* 234.

36. Cited in W. Hagen, "Capitalism and the Countryside in Early Modern Europe; Interpretations, Models, Debates," *Agricultural History* 62 (1988): 14.

37. *Ministerstvo finansov, 1802–1902* (St. Petersburg, 1902), vol. 1, 444–45, 452.

38. A. I. Koniaev, *Finansovyi kontrol' v dorevoliutsionnoi Rossii* (Moscow, 1959), 69.

39. V. G. Chernukha, *Vnutrenniaia politika tsarizma s serediny 50kh do nachala 80kh gg. XIX veka* (Leningrad, 1978), chap. 3; L. E. Shepelev, *Tsarizm i burzhuaziia vo vtoroi polovine XIX veka* (Leningrad, 1981), 86–87.

40. I. F. Gindin, *Russkie kommercheskie banki* (Moscow-Leningrad, 1948); Crisp, *Studies,* 123, 141.

41. Gindin, *Russkie,* 43; L. E. Shepelev, *Aktsionernye kompanii v Rossii* (Leningrad, 1973), 86, 91–92; Crisp, *Studies,* chap. 5.

42. Shepelev, *Aktsionernye kompanii,* 54, 66, 80–81, 92–93, 99, 116.

43. I. F. Gindin, "Gosudarstvennyi kapitalizm v Rossii domonopolisticheskogo perioda", *Voprosy istorii,* 1964, no. 9, 72–95.

VI

A NEGLECTED GREAT REFORM
THE ABOLITION OF TAX FARMING
IN RUSSIA

David Christian

On January 1, 1863, less than two years after it had abolished serfdom, the Russian government implemented a complex and highly technical law of some 279 articles, which had first been published on July 4, 1861, under the unexciting title "Statute on Liquor Taxes."[1] The immediate effect of the new law was to reform the ways in which the government levied taxes on the trade in liquor. It replaced a hodgepodge of regional systems with a single system of taxation under which excises were levied on distillers and license fees on wholesalers and retailers. In addition, the liquor trade as a whole was freed from most existing forms of state regulation. The new system lasted only until the 1890s, at which point the state itself began to assume direct control over the trade in liquor. So in retrospect the reform of 1863 appeared as an aberration, a passing symptom of that brief flirtation with laissez faire which temporarily disrupted the Russian government's ancient marriage to the economics of monopoly.

Fiscal reforms of this kind do not make for exciting history, and the temptation to ignore them is doubled if they prove so ephemeral. So it is perhaps understandable that historians of the 1860s have tended to overlook the 1863 reform and to concentrate instead on those other changes which make up the conventional roll call of the Great Reforms. Nevertheless, the 1863 reform should be treated more seriously, for its main consequence was to abolish tax farming in Russia. This was an event as significant in the history of the Russian state and economy as had been the abolition of the French "General Farms" in 1791.

Financially, the reform achieved a successful reorganization of the Russian government's most important single source of revenue, the taxes on liquor sales. In this way it contributed much to the financial stability of the Russian government during the era of the Great Reforms and beyond. Economically, the effect of the reform was to divert much Russian entrepreneurial capital, of both noble and merchant origin, from a rather unproductive area of commerce (liquor tax farming) into areas such as banking, railways, transportation, and oil, where it could contribute significantly to Russia's economic development. The reform also had a considerable impact on the development of Russian law, for it abolished the most important single source of bureaucratic corruption in Russia. This, as contemporaries were well aware, was an essential prerequisite for any serious attempt to establish the "rule of law" in Russia. Finally, the reform also marked a profound change in the economic foundations of Russia's ruling elites, for, in combination with the abolition of serfdom, it marked the end of traditional estate rights to the exaction of tribute. Henceforth, all upper-class revenues, apart from those of the state itself, would assume purely commercial forms, taking the form of rents, interest, or profits. In this way the reform marked the end of Russia's fiscal *ancien régime,* the point at which Russia's state managed finally to secure a monopoly over taxation, thereby forcing Russia's ruling aristocratic and mercantile elites reluctantly but irrevocably into the chilly world of modern capitalism.

So, despite the apparently narrow goals of the 1863 reform, it was in fact integral to the perestroika of the late 1850s and early 1860s.

Administration of the Liquor Trade before 1863

The system under which the liquor trade was administered and taxed before 1863 was extremely complex, and it varied from region to region.[2] Two regions were of particular significance: first, the thirty "Great Russian" provinces that formed the old Muscovite heartland of the Russian Empire; and second, the Baltic provinces and the sixteen "privileged" provinces along the western borders of the Empire. The second region had been incorporated into the Empire from the seventeenth century.

In most areas of the Baltic and privileged provinces, local nobles as well as other corporate groups, including cossacks and some towns, enjoyed the ancient right of propination, which entitled them to distill liquor freely and to sell their products locally. The government enjoyed limited rights to levy fees on distilling or trading, and these rights varied from region to region. In 1811 it introduced tax farms, which began collecting taxes on the retail trade in urban areas, and in 1851 it introduced so-called excise tax farms, a form of excise on distilling, which was collected by tax farmers. But despite these changes, the various rights of propination in the Baltic and privileged provinces greatly limited the government's control over the liquor trade and the huge revenues it generated. As a result, even after the 1851 reform, the privileged provinces yielded only one-third of total liquor revenues, though they consumed well over half of all the vodka produced in the Empire between 1859 and 1861, and per capita consumption was one-and-a-half times higher than in the Great Russian provinces.[3]

In the Great Russian provinces, the situation was simpler and the government's grip on the trade was firmer. The government had exercised a considerable degree of political and fiscal control over the liquor trade since the first appearance of distilled drinks in Muscovy, probably in the early sixteenth century. Initially it attempted to control the trade through direct control of inns *(kabaki)* which, in the early days of the trade, both distilled and sold liquor. But it soon began farming out liquor revenues, and in 1767 this system was extended to all of the Great Russian provinces. After this, the liquor tax farm survived up to the reform of 1863. In what follows, I will be concerned primarily with the Great Russian provinces, the area in which tax farming flourished most luxuriantly and generated the greatest revenues.

Liquor Taxes and the History of Tax Farming

Despite its significance in Russian history, tax farming is a subject that has been almost entirely neglected by historians of modern Russia.[4]

Tax farms were commercial enterprises, generally funded by an individual entrepreneur (often with backing from others), which contracted to collect taxes in return for the right to make commercial profits from monopolies granted by governments. Tax farming is an ancient fiscal institution, familiar even in the classical world. But it was particularly common in seventeenth- and eighteenth-century Europe; the eighteenth-century French tax farmers were merely the best known of an important and influential group of merchants in Europe in this period. By the eighteenth century, tax farming had come to be seen as one of the most deeply entrenched features of France's ancien régime, and it was one of the first aspects to be overthrown during the revolution, by a law of March 27, 1791.[5]

In Russia, as in Western Europe, forms of revenue or tax farming emerged as soon as there developed a significant monetary sector. Indeed, as Richard Pipes argues, the Muscovite princely family rose to power by acting as efficient tax farmers for the Mongol horde in the fourteenth century, with the most spectacular success in the reign of Ivan "Kalita," or "Moneybags" (1325–40).[6] But once they had asserted their independent sovereignty, the rulers of Muscovy, in their turn, found it convenient to farm out taxes to others. The system of *kormlenie,* under which government officials were allocated a given territory from which they were allowed to support themselves in return for administering it and collecting taxes for the court, is itself a crude form of tax farming. But with the formal abolition of kormlenie in 1555, tax farming assumed more modern forms when, in a number of different regions, the right to collect tolls was farmed out.[7] Tax farming was extended to the collection of taxes on liquor sales toward the end of the sixteenth century.[8] By the seventeenth century several different taxes were being farmed out, including tolls, salt taxes, and liquor taxes, but already liquor taxes had replaced tolls as the most important arena for tax farming.[9] In the late seventeenth century, salt taxes emerged as another important arena for tax farming, but in the middle of the eighteenth century, the government began to relax its grip on the salt trade, as it simultaneously extended tax farming to all of the Great Russian provinces.[10] As a result, while in France tax farming was associated above all with taxes on salt (the infamous *gabelle*), in Russia tax farming, at its apogee, came to be associated above all with taxes on liquor (the *piteinyi oktup*). Liquor tax farming in Russia became synonymous with the institution of tax farming, and the word for "tax farmer" *(otkupshchik)* came to mean, in practice, "liquor tax farmer."

In Russia the period from 1767 to 1863 was the heyday of both tax farming and the liquor tax farmer. And it is in this period that one can see most clearly the extent of the contribution made by liquor tax farming to the financial power and stability of the Russian government and to the growth of the Russian economy. By the middle of the eighteenth century, liquor taxes were already the major form of indirect taxation and by the 1830s they were the single most important tax in the government's fiscal arsenal. They outdistanced the revenues generated by the major direct taxes: the poll tax and the obrok payments of state peasants. As figure 1 shows, between 1763 and 1863, liquor taxes generated on average 33 percent of government revenues; in the 1850s, that proportion rose to over 40 percent.[11]

Another way of demonstrating the fiscal importance of liquor tax farming is by comparing the revenues it earned with government expenditure on defense. As figure 2 shows, in the same period liquor revenues covered a significant proportion of the large defense budget that accounted for Russia's status as a great European power. So dependent was the government on the huge revenues generated by the liquor tax farm that if, at any point in the nineteenth century, all Russians had suddenly decided to stop drinking vodka, the government would have faced bankruptcy.

But the government also had other reasons for favoring the liquor tax farm. Under the tax farm system, liquor taxes were extremely cheap to raise, as most of the administrative costs were carried by the tax farmers. Something like 80 percent of the gross revenues from liquor sales were generally available to the government in the nineteenth century, and only slightly less in the eighteenth century.[12] Liquor revenues were also among the more reliable forms of government revenue. As a government treasurer, F. A. Golubtsov, commented soon after the Napoleonic Wars, "No other government revenue of this size is received by the treasury with such regularity, completeness, and convenience as the liquor farm taxes, which, by arriving regularly on a particular date each month, significantly ease the handling of government expenditures."[13] In the years after the Crimean War, the reliability of liquor taxes was equally striking: as other taxes declined in value or ceased to grow as a result of the dislocation caused by war, the

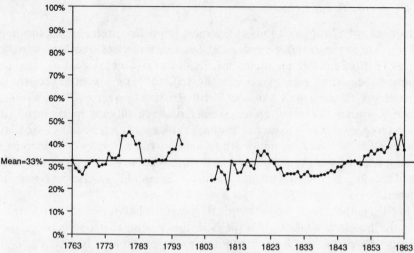

Figure 1. Gross liquor revenues as a proportion of the Russian government's total revenues, 1763–1863. From Arcadius Kahan, *The Plow, the Hammer and the Knout* (Chicago, 1985), and *Ministerstvo finansov, 1802–1902* (St. Petersburg, 1904), vol. 1, 616–19, 624–27, 632–33.

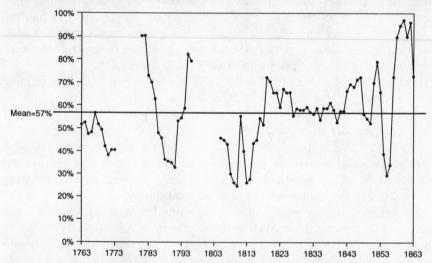

Figure 2. Gross liquor revenues as a proportion of the Russian government's defense budget, 1763–1863. From Kahan, *The Plow, the Hammer and the Knout,* 325, 337, and *Ministerstvo finansov,* vol. 1, 616–19, 626–27, 632–33.

liquor taxes continued to rise, thereby protecting the government from bankruptcy.

The scale of the liquor trade also ensured that it had an economic significance quite distinct from its fiscal role. In practice, vodka was an item of necessity in Russian working-class life in town and country, so those who sold vodka could count on a huge, and in the long run very reliable, demand for their product.[14] The most plausible estimate of the trade's total turnover is probably that of the government commission which prepared the 1863 reform; it put turnover for the Empire as a whole in the period from 1859 to 1863 at 180–200 million rubles per annum.[15] If we accept Druzhinin's estimate that in the 1850s the total turnover of internal trade in Russia was about 1,000 million rubles, this suggests that the liquor trade accounted for as much as 20 percent of all internal trade.[16]

Money of this kind inevitably played a significant role in Russia's economic history. The liquor trade was one of the most important branches of commerce in the middle of the century, and the leading liquor traders were among the country's most influential capitalists. D. E. Benardaki, the wealthiest liquor tax farmer in the late 1850s, paid the government over nineteen million rubles a year in liquor revenues between 1859 and 1863.[17] Another twenty-seven tax farmers owed over one million a year, while thirty owed over 500,000. Altogether, some 145 tax farmers out of a total of 216 (63 percent) owed more than 100,000 rubles a year.[18]

Most of these 145 tax farmers were merchants. But the trade also mobilized the capital of many other investors in a society in which investment opportunities were still restricted. About 20 percent of tax farmers owing over 100,000 rubles a year between 1859 and 1861 were government officials, another 10 percent were retired army officers, and 4 percent were nobles. But more gentry capital was mobilized through the tax farms than these figures suggest, for many nobles participated indirectly in the business either by funding front men (presumably because they lacked the capital, the business experience, or the moral effrontery needed to participate more directly in the trade) or by buying shares in tax farms headed by members of other estates.[19] Some nobles, however, including the gentry liberal A. I. Koshelev, participated in the liquor trade quite openly.

Causes of the 1863 Reform

Given the benefits the Russian government derived from tax farming why did it decide to abolish the tax farm in 1863? The answer is that despite the system's many advantages, it also suffered from a number of drawbacks, the most worrying of which was its propensity to generate widespread networks of corruption.

The government's dilemma was that while keen to enjoy the revenues generated by the aggressive techniques of the tax farmers, it still shared the "moral economy" of the landed aristocracy.[20] This meant that it shared the aristocracy's traditional contempt for commerce and felt obliged to distance itself to some extent from a grubby trade. It did this by issuing regulations designed to control the more outrageous commercial activities of the tax farmers. However, it soon became clear that the strict enforcement of detailed regulations on pricing, quality, and so on, while good for morale, was bad for business. And so the government compromised during most of the century between 1767 and 1863 by issuing strict regulations which it knew it could not enforce. The result was that liquor traders and the tax farmers who employed them were forced to engage in various forms of "commercial corruption"; this in turn meant that they had to protect themselves from overzealous officials through various forms of "bureaucratic corruption," or bribery.[21] It seems likely that by the late 1850s the tax farmers were paying most senior local government officials bribes comparable in size to the salaries these officials received from the government. It was this compromise between the moral economy of the government and its fiscal interests which generated the corrupt practices for which the tax farm became so notorious.

Corruption on such a scale had financial as well as moral consequences, for the government could never be sure that it was receiving an appropriate share of the profits of the liquor trade when the real scale of the trade's turnover was veiled by corrupt practice. As an official of the Ministry of Finance put it in 1819, "the amount of vodka sold and the real revenues from sales became secrets, hidden from the government and known only to the tax farmers, so that the government's income from vodka came to depend, so to speak, on the whims of the tax farmers."[22]

These serious drawbacks ensured that the government was never entirely happy with tax farming. Indeed, it abolished tax farming entirely for a brief period in the 1820s, and during the 1840s there were many discussions within government circles about alternatives. By the late 1840s, most government officials realized that tax farming, like serfdom, would eventually have to go. Yet, as with serfdom, the government was so dependent on the system that despite endless discussions it could never quite bring itself to act.

Several factors combined to clinch the issue in the late 1850s. Most important of all, perhaps, was the fact that the commitment to abolishing serfdom had put the government in the appropriate frame of mind for abolishing other relics of the old regime. But other, more specific, factors operated as well. Four were of particular importance: a sharp increase in corruption in the liquor trade in the 1840s and 1850s; realization on the part of gentry distillers that they were not benefiting from the increasing profits enjoyed (illicitly) by the tax farmers; an increased commitment within the government itself to the abolition of traditional monopolies; and consumer protests, which broke out in 1859 against the widespread corruption in the liquor trade.

These issues were closely linked. The booming liquor trade profits of the 1840s and 1850s, from which the treasury benefited so much during the years of the Crimean War, were generated primarily by an increase in corruption, in particular through increased adulteration and illegal price rises.[23] But extensive infringement of government regulations required in its turn an increase in the extent to which the trade depended on the bribery of government officials and an increase in the government's own willingness to ignore such corruption. Once the government had committed itself to reform and had simultaneously allowed extensive press discussions of reform, the extent of corruption became a matter of extreme, and very public, embarrassment. But the fact that tax farm profits were increasingly generated through adulteration or illegal price hikes also ensured that they were *not* shared with the distillers, who came from the gentry. As tax farm profits rose, the actual amounts of vodka purchased from distillers (and the amounts of grain purchased from other landlords by distillers) remained more or less static; indeed, government purchases of vodka in 1859 were barely above the quotas forty years earlier.[24] This ensured that by the late 1850s, distillers and landlords in general were for the most part opposed to the tax farm system, at least in the Great Russian provinces. These changes played into the hands of the generation of younger, "progressive" bureaucrats who were, on principle, opposed to monopolies of most kinds, including those over serf labor and the sale of vodka. The combination of their theoretical objections and the less disinterested hostility of gentry distillers explains the overwhelmingly critical tone of the prolonged journalistic discussion of the tax farm which continued over several months late in 1858, in most of the major "thick journals."

This debate may have played a role in triggering the consumer protests which broke out at the end of 1858, for consumers as well suffered from tax farm corruption by paying higher prices for a product whose quality was steadily declining despite government regulations on strengths and prices. Indeed, it seems that the effective tax on vodka in the Great Russian provinces rose from 1.68 rubles per capita in 1855 to 2.41 rubles in 1859, while the amounts of alcohol these sums purchased steadily declined.[25] Given the obligatory nature of such purchases for peasant households and the absence of a tradition of illegal home distilling in Russia,[26] these increases in the cost of vodka were as severe in their impact as a similar rise in the level of any major tax or feudal due would have been. Eventually, in the first half of 1859, consumer dissatisfaction assumed threatening forms: first a nationwide boycott of vodka, then violent attacks on taverns.[27] So numerous were these protests against the tax farm that they account for as many as 636 (or 68 percent) of the 938 "disturbances" of various kinds recorded by police officials in 1859.[28]

Two other factors seem to have influenced the government. First, the growing commitment of reformers within the government to the notion of *zakonnost'* persuaded many that the tax farm had to go, for as long as it existed so would the huge networks of bribery and corruption which made a mockery of the notion of a "rule of law" in Russia. Most influential of all the converts to this position were the Grand Duke Konstantin and General Rostovtsev. Indeed, Rostovtsev seems to have extracted a promise from the emperor, in February 1860, to deal with the issue of tax farming immediately after the emancipation of the peasantry.[29] Second, pro-reform officials, of whom the most important were K. K. Grot and A. Zablotskii-Desiatovskii, persuaded the government, despite its tradition of mistrust for its own officials, that if the reform was well handled, government officials would prove quite capable of collecting a new excise honestly and efficiently. They also persuaded a nervous treasury that reform would not lead to a fall in liquor revenues.

So by 1860 there existed within the government a powerful coalition of interests opposed to the tax farm and armed with persuasive arguments as to the necessity of doing away with it. This coalition soon carried the day within the State Council, to whom the issue had been referred by the emperor in 1859. And it was a special royal commission set up at the instigation of the State Council in November 1860 and headed by Andrei Zablotskii-Desiatovskii that prepared the final reform. But despite this, the issue remained in doubt, for as late as 1862 a powerful group of tax farmers persuaded the Ministry of Finance to give close scrutiny to a proposal under which they would have continued to collect an excise on liquor throughout the country while undertaking to build an extensive railway network for the government.[30] Only after the Ministry of Finance, now under the management of the reformer Reitern, had advised the emperor to dismiss the tax farmers' proposal was the fate of the tax farm finally sealed.

Significance and Implications of the 1863 Reform

The 1863 reform simplified an extremely complex body of legislation on the liquor trade by introducing uniform regulations throughout the Empire and abolishing the traditional monopolies attached to particular social "estates." In the Great Russian provinces the reform abolished the commercial monopolies of the tax farmers, while in the privileged provinces it ended the traditional right of propination, which was enjoyed mainly by members of the nobility. Finally, the act replaced the previous taxes on sales with an excise on distillers of four rubles for every bucket of pure vodka they distilled, or the equivalent of about 1.60 rubles for each bucket (12.3 liters) of standard vodka (40 percent alcohol by volume).

The first effect of the reform was financial. Although the government's massive dependence on liquor revenues, particularly in the precarious years after the Crimean War, made it a dangerous matter to tamper with the way in which they were collected, the reform abolished tax farming without endangering the financial stability of the government. After a slight drop in gross revenues to a level just below those for 1859, revenues soon rose again, and they continued to rise until the introduction of the state monopoly in 1894 led to a further increase. The reform also increased the revenues potentially available to the government by abolishing the right of propination in the Baltic region and the privileged provinces. This change strengthened the government's fiscal grip on the vodka trade throughout the Empire. In these ways the 1863 reform made a significant contribution to the financial stability of the government during the Great Reforms and in the decades that followed.

The reform also made a significant contribution to the economic growth of Russia in the postreform period. We have seen the extent of the liquor trade's turnover and the amount of domestic capital locked up in the tax farm business. The abolition of tax farming released this huge amount of capital for more productive uses. It almost certainly gave a significant boost to domestic investment in railways, banking, and other forms of industrial development in the second half of the nineteenth century. Vasilii Kokorev, for example, after some difficulties early in the 1860s, invested in railroads, steamships, banking, oil refineries, foreign trade, agricultural experimentation, art, and real estate; and many of his enterprises were undertaken in conjunction with other former tax farmers.[31] Their money also made a profound impact on Russia's cultural life in the late nineteenth century. It was tax farm money that built some of the first great collections of Russian art. And in the hands of Savva Mamontov, it did much to make Moscow once again the center of Russian artistic and cultural life.[32] Thus the 1863 reform seems to have diverted considerable sums of domestic capital out of the stagnant waters of a corrupt, archaic, and rather unproductive line of business into the faster-moving currents of an emerging Russian capitalism.

The 1863 reform also had considerable legal implications, for it marked an end to the systematic corruption associated with the tax farm. Of course, critics were able to point to new forms of corruption. Distillers engaged in a complex technological war with excise officials to hide the real amounts of liquor they produced so that they could sell their surpluses without paying excise on them.[33] And the reform failed to eliminate the petty commercial corruption of tavern keepers: watering down, undermeasuring, and monopolistic practices of various kinds were again familiar charges against the trade by the 1880s. But what the reform did do was to end the systematic, large-scale corruption of the 1850s. The tax farm system had forced tax farmers to buy protection and had forced officials to collude. Under the new system, liquor traders did not have to be corrupt, and the government had no need to collude with corruption. Corrupt trading was merely one possible commercial strategy; it was no longer the lifeblood of an entire system.

This was a change of immense significance for Russian local government and for the establishment in Russia of a sense of the rule of law. Indeed, the 1863 reform was a necessary preliminary to any serious attempt to establish in Russia some form of rule of law, for, as a government historian wrote fifty years later,

> [Alexander II] saw that, given the corrupting influence of the tax farm, all political reforms, like seeds cast on unprepared soil, will be doomed to a pitiful growth or even to extinction. This is why the abolition of tax farming . . . was seen as the cornerstone of his reforms. . . . Along with the other great reforms of the second half of the nineteenth century—the abolition of serfdom, the introduction of a new judicial system, and the introduction of local and municipal self-government—there should also be placed the reform of the methods of collecting liquor taxes.[34]

There is a deeper significance to the abolition of tax farming in Russia. One of the main characteristics in premodern polities (or "tributary societies," as Eric Wolf has described them) is that fiscal powers are not monopolized by governments but shared by several different groups within the ruling elite.[35] States levy tributes or taxes in labor, in kind, and in cash (and even, in the case of military conscription, in human bodies). But so do nobles, merchants, and organizations such as the church. In contrast, modern states assume an exclusive right to exact tributes of this kind, while other upper-class incomes are secured indirectly, in capitalist societies at least, through the mechanisms of the market, which yield revenues in the guise of rents or profits.

Tax farming was an ambiguous, transitional form between taxes or tributes and commercial forms of revenue. The state leased out fiscal powers which were then exercised by merchants, who proceeded to generate commercial profits from them. But the element of taxation or tribute taking remained just below the surface. As the minister of finance, Kniazhevich, admitted in 1859, tax farm profits represented, in reality, a form of tax on vodka sales.[36] With the abolition of tax farming in Russia in 1863, as in France in 1791, it was possible to say that even in this attenuated form, merchants were now excluded from the levying of taxes. In the privileged provinces it was the rights of other estates that were abolished, including the right of propination, which was also, in practice, a right to exact tribute from drinkers.

In conjunction with the abolition of that other great form of tribute, serfdom, in 1861, the effect of these changes was to eliminate the few remaining forms of tribute available to members of Russia's ruling elites. Henceforth, both gentry and mercantile revenues would have to be earned; they could no longer be collected as a matter of right.

Merchants could survive the change after some initial adjustments. But members of the gentry, whose whole life-style was predicated on the receipt of tributary revenues, found the change much harder. For example, gentry distillers in the privileged provinces found themselves facing competition from more highly capitalized commercial distilleries, without the traditional safeguard of protected markets on their own or neighboring estates. Many went under. In 1862–63 there were 4,017 distilleries in operation in the Empire; by 1876–77 the number had declined to 2,596.[37] In this way the 1863 reform marked a significant stage in a process to which several of the Great Reforms contributed: the dismantling of estate privileges.

So the reform marked the achievement of a state monopoly over the form of tribute known in the modern world as taxation. By abolishing the fiscal privileges of the gentry in the western provinces and the tax farmers in the Great Russian provinces, the state assumed a clear monopoly over taxation. The 1863 reform marks the arrival of the Russian polity in the modern world—at least from a fiscal point of view. It marks the end of Russia's fiscal ancien régime.

NOTES

This essay is based on a larger study of the liquor trade in early nineteenth-century Russia: *"Living Water": Vodka and Russian Society on the Eve of Emancipation* (Oxford, England, 1990). I would like to thank Linda Bowman, John Bushnell, and Ben Eklof for comments on earlier drafts.

1. *Polnoe sobranie zakonov*, 2d ser., 37197, "Polozhenie o piteinom sbore."
2. On the early history of the liquor trade, see Christian, *"Living Water,"* chap. 1, and R. E. F. Smith and David Christian, *Bread and Salt: A Social and Economic History of Food and Drink in Russia* (Cambridge, England, 1984).
3. Figures on revenues come from *Svedeniia o piteinvkh sborakh* (St. Petersburg, 1860–61), vol. 3, 6–7, 10. Figures on consumption are more difficult to calculate; they are based on estimates from *Svedeniia*, vol. 3, 36, and vol. 4, 214. Estimates of illegal sales come from A. Korsak, "O vinokurenii," *Obzor razlichnykh otraslei manufakturnoi promyshlennosti Rossii*, (St. Petersburg, 1865), vol. 3, 288–89. See Christian, *"Living Water,"* 45, 395, for more details on these calculations.
4. Even in Arcadius Kahan, *The Plow, the Hammer and the Knout* (Chicago, 1985), which deals extensively with taxation, there is no reference to tax farming in the index. One of the few articles in English to discuss the subject is Paul Bushkovitch, "Taxation, Tax Farming, and Merchants in Sixteenth-Century Russia," *Slavic Review* 37 (1978), no. 3: 381–98.
5. The classic study of tax farming in France is G. T. Matthews, *The Royal General Farms in Eighteenth Century France* (New York, 1958).
6. R. Pipes, *Russia under the Old Regime* (London, 1974), 60–61.
7. Bushkovitch, "Taxation, Tax Farming, and Merchants," 385.
8. Ibid., 390–92.
9. *Ocherki istorii SSSR XVII v.,* ed. A. A. Novosel'skii, (Moscow, 1955), 424; Bushkovitch, "Taxation, Tax Farming, and Merchants," 397.
10. On the demise of the salt tax, see R. M. Vvedenskii, "Soliarnaia regaliia i uchrezhdenie vol'noi prodazhi soli v Rossii," *Istoriia SSSR*, 1986, no. 1, 171–81.
11. Calculated from figures in *Ministerstvo finansov, 1802–1902*, (St. Petersburg, 1904), vol. 1, 616–21, 624–29.
12. Calculated from figures in Kahan, *The Plow, the Hammer and the Knout*, 324–25; *Svedeniia*, vol. 3, 6–7, 10; *Ministerstvo finansov*, vol. 1, 616–19, 624–27, 632–35, 640–41, 646–47.
13. *Ministerstvo finansov*, vol. 1, 110.
14. On consumption patterns, see David Christian, "Traditional and Modern Drinking Cultures in Russia on the Eve of Emancipation," *Australian Slavonic and East European Studies* 1 (1987), no. 1: 61–84.
15. *Trudy komissii Vysochaishe uchrezhdennoi dlia sostavleniia proekta polozheniia ob aktsize s pitei* (St. Petersburg, 1861), pt. 1, no. 12, 12–13.
16. Druzhinin's estimate is discussed in P. G. Ryndziunskii, *Utverzhdenie kapitalizma v Rossii* (Moscow, 1978), 10.
17. Benardaki was an old hand. Indeed, he had loaned Gogol money in 1839, and it may be that a grateful Gogol took him as his model for the virtuous tax farmer, Murazov, in the second part of *Dead Souls*. David Magarshak, *Gogol: A Life* (New York, 1969), 178, 183.
18. *Svedeniia*, vol. 3, 61–66.
19. The best example is probably S. P. Shipov, whose career is described in A. J. Rieber, "The Moscow Entrepreneurial Group: The Emergence of a New Form in

Autocratic Politics," *Jahrbücher für Geschichte Osteuropas* 25 (1977): 5–6, and in *Russkii biograficheskii slovar'*, (St. Petersburg, 1911), vol. 23, 296–99.

20. E. P. Thompson first put the notion of a "moral economy" into circulation in "The Moral Economy of the English Crowd in the Eighteenth Century," *Past and Present* 50 (February 1971): 76–126. It has since been developed in the work of James Scott, *The Moral Economy of the Peasant* (New Haven, Conn., 1976).

21. These distinctions, and the subject of corruption in general, are discussed more fully in David Christian, "Vodka and Corruption in Russia on the Eve of Emancipation," *Slavic Review* 46 (1987). nos. 3 and 4: 471–88.

22. *Svedeniia*, vol. 1, 37.

23. See Christian, "Vodka and Corruption."

24. *Svedeniia*, vol. 4, 214.

25. Calculated from figures on gross liquor tax revenues in *Svedeniia*, vol. 4, 70–71, 266–69.

26. There is no evidence for the widespread manufacture of *samogon* in nineteenth-century Russia. Samogon making is a product of the unsuccessful experiment with prohibition initiated by Tsar Nicholas II during mobilization for World War I in 1914. See, for example, D. N. Voronov, *O samogone*, 2d ed. (Moscow-Leningrad, 1930), 6.

27. These consumer protests are discussed in David Christian, "The Black and Gold Seals: Popular Protests against the Liquor Trade on the Eve of Emancipation," in Esther Kingston-Mann and Timothy Mixter, eds., *Peasant Economy, Culture and Politics of European Russia, 1800–1917* (Princeton, N.J., 1991), 261–93.

28. V. A. Fedorov, "Krestianskoe trezvennoe dvizhenie. 1858–1859 gg.," in *Revoliutsionnaia situatsiia v Rossii v 1859–1861 gg.*, vol. 2 (Moscow, 1962), 125; S. B. Okun', ed., *Krestianskoe dvizhenie v Rossii v 1857–1861 gg. Dokumenty* (Moscow, 1963), 736.

29. P. P. Semenov, obituary of K. K. Grot, *Russkaia starina*, 1898, no. 4, 220; and see P. P. Semenov-Tian-Shanskii, *Epokha osvobozhdeniia krest'ian v Rossii (1857–1861 gg.) v vospominaniiakh*, (St. Petersburg-Petrograd, 1911–16), vol. 1, 418–39. Rostovtsev's assistant, Semenov, claimed that Rostovtsev had wanted to oversee the abolition of the tax farm. *Konstantin Karlovich Grot kak gosudarstvennyi i obshchestvennyi deiatel': Materialy dlia ego biografii i kharakteristiki* (Petrograd, 1915), vol. 1, 160.

30. The proposal was published in *Moskovskie Vedomosti* 8–10, nos. 124–26 (June 1862).

31. P. L. Lieberman, "V. A. Kokorev: An Industrial Entrepreneur in Nineteenth Century Russia" (Ph.D diss., Yale University, 1981), iii and chaps. 4 and 5.

32. Rieber, "The Moscow Entrepreneurial Group," 11–12.

33. This complex game is described in vivid detail in P. V. Berezin, *Na sluzhbe zlomu delu. Khronika iz zhizni na vinokurennykh zavodakh* (Moscow, 1900); see also M. M. Fridman, *Vinnaia monopoliia* (St. Petersburg-Petrograd, 1914–16), vol. 2, 70–74.

34. *Kratkii ocherk 50-letiia aktsiznoi sistemy vzimaniia naloga s krepkikh napitkov . . . 1816–1913* (St. Petersburg, 1913), iii.

35. The concept of tributary societies is developed with great rigor in Eric Wolf, *Europe and the People without History* (Berkeley, Calif., 1982), particularly chap. 3.

36. A. I. Gertsen and N. P. Ogarev, *Kolokol* (Moscow, 1962), vol. 2, 455 (Nov. 1, 1859).

37. Fridman, *Vinnaia monopoliia*, vol. 2, 91–92.

VII

THE RUSSIAN NAVY AND THE PROBLEM OF TECHNOLOGICAL TRANSFER

TECHNOLOGICAL BACKWARDNESS AND MILITARY-INDUSTRIAL DEVELOPMENT, 1853–1876

Jacob W. Kipp

Over the past century and a half the application of industrial techniques to the manufacture and production of weapons within the context of an ongoing scientific-technical revolution has substantially altered the relationship between the military and the institutions that produce those modern weapons. New technologies have fostered profound changes within the military itself—changing doctrine, strategy, and tactics; accelerating and redefining the process of professionalization among the officer corps; and increasing the skills and status of enlisted personnel. At the same time, the advent of an industrial and technological society has altered the relationship between the military and civil society.

By 1850 Western Europe, especially Great Britain, had begun the shift toward an industrial mode of production occurring in the dynamic civilian economy. In Britain and France the resulting military-technological changes first appeared in naval affairs, where the shift from sail to steam and screw-propelled warships had set off a naval arms race in which both powers sought to replace sailing ships-of-the-line and frigates with screw-propelled vessels. Great Britain clearly and decisively was winning that race when the Crimean War broke out.[1]

The reasons for England's success were complex and depended upon the connections between its dynamic civil economy and the Admiralty. Although England maintained a substantial naval establishment during the nineteenth century, British private shipyards and engine works were not dependent upon the Royal Navy, thanks to a vital merchant marine and an expanding world market for British-built merchantmen and warships. The Royal Navy had the enviable position of maintaining its own modern dockyards for the construction of large warships, while being able to count upon a network of private yards that could be mobilized in times of crisis. Indeed, these private yards were, in many ways, more innovative in the field of maritime technology than the naval yards. The private yards on the Thames and the Clyde and at Bristol introduced the Halifax packets and the iron hull. British engine works, such as Maudsley and Field, pioneered in the development of steam propulsion as well. British shipping lines were the first to purchase such ships. With the world's largest merchant marine and the lion's share of the world's industrial production, Britain could depend upon the Royal Navy to ensure the empire's maritime communications and thereby maintain its prosperity. That prosperity kept British yards and works from settling into a dependence upon the Admiralty's orders. When steam and later screw-propulsion superseded sail as the foundation of naval power, Britain was in an excellent position to meet that challenge. In the Anglo-French naval race of the late 1840s and early 1850s, England and its mixed system of state and private yards proved more robust than France's centralized, bureaucratic, state-owned works, a lesson not lost on Russian reformers.[2] Overall economic power was, as Paul Kennedy has asserted, the foundation of British naval power during the Pax Britannia.[3]

As the Crimean War revealed, Russia's situation was quite different. By the middle of the nineteenth century Russia had fallen behind economically and technologically. Whereas in the eighteenth century its metallurgy had been sufficient to guarantee it a place among the world's leading producers of iron, by the 1850s it no longer could compete with them. Its merchant marine was almost nonexistent. Only Moscow and St. Petersburg were connected by railroad, and a domestic industry to produce engines, cars, and rails was in its infancy.

Until the Crimean War, Russian statesmen, with a few exceptions, were not aware of what a difference this relative decline in the empire's economic position made to its status as a great power. Defeat during the Crimean War brought that lesson home. At the Alma, Russian columns armed with smooth-bore muskets and cold steel melted away under rifle fire of the British and French before they could close. To its embarrassment, the tsarist government found that the British and French, particularly the latter, could supply their troops in the Crimea more efficiently. The absence of a national system of railroads linking the empire's population and industrial centers with the battlefields in the south proved logistically and strategically disastrous. Lacking modern vessels, Russian admirals were either forced to keep their ships under the guns of their own fortifications or to scuttle them because they could not risk open battle with the Anglo-French.[4]

In the wake of the war, reform-minded Russian statesmen accepted the need for sweeping reforms if the empire was to recover its position as a great power. To them, Russia needed a general European peace while it undertook those reforms, beginning with the emancipation of the serfs but including a far wider program that embraced the reorganization of the government and the modernization of the economy. As the United States minister to St. Petersburg noted in 1857, "The policy of those who govern Russia is peace in all her external relations, for she has more to hope for in the development of this new system and her internal resources—vast forest regions and mines, her industry and communications and the peopling of her extensive territory—and through the arts of negotiations than from any foreign wars at present."[5] The Russian autocracy thus began a program of "reforms from above" that would make the empire a great power again, but combined with it a policy of international restraint and the reduction of her military forces.

Because of the persistent financial crisis that confronted the tsarist government following the Crimean War, Alexander II reduced the number of men under arms to well below the levels of the 1840s and sought to check military spending. Russian statesmen such as L. Tengoborski and M. Kh. Reitern stressed the need to cut the military to safeguard the state's fiscal integrity and to increase the amount of capital that could be invested in private industry, commerce, and agriculture. For the reformers the expansion of the civil economy seemed the key to Russia's economic modernization and the strengthening of Russia's international position.[6]

Russian naval reformers shared such sentiments. In a letter to Prince A. I. Bariatinskii, the commander of the Caucasian Army, the General-Admiral Konstantin Nikolaevich noted the absolute need for fundamental internal reforms to stimulate national economic development and stated that he considered the postwar period a time "to work for the future so that our children will reap the fruits from the soil . . . that we can till, enrich, and sow."[7]

It might appear, then, at first glance to be a paradox to seek the origins of a Russian technological modernization in such a period. True, some historians, notably Alfred J. Rieber, have suggested that military modernization lay at the very base of Alexander II's commitment to domestic reform. But this interpretation, for all its straightforwardness when applied to the emancipation of the serfs—the keystone of any civil reforms—has been sharply criticized.[8] Supporting that criticism is a mass of evidence that underscores how slow the Russian Army was to reform following the Crimean War. Most scholars would agree with P. A. Zaionchkovskii's judgment that fundamental changes did not commence until the appointment of D. A. Miliutin as minister of war in the early 1860s.[9] Regarding the emergence of a military-industrial complex, the same scholar makes a telling point when he calls attention to the War Ministry's reluctance to encourage private arms works or to shift from artisans to hired labor in its own arms works and arsenals.[10] Our apparent paradox becomes lessened when we turn to the transformations that were transpiring during this period in the area of military and naval procurement.

Down to the middle of the nineteenth century Russia's military establishment continued to rest upon those institutional pillars that Peter the Great had fashioned during his drive for the Westernization of the empire in the early eighteenth century. During the Northern War Peter I had instituted his own sweeping program of reforms from above to make Russia a match for Sweden, and down to the Crimean War his successors had expanded upon it. The repeated successes of Russian arms affirmed the program's continued vitality. On the eve of the Crimean War the image of Russian military power still captivated European statesmen and generals.[11]

This system, which had permitted Russia to create a large standing army and sailing navy, involved the Westernization of the empire's service elite, the enserfment of the vast majority of Russia's population, the conscription of common soldiers for what amounted to permanent military service, and the organization of a domestic arms industry along artisan, workshop, handicraft lines.[12] In the preindustrial world with its relative technological stability, such a system had allowed Russia to become a great power. Under those conditions the autocratic state had been able to devote a major portion of its military budget to the maintenance of a large standing army and navy— 800,000 men in the former and 100,000 men in the latter in the 1840s— while spending a relatively small share of that budget on the procurement of weapons, whose life in service could be extended into several decades and even a half century.[13]

The Crimean War revealed major flaws in the existing military establishment, the two most important being the absence within the military system of a mechanism for the rapid and large-scale expansion of the army in time of war and the inability of Russia's arms industry to match the production of new technology or absorb it from the West.[14] The former weakness can be seen as an inability to achieve the mobilization potential which the French Revolution had raised under the concept of "nation in Arms." The sociopolitical content of exploiting such a mobilization potential raised the question of shifting from an army based on estate principles to one composed of citizens. The problem of matching the latest military technology of England and France was a much newer and more immediate problem, intruding directly upon the economic foundations of military power; imposing changes on military doctrine, strategy and tactics; and making new demands in the education and training of military personnel. This issue did emerge within the Russian Army after 1856, but debate focused on three interconnected but not fully understood problems: the martinet spirit of Nicholas I's army, the advantages of open over closed tactical formations, and the costs and pace of rearming the army with rifled weapons.[15]

For the Russian Navy, even the limited tactical experience with combat under steam power obtained during the Crimean War was already setting in motion profound changes. Rear Admiral G. I. Butakov had commanded the British-built paddle-wheel frigate *Vladimir* during its successful three-hour battle with the Turkish-Egyptian paddle-wheel frigate *Pervaz-Bakhri* on November 5, 1853 (O.S.). Following the war he began a systematic study of foreign works on steam tactics and speculated about a turning point in naval warfare in which complex maneuvers replaced the conventional battle line of broadside-armed ships. His speculations on a tactical revolution were endorsed by the Naval Ministry, which placed him in command of a practice squadron of forty screw gunboats in the Gulf of Finland. Each summer between 1860 and 1862 Rear Admiral Butakov exercised this squadron in the skerries there. In 1863, following the battle between the *Monitor* and the *Merrimack*, Butakov extended his speculations to the employment of the ram in ironclad naval combat to exploit the maneuver advantages of steam propulsion. Butakov believed that "steam must bring about in naval tactics the sort of revolution [*perevorot*] which took place in army tactics at the end of the last century."[16]

Industry and Armaments

The inability to produce the modern arms required by this revolution provided the point of departure for the development of a new Russian arms industry during the Crimean War. Russia's prewar arms industry, a complex of state-owned works, arsenals, and admiralties located at the two capitals (St. Petersburg and Moscow), at Tula, in the Urals, and in the south still relied upon various forms of "obligated labor" to man the facilities. Since this labor force, composed of state peasants, conscript labor, and obligated artisans, was both cheap and relatively unproductive, the state administration concentrated its attention upon policing its workers in the hope of raising labor discipline, while paying little or no attention to technical innovation. The artisans viewed such innovation as a threat to their status and position. Thus, while some Russian naval officers grasped quite early the implication of the new technologies of steam propulsion, the screw, and the construction of vessels from iron, the state arms industry proved slow and ponderous in its response. Critics of the existing system emphasized the inapplicability of its artisan mode of production to the emerging machine techniques then being employed in the United States and Western Europe. In their concern to increase the productivity of Russia's state yards and works, reformers advocated the shift from "obligated labor" to hired labor and emphasized the inherent advantages of a labor market over the existing bureaucratic-police methods in maintaining worker discipline within a factory system.[17] Although Leskov's "cross-eyed artisan from Tula" might shoe Sheffield's mechanical flea, Russia needed captains of industry to match Sheffield and Manchester.

Private enterprise seemed to these reformers to be an integral part of their solution to Russia's economic backwardness.[18] Enterprise and entrepreneurship were seen as powerful engines of economic production and progress. The model of such entrepreneurship was the U.S. capitalist with his "go ahead" and "never mind," who was "willing to put everything on a single card" to transform a continent. These forces would only be unleashed when the state finances, the monetary system, and the banks were placed on a sound foundation to create a climate for capital investment. Russia's naval reformers were well aware of the avarice and greed at the heart of this engine but believed that these could be harnessed by *glasnost'* and public scrutiny.[19]

The advocacy of private enterprise in the cause of national rejuvenation and defense did not imply that Russian naval reformers were intent upon creating a vast navy through this new relation between the state and Russia's private shipyards and machine works. Their emphasis rather was upon replacing quantity with quality. Indeed, a superficial examination of the evidence would lead to the conclusion that the years following the Crimean War were a period of declining Russian naval power. In 1850 the empire had 100,000 men and over forty ships-of-the-line in its two fleets, but by 1860 those figures had declined to about 54,500 men and eight ships-of-the-line in one fleet. The navy's total budget in 1860, with inflation taken into account, was slightly smaller than in 1853.[20]

Such comparisons in an era of rapid technological change are quite deceptive. Between 1853 and 1860 the Russian Navy had made the transition from sail to steam-screw propulsion. Furthermore, owing to the demilitarization of the Black Sea and the decision to terminate shipbuilding at Archangel, the empire's shipbuilding programs had become concentrated at Kronstadt and St. Petersburg. By decommissioning sailing ships and demobilizing surplus personnel, the Naval Ministry had dramatically increased the share of its budget that went into the procurement of new ships. Russia's shipbuilding program following the Crimean War was vigorous, and it had a disproportionate impact upon the economy of St. Petersburg and its environs.[21]

The Navy and Private Yards during the Crimean War

The origins of the Russian Navy's intimate relationship with private industry are to be found in the technological changes of the late 1830s and the 1840s. For the first time since the reign of Peter I, naval planners addressed the question of technological transfer, since they understood that the navy had to assimilate a host of new inventions in one fashion or another. While Russia built its first steam warship in 1826, this process of technological assimilation became an important naval issue only in the late 1830s; but it continued to be so throughout the nineteenth century down to the current era. In the initial phase the navy tended to utilize Russia's state yards and works to produce most of the steamships for the Baltic fleet. But in the absence of modern yards and large-scale machine-building works in the south, it opted to procure steamships for the Black Sea fleet by purchase from England. Commercial agents and naval officers were dispatched to the

United States and England to conclude contracts with private yards and works for the construction of such ships. These naval missions, which introduced Russian officers to private yards and engine plants, provided the first, however unsystematic, naval intelligence about new technologies.[22] To oversee the procurement of such vessels the Naval Ministry organized ad hoc a Steamship Committee to serve as both a planning agency and an intelligence clearinghouse.[23] At the same time, efforts were made to recruit foreign naval engineers and mechanics into Russian service. Work was also begun on modernizing Russia's yards and works at Kronstadt, Nikolaev, and Izhora. But these efforts were meager and provided a domestic repair capability rather than the construction of the latest wood or iron hulls, engines, and screw machinery.[24]

Purchasing ships from England, however justified on the basis of the existing Russian shipbuilding and engine-making capabilities, had numerous disadvantages. For one thing, commercial agents were paid a commission based on the total cost of the ship and therefore had an incentive for negotiating contracts for a sum higher than the market price. This often meant that Russia paid more than other states for similar warships.[25] A more serious liability was the reality of the foreign dependence that such procurement fostered. In the case of England such orders gave a potentially hostile power a stranglehold on the procurement of modern warships. This became apparent during the Crimean War. On the eve of the war, Russo-British relations deteriorated to open confrontation short of war; the British government confiscated the engines and machinery that Russia had ordered from Robert Napier and Penn for the completion of several screw-propelled ships-of-the-line and frigates. This action delayed the completion of these vessels for the duration of hostilities and served as an important lesson for Russian naval planners on the need to emancipate the empire from dependence on foreign yards and works for the latest technology.[26]

The Russian Navy had not enjoyed great success with screw technology prior to the Crimean War. In 1846 the naval architect Colonel Amosov had overseen the construction of the 300-horsepower frigate *Arkhimed*. The frigate, however, was lost in a storm off Bornholm in 1850. The Naval Ministry did not launch its next screw-propelled warship, the frigate *Polkan,* until 1853, and its first screw-propelled ships-of-the-line, *Vyborg* and *Orel,* were not yet launched when war began.[27] Thus, while England and France had engaged in a naval arms race, competing for the acquisition of the largest number of screw-propelled battleships and frigates, Russia had scarcely entered into the competition. Indeed, in this same period the Naval Ministry reduced the rate of new warship construction at Russian yards and devoted resources to the retimbering of older sailing ships to extend their service.[28]

During the Crimean War the Naval Ministry took its first steps toward ending such dependence by turning to private Russian firms. As soon as the ministry learned of the British confiscation of the Napier and Penn engines, it sent out invitations to Russian engine works to bid for contracts on the engines for the ships-of-the-line. Since one example of the Napier machinery had already arrived, the Naval Ministry proposed that it be used as a prototype. On the basis of its low bid the Nobel works received a 592,500-ruble contract for the production of three 500-horsepower Napier-type engines and screw machinery to be ready no later than the spring of 1856. Nobel, however, stipulated in the contract that the fulfilling of its terms was conditional upon the ability of its plant to import certain machined parts from abroad. The British declaration of war and subsequent blockade made that impossible. In addition, as both the Naval Ministry and Nobel sadly soon discovered, the choice of the Napier prototype had been an expensive mistake. The original engine, when installed on the *Vyborg*, proved unreliable and subject to frequent breakdowns. Delays in the deliveries of the engines and disputes over the costs of redesigning the engines to meet performance specifications ended in litigation that dragged on into the 1850s and poisoned relations between Nobel and the Naval Ministry.[29]

While Nobel went ahead with the preparation of its engines, the Naval Ministry moved to prepare hulls for them. In November 1853 it concluded a contract with Honorary Citizen S. G. Kudriavtsev for 408,000 rubles, under which he agreed to undertake the construction of two ships-of-the-line and the conversion of two sailing ships-of-the-line. This work was to be done at state yards with government materials, but Kudriavtsev was to provide the labor force.[30] The conversions, done in haste with poor materials, had serious design and structural weaknesses.

Fortunately for Russian naval planners, the situation with regard to the manufacture of smaller engines at private domestic works was more advantageous. The 360-horsepower Penn engine proved more reliable and served as a model for Russian-produced machinery for frigates and corvettes during and after the Crimean War.[31]

Under the impact of the Anglo-French expedition to the Baltic in 1854, the Naval Ministry embarked upon a program to strengthen its forces for operations in the skerries of the Gulf of Finland by replacing galleys with steamships. In the summer of 1854 two prototypes of screw-propelled gunboats were begun, and in late 1854 the Steamship Committee, after an analysis of these designs, drew up its own plans for a ship of this type. In January 1855 work began on the construction of thirty-two gunboats. The engines (50-75 horsepower) were built by many St. Petersburg firms. The Aleksandrovskii plant built five mechanisms and boilers; Thomson, Isherwood, and Fricke provided nineteen engines; while the Baird, Ashworth & Stevens and Semenov plants produced the boilers for nineteen gunboats. The Naval Ministry's own plant at Izhora manufactured six engines and boilers. By May 15, twenty-three mechanisms and twenty-six boilers were ready.[32]

In this venture the naval leadership, particularly the Grand Duke Konstantin Nikolaevich, "turned to private enterprise and entrusted the matter to trustworthy persons outside the regular bureaucratic order."[33] Unquestionably the most important "trustworthy person" to whom the grand duke turned was N. I. Putilov, whom he made his plenipotentiary. Putilov, a man of extraordinary energy and managerial talents, had already taken on the role of editing a periodical devoted to news and patriotic propaganda about the war.[34] He now took on the task of coordinating the manufacture of the gunboats' machinery at private and state works. With a line of credit of 640,000 rubles and the charge that he deliver thirty-two sets of machinery by the summer of 1855 at a price of less than 20,000 rubles each, Putilov set about mobilizing labor and management. In a few months the labor force of St. Petersburg's engine shops and boiler works increased twentyfold. In the final accounting it turned out that Putilov delivered all thirty-two sets of machinery for a total cost of 619,870 rubles, a saving of 20,130 rubles to the treasury.[35] In 1855 the Naval Ministry decided to repeat the same methods in a larger program that included thirty-five gunboats and fourteen corvettes. This time Putilov received a line of credit for 1,470,000 rubles and enlisted ten private plants in the effort. The Galvano-Plastic Works, Nobel, Baird, Aleksandrovskii, Thomson, Fricke, Ashworth & Stevens, and Mershchan-skii received major contracts.[36]

While Putilov directed the acquisition of the gunboats' engines, S. G. Kudriavtsev oversaw the construction of their hulls. The honorary citizen agreed to build twenty gunboats and fourteen corvettes at state yards from government materials with his own laborers at a cost of 5,500 rubles per gunboat and 27,750 rubles per corvette. The other fifteen gunboats Kudriav-tsev agreed to build from his own materials at a cost of 13,250 rubles each. The total cost of this program of 1855 came to 2,125,000 rubles.[37]

The Creation of a Screw-Propelled Navy

The birth of a Russian screw-propelled navy during the Crimean War was thus linked with the development of a relationship between the private yards and works of St. Petersburg and the Naval Ministry. Following the war, the Navy sought to make what had been a heady but stormy courtship into a permanent engagement. Russian naval officers had for many years been dissatisfied with the warships produced by government dockyards and blamed the inferior workmanship and materials upon the existing order. In the wake of the Crimean War naval reformers began to transform that sys-tem by emancipating both the admiralty serfs at Okhta near St. Petersburg and those in settlements near Nikolaev, a process completed in 1860. At the same time naval reformers also reduced the number of conscript workers in other naval yards and in the early 1860s replaced all obligatory labor with a two-tier system: a cadre force of skilled labor to staff all naval yards and an unskilled mass of laborers that could be more easily expanded and contracted.[38] In the interim the Naval Ministry relied increasingly upon the services of entrepreneurs like Kudriavtsev to supply labor for the govern-ment's yards, and it set aside the dockyards on Galernyi Isle for their opera-

124   Jacob W. Kipp

tions. Under such projects the entrepreneur recruited the skilled labor, organized the construction work, and sometimes provided a portion of the building materials, while a naval officer-engineer oversaw the technical and architectural aspects of the project.[39]

Following the Crimean War the Russian Navy pressed forward with the conversion from sail to steam and screw propulsion. The Naval Ministry replaced the Steamship Committee with two distinct organizations: the Shipbuilding Department, charged with handling the financial side of all construction projects, and the Shipbuilding Technical Committee, which monitored foreign technical developments, kept track of Russia's own domestic shipbuilding capacity at state and private yards and works, and formulated the final plans for each new ship and the conversion of older vessels.[40]

Under the new organization that Alexander II instituted in the spring of 1855, the General-Admiral Konstantin Nikolaevich assumed direct supervision of the technical side of naval affairs. The rallying cry of naval officers associated with the grand duke now became "making the ministry serve the navy and not the navy the ministry." After the war he dispatched some of his most talented young officers abroad to serve as naval agents.[41] In contrast with the prewar period, the Naval Ministry now followed a consistent policy of using a limited number of foreign orders for warships and machinery as prototypes. The French naval architect Armand built a wood-iron frigate, the *Svetlana,* at Bordeaux, and the Webb Yards in New York completed the seventy-gun cruiser-frigate, the *General-Admiral,* under the supervision of Captain 1st Rank A. I. Shestakov, an officer who would in the 1880s lead the Russian Navy into the era of the steel battleship.[42] The ministry also continued to place orders for the latest and most powerful engines with private firms in England. In all these cases the orders were for single copies that could be used as models by Steamship-Technical Committee to aid Russian yards and works in their own projects.

By the late 1850s the prototype system had begun to pay handsome dividends. The availability of these foreign models and the continuous flow of contracts to St. Petersburg's engine plants allowed them to expand their production to engines of the largest type. In 1859 the Naval Ministry awarded Baird the contract for the 800-horsepower engine for the frigate *Dmitrii Donskoi* and assigned to the Izhorskie State Works the order for a similar one for the frigate *Aleksandr Nevskii.*[43] Such engine building meant an expansion of St. Petersburg's iron industry, and in 1858 the Naval Ministry concluded a contract with Putilov, its former official, to turn scrap iron into boiler plates at his private mill.[44] A sustained building program for steam-propelled, capital ships, corvettes, and clippers kept Russian dockyards, private yards, and works, as well as yards in Finland, fully engaged.[45]

The Naval Ministry did not confine its engagement with private enterprise to shipbuilding and engine construction. Confronted with the demilitarization of the Black Sea, the navy sought to augment its residual maritime capacity in the theater by fostering the foundation of the Black Sea Steamship and Navigation Company. The general-admiral secured for the new company operation capital and a mileage subsidy from the state treasury and turned over to it naval stores and facilities that were left in the naval yards and ports of south Russia.[46] To stimulate passenger business in the Mediterranean, he sent B. P. Mansurov to Palestine, where he was to oversee the improvement of hostels for Orthodox pilgrims to the Holy Land. That nineteenth-century novelty, tourism, could serve the navy.[47]

Naval reformers took a serious interest in the development of Russia's merchant marine, collected extensive statistical evidence on that topic, and proposed various schemes to organize public and private institutions for the training of merchant seamen. About two hundred retired naval officers had been transferred to the merchant marine by 1860.[48]

For all their efforts, however, the naval reformers could not overcome the tremendous economic and social barriers that confronted the Russian merchant marine, and it lagged far behind other maritime powers. The small sailing coasters, which made up most of the empire's shipping, hardly benefited from the Naval Ministry's efforts. Weighed against the risks, steam navigation companies without generous state subsidies and contracts just did not return enough profit to attract private investors. What naval reformers did achieve was the creation of a de facto naval reserve in the Black Sea, which could be effectively mobilized for wartime use, as was the case with the vessels of the Russian Society of Steam Navigation and Trade during the Russo-Turkish War of 1877–78, when Russia still lacked an effective battle fleet there.[49]

The Ironclad Revolution

The postwar engagement with private enterprise, which inspired so much hope among naval reformers, became an outright marriage with St. Petersburg's shipyards, iron works, and machine-building plants in the 1860s, when the Naval Ministry had to confront the next round in the revolution in naval technology that began with the construction of the French and British seagoing ironclads, *La Gloire* and *HMS Warrior.*[50]

In October 1860 R. Musselius, one of the navy's leading experts on artillery, declared in *Morskoi sbornik* that the new ironclads threatened to make the latest screw-propelled, wooden ships of all navies obsolete. A new naval race had begun, and Musselius anticipated rapid progress in both ship's armor and artillery.[51] Musselius's article was the first shot in the Naval Ministry's public battle to secure funds for Russian ironclads, a struggle which had been going on for two years in camera within the Tsarist government.

In 1858 Konstantin Nikolaevich had called the tsar's attention to ironclads as a potentially radical innovation in naval architecture. Having followed the

French and British development of armored floating batteries during the
Crimean War, he became alarmed when France announced its intention to
build an ironclad frigate. In 1859 he again sought funds from the State Council to build one such ship, but the council rejected the request because of a
continuing crisis of state finances.[52] In 1860 the general-admiral included in
the ministry's budget items for the construction of three such ships and
carried the campaign to the State Council. At the council's meeting on
November 29, 1860, he presented the threat posed by such ships in the
starkest terms: "There can be no doubt that ironclad frigates are ships which
in naval combat and especially coastal defense will have a decisive superiority over all other ships known down to the present."[53] Further delays, he
warned, would leave Kronstadt and St. Petersburg defenseless. At the same
time, he informed Alexander II that naval experts were agreed that "the
future of navies lies in iron-hulled ironclads, armed with artillery of the
largest caliber and long-range."[54] While the grand duke and other advocates
of heavy naval artillery did not appreciate the tactical problems associated
with aiming and firing such large naval guns in an engagement at sea, they
did appreciate the dialectical relationship which was emerging between
armor and artillery. After a two-year delay and in spite of strenuous objections on fiscal grounds by some officials, the emperor authorized the purchase of Russia's first ironclad battery in England.[55]

While the State Council debated and Russian naval architects prepared
the specifications for an ironclad battery, Russian private yards were at
work. Carr & MacPherson of St. Petersburg, in collaboration with the Shipbuilding Technical Committee, built a 270-ton ironclad gunboat, the *Opyt*
(experiment). The Baltic Yards installed the 70-horsepower engine built by
Thomson & Company. Launched in October 1861, the *Opyt* with its single
cannon behind a 4.5-inch bow plate armor was the best that Russian yards
and works could yet accomplish in this new field of endeavor. Its armor,
because of the inability of Russian mills to cast plates of such thickness,
had come from England.[56]

From the outset the Naval Ministry was determined to change that situation. The *Pervenets,* a 3,277 ton ironclad battery built at the Thames Iron
Works, would be the first and last Russian ironclad battery constructed
abroad. The naval mission sent to London to oversee its construction, which
included naval architects, engineers, shipwrights, and mechanics, was one
part oversight and one part naval intelligence.[57] At the Thames these officers
and men were expected to learn the latest techniques used in iron shipbuilding and ironclad construction.

In 1862 the Naval Ministry took an important step toward the creation of
a Russian iron shipbuilding industry by concluding with the British ship-
builder Mitchell a contract for the construction in Russia of a second ironclad battery, the *Ne Tron' Menia.* Under the term of the contract the Naval
Ministry agreed to provide Mitchell with the use of the dockyards on Galernyi Isle and to undertake the modernization of the yard. In exchange he

agreed to recruit British engineers and shipwrights and to train Russians.[58] At the same time and following the decision of the Royal Navy to adopt such a course, the Naval Ministry decided to convert two new wooden frigates, the *Sevastopol* and *Petropavlovsk,* into the ironclads. The ministry awarded the conversion projects to the Baltic Yards of Carr & MacPherson and the Naval Yards of Semiannikov and Poletika.[59] While Mitchell continued work on Russia's second ironclad battery at Galernyi Isle, the Naval Ministry turned to Semiannikov and Poletika for the construction of the third and final ship of this class, *Kreml',* in 1863.[60]

In the space of three years the Naval Ministry had moved in rapid succession from foreign purchase to domestic construction of ironclads and had given St. Petersburg's private yards a conspicuous part in the undertaking. The domestic construction of ironclad batteries and the conversion of wooden frigates into ironclads were not, however, independent from foreign know-how or materials at this stage. The ministry's arrangement with Mitchell certainly promised the domestication of the former in the not-too-distant future. But materials in 1862-63 still seemed a problem. Russian mills could not yet forge the armor for the ironclads, and Brown and Co. of Sheffield produced the plate for all five ships.[61]

The cosmopolitan spirit of this most bourgeois of eras certainly aided the Russian Navy in its ironclad program. The Thames Iron Works, like Messers or Baird of Merseyside, had no objection to selling ironclads to foreigners—even to the tsar—and Mitchell's contract was hardly more than an extension of the same attitude. In Russia itself, many of the firms with which the Naval Ministry dealt could be called foreign, including Baird, Carr & MacPherson, Thomson, and Ashworth & Stevens. Baird, the latest private engine maker in St. Petersburg, recruited some of its engineers from abroad, one of them the son of the famous naval architect and engineer, John Scott Russell.[62] Science and technology, as M. Kh. Reitern observed, had no homeland. They could be put into the service of any society that would accept the advantages of free labor and private enterprise.[63] Likewise, there were few reservations in Manchesterian England. Self-confident and assured about England's preeminent position as the "workshop of the world," British society and Her Majesty's government saw little reason to curtail the blessings that free trade and commerce—even in warships—bestowed upon the empire. If foreign complications threatened British security, the government could act. But such an eventuality was seen as an exceptional situation.

Such an exceptional situation did, however, shortly develop when British relations with the Tsarist government deteriorated in 1863 over the Polish question. To forestall the confiscation of the still-unfinished *Pervenets,* the Naval Ministry had the battery brought back to Kronstadt for final completion in August of that year. On its passage down the Thames with a British pilot at the helm, *Pervenets* struck and severely damaged one of the hulks used by the Royal Navy at Greenwich. This proved to be the only "hostile" act that took place between the navies during what both powers considered a threatening period.[64]

The battle between the USS *Monitor* and the CSS *Virginia* in 1862 had already turned Russian naval planners' attention to ironclad development in the United States. The Shipbuilding Technical Committee sent a three-man mission to investigate U.S. ironclad technology, especially Ericcson's *Monitor*. Captain First Rank S. S. Lesovskii, N. A. Artseulov, a naval engineer, and F. N. Pestich, an artillery specialist, came back with an enthusiastic report on the *Monitor's* many advantages as a coastal defense craft.[65] The ship's small size, shallow draft, and heavy artillery, mounted in a revolving turret, made it ideal for operations in the skerries of the Gulf of Finland and for the defense of Kronstadt and St. Petersburg. In early 1863 Artseulov returned to Russia with the plans of Ericcson's *Monitor* and stressed in his report to the Shipbuilding Technical Committee the advantages that could be gained by adopting the U.S. layer technique for the production of armor plate—the joining together of single one-inch curved plates to achieve the desired thickness. This method would permit Russian mills to manufacture the armor for the craft and thereby reduce the empire's dependence on Britain.[66]

The size of the *Monitor* and the relative simplicity of its construction appealed to Admiral N. K. Krabbe, the acting naval minister during the general-admiral's absence. Monitors cost substantially less than either batteries or converted frigates and could be completed much more rapidly.[67] Ericcson's first ship of the monitor type had taken just a hundred days from the laying of the keel to commissioning. The financial savings were also enormous. The *Pervenets* had cost over a million rubles, and the total cost of a converted frigate was close to 1.5 million rubles. Russia's monitors cost about 575,600 rubles each.[68]

Given what seemed to be a likelihood of war with England and France, the Naval Ministry's endorsement of the *Monitor* received a favorable response from General Kryzhanovskii's special committee on the defenses of Kronstadt and St. Petersburg.[69] By the summer of 1863 Russia's preparations for war had taken on a feverish pace, as the U. S. consul in St. Petersburg observed: "Russia is making the most wonderful preparation for war. The work at Petersburg, Cronstadt, Sweaborg, Viborg and other ports on fortifications has been pushed night and day. The new monitors are going ahead rapidly."[70]

As Russia's soldiers and sailors went about improving the Gulf's defenses, the Naval Ministry, under a cloak of secrecy, prepared to dispatch its best screw-propelled ships to sea. Admiral Krabbe ordered Rear Admiral S. S. Lesovskii to take his squadron across the Atlantic to Union ports, and Rear Admiral A. A. Popov took the Russian Pacific Squadron to San Francisco on his own initiative. In this threat to initiate *guerre de course* against the British merchant marine in the Atlantic and Pacific, the Russian government had embarked, with the implied consent and support of the Union, upon an act of naval deterrence. Meanwhile the frigate *General-Admiral* sailed to England to escort the unfinished *Pervenets* back to Kronstadt. Russian naval planners were making every effort to improve the empire's maritime posture before the outbreak of hostilities and to prevent a recurrence of the situation that had forced the navy to seek protection under fortress guns during the Crimean War.[71] New technology had been used to forge a very different naval strategy for Russia.

Technologically, Russia had come far in the decade between the Crimean War and 1863. It had begun that war with a fleet of obsolete galleys in the Baltic and had ended it with a flotilla of screw-propelled gunboats. Each of these craft had cost less than 40,000 rubles. In 1861 the Naval Ministry and Carr & MacPherson had built Russia's first ironclad gunboat, the *Opyt*. By 1863 the Naval Ministry had adopted the monitor for the same mission that the galley had served only ten years before.

The ironclad program of 1863 brought a substantial increase in shipbuilding expenditures to 7.9 million rubles, including an extraordinary credit of 3.6 million. With these funds the navy procured ten single-turreted monitors; one twin-turret ship, the *Smerch'*, that incorporated Captain C. P. Coles's turret system; thirteen armored rafts; and the already mentioned ironclad battery, *Kreml'*. For so large and ambitious a program the Naval Ministry mobilized all available shipbuilding facilities—state admiralties, private domestic yards, and foreign facilities. Two of the monitors were built at the New Admiralty, two more by Kudriavtsev at Galernyi Isle, two at the Baltic yards of Carr & MacPherson, and two at the Neva Yards of Semiannikov and Poletika. Two others were prefabricated at a private yard in Belgium and brought to Kronstadt for assembly. The *Smerch'* was built by Mitchell at Galernyi Isle.[72] Under the threat of war the Naval Ministry's engagement with private shipbuilding yards and machine works became a marriage.

In 1863, over the strong objections of the War Ministry, the navy oversaw the founding of Russia's first private steel mill and cannon works, the Obukhov Mill, at the site of the former Aleksandrovskii Works in St. Petersburg. This cooperative arrangement among Colonel P. M. Obukhov, the former director of the State Cannon Works at Zlatoust, and his partners, Putilov and Kudriavtsev, and the Naval Ministry was intended to provide the navy with the most powerful steel, rifled artillery with the ability to penetrate the latest armor. One of the strongest supporters of this venture within the Naval Ministry, R. Musselius, in commenting on the establishment of the Obukhov Mill wrote that such a mill would guarantee Russia a domestic source of the latest type of ordnance and reduce the costs and delays in providing warships with such large guns, but its steel-making capacity could be put to use for the further development of the empire's "shipbuilding industry, railroads, and industry in general."[73] In the wake of the Polish crisis, Russian naval planners had become convinced that private entrepreneurship had a key to play in solving the empire's long-term problems of maritime defense. *Morskoi sbornik* carried articles on St. Petersburg's iron industry, and naval authors had few doubts about what an alliance between the ministry and business could accomplish.[74]

The Continuing Challenge of Technological Innovation

The founding of the Obukhov Mill and the monitor program of 1863–64 were the honeymoon of Russia's naval-industrial complex. Forged under the impact of foreign technological development, the immediate threat of war, and an enthusiastic belief in the economic potential of private enterprise, these programs created intimate ties between the Naval Ministry and St. Petersburg's leading entrepreneurs. After 1864 the Naval Ministry's efforts to deepen that commitment ran into serious difficulties. The dialectics of artillery versus armor had set in motion another arms race in which each new gun demanded better armor and each improvement in armor stimulated cannon makers to create new guns with ever-greater penetrating power. Stimulated by British efforts to develop true ocean-going ironclads, the Naval Ministry undertook yet another eight-ship ironclad program in 1864. This program was supposed to be completed by 1869.[75]

This effort, following on the heels of the monitor program of 1863, provided a powerful stimulus for the development of industry in St. Petersburg. During the period 1863–66 the Naval Ministry spent over thirty-seven million rubles on shipbuilding, machinery, and artillery. Most of the sum went toward the construction of ironclads, and a great majority of the funds were spent in St. Petersburg.[76]

When General-Admiral Konstantin Nikolaevich initially sought funding for this program he drew upon a number of arguments that were as much economic as technical. He pointed to the advantages to be derived by giving St. Petersburg's private yards and admiralties such orders. During the monitor program a materiel and manpower pool had been assembled in the capital. New contracts over a longer period would keep the shipbuilding capacity intact, especially the skilled labor force. Finally the program would sustain St. Petersburg's iron and steel, shipbuilding, and mechanical industries, whose health, the general-admiral asserted, was vital to the national defense.[77]

The Naval Ministry was shortly forced to renege upon the general-admiral's implicit promise of continued funding. Another crisis of state finances hit the Naval Ministry hard. In 1867 the ministry's budget was cut from twenty-four million to sixteen million rubles.[78] The combination of a decline in the general-admiral's political fortunes after the attempted assassination of Alexander II, which many conservatives blamed on liberal sentiments emanating from his brother's residence, the Marble Palace, and another crisis of state finances proved overwhelming. This period of reduced spending for naval affairs came at a time when the Naval Ministry had no alternative but to cut back upon its capital programs. There was no surplus manpower in the navy that could be sacrificed this time. Naval appropriations for shipbuilding continued to decline for the rest of the decade until in 1869 they bottomed at 5.5 million rubles. In 1870 they recovered slightly, to 7.1 million, but were still less than at any year during the peak of the ironclad programs of 1863–66. How serious this situation had become by the late 1860s can be seen in the figures spent on engines and machinery: in 1869 this item declined to 267,230 rubles.[79] These budget cuts forced the Naval Ministry to stretch out its ironclad construction projects. As a result the later ironclads were obsolescent by the time of their completion.

The long-term negative effects of this budgetary crunch were profound. For Russia's recently expanded private yards it meant, as Alfred Nobel observed, bankruptcy.[80] Some firms were able to shift their production to other markets, particularly to the state-subsidized railway industry.[81] Some were not; Carr & MacPherson went bust during the economic depression of the 1870s and the Baltic Yards were reorganized as a Russian enterprise. The private firms were not the only losers. When the Naval Ministry came back into the market for new orders, it had to face a reduced capacity and an inferior product. By the mid-1870s the general-admiral was threatening to curtail the navy's longstanding association with Baird because of the decline in the firm's marine engines.[82]

Russia's machine builders and shipwrights, when faced by sudden and prolonged decline in naval contracts, had neither domestic nor foreign orders upon which to rely. Russia's own merchant marine was too small and undercapitalized to purchase the iron-hulled steamships that the Baltic and Neva Yards could produce. A great portion of the empire's merchant marine still consisted of small sailing ships for the cabotage trade. This situation had not changed even by the last decade of the century.[83]

The Naval Ministry's courtship of private enterprise did not produce the results that its architects intended. The constraints of economic backwardness and of the government's other economic policies made their hopes for a rapid economic takeoff in the 1860s unrealistic. When announcing the establishment of the Obukhov Mill, they had spoken of both swords and plowshares. But the results were products for the military or the state-subsidized railway industry. And the mill itself became a state enterprise when the partnership collapsed after the death of Obukhov and Kudriavtsev and its debt to the Naval Ministry had reached 1.3 million rubles.[84] In shipbuilding and the mechanical industry too the Naval Ministry's alliance with private entrepreneurs proved ambiguous. The high costs of the new technology, combined with grave doubts about the profitability of such ventures, made many Russian entrepreneurs shy away from maritime investments. Those who did invest risked dependence and possible bankruptcy. The only real enthusiast among St. Petersburg's industrialists for maritime projects was N. I. Putilov, who after his involvement in the Obukhov Works had gone on to organize his own works to produce rails for Russia's railway boom. Putilov kept his interest in maritime and naval affairs, and in the

1870s his fanatical devotion to the construction of a deepwater canal linking Kronstadt and St. Petersburg cost him his fortune.[85]

The same technological impulse that had prompted naval reformers to embrace private enterprise during the Crimean War and then to court it during the early 1860s now reinforced the trends towards economic dependence on state contracts by Russian private yards and works. In the two cases where the navy's experiment had enjoyed its clearest and most unambiguous success, the private yards and works had been mobilized for the construction of relatively numerous low-cost units, based upon technologies that did not demand immediate and large-scale investments of capital—the gunboat-corvette programs of the Crimean War and the monitors of 1863–64. In the first case unit costs for hull and machinery had not exceeded 40,000 rubles. In the second case these figures had increased by more than twelve-fold. And the trends toward larger seagoing ironclads of the 1864 program, the battleship *Petr Velikii* and later the oceanic cruisers, brought further increases in unit costs. The Naval Ministry spent over 5.5 million rubles for the *Petr Velikii*, Admiral A. A. Popov's answer to HMS *Devastation*.[86] Given the navy's meager resources and the chronic crisis of state finances, the later ironclads could only be produced in fewer numbers, insufficient to keep Russia's state and private dockyards at full employment. These few government contracts became matters of life and death for the private yards in St. Petersburg. And their situation deteriorated still further after 1870, when Russia again had an opportunity to rebuild its Black Sea Fleet, since after 1876 the Naval Ministry had devoted significant funds to the development of the state's admiralties in the south. The general economic depression of the 1870s only intensified their dependence.[87]

In spite of these problems, Russian naval reformers viewed the alliance between the state and private enterprise as a success. As General-Admiral Konstantin Nikolaevich stated in his report to Alexander II in 1880, the basic objectives had been achieved:

> Without a doubt, in this very difficult area [the policies] did not go forward without failures and major setbacks, but still they rendered a timely service not only to the Russian Navy but also to general mechanical affairs in Russia. The existence of those [plants] that survived this difficult period has now made us independent from foreign works not only in shipbuilding but also in other important areas of the iron and machine-building industry.[88]

Conclusion

The Naval Ministry's cooperation with St. Petersburg's private shipyards, machine-building works, and iron industry during the mid–nineteenth century represented the Russian response to the problem of economic backwardness and technological inferiority. The Naval Ministry's successes came most markedly in those areas when available alternative technologies could be easily produced and quickly adapted to Russia's maritime defense needs. The two most outstanding examples of these were the gunboat program during the Crimean War and the monitor program during the Polish crisis of 1863. Naval Ministry policy sought to find a happy medium between dependence on foreign technology, as had been the case prior to the Crimean War, and economic autarky, which would have flown in the face of their most basic assumptions about markets, innovation, and progress.

The particulars of the Russian shipbuilding industry during this period hardly resembled those then existing in England or the United States. Three basic features defined Russia in this case: it was at once economically backward, politically autocratic, and geostrategically a continental power.

Economic backwardness meant that the Russian state, acting through the Naval Ministry, sought to overcome a perceived technological inferiority in an area vital to the national defense through the importation of foreign technology and by harnessing private enterprise to the needs of the state. This policy created a kind of economic greenhouse for certain industries in St. Petersburg but isolated them from the rest of the national economy and thereby promoted an economic and political dependence upon the state: The more advanced the technology and the greater the costs of production, the more probable an immediate dependence upon state orders and subsidies. Both advanced maritime steam engines and heavy rifled, breech-loading steel artillery fit this category.

Gambling on the domestic production of very advanced weapons systems based upon untested foreign or domestic concepts proved particularly costly, as was the case with the *Minin,* built along the lines of Coles's HMS *Captain* and the *Popovka,* circular coastal-defense ironclads especially designed for use in the Black Sea. The best course proved to be the adaption of proven foreign and domestic designs to specific strategic needs and roles, i.e., gunboats and monitors to coastal defense or frigate-cruisers to *guerre de course.* The Naval Ministry was beginning to deal with the perpetual challenge of technological change and innovation in the wake of the industrial revolution.

Autocratic politics, especially Alexander II's habit of playing his ministers off against one another, meant that the Naval Ministry's policy, in spite of its long-term implications for Russia's defense and economy, remained uncoordinated with other ministries and unsupported over the long run. At the same time the long tenure of General-Admiral Konstantin Nikolaevich provided continuity of leadership; his close ties with his brother Alexander II enhanced the stature of the navy, certainly during the first decade of the reign, 1855–66.

Finally, although the very special circumstances of Russian naval affairs after the Crimean War led to a temporary concentration of engine, shipbuilding, and artillery facilities in St. Petersburg, it was the needs of the army, based upon Russia's geostrategic situation, which received the lion's share of the budget. The best the Naval Ministry might achieve was a temporary recognition of the wisdom of Peter I's injunction: "A potentate who has only an army has but one arm, but he who has an army and a navy has two."

The Naval Ministry's experiment does shed some light on the relationship between Tsarist economic policy in the era of the Great Reforms and what Alexander Gerschenkron described as Petrine mercantilism, that "specifically Russian pattern of economic development."[89] It is true that one critic of Konstantin Nikolaevich and his associates described them as men who had set out to be "the Peters the Great of the present century."[90] But the operative portion of that phrase here relates directly to their understanding of the demands of the nineteenth century, i.e., their efforts to import new techniques and radically different modes of organization from the West with the overt aim of liberating the productive capacity of Russia while mobilizing it for the purposes of the state. As agents of the autocratic state, these naval reformers sought to maintain governmental initiative even as they heralded private enterprise, hired labor, and the factory system. Such preponderant influence by the state, so in keeping with Russia's past and so different from conditions in the industrial West of the mid–nineteenth century, is the paradox of Russia's naval-industrial complex. This problem, in turn, raises serious questions about the political economy of reform.

NOTES

1. C. I. Hamilton, "The Royal Navy, Seapower, and the Screw Ship of the Line, 1845–1860" (Ph.D. diss., University of London, 1974).

2. M. Kh. Reitern, "Opyt kratkago sravnitel'nago izsledovaniia morskikh budzhetov angliiskago i frantsuzskago," *Morskoi sbornik,* January 1854, uchen-lit., 1-36. On the relationship between industrialization and naval modernization, see Wilhelm Treue, *Der Krimkrieg und seine Bedeutung fuer die Entstehung der modernen Flotten,* 2d ed. (Herford, 1980).

3. Paul M. Kennedy, *The Rise and Fall of British Naval Mastery* (Malabar, Fla., 1982), 149ff.

4. Jacob W. Kipp, "Consequences of Defeat: Modernizing the Russian Navy, 1856–1863," *Jahrbücher für Geschichte Osteuropas,* June 1972, 210ff.

5. National Archives of the United States, Record Group 59, Department of State, Dispatches from U.S. Ministers to Russia (hereafter cited as RG 59), vol. 18, no. 11, September 1858 (n.s.).

6. GPB, f. 208 (A.V. Golovnin), d. 10/266, "E'trats du Memoire du Conseiller Prive Actuel Tengoborskii," and d. 67/1–12, "Dokladnaia zapiska v. kn. Konstantinu Nikolaevichu o finansovom polozhenii Rossii," Paris, November 8/20, 1857.

7. N. P. Pavlov-Sil'vanskii, "Velikii kniaz' Konstantin Nikolaevich," *Sochineniia* (St. Petersburg, 1910), vol. 2, 330–31.

8. Alfred J. Rieber, *The Politics of Autocracy: Letters of Alexander II to Prince A. I. Bariatinskii, 1857–1864* (Paris/The Hague, 1966), 15ff., and Daniel Field, *The End of Serfdom: Nobility and Bureaucracy in Russia, 1855–1861* (Cambridge, Mass., 1976), 51ff.

9. P. A. Zaionchkovskii, *Voennye reformy 1860–1870 godov v Rossii* (Moscow, 1952); Forrestt A. Miller, *Dmitrii Miliutin and the Reform Era in Russia* (Nashville, Tenn., 1968); and L. G. Beskrovnyi, *Russkaia armiia i flot v XIX veke* (Moscow, 1973).

10. Zaionchkovskii, *Voennye reformy*, 138–48. On the War Ministry's approach to the modernization of its arsenals, see Joseph Bradley, *Guns for the Tsar: Technology Transfer and the Small Arms Industry in Nineteenth-Century Russia* (DeKalb, Ill., 1990).

11. Constanin de Grunwald, *Tsar Nicholas I.*, trans. Brigit Patmore (London, 1954), 255.

12. L. G. Beskrovnyi, *Russkaia armiia i flot v XVIII veke* (Moscow, 1958), 74–96, 344–64, 635–37.

13. Ibid., 277–93, 330–43.

14. L. G. Beskrovnyi, *Russkoe voennoe iskusstvo XIX v.* (Moscow, 1974), 224ff.; John Sheldon Curtiss, *Russia's Crimean War* (Durham, N.C., 1979), 299–341, 425–71.

15. "Neskol'ko zamechanii po povodu stati: 'Vzgliad na sostoiane ruskkikh voisk v minuvshchuiu voinu,' pomeshennuiu v 1-m No. *Voennago sbornika*," *Voennyi sbornik*, 1858, no. 6, otdel II, 271–88.

16. G. I. Butakov, *Novye osnovaniia parokhodnoi taktiki* (St. Petersburg, 1862), 1-3. On the battle between *Vladimir* and *Pervaz-Bakhri*, see N. V. Novikov and P. G. Sofinov, eds., *Vitse-Admiral Kornilov* (Moscow, 1947), 210–12.

17. B. P. Mansurov, *Okhtenskiia admiralteiskiia seleniia: Istoricheskoe opisanie* (St. Petersburg, 1856), pt. 3, 115ff. Mansurov, in this study of the Okhta admiralty artisans, concluded that emancipation was in the best interests of the Naval Ministry, the artisans, and the government. In more general terms Mansurov concluded that hired labor would be more productive in the shipbuilding industry. In general terms, the Konstantinovtsy supported the broadest possible expansion of free enterprise in the national economy. For the most complete statement of their general position, see M. Kh. Reitern, "Vliianie ekonomicheskago kharaktera naroda na obrazovanie kapitalov," *Morskoi sbornik*, 1860, no. 5, neof., 64ff.

18. GPB, f. 208 (A.V. Golovnin), d. 2/149, and ORGBL, f. 169 (D.A. Miliutin), d. 42, papka 15/7–8.

19. Jacob W. Kipp, "M. Kh. Reutern on the Russian State and Economy: A Liberal Bureaucrat during the Crimean Era, 1854–60," *Journal of Modern History*, September 1975, 438–59.

20. Russia, Morskoe Ministerstvo, *Otchet po morskomu vedomstvu za 1859 g.* (St. Petersburg, 1860). On the impact of inflation on labor and shipbuilding materials, see GPB, f. 208 (A. V. Golovnin) d. 23/7–9.

21. Russia, Morskoe Ministerstvo, *Kratkii Otchet po morskomu vedomstvu za 1856, 1857, i 1858 gg.* (St. Petersburg, 1860), 22ff.

22. GPB, f. 413 (M. P. Lazarev), d. 5/1–180.

23. Russia, Morskoe Ministerstvo, *Obzor deiatel'nosti morskago upravleniia v Rossii v pervoe dvadtsatipiatiletie tsarstvovaniia G. Imp. Aleksandra Nikolaevicha* (hereafter cited as *Obzor*) (St. Petersburg, 1880), vol. 1, 414–22.

24. A. S. Menshikov, "Obzor minuvshago dvadtsatipiatiletiia v otnoshenii k ustroistvu morskikh sil Rossiiskoi Imperii," *SbIRIO* 98 (1896): 454ff and "Deiatel'nost admiralteistv v tsarstvovanie Imperatora Nikolaia I," *Morskoi sbornik*, 1859, no. 11 of., 1–28.

25. GPB, f. 413 (M. P. Lazarev) d. 5/32–42 (letters of Captain Istomin to Admiral Lazarev, London, 2/14 February 1842).

26. Russia, Morskoe Ministerstvo, *Kratkii otchet po morskomu vedomstvu za 1853–1854 gg.* (St. Petersburg, 1860) 8–9.

27. N. Mordovin, "Russkoe voennoe sudostroenie v techenii poslednykh 25 let," *Morskoi sbornik*, 1880, no. 8, 111–20, and Russia, Morskoe Ministerstvo, *Kratkii otchet po morskomu vedomstvu za 1853–1854 gg.* (St. Petersburg, 1860), 6–7.

28. "Deiatel'nost' admiralteistv v tsarstvovanie Imperatora Nikolaia I-go," *Morskoi sbornik*, 1859, no. 11, of., 1 – 28.

29. *Kratkii otchet po morskomu vedomstvu za 1853–1854 gg.*, 198–202.

30. A. V. Voevodskii, "Otchet direktora korablestroitel'nago departamenta za 1859 god,"*Morskoi sbornik,* 1860, no. 5, of., 70–81, and *Kratkii otchet po morskomu vedomstvu za 1856, 1857 i 1858 gg.,* 107–8.

31. *Kratkii otchet po morskomu vedomstvu za 1853–1854 gg.,* 205.

32. A. V. Voevodskii, "Otchet direktora korablestroitel'nago departamenta za 1859 god," *Morskoi sbornik,* 1860, no. 8, of., 111–20, and *Kratkii otchet po morskomu vedomstvu za 1856, 1857, i 1858 gg.,* 107–8.

33. *Kratkii otchet po morskomu vedomstvu za 1855 god,* 54–55.

34. *Sbornik izvestii, otnosiashchikhsia do nastoiashchei voiny, izdavaemyi s Vysochaishago soizvoleniia N. Putilovym* (St. Petersburg, 1854), vol. I, Iff.

35. GPB, f. 208 (A.V. Golovnin), d. 2/149.

36. *Kratkii otchet po morskomu vedomstvu za 1855 god,* 55.

37. Ibid., 58–59.

38. Ibid., 56–57.

39. *Obzor,* vol. 2, 200–207.

40. Voevodskii, "Otchet direktora korablestroitel'nago departamenta za 1859 god," *Morskoi sbornik,* 1860, no. 5, of., 60–78, and *Kratkii otchet po morskomu vedomstvu za 1856, 1857, i 1858 gg.,* 29–34.

41. Russia, Morskoe Ministerstvo, *Obshchee obrazovanie upravleniia morskim vedomstvom* (St. Petersburg, 1959), 28ff.

42. GPB, f. 208 (A.V. Golovnin), d. 52/1–4 (17/29 July 1856).

43. *Kratkii otchet po morskomu vedomstvu za 1856, 1857, i 1858 gg.,* 105, and GPB, f. 208 (A.V. Golovnin), d. 23/96–97.

44. "Otchet direktora korablestroitel'nago departamenta za 1859 god," *Morskoi sbornik,* 1860, no. 5, of., 64–65.

45. Voevodskii, *Otchet o deistviiakh korablestroitel'nago departamenta morskago ministerstva za 1860 god* (St. Petersburg, 1861), 110–11.

46. "Otchet direktora korablestroitel'nago departamenta za 1859 god," *Morskoi sbornik,* 1860, no. 5 of., 60–78. In 1859 the navy had the following steamships under construction: one ship-of-the-line, seven frigates, two clippers, one paddle-wheel steamer. Of these ships, the ship-of-the-line, four frigates, and a corvette were being built in the St. Petersburg area—most at government admiralties by private contractors. Three ships—a corvette and two clippers—were being built at Archangel but later had their machinery installed in St. Petersburg. In addition to the frigates *Svetlana* and *General-Admiral,* which were built in France and the United States, the Naval Ministry had another foreign contract for two iron-hulled schooners with the Thames Iron Works of London. Most of the engines for the Russian-built ships came from the St. Petersburg works of Baird and Carr & MacPherson and the state works at Izhora.

47. Russia, Morskoe Ministerstvo, *Otchet o merakh priniatykh k ulusheniiu byta russkikh pravoslavnykh poklonnikov v Palestine* (St. Petersburg, 1860), Iff, and GPB, f. 208 (A.V. Golovnin), d. 10/192. See also W. E. Mosse, "Russia and the Levant, 1852–1862: Grand Duke Constantine Nicolaevich and the Russian Steam Navigation Company," *Journal of Modern History* 26 (1954): 39–48.

48. Kh. Vol'demar, "Russkii torgovyi flot, v osobennosti baltiiskii, ego sostoianie, razvitie i budushchnost'" *Morskoi sbornik,* 1860, no. 4, neof., 109–32; V. Mel'nitskii, "Russkii kommercheskii flot po 1–3 ianvaria 1858 goda," *Morskoi sbornik,* 1859, no. 3. neof., 213–47, no. 4, 487–500, no. 5, 171–88, and no. 6, neof., 349–54. See also N. Barbatev, *K istorii morekhodnogo obrazovaniia v Rossii* (Moscow, 1959), 161ff.

49. K. Skal'kovskii, *Russkii torgovyi flot i srochnoe parakhodstvo na chernom i azovskom moriakh* (St. Petersburg, 1887), 508–54.

50. Stanley Sandler, *The Emergence of the Modern Capital Ship* (Newark, Del. 1979), 15ff. While the Anglo-French had employed ironclad "floating batteries" against the Russian fortress at Kinburn during the Crimean War, the real ironclad

revolution began with these seagoing screw-propelled ironclads. On the economics of the ironclad revolution, see Philip G. Pugh, *The Cost of Sea Power: The Influence of Money on Naval Affairs from 1815 to the Present Day* (London, 1986).

51. R. Musselius, "O bronenosnykh sudakh," *Morskoi sbornik*, 1859, no. 11, 349–61.

52. *Kratkii otchet po morskomu vedomstvu za 1859 g.*, 48.

53. GPB, f. 208 (A.V. Golovnin), d. 23/5–6.

54. Ibid., d. 22/9–11 and d. 23/7–20.

55. Russia, Morskoe Ministerstvo, *Otchet po morskomu vedomstvu za 1860 god* (St. Petersburg, 1862), 18–21.

56. Russia, Morskoe Ministerstvo, *Otchet po morskomu vedomstvu za 1861 god* (St. Petersburg, 1862), 18–21.

57. Ibid., 86–90.

58. S. V. Cherniavskii, "Otchet o deistviiakh korablestroitel'nago teknicheskago komiteta v 1862 godu," *Morskoi sbornik*, 1863, no. 8, of., 166–73, and "Otchet o deistviiakh korablestroitel'nago tekhnicheskago komiteta v 1863 godu," *Morskoi sbornik*, 1864, no. 8, of., 58–61.

59. Ibid., 166–73.

60. "Otchet o deistviiakh korablestroitel'nago tekhnicheskago komiteta v 1863 godu," *Morskoi sbornik*, 1864, no. 8, of., 61–65.

61. *Otchet korablestroitel'nago departamenta za 1862 god*, 5.

62. George S. Emmerson, *John Scott Russell: A Great Victorian Engineer and Naval Architect* (London, 1977), 291.

63. Reitern, "Vliianie ekonomicheskago kharaktera naroda na obrazovanie kapitalov," *Morskoi sbornik*, 1860, no. 5, neof., 65.

64. "Perekhod iz Anglii v Kronshtadt bronenosnoi batarei *Pervenets*," *Morskoi sbornik*, 1863, no. 9, of., 1–9.

65. "Otchet o deistviiakh korablestroitel'nago teknicheskago komiteta v 1863 godu," *Morskoi sbornik*, 1864, no. 8, of., 65–67.

66. Ibid., 67–68. See also S. S. Lesovskii, "Zamechaniia kon. adm. Lesovskago na stat'iu United Service Gazette o resultatakh ispytaniia bronenostev," *Morskoi sbornik*, 1863, no. 8, neof., 445–51.

67. Mordovin, "Russkoe voennoe sudostroenie v techenii poslednikh 25 let." *Morskoi sbornik*, 1881, no. 10., neof., 67–68.

68. Ibid.

69. Ibid., 73.

70. RG 59 Consular Despatches: St. Petersburg, vol 11, July 20, 1863 (N.S.).

71. V. Goncharov, "Amerikanskaia ekspeditsiia russkago flota v 1863–1864 gg.," *Morskoi sbornik*, 1913, no. 8, neof., 25–58; A. Belomor and A. G. Konkevich, "Vtoraia Tikhookeanskaia eskadra," *Morskoi sbornik*, 1914, no. 10, neof., 509–17; and "Perekhod iz Anglii v Kronshtadt bronenosnoi batarei *Pervenets*," *Morskoi sbornik*, 1863, no. 9, of., 1–9.

72. "Otchet o deistviiakh korablestroitel'nago departamenta v 1863 godu," *Morskoi sbornik*, 1864, no. 8, of., 61–81; and *Obzor*, vol. 1, 509–17.

73. R. Musselius, "O staleliteinon proizvodstve," *Morskoi sbornik*, 1862, no. 9, neof., 210–11.

74. "Metallicheskie zavody, fabriki i remeslennye zavedeniia v S. Peterburge i ego okrestnostiakh v 1863 g.," *Morskoi sbornik*, 1864, no. 10, neof., 187–208; and "Admiralteistva i zavody baltiiskago flota," *Morskoi sbornik*, 1864, no. 11, neof., 55–79.

75. Russia, Morskoe Ministerstvo, *Otchet po morskomu vedomstvu za 1864* (St. Petersburg, 1865), 28–36.

76. Voevodskii, "Izvlechenie . . . 1865 god," *Morskoi sbornik*, 1866, no. 8, of., 7;

Otchet korablestroitel'nago departamenta za 1866 god, 8–10; and *Otchet po morskomu vedomstvu za 1870–1873 gg.,* 51–53.

77. Russia, Morskoe Ministerstvo, Otchet po morskomu vedomstvu za *1864* (St. Petersburg, 1865), 28–36.

78. S. O. Ogorodnikov, *Istoricheskii obzor razvitiia i deiatel'nosti Morskogo Ministerstva za sto let ego sushchestvovaniia* (St. Petersburg, 1902), 215.

79. Voevodskii, "Izvlechenie . . . 1865 god," *Morskoi sbornik,* 1866, no. 8, of., 10, and *Otchet korablestroitel'nago departamenta za 1866 god,* 8–10. On the *Minin's* metamorphosis, see *Otchet po morskomu vedomstvu za 1868 god,* 21; *Otchet po morskomu vedomstvu za 1870–1873 gg.,* 59–63; and *Otchet po morskomu vedomstvu za 1874–1878 gg.,* 32–33.

80. *Zapiski russkago tekhnicheskago obshchestva,* vol. 10, 1876, "Prilozheniia," 233–34.

81. "Nasha zheleznodorozhnaia politika po dokumentam arkhiva Komiteta ministrov," *Istoricheskii ocherk,* vol. 4, 1902, 235, as cited in I. Gindin, *Gosudarstvennyi bank i ekonomicheskaia politika tsarskogo pravitel'stva* (Moscow, 1960), 35.

82. *Otchet po morskomu vedomstvu za 1874–1878 gg.,* 33–34.

83. Brokgauz-Efron, *Entsiklopedicheskii slovar'* (St. Petersburg, 1901), vol. 32, 603–4, and *Lloyd's Calendar* (London, 1899), 123.

84. *Obzor,* vol. 2, 84–85.

85. M. Mitel'man, B. Slebov, and A. Ul'ianskii, *Istoriia putilovskogo zavoda* (Moscow, 1961), 18–27.

86. Russia, Morskoe Ministerstvo, *Vedomost' o sravnenii kreditov, otkrytykh po smetam Morskago Ministerstva na 1862–1884* (St. Petersburg, 1885).

87. On naval policy during this period and the connection between naval strategy, force structure, and warship procurement, see Jacob W. Kipp, "Tsarist Politics and the Naval Ministry, 1876–1881: Balanced Fleet or Cruiser Navy?" *Canadian-American Slavic Studies,* Summer 1983, 151–79.

88. *Obzor,* vol. 2, 111–12.

89. Alexander Gerschenkron, *Europe in the Russian Mirror: Four Lectures in Economic History* (Cambridge, England, 1970), 94ff.

90. P. V. Dolgorukov, *Peterburgskie ocherki: Pamflety emigranta, 1860–1867 gg.* (Moscow, 1927), 114–22.

VIII

MILIUTIN AND THE BALKAN WAR
MILITARY REFORM VS. MILITARY
PERFORMANCE

John S. Bushnell

In the predawn darkness of June 15, 1877 (O.S.), Russian troops crossed the middle course of the Danube into Bulgaria.[1] The first party took the small Turkish force at Sistovo by surprise; the next wave crossed successfully under fire, and the Russians secured a beachhead. Within a few days they had constructed a pontoon bridge; by early July they had 120,000 men south of the river. The crossing, an unqualified success, had been well and carefully prepared. The Turks guessed the general area of the attempt, but the Russian high command decided on the precise point of crossing late, and kept it secret even from the troops involved until the last minute. More important, the Russians overcame the complete control that the Turks exercised over the Danube at the outset of the campaign. With no naval forces in the Black Sea to speak of since the Crimean War, the Russians could not confront the Turks' river fleet with main force. Instead, they systematically employed mines, nighttime torpedo attacks by small cutters, and shore fire from mortars to drive the Turkish ships under the shelter of fortress guns, segment the river, and win secure passage.

The entire crossing operation, carried out almost exactly as scheduled, was the culmination of a highly successful Russian mobilization. The Russian army did have considerable time to prepare. The Turks' brutal suppression of rebellions in Bosnia-Herzegovina in 1875 and Bulgaria in 1876 and their crushing defeat of Serbia in 1876 gradually brought Russia and Turkey to the brink of war. On November 1, 1876, Alexander II ordered the mobilization of one-third of the army; 225,000 men were called up from the reserves, and 33,000 cossacks were recalled from their villages. Making use of the newly built railways, all four corps designated for the Balkan theater had taken up their stations along the Pruth River by January 7, only six days behind schedule. When Russia declared war on Turkey on April 12, other partial mobilizations—three more corps for the Balkan theater—had

put half of the Russian army on a war footing. Russia's new machinery for calling up and equipping reserves and for moving troops toward the theater by rail worked well. Inadequate railways and heavy spring rains that turned roads to mud hampered movement across Romania, but even that had been anticipated. By the end of May, on schedule, all seven corps were encamped north of the Danube, where the river bulges south closest to the Balkans. By then, the Turks' river flotilla had been neutralized.

The Russians' plans went awry as soon as they crossed the Danube and engaged the Turks in the field. The problems began at the very top, with ineffectual leadership by the commander in chief, the Grand Duke Nikolai Nikolaevich, younger brother of Alexander II, and his chief of staff, General Nepokoichitskii. The plan of campaign drawn up by General Nikolai Obruchev called for Russian forces to bypass the quadrangle of Turkish fortresses in eastern Bulgaria, at Silistria, Varna, Rushchuk, and Shumla. Those fortresses, which lay athwart the direct route to Constantinople, had entangled every prior Russian invading force in sieges and frontal assaults. To avoid prolonged fortress warfare and achieve a decisive victory before the European powers could intervene, Obruchev called for invasion through the center of Bulgaria. Russian forces would be divided into two armies. One would plunge immediately over the Balkan range through the Shipka pass and push as quickly as possible toward Constantinople, the strategic objective of the war. The second would protect the flanks of the first by blocking troops coming from Vidin and taking the weakest fortress, at Rushchuk.[2] Speed of movement was at a premium, and siege warfare was to be avoided at all costs. But costly assaults and prolonged sieges were precisely what the Russian high command's inept and dilatory dispositions imposed on the Russian army.

Rather than pushing half of his army rapidly across the Balkans, Nikolai Nikolaevich divided his forces into three contingents, no one of which was adequate to achieve its objective. Half his force he used to invest Rushchuk, more or less as planned, but this detachment was larger than needed for the entirely passive blocking operation that it at first undertook. Nikolai sent IX Corps and then miscellaneous other units to take the small Turkish fortress at Nikopol and secure the Russians' western flank. And he gave General Gurko 12,000 men to cross the Balkans. Since they were too few to press on toward Constantinople, Gurko's forces were merely to seize the passes, then act as circumstances warranted. The Russians further weakened their ability to strike by leaving units north of the Danube opposite Rushchuk, guarding against the nonexistent threat of a Turkish breakthrough there, and by placing an entire corps into the Dobrudja, where it sat inactive for the duration of the war.

The grand duke thus reduced the strategic objective of the war, the thrust on Constantinople, to a secondary or even tertiary goal in a diffuse plan of campaign. Rather than bypassing the Turkish army, which was tied to its own fortresses, the Russians let Turkish dispositions dictate their own operational plans. And rather than concentrating every unit possible to break through the Balkans and carry the war to Constantinople, they sent inadequate detachments in several directions. This was precisely the kind of campaign that Obruchev had sought to avoid.

The slow deliberation with which the grand duke directed the campaign found its match in the operations conducted at lower command levels. On July 3 the western detachment, IX Corps under General Kridener, took Nikopol against little resistance, then did nothing for three days. On July 7

Kridener sent General Shilder-Shuldner with roughly a division (9,000 men) to take Plevna, garrisoned by 3,000 Turks, forty kilometers to the south. But on July 1, Osman Pasha had left the Turkish fortress at Vidin two hundred kilometers to the west and arrived at Plevna with 20,000 men on the 7th. After a preliminary exchange of fire on July 7, the Russians on the 8th attacked Plevna, virtually without reconnaissance and without employing their rifles, in the dense columns that had been disastrously outmoded at the time of the Crimean War. Russian regiments actually penetrated the city but had to fall back because of heavy losses, 2,400 men in all.

Dilatoriness contributed to the defeat of the second assault on Plevna as well. By the time the Russians attacked again on July 18, the Turks had dug in and erected a system of immense earthworks. Kridener had 26,000 men at his disposal, a slight numerical advantage, but he attacked the Turkish positions where they were strongest; thinking he was outnumbered two to one, he chose to attack at the point from which retreat would be most convenient. Once again the Russian regiments marched into Turkish fire in company columns; some still marched without returning fire. Seven thousand Russians were killed or wounded, their units shattered and scrambled, and the entire western operational detachment teetered on the edge of a disorderly rout even though the Turks never left their redoubts. The Russians thereupon ordered two and a half divisions already mobilized but still in Russia to proceed to the theater of operations, and in addition ordered the mobilization of the Guards and Grenadier corps and three other divisions, 110,000 more men in all. But those reinforcements could not arrive until fall.

At that point, the Russian army had managed to trap itself within a semicircular pocket, with the quadrangle on the east, Plevna on the west, and the Balkans in the south. The Russian perimeter was three hundred kilometers long; there were considerable gaps through which the Turks could penetrate and no strong points east or west onto which Russian units could fall back in the event of a Turkish attack. They had turned what ought to have been, even in this campaign gone awry, the advantageous interior position into the peril of double encirclement.[3] It was only because of genuinely heroic fighting by the small Russian force at the Shipka pass in August and the gross incompetence of Turkish commanders in the quadrangle that the Turks did not push the Russians north from the Balkan range and threaten their entire position in Bulgaria. When a third, incompetently conducted assault on Plevna failed with the loss of 16,000 men at the end of August, the grand duke and his chief of staff urged withdrawal back across the Danube and suspension of the campaign until spring. Only because of the insistence of Minister of War Miliutin, traveling with Alexander just behind the front, was it decided instead to invest and starve Plevna into submission.

On November 27 Osman tried but failed to break out of Plevna, then surrendered, and that unblocked the Russian forces that now—with the arrival of the Guards and Grenadier corps—enjoyed overwhelming numerical superiority. Suffering far more from the weather than Turkish resistance, Russian units forced the icy Balkan passes in late December; Turkish units south of the Balkans fled in panic, and the Russians marched rapidly toward Constantinople. They were halted outside the city only by an armistice on January 19. Turkish troops in the quadrangle had been unable to protect their capital against the Russians who had cut around behind them. That was how Obruchev had envisioned the campaign in the first place.

Failures in the overall strategic direction might be charged to a handful of individuals with the Grand Duke Nikolai Nikolaevich at their head, but command failed at lower levels as well. Time after time—not just at Plevna—Russian troops attacked in dense company columns, did not bother to fire on the enemy until they had closed to within a few hundred paces if they fired at all (while the Turks blazed away at two thousand or even three thousand paces), and failed to entrench themselves. In one battle, a Russian regiment did not use rifles even in defense, instead repeatedly charging the advancing Turks with bayonets.

Russian officers and soldiers did learn the value of dispersal and cover. By the middle of the war many Russian units were attacking in skirmish lines; by the end they were quite as skilled at entrenching themselves as the Turks. What was remarkable was that every unit newly arrived at the front had to learn those lessons for itself: divisions brought from Russia when the war was already well under way entered combat in company columns. Indeed, the charismatic Skobelev, popularly lauded as Russia's best battlefield general, continued throughout the campaign to value the moral effect of units marching into battle with banners waving and bands playing. Skobelev's white horse epitomized the romantic and heroic view of combat that he and lesser commanders brought to the war. The inevitable result was that the Russians sustained very heavy losses attacking even small Turkish redoubts, and no Russian victory was considered worthy unless the cost in blood was high. All observers praised the determination and bravery of Russian soldiers and officers just as they had since the eighteenth century, but those qualities were ill employed by Russian commanders.

Between strategic dispositions and battlefield tactics lay operational command of various kinds, and the Russian Army showed itself woefully deficient in this area, too. Most Russian generals—like Kridener and Shilder-Shuldner—were slow to move against objectives, incapable of formulating precise plans and issuing clear directives, slow to press an advantage, and quick to panic and retreat. The cavalry showed itself poorly, time after time failing to act when action was called for. Large cavalry formations outside Plevna failed twice to obstruct supply convoys that could easily have been blocked, and for an entire month a road on the Rushchuk front vital to Turkish movements and completely vulnerable to Russian cavalry interdiction was not disturbed. Time and again Russians attacked fortified positions, as at Plevna, where they were strongest rather than where they were most vulnerable. Time and again the Russians escaped payment for their operational errors only because Turkish generalship was even worse.

Compared to these failures in Russian command, all other problems were irrelevant, or at least not unusual in the confusion of war. Some Turkish artillery was superior to Russian artillery, and Russian shells were quite ineffective against the earthworks the Turks were so skilled at erecting. Some Russian units were armed with rifles that were inferior to the rifles used by some Turkish units, while the Russians' use of two different models of rifle complicated cartridge supply. Staff work was so poorly organized that once the Russian Army began to move in December 1877, orders arrived days after they were to take effect. The commissariat and its notorious supplier, Gregor, Kogan, and Gorvits, were grossly incompetent and corrupt. Every one of these factors did handicap Russian operations, but only marginally. The weight of numbers, guns, unity of command, and clear strategic objective ought to have given the army the kind of decisive superiority around which Obruchev had built his war plan. The campaign went badly because command was incompetent.

Even the great accomplishment of the winter crossing of the Balkans and swift push to Constantinople could not cover the Russians' embarrassment. The Grand Duke Nikolai Nikolaevich as commander in chief received the brunt of criticism, but he was only one of the twelve grand dukes who fought in what by the late summer of 1877 was already being called caustically "the Grand Dukes' War." The grand dukes did not make good commanders. But their nonimperial chiefs of staff, from Nepokoichitskii on down, performed just as poorly. A few generals—Gurko, Radetsky, Skobelev—passed for competent commanders, but they often committed costly blunders. The utterly hapless performance of a much longer list of generals created a desperate need to find luster somewhere.

The difficulty of putting a good face on the campaign resulted in a very long delay in the publication of an official account of the war. A commission charged with writing the history of the war was in place as early as 1879, but it did not publish anything until 1898. It demonstrated a preference for documentary compilations, publishing ninety-seven volumes of documents relating to the war by 1912. What most of the unit records and after-action reports revealed was Russian commanders' obsession with self-justification. When the first historical volumes were ready to go to press in 1897, Minister of War Kuropatkin (who had served on Skobelev's staff) intervened and commanded that criticism of individuals be omitted, heroic actions stressed. The head of the commission resigned, and the official history was further delayed.[4]

The Russo-Turkish War provided a test and exposed the limits of the military reforms that had been enacted after the Crimean War debacle. Dmitrii Miliutin, minister of war since 1861, believed that the war fully vindicated the reform program he had carried out. During the mobilization of late 1876 and early 1877, he remarked repeatedly in his diary that the reforms had proved their worth, that the many voices that had accused him of destroying the army had been stilled, and that the emperor Alexander had congratulated him. In a more cautious moment Miliutin observed that while the army was in good shape, that alone did not ensure success; much would depend on the diplomatic situation and the quality of command. Miliutin professed to see among Russia's generals "not a single individual who can inspire confidence in his strategic or tactical capabilities. Our troops and materiel are prepared, but we have neither commanders in chief nor corps commanders ready."[5] The ministry had indeed modest leverage over international politics, but Miliutin's plea of helplessness as to quality of command ought to have been a confession of failure. He did not mean it that way.

Appointment to command remained the personal prerogative of the tsar, and he exercised it. Miliutin could not or would not blame him for appointing one brother to command the army in the Balkans, another brother to command the Russian forces in the Caucasus, his oldest son to command the force blocking Rushchuk, and a younger son to command a Guards infantry division. Nor did he criticize the tsar for appointing nonimperial incompetents to high command. Only occasionally did the tsar seek Miliutin's advice when filling command positions. Before the war began, he noted that he had no idea whether or not the tsar had already compiled the list of generals to whom he would entrust the army.[6]

The unfortunate consequences of the tsar's deep involvement in military affairs were evident even in the preparation for the successful restructuring of the army. The Crimean War left no doubt in anyone's mind that the army needed to be rebuilt. Generals submitted memoranda and the tsar named a committee to make recommendations. But he also appointed General N. O. Sukhozanet, widely viewed as an ignoramus, as minister of war. The tsar commanded Sukhozanet to carry out reforms, but although obedience was the virtue that had won Sukhozanet his appointment, he had no idea what to do. Alexander provided his own ideas, but many of them involved redesign of uniforms. Sukhozanet did strip away some of the most useless appendages from the old army, more for economy's sake than to increase military efficiency. But except for the removal of a certain amount of debris, there were no serious steps toward military reform until Dmitrii Miliutin was appointed minister of war in November 1861, more than five years after the conclusion of the war.[7]

Miliutin submitted a comprehensive plan of reform to the tsar on January 15, 1862, only two months after his appointment. He had been thinking about how to overhaul the army for some time.[8] He had sat on the committee the tsar set up to recommend military reforms and had tried out new principles of military administration when he served as chief of staff under Prince Bariatinksii in the Caucasus in 1856–59, and the tsar (at Bariatinskii's urging) had appointed him assistant minister of war under Sukhozanet in 1860. Miliutin had two overriding goals: to cut costs and at the same time increase the army's wartime strength. He believed he could achieve both objectives by restructuring military administration and reducing the term of service. Maladministration cost money and undermined effectiveness. Excessive length of service—fifteen years prior to the Crimean War (twenty-five years in principle, but in practice ten years were forgiven for good behavior)—meant the army had few reserves and required a correspondingly large and expensive permanent establishment. The shorter the term and the more quickly trained manpower could be discharged into the reserves, the larger the reserve available for war and the smaller the peacetime army need be. Miliutin suggested in his 1862 report that the term of service might be reduced to eight years. He wanted to, but dared not, recommend that service be shorter than that.

Miliutin also proposed a host of subsidiary reforms, the need for which was in almost every case pressing and had been demonstrated by the recent unhappy experience of the Crimean War. The Russian army needed to improve officer training (at the time, only about one quarter of the officer corps had formal military instruction) and the procedures for selection to command. Soldiers needed training in adapting to terrain rather than parading on level fields. They needed to be made literate so that they could serve more intelligently. Infantry and artillery needed rifled weapons. The supply system needed change from the commissariat at the top to the regiments at the bottom. And there was a pressing need for more barracks; just over one-fourth of the soldiers lived in barracks, while the rest were quartered on the population and assembled in their units only during the summer encampments.[9]

Alexander approved this ambitious agenda. It served as the blueprint for Miliutin's activity until his retirement in 1881, and he actually accomplished most of what he set out to do. Of course, there were constraints. Money was one, and Miliutin complained constantly about its absence and about Minister of Finances Reitern's indifference to military requirements. Yet for all the pleas of penury, the military budget grew steadily and in proportion to the growth of total government spending. The army claimed an average of 27 percent of the budget in the years 1858–62 and 29 percent from 1865 through 1875; during the years of the Polish and Balkan crises the army of course received considerably more than that. Excluding the government's railway program, which was not part of the regular budget, the army's share of government spending averaged 31 percent between 1865 and 1875.[10] After a false start or two, by the end of Miliutin's tenure Russian arms were roughly up to the European standard. By 1881 better than half of the army was in regular barracks, another quarter in converted civilian structures, and a corresponding proportion of regiments existed the year round.[11] With more money at its disposal the Ministry of War might have rearmed and constructed barracks more rapidly, but the military probably received about as much money as was feasible. National poverty did sap military efficiency, but given the realities of Russia's financial situation Miliutin had little cause for complaint about funding, and in fact probably complained no more than was the custom.

Demands on the army and resistance from traditionalists—Alexander included—delayed the achievement of Miliutin's principal objective, a small peacetime army that could expand rapidly by mobilizing trained reserves. The term of service had been officially reduced to fifteen years in 1856, which merely regularized longstanding practice, then to twelve years in 1859. With demobilization after the Crimean War, the reduced term of service, and suspension of the draft until 1863, army strength fell from a peak of 2,300,000 in 1856 to just over 800,000 by 1863. The reduction might have been more substantial if the army had not turned immediately after the war to the final conquest of the Caucasus (completed by 1864). Renewed conscription in January 1863 touched off full-scale rebellion in Poland, which led to the recall of soldiers from reserve. By 1864 the army again numbered over a million, with no reserve left. But by gradually reducing peacetime strength, shaving active service to ten years in 1868, and by annually drafting somewhat more men than needed and demobilizing a like number ahead of term, by 1870 the army had 700,000 men on active duty and 500,000 available to be called up.[12] Thus Miliutin in piecemeal fashion gradually built up a reserve. But Russia still lagged behind the major European powers in potential wartime strength. Miliutin wanted drastically shortened active service and a vastly expanded reserve so that Russia could put two million trained men in the field. Prior to the Franco-Prussian War, however, Alexander was unwilling to make a clean break with traditional conceptions of military service.

Miliutin effected a far more rapid and thoroughgoing reform of the military administration that he inherited. In the prereform army, units in the field were administered by order of battle: First Army headquarters in Warsaw exercised both command and supply functions for its subordinate units, and the various corps headquarters also had both command and administrative duties. In principle, army and corps were ready to march, ponderously, from peacetime bivouac to battle. In practice, the headquarters could not perform either command or administrative functions effectively, especially with the subordinate units scattered over several provinces. Miliutin proposed the establishment of a territorial, district system that would separate command from supply. The district staff would carry out supply and support functions, while operational command would be left to division commanders. In Forrestt Miller's felicitous figure, the districts would provide umbilical cords to which divisions could attach themselves wherever they happened to be stationed.[13]

There was at first no more than marginal opposition to the military district system, but only in part because the order of battle administration was thoroughly discredited and the new system admirably streamlined. Miliutin was able to test the system of territorial administration while he was chief of staff in the Caucasus, and it worked there. In 1862, in order to respond more effectively to the deteriorating situation in Poland, the First Army was replaced by the Warsaw, Kiev, and Vilna military districts. During the 1863 rebellion, the system of territorial commands (in this case, small districts within the Polish provinces) proved invaluable in coordinating operations against insurgents.[14] Or so Miliutin reported to Alexander, who thereupon enthusiastically endorsed complete conversion to the military district system.

But in addition to the opportunity to field test the district system, there was almost certainly another reason for the rapidity with which it gained assent: the new structure conformed to the wisdom of the day on proper administration. The commander of the military district had great responsibility and authority independent of the center, and he presided over a council consisting of representatives of the various support and supply services in his district. That corresponded perfectly to the civilian ideal of the powerful and independent governor commanding the civil administration of his province and assisted by a council coordinating the activities of the various civilian agencies. The ideal was more nearly implemented in the military sphere than in the civilian, no doubt because governors had to contend with agencies subordinate to a variety of ministries jealous of their own prerogatives, while all military agencies were subordinate to a single ministry.[15]

Meanwhile, the Ministry of War was itself reorganized, on the model of the military district. Prior to 1862, not only was the minister of war detached from the chain of command of the army in the field but many central military departments and agencies were also independent of the ministry. By the time reorganization was complete in 1869, the ministry had consolidated departments and gathered them all under the authority of the minister, who was assisted by a council. There were institutional links between the ministry and the districts, but the district commanders were appointed by the tsar. Giving the tsar the right to appoint military chieftains was the price Miliutin had to pay to get his administrative reforms through.

There was a consensus almost equally broad for fundamental changes in the system of officer training, although eventually Miliutin's educational reforms produced a backlash from military traditionalists and those who supported noble privileges (for the most part one and the same group). As of the 1850s, roughly one-fourth of the army's officers were educated for eight years at state expense in cadet corps; upon graduation almost all became officers in the socially exclusive Guards regiments. The rest, mostly from the lower reaches of the nobility, served a brief stint in the line as junkers, then became officers on the basis of an examination that tested their knowledge chiefly of military regulations. Their ignorance was much commented upon after the Crimean War.

Beginning in 1864 Miliutin, following the example of a few corps commanders who after Crimea set up schools for junkers at their headquarters, attached junker schools to the new military districts; they provided a basic two-year military education to volunteers serving in the ranks who had the requisite general education. A small number of military gymnasia, offering basically a civil education, were created for youngsters already in the system, but most of the cadet corps were abolished and replaced by new four-year military schools *(voennye uchilishcha)*, open to those sixteen years of age or older who had the equivalent of a gymnasium (college preparatory) education or better. The Russian Army still had a two-track educational system: children of the elite moved through the military schools into the Guards, the rest (at first still mostly from the noble estate) passed through junker schools into the regular army. But the overall level of officer education rose substantially.

Simultaneously with the reform of officer training, Miliutin oversaw reform of the system of military justice. This followed the civilian judicial reforms of 1864 very closely. Like prereform civilian justice, prereform military courts conducted trials entirely by written inquiries, with no provision for defense counsel. Commanders had the authority arbitrarily to raise or reduce sentences the court handed down. The reformed military justice system as codified in 1867 was founded on trial in open court, with oral argument and counsel for the defense. Regimental courts martial, appointed by the regimental commander, dealt with enlisted men, military courts attached to the military districts tried officers and some categories of offenses by soldiers, and a Military Supreme Court in St. Petersburg handled appeals and offered advice on proposed changes in punishments. Judges at the district and supreme court levels were appointed by the tsar, and were thus independent of command personnel. Also in 1867, Miliutin opened the Military Law Academy to provide trained personnel for the new legal system.

Early in his administration Miliutin also acted to make conditions for soldiers more humane. In 1863 a new statute on penalties for infractions of discipline abolished particularly cruel punishments such as the gauntlet and greatly reduced the severity and application of other corporal punishments. When in 1863 the army conducted its first draft since the Crimean War, conscripts were allowed to wear shifts while waiting for their medical examinations rather than standing naked for hours as had been practice before. When they marched off to join their units, they were not dressed in convicts' clothing; nor did they have the front of their scalps shaved—the old precaution against desertion that had marked the conscript as a social outcast.[16] And Miliutin pushed the literacy programs that had already begun in the aftermath of the Crimean War. He and others believed that literate soldiers would understand their duties better, serve more conscientiously, and commit fewer disciplinary infractions. Even though literacy instruction was made absolutely mandatory only in 1875 (and that requirement lasted only until 1880), the ministry's encouragement of schooling brought results. By the end of the 1860s, when only about 10 percent of conscripts could meet the army's minimal test for literacy, statistics the ministry collected indicated that 50 percent of enlisted personnel could read and 28 percent could write. Inspectors believed those reports were inflated by a third, but there is no question that a substantial proportion of soldiers became literate while in the army.[17]

In his first few years as minister, Miliutin laid the basis for the organization and administration of the Russian army down to 1917. The structure of the Ministry of War and the powers of the minister, the military districts, the junker and military schools, the system of military justice, and many other lesser reforms enacted in the 1860s endured long after Miliutin departed. Although he could not persuade the tsar to adopt the short-service army with substantial reserves that he wanted, he did nevertheless gradually reduce the length of service and build up reserves.

By the end of the decade, resistance to military reform was building, in part because of the antiliberal sentiment following the attempt to assassinate Alexander in 1866. Miliutin himself was suspected of harboring liberal thoughts, of being a red like his brother Nikolai, who had played so important a part in the emancipation of the serfs. Actually, Miliutin had urged a harshly anti-Polish policy; he oversaw the expansion of the Russian Empire into Central Asia and longed for revenge on the British, whom he considered chiefly responsible for thwarting Russia's national destiny. Furthermore, he subscribed to widely shared notions about Russian exceptionalism and believed that foreign institutions were inappropriate for Russia. On the other hand, Miliutin placed the interests of state and autocracy over the selfish interests of nobles: he opposed any institutions that gave nobles a corporate voice in policymaking and was willing to abridge privileges that the nobility had traditionally enjoyed but that obstructed national development and state power. He knew the reform of military education threatened time-honored educational prerogatives of the upper strata of the nobility and would make it somewhat easier for commoners to advance to high rank. He saw no reason to sacrifice military efficiency to privilege.[18] Thus Miliutin was a logical target for the ascendant party of Petr Shuvalov and the aristocrats after 1866, and he had constantly to fight off efforts to discredit him and his reforms in the eyes of the tsar.

Miliutin had opponents within the military, too. The many changes unsettled some generals, while the social implications of the reforms offended others. They may or may not have understood the virtues of military districts, but many generals saw no particular need to educate soldiers. Others believed that locking soldiers up for a few days for minor infractions rather than flogging them actually gave them an unjustified vacation. The same conservative generals also maintained that soldiers themselves preferred to be flogged. Traditionalists especially resented the closing of the cadet schools, which they had attended as boys and saw as the seedbed of a proper military spirit; they balked at the very sound of "military gymnasium." After Miliutin's resignation in 1881 the gymnasia were abruptly converted back to cadet corps, with something like their old-time drill and mock formations.[19]

The most ferocious attack on Miliutin and his reforms came from Prince Field Marshal Aleksandr Bariatinskii, his former patron. Bariatinskii had believed the Russian Army would be remodeled along Prussian lines, with Miliutin as minister overseeing administration and support services and himself as warlord in a new office of chief of staff. Expectations shattered and suffering from gout, he retired to his estate. In 1868 he launched a verbal assault on the military districts and on the new wartime field statute; both of these, he and his confederates charged, gave precedence to administration over command, while the field statute actually denigrated the tsar. Bariatinskii also cited excessive paperwork and corruption within the Ministry of War. Because he had been Alexander's childhood friend and longtime faithful servitor, Bariatinskii was sure of a hearing for his charges, and he harassed Miliutin into the early 1870s. Bariatinskii's campaign undergirded a widespread belief that Miliutin had indeed emphasized administration and book learning at the expense of martial spirit.[20] That was one reason why Miliutin repeatedly recorded in his diary the compliments he received during the army's successful mobilization in 1876–77.

Miliutin and his program survived the considerable assault because the state's interest in a strong army took precedence over every other consideration. The Franco-Prussian War of 1870 was a timely reminder of that point. Peter Valuev, former minister of interior and current member of the State Council, was in Germany when war broke out, witnessed the stunning success of the German mobilization and German arms, and returned to Russia a convert to Miliutin's vision of short-term service and large reserves. Moreover, he supported Miliutin's view that in order to expand the manpower resources at the army's disposal, everyone in society should be subject to military conscription—clergy excepted but nobility included. A true reserve system and universal liability to conscription were in fact separable issues. Under current law only about 20 percent of the population was exempt from the draft, and Miliutin could have achieved his strictly military objectives without abridging the nobility's prerogatives. But he saw no reason to respect noble privilege in this matter any more than in any others.

Somewhat surprisingly, at Miliutin's and Valuev's urging the tsar in November 1870 announced publicly that a new military statute embodying universal liability and a regular reserve system would be adopted. But it took more than three years of fierce debate, with Bariatinskii and Shuvalov still fighting Miliutin tooth and nail, before the details could be worked out. Bariatinskii made one last assault on the entire system of military reforms. Shuvalov directed the defense of the privileges of the nobility in a fight over educational deferments and the conditions under which volunteers with education could become officers. On January 1, 1874, Alexander finally enacted six-year service and nearly universal liability to conscription into law, thus completing Miliutin's basic reform program.[21] The interests of state had triumphed over privilege.

Miliutin thus managed to enact the principal reforms that he had outlined in the program he had submitted to the tsar in 1862. He himself wrote in 1874:

> The fundamental reforms in the structure of our forces begun in 1862 . . . have been systematically implemented over a number of years and have raised our army and our entire military system to a degree of strength and order that corresponds fully to the highest missions of state.[22]

But as the war of 1877–78 showed, the reforms did not justify that claim; they did not produce an effective military machine. The army was better adminstered and the fruits of able administration were plain to see during the mobilization of 1876–77. But good administration did not win battles. Neither did literate soldiers humanely treated, nor the officers (still junior) produced by the new junker and military schools. Miliutin's views on the treatment of soldiers and the proper education for officers were liberal, sensible, and commendable, but the reforms that made the army a better human institution had no visible military effect. The officers and men of the bad old prereform army had fought just as bravely. They had fought in almost the same manner, and that was the problem: Miliutin's reforms did not signally alter the way the Russian army fought.

Miliutin did bear part of the responsibility for that, because he approved regulations that gave training an unfortunate nationalist twist. The principal architect of Russian combat doctrine and of the new infantry regulations was Mikhail Dragomirov, who from 1860 taught tactics at the General Staff Academy and whom Miliutin in 1862 put on the committee that planned reforms in training and force structure.[23] Dragomirov sought to adjust Russian practices to changing conditions of war while reviving national military traditions that he traced back to the late eighteenth century and Suvorov. Miliutin himself helped foster the Suvorov cult: he had begun his academic career with a history of Suvorov's 1799 campaign, took Suvorov's military practices as the model for the modern Russian army, and appears never to have doubted Dragomirov's neo-Suvorovite doctrine.[24]

Some of the lessons that Dragomirov derived from Suvorov, such as that soldiers should be drilled only in skills they would apply on the battlefield, were apt. Dragomirov urged an end to the army's parade ground traditions and the adaptation of formations to terrain. And he believed in the importance of education and motivation as opposed to blind discipline. But Dragomirov also taught the decisive importance of will and inspiration, and in this his thinking scarcely differed from the sentimental nationalism of military conservatives who argued that martial spirit was the soul of Russia's military tradition and the only certain support for Russian arms. Dragomirov traced the Russian doctrine of willpower back to Suvorov, too. It had been Suvorov who devised the maxim that "the bullet is a fool, the bayonet a hero." Dragomirov insisted that the issue of battle would still be decided by the bayonet and that fire was at most preparatory and subordinate to the final clash of cold steel. He did recognize that rifle fire could inflict tremendous casualties on the attackers, that battalion formations now presented too large a target and thus the company must be the basic tactical unit, and that the skirmish line and dispersed formations were crucially important. But he insisted that the closed formation should remain the premier assault technique. Moreover, he insisted that soldiers should fire their rifles as little as possible—and invoked another Suvorov maxim, that soldiers should shoot "rarely but squarely" *(redko da metko)*—because aiming and firing slowed their advance. He recommended against too much training in riflery and use of cover, because that would increase the soldiers' instinct for self-preservation and undermine their will to attack. Dragomirov articulated these views more fully than anyone else, but they were widely shared.

Dragomirov's precepts were embodied in the new infantry regulations adopted between 1862 and 1866. One company of the five in a battalion was designated a rifle company and advanced into attack in a skirmish line; the rest followed behind in the old column formation. Skirmishers were permitted to open fire at a massed target at six to eight hundred paces, at individual targets from three hundred paces. Volley fire was preferred. Four-fifths of the battalion were not expected to fire at all. Revisions of the statutes in the 1870s barely altered the emphasis on volley fire, column assault, and bayonet charge.[25] The Russian Army was not alone in having difficulty adapting tactics to the evolution of weaponry, but it had more difficulty than other armies. And so in the years prior to the Balkan War the Russian Army prepared to march gallantly into fire, in keeping with national tradition. Miliutin seems to have found no fault with this doctrine, presumably because he shared the nationalist premises on which it was partially founded.

The reality was worse than the doctrine, because even the quite inadequate attention the regulations gave to rifle fire and dispersed formations far exceeded what officers and soldiers actually practiced. During summer training exercises regimental commanders drilled their men most assiduously in closed formations with ranks dressed, rather than open formation and skirmish lines. The bulk of the soldiers practiced only the bayonet attack. When infantry did fire their expensive new rifles (testing in riflery was not even required at summer inspections until 1871), they trained in volley fire. Rather than soldiers learning to adapt to terrain, terrain was chosen for handsome visual effect. Soldiers were told to hold rank rather than use cover, and officers scuffed trails in the dirt so that soldiers would converge uniformly in the bayonet charge. And at that the infantry may have trained more productively than any other service. Even before the Balkan War the cavalry was notorious for its lack of exercise and utter inability to shoot from horseback. During maneuvers the artillery rolled their guns to within hailing distance of the enemy before taking firing positions. Military district commanders upbraided the winning generals in combat exercises if they did not give their opponents an opportunity to recover from their mistakes. Miliutin confided to his diary after a war game at Krasnoe Selo in 1874, in which the Grand Dukes Nikolai Nikolaevich and

Mikhail Nikolaevich commanded the two sides: "Many foreign officers were present at the maneuver; more than once our generals and unit commanders embarrassed us."[26]

To some extent these old traditions were perpetuated by the stringent military budget. During the 1860s and 1870s the Russian Army was in transition, from quartering on the civilian population during all but the months of summer encampment to quartering in regular barracks. Training in those many units whose soldiers lived among peasants could only be episodic, but even when men lived together in units they had little time for drill because they had to produce necessities that the Ministry of War did not provide. Every year soldiers left their units to earn thousands of rubles for their own and regimental needs; other soldiers labored in the regimental gardens, sewed the regiment's uniforms, and cobbled the regiment's boots. And there were innumerable housekeeping and other chores that soldiers performed. At the close of the Miliutin era, on a very good day during the winter months, ten men out of a hundred in a company might report for drill. Even during summer encampment, less than half of the strength of the regiment turned out. Even if officers had wanted to, they could not train their men in much else besides basic marches.[27]

Defects in tactical doctrine and training caused grievous loss of life, but as the Balkan War demonstrated they undermined the performance of Russian arms far less than did the failure of generalship. After the Crimean War Miliutin and many other ranking officers excoriated the quality of command and recommended that new criteria be applied to the selection of military leaders. For his part, Miliutin upgraded the admissions standards to the General Staff Academy and improved the curriculum, and by the 1870s he had turned the academy into a center of military professionalism. The professors and graduates, although not always admired by their less scholarly comrades, were without question the elite of the army; they filled the pages of the fledgling military press with useful discussions of military affairs. Relatively few officers went through the academy while Miliutin was in office, and they did not rise to command rank by 1877. But by the early twentieth century GSOs dominated high command, and that should certainly be credited to Miliutin. Probably he should not be blamed for the fact that the academy graduates led Russian armies into disaster during the Russo-Japanese and world wars. Still, the fact that the post-Miliutin GSOs rose to high command chiefly through able staff work rather than through a series of field commands might be considered a distant consequence of the emphasis that Miliutin—of necessity—put on proper administration.[28]

But the characteristics of the General Staff career ladder were of less moment than the example of a single academy graduate of 1876. That was the year when the Grand Duke Nikolai Nikolaevich the younger, future commander in chief of the Russian Army during the world war, passed his examinations in the presence of his overwrought father, Nikolai Nikolaevich the elder, soon to be commander in chief in the Balkan theater.[29] The younger Nikolai may or may not have merited his GSO status and may or may not have been a good choice as commander in chief in 1914. His qualifications were almost irrelevant, because it was the tradition of grand dukes in high military office that accounted for his own and his father's appointments. That was not Miliutin's doing, nor could he have put an end to the tradition if he had tried.

The Russian autocrats and their relatives loved their military duties too well. They were appointed to regiments as children, spent time in the company of officers as they grew up, took part in maneuvers, and when on the throne treated the young Guards officers of the day as guests. Alexander II wept when he read the list of Guards officers who had died in the attack on Gornyi Dubniak on October 12, 1877, because he knew so many of them personally.[30] Not only did the tsars associate with officers throughout their lives; they unfailingly exercised their autocratic prerogative to fill the top military posts. Miliutin could do no more than offer his opinion—and not always that—about the generals the tsar chose as military district commanders. Because the many grand dukes also took their military careers seriously, Alexander and his successors routinely appointed them to high office. Inspectorates, the military educational system, military districts—under Alexander II and his successors all were at one time or another headed by grand dukes.[31]

And so an imperial patronage network was formed, with the tsar as the patron in chief, appointing relatives, or the military friends of his youth, or those whom relatives and friends brought to his attention, to the key positions. Some of these appointments were good: probably Bariatinskii, his longtime friend, to command the army of conquest in the Caucasus; obviously Miliutin to the Ministry of War. But patronage was the only route to top office; without Bariatinskii's backing and without his uncle Count Kiselev's support before that, Miliutin's military career would not have gone very far. The mix of circumstances that brought Miliutin to the fore would just as often produce a Sukhozanet. The most likely candidates of all for high military office were cautious mediocrities like Miliutin's successor, Petr Vannovskii. During the Russo-Turkish War Vannovskii served as chief of staff in the Rushchuk detachment under the Grand Duke Aleksandr Aleksandrovich, where he displayed no particular talent. But when the grand duke became Tsar Alexander III, he naturally picked as his minister of war a general with whom he was comfortable.

Only a fundamental change in the political system could make it possible to establish professional competence as the criterion for advancement to the top military posts. Just as with other of the reforms of the 1860s and 1870s, maintenance of the principle and practice of autocracy set bounds beyond which military reform could not go. But the connection between autocratic politics and the failure of reformed institutions to perform adequately emerged much more clearly in military than in civilian affairs. The Russian Army's embarrassingly difficult victory over a third-rate power in the Balkan War was an unambiguous sign of failure, and the manner in which the army failed implicated the autocracy.

The reformed army was of course better than the prereform army. One can find evidence of improved performance even in the Balkan War. The Russian Army of 1877–78 had become modern—in structure, in weaponry, in education—while the army that had fought in the Crimea had been distinctly premodern. But the inability to achieve what ought to have been an easy victory was not the result of a few mistakes or unlucky circumstance. The tactical training that prepared the way for lengthy casualty rolls sprang directly from the military variant of Russian exceptionalism and from underfunding of the regiments that diverted men from drill and encouraged commanders to fall back on familiar exercises with compact columns and dressed ranks. Inept command grew out of the practice of autocracy. Fundamental political, intellectual, and social characteristics of Imperial Russia produced faulty military performance. If Miliutin's military program mirrored the reforms in civilian society, perhaps the army's difficulties in 1877 anticipated the failure of the Great Reforms as a whole to save the Tsarist system from collapse forty years later.

NOTES

1. The description and analysis of operations in the Balkan theater are based on N. I. Beliaev, *Russko-turetskaia voina 1877–1878 gg.* (Moscow, 1956); V. A. Zolotarev, *Rossiia i Turtsiia, voina 1877–78 gg.* (Moscow, 1983); A. Kersnovskii, *Istoriia russkoi armii,* vol. 2: *Ot vziatii Parizha do pokoreniia Srednoi Azii (1814–1881)* (Belgrade, 1934), 416–62; D. A. Miliutin, *Dnevnik D. A. Miliutina,* vol. 2 (Moscow, 1949), devoted largely to the preliminaries and the campaign; F. V. Greene, *Report on the Russian Army and Its Campaigns in Turkey in 1877–1878* (New York, 1879); F. V. Greene, *Sketches of Army Life in Russia* (New York, 1880); Lt.-Gen. Valentine Baker-Pasha, *War in Bulgaria: A Narrative of Personal Experiences,* 2 vols. (London, 1879); P. Parensov, *Iz proshlogo, Vospominaniia ofitsera General'nogo shtaba,* vol. 1 (St. Petersburg, 1901); M. Gazenkampf, *Moi dnevnik, 1877–78 gg.,* 2d ed. (St. Petersburg, 1908); A. N. Kuropatkin, *Deistviia otriadov generala Skobeleva v Russko-turetskuiu voinu 1877–78 godov,* 2 vols. (St. Petersburg, 1885); D. A. Skalon, *Moi vospominaniia 1877–1878 gg.,* vol. 1 (St. Petersburg, 1913); A. Puzyrevskii, *Vospominaniia ofitsera General'nogo shtaba o voine 1877–1878 gg. v evropeiskoi Turtsii* (St. Petersburg, 1879); P. P. Kartsov, *Iz proshlogo, Lichnye i sluzhebnye vospominaniia,* vol. 2 (St. Petersburg, 1888); *Sbornik materialov po Russko-turetskoi voine 1877–78 gg. na Balkanskom poluostrove* [henceforth *Sbornik materialov*], vol. 14 (St. Petersburg, 1898) and vols. 25 and 26 (St. Petersburg, 1899); and numerous articles in *Voennyi sbornik,* 1878–80.

2. Obruchev's strategic plan is in Gazenkampf, *Moi dnevnik,* appendices 1 and 4. See also A. P. Barbasov, "Novye fakty o planirovanii russko-turetskoi voiny 1877–1878 gg.," *Voenno-istoricheskii zhurnal,* 1976, no. 2, 98–104.

3. On the Russian army's infelicitous position, see Miliutin's recommendations to the tsar after the second battle of Plevna, "Zapiska Voennogo Ministra ob izmenenii plana kampanii, dolozhennaia 21 iiulia 1877 g. Imperatoru Aleksandru II," *Sbornik materialov,* vol. 26, 152–56.

4. Zolotarev, *Rossiia i Turtsiia*, pp. 78–83, provides a nice account of the commission's work. Official embarrassment over the Russo-Turkish War was well known in military circles at the turn of the century.

5. Miliutin, *Dnevnik*, vol. 2, 65; also 52, 64, 109, 117, 131, 164.

6. Ibid., 65.

7. E. Willis Brooks, "Reform in the Russian Army, 1856–1861," *Slavic Review*, Spring 1984, 63–82.

8. Miliutin's January 1862 report is in *Stoletie Voennogo ministerstva, 1802–1902*, vol. 1 (St. Petersburg, 1902), "Prilozhenie," 70–183. Unless otherwise noted, I follow the standard accounts in outlining Miliutin's plan and the ensuing reforms: P. A. Zaionchkovskii, *Voennye reformy 1860–1870 godov v Rossii* (Moscow, 1952); Forrestt A. Miller, *Dmitrii Miliutin and the Reform Era in Russia* (Nashville, Tenn., 1968); and General M. Bogdanovich, ed., *Istoricheskii ocherk deiatel'nosti voennogo upravleniia v Rossii v pervoe dvadtsati-piatiletie blagopoluchnogo tsarstvovaniia Gosudaria Imperatora Aleksandra Nikolaevicha (1855–1880 gg.)*, 6 vols. (St. Petersburg, 1879–81). Also useful is Miliutin's explanation of key reforms: "Voennye reformy Imperatora Aleksandra II," *Vestnik Evropy*, 1882, no. 1, 5–35.

9. On quartering: V. Anichkov, *Voennoe khoziaistvo, Sravnitel'noe issledovanie polozhitel'nykh zakonodatel'stv Rossii, Frantsii, Prussii, Avstrii, Sardinii, Bel'gii i Bavarii* (St. Petersburg, 1860), 223.

10. *Ministerstvo finansov 1802–1902*, vol. 1 (St. Petersburg, 1902), 636–39, and vol. 2 (St. Petersburg, 1902), 642–43.

11. On barracks: P. A. Zaionchkovskii, *Samoderzhavie i russkaia armiia na rubezhe XIX–XX stoletii* (Moscow, 1973), 270–71; Dietrich Beyrau, *Militar und Gesellschaft im vorrevolutionaren Russland* (Cologne-Vienna, 1984), 328–34.

12. Bogdanovich, *Istoricheskii ocherk*, vol. 3, 90–97, 112, 118, and Prilozhenie 38.

13. Miller, *Dmitrii Miliutin*, 61.

14. For a detailed account, see P. P. Kartsov, *Iz proshlogo, Lichnie i sluzhebnye vospominaniia*, vol. 1 (St. Petersburg, 1888), chap. 7–10.

15. S. Frederick Starr, *Decentralization and Self-Government in Russia, 1830–1870* (Princeton, N.J., 1972).

16. "O rekrutskom nabore v 1863 godu," *Voennyi sbornik*, vol. 28 (1862), 385–92.

17. See John Bushnell, *Mutiny amid Repression* (Bloomington, Ind., 1985), 8 and n. 24, 260–61. In the 1860s and the 1870s, *Voennyi sbornik* published many articles on the practice and results of education of enlisted personnel.

18. The four published volumes of Miliutin's diary are the best source on his views. The introduction by P. A. Zaionchkovskii in volume one is a useful overview; Miliutin, *Dnevnik*, vol. 1 (Moscow, 1947), 5–72. See also E. W. Brooks, "D. A. Miliutin: Life and Activity to 1856" (Ph.D. diss., Stanford University, 1970).

19. P. P. Kartsov, *Iz proshlogo*, vol. 1, 51, 54, 232–34, 236–38, 374–76, 492; vol. 2, 536–37, 650–51; Kersnovskii, *Istoriia*, vol. 2, 400–401.

20. Zaionchkovskii, *Voennye reformy*, 115–19, 126–33; Rostislav Fadeev, *Russlands Kriegsmacht und Kriegspolitik* (Leipzig, 1870), 197–202 and passim; Rostislav Fadeev, *Russkoe obshchestvo v nastoiashchem i budushchem. (Chem nam byt'?)* (St. Petersburg, 1874), 132–54; Kartsov, *Iz proshlogo*, 484–86. [Miliutin], "Voennye reformy," is in large part a response to such charges.

21. In addition to Zaionchkovskii, *Voennye reformy*, 257–61, 304–31, and Miller, *Dmitrii Miliutin*, 194–225, see P. A. Zaionchkovskii, "Podgotovka voennoi reformy 1874 goda," *Istoricheskie zapiski* 27 (1948): 170–201, and Miliutin, *Dnevnik*, vol. 1.

22. Cited in Zolotarev, *Rossiia i Turtsiia*, 29.

23. In assessing Dragomirov's thinking and influence I have drawn particularly on M. Dragomirov, *Uchebnik taktiki*, 2d ed. (St. Petersburg, 1881), 40–45, 63–65, and passim; M. Dragomirov, *Sbornik original'nykh i perevodnykh statei, 1850–1889* (St. Petersburg, 1881), 291–354 and passim; G. P. Meshcheriakov, *Russkaia voennaia*

mysl' v XIX v. (Moscow, 1973), 196–203, 215–16; and an unpublished paper by Bruce Menning, "The Army of D. A. Miliutin and M. I. Dragomirov," 1984. The stress on Dragomirov's nationalism and its consequences is my own.

24. See D. A. Miliutin, "Suvorov kak polkovodets," *Otechestvennye zapiski,* April 1839, 1–32, and May 1839, 71–94; and Brooks, "D. A. Miliutin," 67–68, 127–132.

25. N. Z., "Nash pekhotnyi stroevoi ustav," *Voennyi sbornik,* 1878, no. 5, 29–65, and no. 6, 191–216; Zaionchkovskii, *Voennye reformy,* 187–191, 246–47; Meshcheriakov, *Russkaia voennaia mysl',* 203–4; Menning, "The Army."

26. Miliutin, *Dnevnik,* vol. 1, 164; A. K. Puzyrevskii, "Otryvochnye zametki iz opyta minuvshei kampanii," *Voennyi sbornik,* 1878, no. 7, 70; Zeddeler, "Neskol'ko prakticheskikh vyvodov," *Voennyi sbornik,* 1878, no. 6, 220–22; N. Z., "Nash pekhotnyi ustav," *Voennyi sbornik,* 1878, no. 6, 195; Kartsov, *Iz proshlogo,* vol. 1, 384–85, 458–66; Nikolai Epanchin, "Na sluzhbe trekh imperatorov," 1939 typescript, Bakhmeteff Archive, Columbia University, 36; Zaionchkovskii, *Voennye reformy,* 192–200; Kersnovskii, *Istoriia,* vol. 2, 404–5; N. Butovskii, *Novoe napravlenie v smotrovykh trebovaniiakh* (St. Petersburg, 1893), 3–6. These points are also brought out in what was reported and omitted in the many official reports on summer inspections and maneuvers contained in the two tomes of *Sbornik materialov,* vol. 21 (St. Petersburg, 1903).

27. John Bushnell, "The Russian Soldiers' Artel, 1700–1900: A History and an Interpretation," in *Land Commune and Peasant Community in Russia* (London, 1990), 376–94; John Bushnell, *Mutiny amid Repression,* 11–15.

28. Meshcheriakov, *Russkaia voennaia mysl',* 181, 183–90, 218, 222; Zaionchkovskii, *Voennye reformy,* 231–36; William C. Fuller, Jr., *Civil-Military Conflict in Imperial Russia 1881–1914* (Princeton, N.J., 1985), 9–10, 31–46, and passim; John Bushnell, "The Tsarist Officer Corps, 1881–1914: Customs, Duties, Inefficiency," *American Historical Review,* October 1981, 771–73.

29. Miliutin, *Dnevnik,* vol. 2, 33.

30. Miliutin, *Dnevnik,* vol. 2, 231–2.

31. See, for example, Zaionchkovskii, *Voennye reformy,* 100, 106, and elsewhere; and P. A. Zaionchkovskii, *Samoderzhavie i russkaia armiia na rubezhe XIX–XX stoletii* (Moscow, 1973), 31–77.

Part II
State and Society

IX

ACCOUNTABLE ONLY TO GOD AND THE SENATE

PEACE MEDIATORS AND
THE GREAT REFORMS

Natalia F. Ust'iantseva
Translated by Ben Eklof

The middle of the nineteenth century witnessed a fundamental transformation of economic relations in Russia. The old economic system, rooted in compulsory labor and nonmarket mechanisms, had outlived its time and was fated to change. The turnabout was initiated "from above," and began with the thorniest of issues—the abolition of serfdom.

The nature of the transformations wrought by the reforms depended upon the mechanisms of implementation, for, in the prevailing conditions, even the best conceived project could easily be obstructed, even buried. Therefore, the issue of who would be placed in charge of implementing the forms *in situ* was of utmost importance, and provoked much argument. N. A. Miliutin, the leader of the liberal bureaucrats and head of the commission drawing up the draft legislation on peasant institutions, noted:

> No matter what we might write here, no matter how hard we try to defend the interests of the peasant estate, now entirely lacking legal rights, the success of our great enterprise is entirely dependent upon how we carry it through. The process of implementation could entirely distort, even render lifeless, the best intentions of the lawgiver.[1]

In the circumstances of midcentury Russia, it was the liberal bureaucracy rather than an independent middle class which displayed the greatest energy in pushing forward reform. It was precisely this liberal bureaucracy which, in the tense situation then prevailing in the country, was summoned by the government to work out the terms of the series of bourgeois reforms. In turn, this liberal bureaucracy, in the course of the reform, sought to enlist the support of the liberal segment of the nobility without relinquishing control over the reform process itself. That this was so is amply demonstrated by the way in which the post of peace mediator was staffed, for the peace mediator was to be the chief agent of reform in the countryside.

The history of the establishment of the institution of peace mediators is a component of the larger prehistory of the Emancipation of 1861.[2] At the initial stages, legislative drafts envisioned making the local landed nobility, through provincial committees of the nobility, responsible for implementing the reforms. But the government was soon forced to adopt a more radical approach to peasant reform, fundamentally altering the contours of legislation. Specifically, a new institution—that of the peace mediator—was devised to help implement the reform in the field.

All told, in 444 districts of 44 provinces of Russia some 1,700 peace mediators were appointed in 1861. Peace mediators, along with a "representative from the government," comprised the district *mirovoi s"ezd* (the next higher echelon, according to the Judicial Reform of 1864). As for who would lead this body, originally the Miliutin commission proposed making one of the mediators, elected by his peers, chairman of the mirovoi s"ezd. However, conservatives managed to have this amended in the State Council so that the district marshal of the nobility would now be the chairman.[3]

In addition to the peace mediators and the district mirovye s"ezdy, another institution was established to oversee the implementation of the Emancipation Statute. This was the provincial Office of Peasant Affairs, including among its members the governor, the head of the office [*palata*] of state domains, the provincial marshal of the nobility, the local procurator, two elected delegates from the nobility, and two representatives of the government, who also had to be from among the local nobility. All in all, the number of peace mediators [along with candidate members], government representatives on the mirovye s"ezdy, members of the provincial Office of Peasant Affairs from both bureaucracy and nobility, totaled some five thousand people. In the course of the thirteen years during which the peace mediators existed, some nine thousand people held these positions.[4] Undoubtedly the most important in this group were the peace mediators themselves, for it was they who were primarily responsible for carrying out the emancipation legislation.

Peace mediators were to be recruited from the local hereditary nobility owning no fewer than five hundred *desiatinas* [one desiatina equals 2.7 acres] of land [or 250 desiatinas for those with a higher education]. The personal nobility were eligible only in the event of a shortage of eligible hereditary nobles and if they held twice the minimum size holding of land [i.e., one thousand desiatinas, or five hundred with a higher education].[5]

The property qualification was based on all the holdings of the *pomeshchik* within the district, including land in use by the peasantry. If necessary, land held in other districts or even provinces could be included. Even land held by parents or one's spouse could be counted; this of course significantly enlarged the pool of eligible candidates. To expand this pool yet further, an imperial order [*povelenie*] of February 18 and a circular to the governors dated February 26, 1861, allowed those actively employed in the military or the civil bureaucracy to take leaves of absence within their province if appointed to a post having to do with peasant affairs. In such an event, candidates were to retain all rights and privileges attached to their position but were to forego their salaries from their office. Officers were to be transferred to the reserves or to be given indefinite leave; civil servants either retained their previous position or remained attached to their ministry.[6]

All of these measures helped establish a large pool of candidates for selection; on average in Russia each mediator was chosen from ten to fifteen candidates. A universal property qualification, to be sure, took no account of the specificities of those provinces with land deficiencies or an abundance of land. So if in Kovno Province each mediator was chosen from a field of twenty-one candidates, in Kursk the number was only nine. Even within the boundaries of a province there were significant discrepancies.

The property qualification for peace mediators was roughly equivalent to that providing the right to a full vote at the provincial assembly of the nobility. It served to eliminate the small-holding nobility, leaving eligible that segment most active and competent in public affairs. This property qualification, however, was not of decisive significance; once a mediator took office other factors came into play, notably the individual's attitude toward the reforms. It was precisely this unwritten qualification—a positive attitude—which intensely interested the liberal bureaucrats supervising the preparatory stages and initial steps of the Emancipation. A circular from Minister of the Interior S. S. Lanskoi to the governors, dated March 22, 1861, delineated the qualities each mediator was to have: impartiality, genuine dedication to the cause of liberating the peasantry, education, and the trust of the peasantry. Special attention was directed to former members of provincial committees and to other local pomeshchiki known for "unflinching sympathy for the reforms and good relations with the peasantry."[7]

In the course of deliberations of the draft statute, the Miliutin commission succeeded in rejecting reactionary designs to turn over the selection of peace mediators to the nobility's corporate organizations. But the bureaucracy also rejected the notion of a selection process giving all estates a voice, arguing that

> in the initial period ensuing upon Emancipation such [all-class] gatherings will be dominated by the upper classes by virtue of their superior education or, on the contrary, the uneducated masses, through force of numbers, will take control. In the latter case, the educated classes will not have the desired influence or, finally, the nobility will consider it beneath their dignity to participate on the same level as the peasantry, and will decline to take part in public affairs.[8]

Eventually it was decided that for the first three years the selection of peace mediators would be left up to the local governor, with a final decision on procedure left for future resolution. In fact, this is how matters stood as long as peace mediators existed, with the government renewing their appointment every three years. Appointed by the governor, peace mediators were confirmed in office by the Senate, which, verifying only that correct procedures had been followed, did not intervene in matters of substance.

Lists of all the eligible candidates [candidates, in addition to meeting the property qualification, had to be at least twenty-one years old] in a district were drawn up by the local marshal of the nobility and verified by the noble assembly. We should note that the right of the local nobility to compile and verify such lists was, basically speaking, a mere formality, since such lists included all eligible candidates without exception, and only those under investigation or convicted of crimes could be excluded during the verification process. Some opportunity to influence the selection of candidates for the post of peace mediator was offered by the right exercised by the marshal of the nobility to meet with the governor. The governor retained the final word, however; the marshal held only a consultative voice, which did not bind the governor to heed his advice. In this manner, the statute reduced to a minimum participation by the nobility as a corporate entity in the selection of peace mediators, particularly in the early period following the Emancipation.

As early as the deliberations in the State Council over the draft statute, the planter majority [thirty-one members] in the council declared that leaving the choice of peace mediators to the governor would reduce the rights of the noble assembly to a mere formality and "in general would allow the nobility no real opportunity to participate in the selection process. . . . Consultation with the governor alone, as proposed in the draft, gives the nobility no guarantee that individuals will be selected as peace mediators whom the nobility itself considers worthy of that post, for there is nothing binding in this consultation."[9] Nevertheless, Alexander II upheld the minority opinion [thirteen votes], thereby defending the procedures contained in the draft.

After promulgation of the Emancipation Statute, when the issue of selecting peace mediators came to the fore, the struggle heated up with new intensity.[10] Thus, for example, the gendarme officer Khodkevich reported from Pskov Province on April 18, 1861, that "ninety-nine out of a hundred pomeshchiki are unhappy for various reasons [with the Emancipation], and for that reason they are preoccupied at this time primarily with selecting peace mediators. And the nobility is very unhappy that the governor, and not they, have been given the right to make the choice in this area."[11] In Kholmsk District the assembly of the nobility petitioned for the right to have, instead of three paid peace mediators, twelve unpaid mediators, selected, however, by the nobility. Pomeshchiki from Chern' District in Tula Province proposed increasing the number of peace mediators and alternates so much as to encompass everyone having the right to vote at the local noble assembly.[12] Members of the nobility, which had always dominated local affairs, could not reconcile themselves to the fact that in such a vital matter, directly bearing upon their personal interests, they had been pushed to the side. Precisely for this reason they persistently endeavored to alter the selection process, bringing it in line with traditional local corporate elections.

The selection process took place under a variety of conditions, depending upon the specific locale, the local balance of forces between liberal and conservative nobles, the amount of influence exerted by the liberal opposition, and the views held by the provincial governor on peasant reform. In these circumstances the liberal bureaucracy relied primarily upon its own resources. Here a major factor was the March 22 circular already mentioned. This circular made the governor responsible for drawing up the preliminary list and making the initial selection of candidates fitting the profile called for by the government. Here the ministry promised to help by providing the names of "educated and reliable nobles serving in St. Petersburg but not necessarily personally known to the governor." The circular concluded with a request to keep the ministry informed of all instructions issued pertaining to the peace mediators.

The ministry followed this circular with a list, stamped secret, of its preferred candidates to the post of peace mediator. A. N. Kulomzin, who served as a mediator and was subsequently a high-ranking official, recalled the approach that was followed: "although officially the selection of peace mediators was in the hands of the governor . . . Miliutin endeavored to place at least one fully reliable individual, i.e., one who genuinely supported the reform, in each district. The ministry made known the names of such individuals to the governor, and they were in fact selected."[13] Of 166 names recommended by the ministry, 112, or 70 percent, were actually appointed. Similar, confidential, lists were sent out containing the names of officials to be appointed to the mirovye s"ezdy.

Appointed by the governor and confirmed in office by the Senate, the peace mediators could be removed only by the latter institution, and only for violations of the law subject to criminal prosecution. Such protection from arbitrary removal gave the peace mediators freedom to stand up to pressure from the local nobility.

Dissatisfaction with peace mediators surfaced as early as late 1861 in the elections to the noble assemblies. For example, in Smolensk Province, despite the efforts of the governor—including threats to terminate the assembly—open expressions of hostility to the new institution were voiced. Nobles called for "protection from the tutelage [*opeka*] and surveillance [*nadzor*] of peace mediators"; a reduction in the number of peace mediators, who were "burdensome for the province"; salary cuts of more than half for those serving in the post; and election [rather than appointment] of noble representatives to the provincial Office of Peasant Affairs. Nobles from Bel'sk District went even further in calling for the election of two representatives from the nobility to the mirovye s"ezdy. Only then, in their opinion, would the rights of both peasants and nobles be protected, for the peace mediators, so they said, as representatives of the peasantry, would continue to defend the latter's interest, while nobles elected by their own corporation would serve as mediators for the upper order.[14]

The new minister of internal affairs, Petr A. Valuev, who replaced S. S. Lanskoi in April 1861 and who looked askance at the institution of peace mediator as shaped [staffed] by N. A. Miliutin and his allies, was nevertheless compelled to turn down such petitions as illegal. Thus the liberal bureaucracy, now on the way out, had managed to put down roots for the peace mediators. But Valuev's true attitude toward the peace mediators was eloquently formulated in a letter to A. G. Troinitskii in August 1862: "I insist on the general principle that the peace mediators shouldn't be given any extra rope; on the contrary they should be reined in whenever possible. I don't like the friends of my enemies, and as long as we don't have judges who cannot be removed from office, I don't understand the principle of irremovability applied to peace mediators. . . ."[15]

The peace mediators disposed of considerable plenary powers in both administrative and judicial affairs. Their basic task was to regulate [mediate] land relations between lord and peasant: to verify, implement, and in certain cases even draw up land charters, to supervise the allocation of holdings, to increase or decrease peasant obligations, to conclude agreements on redemption payments, to collect arrears, etc., and even to confirm in office locally elected peasant officials.

In judicial affairs their authority extended to investigating conflicts and disputes, as well as complaints leveled against pomeshchiks, peasants, peasant land societies, and institutions of peasant self-government. The peace mediators functioned as notary publics in witnessing various legal documents concluded between pomeshchiki and the temporarily obligated peasantry.

The peace mediators were also entrusted with judicial and police powers in certain matters: disputes over *potravy, porubki,* etc. In addition, affairs concerning rental of land and agricultural labor when estates other than the peasantry and nobility were involved. After a few years, however, those juridical functions entrusted to the peace mediators were turned over to the newly created district courts [*mirovoi sud*].

Particularly in the initial period, when the government was endeavoring to move quickly in drawing up land charters, the position of peace mediator required feverish efforts day in and day out. The peace mediator had to be constantly on the road, traveling his district [*uchastok*], which comprised on the average an area of thirty square versts [one verst equals roughly two-thirds of a mile], but in more remote regions was often far larger [in Perm sections were one hundred square versts and larger]. It does not take much effort to imagine the hardships endured during the winter frosts, summer heat and dust, or the spring and fall muddy seasons.

In the territory entrusted to each peace mediator there were roughly six thousand inhabitants in several dozen settlements and landed estates. And so the peace mediator, usually employed in his native district, found himself in the middle of several thousand local peasants insistent upon receiving land without compensation and numerous neighbors and acquaintances generally anxious to preserve the status quo.

The enormity of the expanse of territory for which they were entrusted, the complexity and sheer volume of their tasks, and the conflicts built into the situation all tell us how difficult it must have been for the peace mediators to live up to their calling. Nevertheless, despite the hardships and complexity accompanying the position, there was initially no shortage of candidates. The liberal, enlightened segment of Russian society was determined to liberate Russia from that shameful bondage which so compromised the country in the eyes of Europe, to cleanse the country of Asiatic traits, to "Europeanize" Russia, and this desire led many to seek the post of peace mediator. The wave of social activism which swept over Russia after the period of stagnation and obscurantism under Nicholas I extended even into the far corners of provincial Russia. Many students from the gentry put aside their bureaucratic careers and returned home from the universities inspired by abolitionist fervor and the determination to apply their energy to the effort to liberate the serfs.

The liberal euphoria over the magnitude of the transformation under way in Russia affected a significant proportion of the young, educated nobility. A. M. Lazarevskii, a peace mediator from Chernigov Province and later a renowned archaeologist, recalled: "When I read the statute, I was swept away with the desire to be included among the numbers of those who had been summoned to 'bring into reality' this great legislation. I felt willing to dedicate all my youthful energies to this noble and joyous cause."[16]

The writer Saltykov-Shchedrin, depicting the public mood at the turn of the decade, wrote: "In one fell swoop to liberate an entire people from Egyptian captivity, in one act to put an end to those lugubrious moans sounding forth from every corner of Russia, such a cause is capable of inspiring boundless enthusiasm."[17]

Testimony to the fact that when the position of peace mediator was first established it enjoyed great popularity and prestige can be found in the periodical press of the time. *Moskovskie vedomosti* wrote: "One can confidently say that at present in Russia there is no calling more honored, more noble, more elevated, but at the same time more difficult, than that of peace mediator." And the current events column of *Russkii vestnik* asserted that the post of peace mediator had attracted many worthy individuals from the local nobility who had "made a commitment based not upon personal profit, upon career considerations, but rather exclusively upon selfless support for the transformation that has been wrought in our country." As early as March 1861, testing the mood in the capital, the editors of this journal concluded that "today it is even fashionable to make for the countryside and become a peace mediator. This will significantly ease the work of the governors in making appointments."[18]

In March 1862 *Sovremennaia letopis'* published a sketch of district life drawn from the previous summer. After visiting six districts in his province, the author of this sketch was persuaded that the only topic of conversation was the peasant question: "The central figures in the district are, of course, the peace mediators. Everyone is talking about them, and if we were living in France, no doubt, we would be wearing chapeaux à la peace mediator, ties, boots, and brandishing walking sticks à la peace mediator. . . . The majority of the peace mediators are young men, the best young men in the district. The real 'bigwigs' themselves did not aspire to the post, because they understood that it would require much effort, concern, attention to petty detail, and even personal sacrifice as well as personal discomfort."[19]

Irremovability, independence, autonomy, and glasnost all contributed to enhancing the position of peace mediator. The peace mediator could not be removed from office through administrative measures; nor was he directly and immediately subordinate even to the mirovoi s"ezd or the provincial office of peasant affairs. On many matters to be adjudicated the law gave the peace mediator the final word. In March 1861 the minister of internal affairs wrote to the governors in explanation: "In certain cases, the activities of the peace mediator fall under the purview of the provincial office [of peasant affairs], but we are not dealing here with a relationship of *subordination*."[20]

The law also limited the degree of subordination of the peace mediator to the minister of internal affairs, for the latter could neither directly remove the peace mediator nor intervene [intercede] directly in his activities. The only lines of control came through circulars and other legal documents "clarifying" the February 19 Statute. Of course this did imply a certain degree of subordination, but the peace mediators were not hampered in their activities by petty regulations. In fact, the governor of Smolensk Province wrote to the ministry that the peace mediators in his area claimed that they were "accountable only to God and the Senate."[21]

Glasnost, pertaining both to the activities of the peace mediators and to the sessions of the mirovoi s"ezd, was a completely new development for Russian provincial life. Investigations were carried out and resolutions arrived at in the presence of the general public as well as of those involved in the matter at hand. Thus in the workings of the new institution we see embodied in embryonic form those principles which were developed more fully in the subsequent reforms.

Contemporaries, who generally gave high marks to the peace mediators, placed particular emphasis upon the fundamental novelty of the institution and the link between the peace mediators and the local institutions subsequently established. Thus P. N. Obninskii, a well-known liberal legal specialist and publicist, a peace mediator of the "first muster," and district [*uchastkovyi*] justice of the peace in Kaluga Province, recalled in his memoirs:

> One has also to bear in mind what service in our bureaucracy was like before February 19, 1861, and what it became after this *perelom*, which so abruptly impinged upon all spheres, leading to the creation of the peace mediators, zemstvo activists, and judges who mete justice according to the dictates of their conscience. The passive, almost mechanical, carrying out of instructions issued from above, the blind adherence to routine, the pursuit of career, salary, protectionism—here you have the sum and substance of matters before the reforms; activity more frequently labeled marking time . . . and suddenly, into this stagnant, moribund milieu burst a new spirit, replacing the familiar blind imitation and accommodationism with creativity and determination. . . . the chinovnik becomes a missionary, and genuine ideals [*ideia*] grasp the heart, take over matters."[22]

The peace mediators did not provide their services gratis, as was the case with the marshals of the nobility. They received 1,500 rubles a year to compensate for their expenditures, including travel, office outlays, etc. This was no mean sum in those days, and the peace mediators did not have to provide records of their expenses. But it wasn't the money that made the position attractive, especially to the "first muster." Owning, on the average, two or three hundred peasant souls and around two thousand desiatinas, the peace mediators were sufficiently well off to be economically independent. This fact was noted by contemporaries. The newspaper *Mirovoi posrednik* [Peace Mediator] even opined that having adequate means and not relying exclusively upon salary for existence, the peace mediator who was simultaneously a large landowner had more free time to devote to public concerns.[23] It followed that few peace mediators looked upon their position as a source of profit, or even of earning a living. Moreover, being men of means permitted them to interact as equals with the other district pomeshchiki, especially since most peace mediators enjoyed a full vote in the provincial assembly of the nobility.

Hidden behind the averages one can find significant diversity in the pool of peace mediators. As A. M. Lazarevskii recalled,

> They were an extremely variegated group, in terms of age, education, and degree of independence. . . . There were those from the older generation as well as those who came to the post directly from the school bench; there were those with university degrees and those who had dropped out of the gymnasium; there were rich men like Vasilii Arkad'evich Kochubei, and there were those, to be sure only a few, who were so impoverished they barely met the minimum requirements in land holdings. Among this diverse group there were also differences in attitudes about the meaning of the emancipatory legislation.[24]

Contemporaries often based their estimate of the views and convictions of the peace mediators upon attributes such as age and education. Although the statute did not include minimum requirements of age or education, a circular dated March 22, 1861, proclaimed, according to P. N. Obninskii, a "moral qualification." And so who could best meet such a requirement? We find the answer in the words of Saltykov-Shchedrin, who took part in the deliberations of the Miliutin commission and later served as vice-governor in Riazan and Tver Province. Saltykov-Shchedrin thus could observe first-hand all the ebb and flow of conflict around the reform, beginning with the work of the provincial committees of the nobility and ending with the activities of the peace mediators themselves. He wrote: "Among no group did the ideas underlying the Emancipation Statute of February 19 encounter such enthusiastic support as among the 'children' [the reference is to Turgenev's recently published *Fathers and Sons*], and no group has been so severely criticized from all directions . . . as have the younger generation." In his opinion, the peasant reform mobilized young people above all: "Only from among the ranks of young people do we see a passionate desire to serve the cause of emancipation, and it was from this younger generation that the largest numbers of activists came."

In distinguishing between fathers and sons, between planters and die-hard reactionaries on one hand and emancipators and liberals on the other, Saltykov saw a close correlation between age and views: "The younger generation has no natural affinity for the ways of serfdom, if only because they had never tasted its fruits, they hadn't had time. . . . they are more moderate in their views if only because they are not haunted by memories of past grandeur." On the other hand, "in order to be such a died-in-the-wool planter [advocate of serfdom] that one would resort to one's fists in defense of the now-abolished privileges conferred by serfdom [the reference is to a notorious incident in which a peace mediator was severely beaten by pomeshchiki at the Pskov meeting house of the assembly of the nobility], it was necessary that such individuals had drunk deeply of the pleasures of serfdom, were satiated not merely with the external niceties but also with its deepest, surreptitious joys. Apparently such a state is possible only through prolonged, persistent practice, and only for those who have not merely sown the seeds but also brought in the harvest more than once." Saltykov concluded that "the hopes aroused by the February 19 Statute rest exclusively on the younger generation, which has such natural empathy for its goals."[25]

My calculations show that the average age of the peace mediators was thirty-seven years, that two-thirds of them were forty or younger, and that one in every four was literally a youngster. Older men with prolonged experience living under serfdom comprised only 2 percent of the group.

Obninskii discussed the issue of a "moral qualification for office" from a different, though related, perspective. He attributed the success of the peace mediators to their excellent education, received in the years prior to the Emancipation, when the "spirit of liberation" [*dukh osvobozhdeniia*] extended even into the upper classes of the gymnasia through the inspiration or efforts of Solov'ev, Belinsky, Turgenev, Kostomarov, and Dobroliubov. But this spirit was even more prevalent in the 1850s in the corridors of the universities, where an immortal pleiad of teachers preached their message. Anticipating the question, Obninskii added: "The reader might protest that if the secondary schools and universities exerted such a profound impact, then why was this not reflected in the milieu of the gentry opposition? But the fact is that . . . this opposition was dominated by spiteful old men who had never had contact with schooling of any sort."[26]

Similar observations were made by a peace mediator named N. A. Borovkov from Voronezh Province in his recollections of the work of the provincial committee of the nobility in which he took part. The majority of its members, "ripe in years," were adamant planters, "while the minority, possessing youth, an education, and familiarity with foreign ways, doused the flames of the planters. . . ."[27]

Although the correlation between age, education, and one's views was, of course, not precise in each individual instance, as some liberal contemporaries were wont to argue, nevertheless the general tendency was undeniable. My calculations demonstrate that almost one-half of the peace mediators had a higher education. Such a high proportion would have done credit to any institution of the central government at the time, not to mention local institutions, which could not even dream of recruiting such qualified people. In terms of geographic distribution, we find among the peace mediators graduates of every Russian university [as well as some foreign universities], of the lycées, of the higher—including the most privileged—military institutions. We can say with confidence that virtually every tertiary or secondary educational institution in Russia included in its roll of graduates at least one future peace mediator. This testifies to the high intellectual caliber of the newly commissioned functionaries.

More than half of the peace mediators possessed a rank in the military service; among them were many officers from the military elite, i.e., the guards, the engineer and artillery corps, and the navy. In addition, 5 percent of the peace mediators were from the titled nobility; this compares with a figure of 2 percent for the nobility as a whole. Among the ranks of the peace mediators we find Lev Tolstoy and his brother Sergei, the renowned doctor N. I. Pirogov, the sons of the minister of internal affairs S. S. Lanskoi, the son-in-law of P. A. Valuev, the son of the renowned historian Karamzin, the Samarin brothers who left their mark on Russian history, the sons of the legendary guerrilla hero of the War of 1812 Denis Davydov, and the brothers of M. Saltykov-Shchedrin, of the painter N. N. Ge, of the botanist A. N. Beketov, of the physiologist N. M. Sechenov, of the biologist K. A. Timiriazev, of the mathematician M. V. Ostrogradskii, of the famous public figure K. D. Kavelin, and many others. Many of the more renowned noble families "recruited" from among their ranks at least one "representative," which partially explains the extraordinary composition of the institution of peace mediator.

To cite just one example. Before the reform period the Kaluga noble Prince A. M. Khilkov traveled to America. He was determined to follow the example of Peter the Great, working on a steamship, beginning as a stoker. On the eve of the Emancipation he returned home for a brief spell as a peace mediator, then returned to America, where he took up work with the railroads, advancing to the position of sector chief. Returning home for good, he became the minister of ways of communication. Among the ranks of the peace mediators one could find many such colorful individuals.

The explanation for the unusual quality of those who took up the post of peace mediator rests, in my opinion, in the newness, the untraditional nature, of the goals with which peace mediators were entrusted and in the unusual circumstances in which the position was established. Though drawn from the ranks of the pomeshchik, the peace mediator was set apart both from the nobility as a corporate institution and from the provincial bureaucracy. The new principles underlying this position were intended both to facilitate the work at hand and to attract a significant proportion of the liberal nobility, who saw in the activities of the peace mediators the opportunity to apply their energies to the vital task of transforming the country.

During the thirteen years in which the peace mediators existed, the position underwent significant changes, beginning almost immediately after the enabling legislation. Some peace mediators quit in the first six months after confronting the many cares accompanying the position and the difficulties associated with reconciling the demands of their neighboring pomeshchiki with the terms of the emancipation legislation. However, the number who quit was small and included many of advanced age.

Until the middle of 1863, most of the turnover came from resignations of another sort. The peace mediators often clashed with pomeshchiki who were determined to defend their privileges. To get rid of the independent and legally irremovable peace mediators, these pomeshchiki had to find a way to force a "voluntary" departure. Such clashes demonstrate that the peace mediators were in a way the shock troops of the local landed nobility in its struggle against the peasantry. Nor did the institution serve primarily to defend the interests of the pomeshchiki, as is so often asserted in Soviet historiography.[28] The source of conflicts resided in the nature of the institution itself, its governing principles, the conditions in which it was created, and the status of the peace mediators.

An illustration of this argument is the work of Lev Tolstoy as peace mediator in Krapivna District of Tula Province. Local pomeshchiki believed he was working primarily to serve the peasantry. At the provincial assembly of the nobility in December 1861, the district nobility petitioned that he be removed from his position "because Count Lev Tolstoy had lost the confidence of the pomeshchiki." In January 1862 Tolstoy wrote to V. P. Botkin: "I became a peace mediator quite fortuitously, and despite the fact that I work conscientiously and impartially, I provoked the intense ire of the nobility. They want to beat me up, they want to bring me to court, but they won't get their way. I'm waiting only for them to calm down, and then I'll retire on my own."[29]

In December 1861 the peace mediators in Smolensk Province tried to resign en masse, and the governor had to twist their arms to resist the illegal entreaties of the nobility. Interestingly, in this very province, according to a report by an officer of the gendarmes, the "selection of names for the position of peace mediator had been controlled by the local nobility in each district," and only those individuals who had been deemed most reliable had actually been allowed to take office." Yet despite such credentials the very first steps taken by peace mediators had turned them into "socialists" and "communists."[30]

In a number of provinces the campaign against the peace mediators assumed organized form, and not everyone could withstand such a formidable assault. As F. F. Voroponov, who wrote for several liberal publications at the time, noted, "The legal protection granted the peace mediators on occasion crumbled in the face of pressure by an irate nobility, pressure which many found simply insurmountable and gave up their positions."[31]

The liberal press condemned those peace mediators who yielded to the protestations of the nobility. The newspaper *Moskovskie vedomosti* reprinted articles from *Mogilevskie gubernskie vedomosti* investigating the resignations of two peace mediators from Bykhov District. There the local nobility had drawn up an indictment depicting the peace mediators as "embezzlers of public wealth" and accusing them of "unconstrained activities and neglect of noble interests." Passing the indictment on to the provincial office of peasant affairs, the peace mediators submitted their resignations. The author of the article posed the questions "Were the peace mediators justified in submitting their resignations and bowing to the illegal pressure exerted by eighteen members of the nobility? Can it really be that the interests of more than twenty thousand peasants, the rights of whom the dispassionate activities of the peace mediators are designed to protect, are in reality of secondary importance to them?"[32]

The majority of the liberal peace mediators resisted the encroachments of the nobility. D. D. Bronevskii, peace mediator from Voronezh Province, recalled how, finding himself in a minority at his local mirovoi s"ezd, he nevertheless replied to calls for his resignation by asserting that "the mirovoi s"ezd has no right to make such a demand. . . . I am not serving at the behest of the nobility. At this point everyone shouted, as if stung by the comment, 'Then whom do you serve?' I replied, 'My region, and everyone in it.'"[33] Such stalwart individuals knew who would succeed them should they resign. A. N. Kulomzin wrote: "We knew that in leaving our posts, with the change in direction at the top of the government, peasant concerns would be turned over to people with views diametrically opposed to ours, that our cause would be ruined. So we stayed on, maneuvering between the statute and the circulars subsequently issued, trying to ignore the latter whenever possible."[34]

A new wave of replacement began in the middle of 1863. First the government ordered all military personnel to return to their posts if they had not resigned them in taking up the position of peace mediator in accordance with the circular of February 26, 1861. Then a reduction was carried out in the number of peace mediators, a process meriting special comment. This contraction was connected with the reduced workload [after the feverish activity of the initial post-Emancipation period] and with the need to reduce the financial burden of local peasant-related institutions [amounting to four million rubles annually, of which 2.5 million rubles went to peace mediators].[35] At the same time, this was the only way the nobility could rid itself of troublesome individuals. Requests for cutbacks began to arrive at the Ministry of Interior by the end of 1861. The governors themselves noted that such requests were motivated "not so much by any real need to reduce the number of peace mediators as by the desire to get rid of specific individuals."[36]

Valuev, whose draft legislation to provide for the temporary suspension of peace mediators through adminstrative means had been rejected in 1861 by the Main Committee on Peasant Affairs headed by the Grand Duke Konstantin Nikolaevich, succeeded in July 1863 in winning approval for a measure entitled "On Reducing the Size and Number of Local Institutions of Peasant Affairs." "Soon," wrote Obninskii, "a radical means was devised to get rid of unforgiven and bothersome advocates of legality; one by one, local sectors [mirovye uchastki] were closed down."[37]

Events in Kaluga Province provide a vivid illustration of this process. There a particularly unified group of peace mediators emerged under the sponsorship of Governor V. A. Artsimovich. One of this group later recalled: "After Viktor Antonovich left, reportedly at Valuev's prompting, a reduction in the number of positions was carried out in Kaluga Province; and it was precisely those peace mediators who had encroached upon the interests of the nobility whose positions were eliminated. Once they left, it was proposed to restore the position, and to appoint more desirable individuals to it." The majority of Kaluga peace mediators submitted their resignations without waiting for the cutback; within half a year, some twenty peace mediators quit. Later, five of this number confessed to Artismovich that "we all relinquished our positions, exhausted by the pointless struggle against the reactionary faction which everywhere is now in the majority, in the provincial office of peasant affairs as well as at the mirovoi s"ezd."[38]

In three years the peace mediator institutions in Russia underwent significant turnover, amounting to roughly 45 percent of all personnel. The liberal stratum of peace mediators, upon whose shoulders hopes for successful implementation of the reforms rested, were pressured by changing government policies and by the resolute claims of the reactionary nobility, and the group gradually dissolved.

A distinctive page in the history of the institution of peace mediator was written in the nine western provinces [Vilno, Kovno, Grodno, Minsk, Mogilev, Vitebsk, Kiev, Podolsk, and Volyn'], where almost one quarter of all peace mediators worked. There the Polish insurrection of 1863 led to even greater changes in the institution. The overwhelming majority of the provinces' pomeshchiki were Polish. Disturbances in Poland began early in 1861; thus an oppositional mood surfaced among peace mediators virtually from the start. The governor of Podolsk Province reported in the spring of 1861 that the district marshals of the nobility were using the congresses of the nobility, summoned to draw up lists of candidates for the position of peace mediator, to compose patriotic manifestos.[39] Outright opposition first appeared during the events in Warsaw in the form of patriotic hymns sung in church and the wearing of funereal garb, the cap of the confederacy, buttons, and insignias with the Polish eagle.

By 1863 peace mediator support for the opposition movement was obvious. The government received reports of participation by peace mediators in fund-raising efforts in preparation for the uprising [including even contributions from their government salaries], attempts to influence the peasantry and to recruit their support for the uprising, use of the Polish language in official correspondence with volost officials, military training of the peasantry by the peace mediators, and efforts to create schools for the peasantry in which the Polish language was used. The peasants were told that if they joined the uprising they would be given the land free and would be released from taxation. When they declined to join the revolt, the peace mediators called for troops to put down purported uprisings by the peasantry. In response, in August officials stopped sending troops into the countryside at the request of the peace mediators.

In the western provinces the peace mediators exerted a strong influence on the selection of peasant officials. For example, volost clerks and secretaries were drawn primarily from the ranks of students expelled for their political activities, and only Catholics were appointed as volost elders.

The position of peace mediators was ideal for supporting insurgent activity, since it required constant travel and visits to pomeshchik estates and provided powerful levers with which to influence the peasants and their institutions of self-government. A. Zelinskii, a peace mediator who was in charge of insurgent organizations in one region, testified in a deposition after his arrest that "all my trips, both to collect money, and to arrange clandestine meetings, were done while carrying out official duties."[40]

The insurgents often took as their basic organizational unit the *okrug,* a territory coterminous with the sector [*uchastok*] defining the area of the peace mediator. Soon after the promulgation of the Emancipation Statute in Tsarist Poland, a "Polish catechism" of sorts was drawn up in the native language. In this document, "Polish Instructions for the Peace Mediators of the Northwestern Region," the activities of the peace mediators were enumerated.[41] In its struggle with the Polish liberation movement, the government in August 1861 ordered that, "in accordance with established procedures, untrustworthy peace mediators be turned over to the courts and temporarily replaced by officials from the bureaucracy, if among the ranks of candidates already in line for the position no reliable individuals can be found."[42]

In this period dismissals were infrequent and took place according to regulations, through the Senate. But by 1863, when the insurgency had grown considerably, isolated replacements would no longer do. As a result, on March 7 Alexander II granted the governors-general the right to dismiss peace mediators and volost and village elders "who in the present, extraordinary circumstances they deem insufficiently trustworthy." In the place of dismissed peace mediators the governors-general could make new appointments, both from the list of approved candidates and from the civil and military bureaucracy.[43] So the government resorted to administrative measures to purge the ranks of the peace mediators in the western region. In accordance with the above instruction [ukaz], the ranks of local government were thoroughly purged, with many dismissed officials turned over to the courts.

As we have seen, in the middle of 1863 a new stage began in the history of the peace mediators, with qualitative and quantitative changes occurring in the ranks. In the western region peace mediators were replaced by Russian officials and pomeshchiki, many of whom had formerly served as peace mediators in European Russia. Many such pomeshchiki obtained land sold or granted by the government after confiscation from the Polish nobility. In other outlying areas of the Russian Empire, where, for the most part, the Emancipation was promulgated at a later date, the office of peace mediator took a different shape. Another influence on the institution was the implementation of the reform of the appanage and state peasantry [in 1863 and 1866, respectively]. In those areas, where such categories of peasants were compactly clustered, it was necessary to significantly augment the number of peace mediators; in Perm Province, for example, a doubling of positions occurred.

But the greatest influence on the institution of peace mediator was exerted by the zemstvo, especially by the judicial reforms. From the first drafts of the reforms a close link was established between the office of the justice of the peace and the peace mediator. The Miliutin commission was confronted above all with the question: should separate institutions be established to supervise peasant affairs, or should such matters be entrusted to the regular justices of the peace to be established as part of the judicial reforms? But in fact what was created were not justices of the peace, but peace mediators. Thus a direct link between the peace mediator and the justices of the peace established by the court reform of 1864 did not in fact exist. However, with the establishment of the justices of the peace, those principles tested out through the peace mediators in the years immediately following the Emancipation were now implemented. Moreover, a significant portion of the functions of the peace mediators was turned over to the justices of the peace. It was no coincidence, either, that there was an upsurge of public interest in the peace mediators at the time that the draft legislation for the judicial statute was undergoing examination. In reality, when the office of justice of the peace was established, many of the most active and experienced peace mediators were drawn away from their positions. This tendency was reinforced by a provision of the new law stipulating that a three-year term as peace mediator automatically entitled one to be put forward as a candidate for the position of justice of the peace. Finally, with the zemstvo statute many peace mediators were selected to become chairmen of the provincial and district zemstvo executive boards.

By the early 1870s the institution of peace mediator bore little resemblance to what it had been in 1861. The sphere of competence had been reduced and the levers by which the government could apply pressure increased. N. A. Borovkov recalled that in the margins of his copy of the statute he added all of the "clarifications" issued by the ministry. "My God," he exclaimed, "what a collection of contradictions, distortions, and obfuscations of the original terms of the statute!"[44] The result was to place the peace mediator in the ranks of the traditional local bureaucracy; this, of course, inevitably had an impact on the selection of personnel for the position.

The liberal publicist S. N. Terpigorev left an eloquent description of the changes which took place in the quality of the individuals serving as peace mediators. Initially, he wrote, many who served were distinguished by their honesty, their authentic and profound dedication to the principles and the very cause of reform. However,

> the first wave of enthusiasm, marked by extraordinary force, candor, and ardor, was soon replaced by disillusionment, enervation. . . . One after the other, these "wonder workers" [*chudaki*] lost their drive . . . and this one left for Petersburg, that one for Moscow, and others went abroad. . . . Those who stepped into their shoes were people of a different mold, a different type, with different tastes. This second shift was made up almost entirely of planters, embittered by the Emancipation Statute and by their failure to adapt their own estates to the new economy. . . . Almost none of this type were included in the first muster, because at that time it was still unclear how events would unfold and they were apprehensive of the prospect of dealing face to face with the liberated *muzhik;* after all, we were fearful that we were going to be exterminated to the last man! . . . In recent years this office, so magnificent according to the terms of the Emancipation Statute, has been . . . something . . . moribund, vulgarized, and with a whiff of scandal hovering over it. . . . In recent years we see people trying to gain office for purely, openly, and directly venal and corrupt ends.[45]

In accordance with legislation issued July 27, 1874, the position of peace mediator [along with congresses of peace mediators] was eliminated. The peace mediators were replaced by new institutions, the district and provincial offices of peasant affairs, to which were now transferred the few functions still entrusted to the peace mediators. Within this new institution the responsibilities previously accruing to the peace mediators, that is, the settlement of land relations between pomeshchik or state on one hand and peasant on the other, were now handed over to the so-called permanent members of the district office of peasant affairs. These permanent members, although appointed from among the local landholding nobility, were nevertheless completely under the thumb of the administration; in their service ranking they were equivalent not to the district marshals of the nobility [as the peace mediators were] but to officials within the Ministry of Interior.

After 1874 the peace mediators continued to function in a number of the country's outlying regions where the zemstvo and court reforms had not yet been applied. Then, between 1877 and 1882, district offices of peasant affairs were introduced in Astrakhan, Orenburg, Ufa, Vitebsk, Minsk, Mogilev, Archangel', and Vologda provinces.

The history of the institution of peace mediator is indicative of the course of the reforms of the sixties in general. Such profound changes could not but be accompanied by a certain liberalization and emancipation of the spirit of society. As a result, people were found to implement these changes and new opportunities were opened for those who wanted to dedicate themselves to public service.

On the other hand, in the circumstances of a revolution from above, the only guarantee of a measure of consistency and irreversibility to the reforms was in the initiatory and patronizing role played by the monarchy. Such a role was manifest in the way peace mediators were appointed, in their relative independence and irremoveability. But it could not be a steadfast guarantee.

In the immediate postreform period preceding the zemstvo and judicial reforms, the principles underlying the institution of peace mediator served as a trial balloon of sorts for the new bourgeois legislative norms. The institution was an oasis in the system of absolute monarchy but also bore the stamp of the old ways. For that reason, the activities of the peace mediators were sustained by a high level of personal commitment, occasionally even heroic sacrifice. But this [dependence upon heroic exploits] was also the weakest link in the policies of the liberal bourgeoisie of the epoch of reform.[46]

NOTES

1. *Osvobozhdenie krest'ian v tsarstvovanie imperatora Aleksandra II: Khronika deiatel'nosti komissii po krest'ianskomu delu N. P. Semenova* (St. Petersburg, 1891), vol. 3, pt. 1, 346.

2. The first historian to consider establishing the position of peace mediators in the context of the peasant question as a whole was Larissa Zakharova, in *Samoderzhavie i otmena krepostnogo prava, 1857–1861* (Moscow, 1984), 214–21. Official policy concerning the peace mediators is treated in a chapter of V. G. Chernukha's *Krest'ianskii vopros v pravitel'stvennoi politike Rossii* (Leningrad, 1972), 25–69.

3. *Zhurnaly i memorii Obshchego sobraniia Gosudarstvennogo soveta po krest'ianskomu delu s 28 ianvaria po 14 marta 1861* (Prague, 1915), 56.

4. The data here and later in this essay are based on research done by the author and summarized in N. F. Ust'iantseva, "Institut mirovykh posrednikov v sisteme gosudarstvennogo stroia Rossii," *Kandidat* diss. (Moscow, 1984).

5. The legal aspects of the activities of the peace mediators are treated in "Statute on Provincial and District Offices of Peasant Affairs," in *PSZ* ser. 2, vol. 36, sec. 1, no. 36660.

6. *Sbornik pravitel'stvennykh rasporiazhenii po ustroistvu byta krest'ian, vyshedshikh iz krepostnoi zavisimosti* (St. Petersburg, 1861), vol. 2, pt. 1, 35–38.

7. Ibid., 111–15.

8. *Pervoe izdanie materialov Redaktsionnykh komissii dlia sostavleniia polozhenii o krest'ianakh, vykhodiashchikh iz krepostnoi zavistimosti* (St. Petersburg, 1860), vol. 9: *Ob'iasnitel'naia zapiska*, 45.

9. *Zhurnaly i memorii Obshchego sobraniia Gosudarstvennogo soveta po krest'ianskomu delu*, 41–42.

10. On the establishment of the peace mediators, see the author's "Institut mirovykh posrednikov v sisteme gosudarstvennogo stroia Rossii (formirovanie i kompetentsiia)," in *Gosudarstvennyi stroi i politiko-pravovye idei Rossii vtoroi poloviny XIX stoletiia* (Voronezh, 1987), 24–34.

11. TsGAOR, f. 109, 4 expeditsiia, 1861, d. 225, l. 21 ob.

12. TsGIA, f. 1181, op. 1 (vol. 15), 1861, d. 22, l. 2-2 ob.

13. A. N. Kulomzin, "Vospominaniia mirovogo posrednika," in *Zapiski OR GBL*, vol. 10, 1941, 10.

14. TsGIA, f. 1282, op. 2, 1861, d. 1095, ll. 10–12, 51–54 ob., 58–62 ob., 67–68.

15. *Russkaia starina*, 1905, no. 4, 274.

16. *Kievskaia starina*, 1901, no. 3, 352.

17. M. E. Saltykov-Shchedrin, *Sobranie sochinenii*, vol. 7 (Moscow, 1969), 238.

18. *Moskovskie vedomosti*, Aug. 4, 1862, 1367–69; "Sovremennaia letopis,'" *Russkii vestnik*, 1861, no. 13, 14; no. 40, 23.

19. "Sovremennaia letopis,'" *Russkii vestnik*, 1862, no. 12, 1–4.

20. TsGIA, f. 1291, op. 123, 1861, d. 22, l. 1–4 ob.

21. Ibid., op. 1, 1861, d. 47, l. 264.

22. P. N. Obninskii, "V. A. Artsimovich v Kaluge v 1861–1863 godakh," *Viktor Antonovich Artsimovich: Vospominaniia, kharakteristiki* (St. Petersburg, 1904), 113.

23. *Vestnik mirovykh uchrezhdenii (byvshii Mirovoi posrednik)*, 1863, no. 6, 425–26. For a detailed analysis of the newspaper *Mirovoi posrednik*, see the author's "Institut mirovykh posrednikov v otsenke sovremennikov (po materialam gazety 'Mirovoi posrednik')," *Vestnik Moskovskogo universiteta*, series 8: *History*, 1984, no. 1, 64–75.

24. *Kievskaia starina*, 1901, no. 5, 287.

25. Saltykov-Shchedrin, *Sobranie sochinenii*, vol. 5 (Moscow, 1965), 235–36, 503.

26. *Russkaia mysl'*, 1896, no. 6, 47.

27. N. A. Borovkov, *Iz proshlogo* (St. Petersburg, 1901), 40.

28. M. E. Naidenov, *Klassovaia bor'ba v poreformennoi derevne (1861–1863)* (Moscow, 1955), 175, 181, 190; A. P. Korelin, *Dvor'ianstvo v poreformennoi Rossii, 1861–1904 gg.* (Moscow, 1979), 183.

29. *Obshchestvennaia deiatel'nost L. N. Tolstogo v Tul'skom krae: Sbornik dokumentov* (Tula, 1980), 10–11; L. N. Tolstoi, *Polnoe sobranie sochinenii*, vol. 60 (Moscow, 1949), 415.

30. TsGIA, f. 1282, op. 2, 1861, d. 1095, l. 52 ob., 53; TsGAOR, f. 109, 4 eksp., 1861, d. 231, ll. 76–79.

31. *Vestnik evropy*, 1904, no. 7, 21.

32. *Moskovskie vedomosti,* May 30, 1862, 295–96, and Aug. 2, 1862, 1351–52;
Mogilevskie gubernskie vedomosti, Apr. 18, 1862.

33. *Russkii arkhiv,* 1901, kn. 2, vyp. 8, 561.

34. Kulomzin, *Vospominaniia mirovogo posrednika,* 19.

35. *Obzor deistvii Ministervstva vnutrennikh del po krest'ianskomu delu s ianvar-
iia 1861 po 19 fevraliia 1864 g.* (St. Petersburg, 1864), 17–18.

36. TsGIA, f. 1291, op. 36, d. 8a (chast' 1), l. 204–5; d. 8b (chast' 2); ll. 36 ob., 74.

37. *Sbornik pravitel'stvennykh rasporiazhenii,* vol. 4, chast' 2, 22–23; *Russkii arkhiv,* kn. 1, vyp. 1, 1892, 127.

38. A. A. Muromtsev, "Moi vospominanii o Viktore Antonoviche Artsimoviche,"
in *Viktor Antonovich Artsimovich,* 612; TsGAOR, f. 815 (V. A. Artsimovich), op. 1,
d. 433, ll. 1–2.

39. *Obshchestvenno-politicheskoe dvizhenie na Ukraine v 1863–1864,* vol. 1:
1856–1862 gg. (Kiev, 1963), 114.

40. Ibid., vol. 2: 1863–1864 (Kiev, 1964), 349.

41. *Sbornik dokumentov muzeiia grafa M. N. Murav'eva,* ed. A. Beletsii, vol. 1
(Vil'na, 1906), 229–33.

42. *Revoliutsionnyi pod'em v Litve i Belorussii v 1861–1862 gg.* (Moscow, 1964),
53; *Sbornik dokumentov muzeiia grafa M. N. Murav'eva,* 12.

43. *Polnoe sobranie zakonov,* ser. 2, vol. 33, sec. 1, no. 39354.

44. Borovkov, *Iz proshlogo,* 68.

45. S. N. Terpigorev, *Oskudenie: ocherki pomeshchich'ego razoreniia,* vol. 1 (Moscow, 1958), 276, 284.

46. See L. G. Zakharova, "Samoderzhavie, biurokratiia i reformy 60-kh godov xix
v. v Rossii," *Voprosy istorii,* 1989, no. 10, 18.

X

MUNICIPAL SELF-GOVERNMENT AFTER THE 1870 REFORM

Valeriia A. Nardova

Translated by Lori A. Citti

Changes in economic structure set Russia on a capitalist path and ultimately brought about the emancipation of the serfs in 1861.[1] The emanciation initiated a series of reforms designed to preserve the political structure of the Russian autocracy. Government leaders clearly understood that the peasant reform could not remain an isolated legislative act: "either we move along with the peasant question, or the country will move without us."[2] The reform of local government, especially the zemstvo reform, occupies an important place among the unavoidable changes following the emancipation. In turn, the zemstvo reform had a direct impact on the established system of municipal administration and ushered in a series of city reforms.

The issue of initiating city reforms had been growing for many years. The rapid growth of Russian cities and subsequent changes in the social structure of the urban population marked Russia's initial steps on the road to capitalism.[3] These demographic changes led to the growing influence of city centers on the economic, sociopolitical, and cultural life of the country. For this reason, questions of city administration which affected the national economy acquired particular significance. Up to the beginning of the 1870s, the City Charter of Catherine II (1785) remained the primary legal document regulating the structure of municipal administration. In reality, however, subsequent legislation had nullified several of Catherine's statutes and others simply ceased to exist; but officially, no changes were made. By the 1870s, this intricate and vague legislation no longer reflected the actual level of urban social and economic development.

Prior to the reform, Russian city government had no elected, representative body to carry out administrative functions. Adminstrative duties were performed by assemblies of the "urban elite" *(gorodskoe obshchestvo),* made up almost exclusively from the urban estates: merchants, honored citizens, tradesmen, and artisans. Peasants living in the city, members of the clergy, commoners *(raznochintsy),* and villagers were barred from participation in public affairs. An assembly of the entire "urban elite" was required, for example, in order to pass resolutions and elect an executive body. This arrangement testifies to the inherent inequalities embedded in the structure of urban administration before the reforms. By way of contrast, European municipal government at this time had already been organized on a representative basis. The Russian municipal representative body—the *duma,* or city council—consisted of several elected officials headed by the mayor. In effect, the city council exercised no real power and was completely dependent on the state administration.

By the beginning of the 1860s, St. Petersburg was the only city with a legislatively established municipal administration. In 1846, reform of the capital's municipal administration had reinforced the right of permanent residents to participate in city government. The right to participate in city elections was based not on estate but on property. In another important change, administrative functions were transferred from the "urban elite" to an elected assembly known as the General Council. The General Council was elected by estate and originally consisted of 750 members, 150 from each estate. The executive body, or Administrative Council, was elected not by an assembly of the urban estates as before but by the General Council. The duties of the executive and administrative bodies were clearly delineated, but the overall range of autonomous city self-government remained limited.

Serfdom left its mark on the 1846 reform. The organization of public administration in St. Petersburg was built upon a combination of bourgeois and estate principles; yet, despite all its inequalities, the reform represents a step forward in comparison with the structures of municipal government existing in other cities. In 1862–63, in response to petitions, the state extended administrative structures similar to those in St. Petersburg to Moscow, the second capital, and Odessa, an important trading port on the Black Sea.

With the capitalist development of the country, the further preservation of the existing dual system of city government proved unacceptable. In 1862 the Ministry of the Interior broached the question of city reform and received the tsar's approval. Originally the state put forth a half-hearted program outlining several improvements in the 1846 charter. However, by the beginning of the 1860s it had proved impossible for such a modest measure to attract wide public support. The ministry authorized the creation of special city commissions made up of local bureaucrats and representatives of the urban population. Their views concerning the projected reforms unarguably testify to the project's infeasibility. Given the current social and political situation, the government had no recourse but to take public opinion into consideration. The protracted discussion over the zemstvo reform proved influential in pushing directives for the city reform in a more progressive direction. Adopted in 1864 on the crest of the wave of public enthusiasm, the zemstvo reform engendered a fundamentally new type of social structure premised on all-estate representation, bourgeois property qualifications, and municipal autonomy over economic decisions. The earlier principles governing the zemstvo reform had been kept in mind during the preparation of the first project for the city statute, but with the completion of the zemstvo reform in 1864, officials received instructions to bring the municipal reform into accord with the provisions now in force in the zemstvo reforms.

The draft of a new municipal statute went much further than original government conceptions and moved significantly closer to bourgeois legal norms. In content the draft resembled other progressive reforms initiated at the beginning of the 1860s, such as the zemstvo and legal reforms. The draft principles included all-estate representation, bourgeois property qualifications, separation of administrative and executive powers, and self-government for the urban elite.

The first version of the draft, however, bore little resemblance to its final form. In 1870 the ministry finally approved a third draft and the measure passed into law. In all, preparations for the municipal reform dragged on for eight years. As government interaction with both zemstvo and city institutions undoubtedly shows, during these years a sharp shift in domestic policy provoked changes in the government's approach toward municipal self-government. In the 1860s the city councils of Petersburg, Moscow, and Odessa demonstrated the public's readiness to take up a significantly greater degree of city management than the government had intended. The government deemed tendencies to broaden the scope of city government as unacceptable, especially if they exceeded the boundaries of purely economic matters and weakened municipal dependence on the state administration.

The first time the draft was introduced to the State Council in December 1866, it languished there until the spring of 1867. After the attempt on the tsar's life in April 1866, the climate was not favorable for discussion of a proposed reform implementing principles of self-government. Nonetheless, the need for municipal reform was so pressing that the Ministry of the Interior could not refuse categorically to review the draft project before the tsar. Instead it worked to strengthen conservative tendencies in the future law through the revision of certain articles.

As a result, in the final version of the draft the City Statute assumed a more conservative tone and restricted character in comparison with reforms proposed at the beginning of the 1860s. Nonetheless, the governing principles of the Zemstvo Statute still served as the basis for the City Statute as well. Despite shifts in the internal political situation, the ruling elites remained interested in reorganizing the municipal administration and in laying the foundation for a more effective solution to city problems.

The municipal reforms of 1870 created all-estate institutions of local government. Administrative responsibilities now lay not in the hands of the urban elite but in a representative body—the duma. Elections to the city council occurred once every four years. The number of elected delegates was based on the number of eligible voters in the city and usually numbered from thirty to seventy-two persons. In the capital cities, however, the number of members elected to the city council was much greater: 180 in Moscow and 252 in Petersburg. The executive bodies of city government, the municipal board *(uprava)* and the mayor, served simultaneously as representatives of both the executive and the administrative bodies and were elected by the city council, not by the urban elite as before.

Voting rights were based on "bourgeois" property qualifications. Regardless of estate, city taxpayers owning immovable property and individuals paying specific duties on trade and industry received the right to participate in elections. Furthermore, legal entities such as various government agencies, institutions, associations, companies, churches, and monasteries also held voting rights. Men who had reached the age of twenty-five could vote, but women meeting the prescribed voter qualifications could participate in elections solely through the use of designated proxies. Hired laborers (the overwhelming majority of the population owning no real estate) were deprived of the right to vote, as were educated white-collar people such as engineers, physicians, teachers, and bureaucrats. In essence, voting rights were denied to all who did not own their own homes.

Throughout the entire life of the municipal statute of 1870, the pages of the liberal press bandied back and forth the issue of granting the franchise to persons leasing apartments above a certain rent level. The press emphasized the paradoxical situation created by the lack of an established minimum for property qualification. Under statute provisions, voting rights were granted to indigent owners of hovels and hawkers' stands who paid a kopek for the right to peddle goods. At the same time, sufficiently well-off people renting expensive, comfortably appointed apartments were denied the franchise, even though many of them, thanks to education and professional competence, could have made a real contribution to society as members of city government.

We should note that many people circumvented the law, however, by buying "certificates of small trade" or by acquiring practically worthless real estate. For example, the famous scholar and jurist Boris N. Chicherin was a permanent resident of Tambov and did not meet the necessary property qualifications to participate in Moscow elections. Having made the decision to run for election as mayor of Moscow, he bought a ramshackle hut on the outskirts of the city. As a property owner, he then received the formal right to register as a voter in Moscow. Because the affair concerned such a well-known personality, the press could not let Chicherin's election as mayor go unnoticed. The press quickly exposed how Chicherin had succeeded in "suddenly, through circuitous means, becoming a Moscow citizen."[4]

As for the question of a precise minimum property qualification, the legislators sought instead to adopt measures limiting poor townsmen's influence on the elections. The state proposed the principle of "proportional participation" in city government based on the "number of taxpayers." Modeled after the Prussian Municipal Code, the proposal grouped voters according to the so-called three-curia system. The crux of the code hinged on the fact that the register of voters was drawn up in order of decreasing amounts of taxes paid to the city budget. This sequence divided voters into three numerically unequal groups, the size of each category being determined by the amount of city tax payments. Each of the three categories had the right to elect an equal number of members. Therefore a mere handful of the most well-off (who accounted for one-third of the tax payments) sent as many representatives to city government as the majority of poorer taxpayers lumped together in the ranks of the third category. Take, for example, the picture provided by the first election to the St. Petersburg city council. The first category consisted of 202 persons, the second of 705; the remaining 15,233 voters made up the third category. Each category elected up to 84 deputies. As a result, one city council deputy represented every 2.4 voters in the first category, every 8.4 voters in the second, and every 181.3 voters in the third.[5]

The management of city finances fell to the new city institutions. The state administration transferred a broad range of responsibilities dealing with city finance and management to the municipal government, including water works, sewage, lighting improvements, transportation, the maintenance of city parks, city planning, and so forth. The city council also assumed responsibility for maintaining social welfare by providing assistance that guaranteed food; adopting measures against fire and other accidents; preserving public health through the construction of hospitals and assistance to the police in carrying out sanitary and hygienic measures; taking steps against indigence; and disseminating public education through city schools, museums, and the like.

Agencies of city self-government enjoyed autonomy within their designated framework of activity.[6] The provincial administration's supervisory powers were reduced to verifying the legality of measures taken by the municipality. Legally restricting municipal duma activities to the sphere of economic *(khoziaistvennye)* affairs, the autocracy also took preventive steps to ensure that municipal government did not exceed its authority. In particular the state was concerned that the duma might serve as a tribune for the opposition.

The first draft of the city statute contained an article providing for the creation of an executive body accountable to the city council but retaining the right to veto council decisions. In effect the executive supervised the activities of the administrative body of the city duma. As a result of further changes in the statute, the conservative, status-quo tendencies in the project became more pronounced. In particular the State Council changed the provision providing separate presidents for administrative and executive bodies, concluding that, as the "best guarantee against illegal resolutions both in the city duma and in the city administration," it would be in the state's interest to merge the two posts by strengthening the authority of the city mayor.

With the same goal in mind, the mayor was given the right to prevent the execution of duma measures he deemed illegal.

Conservatives endeavored to secure broader rights of intervention into the activities of the city council. At one of the last legislative stages in producing the statute—a meeting of the joint departments of the State Council—a resolution passed creating local inspectorates to review the activities of the municipal public administration and provincial business affairs. The inspectorates not only retained the authority to approve or veto council proposals but also held the right to propose resolutions on existing issues. Even the Ministry of the Interior had not dared consider taking such extreme measures to limit the city administration's autonomous agencies. Minister of the Interior A. E. Timashev declared that such sweeping powers "would undermine that autonomy in municipal finances and construction assigned to the city administration in the charter's articles, and in that respect, the City Statute effectively deviated from the Statute on Zemstvo Institutions."[7] A general meeting of the State Council found it undesirable to give two bodies of local public administration such disproportionate rights, and it was decided not to give provincial offices the right to intervene directly in the affairs of city government.

As already explained, the reform resulted from, and to a large degree satisfied the requisites for, Russia's capitalist development. For its time, the reform undoubtedly represented a progressive legal act. However, because it had been prepared by the autocratic bureaucracy, the reform remained limited and half-hearted. In the final version of the charter, none of the proposals to strengthen the position of the bodies of city self-government was adopted. The authority of autonomous bodies extended solely to the sphere of economic activities, and although municipal institutions were given autonomy in this area, in general their actual ability to exert influence over city finances was narrowly circumscribed due to their limited budgetary powers.[8] It is impossible to determine what effect the lack of an enforcement arm had on municipal activities. Municipal institutions could only enforce their instructions through the state police. This serious defect in the Municipal Statute came about due to the incomplete implementation of the principle of separation of executive and administrative powers. Finally, the electoral law remained fundamentally undemocratic. In many ways these basic aspects of the Municipal Statute predetermined the condition and scope of the city council's activities and shaped the further development of city self-government.

Many public figures and commentators viewed the Municipal Charter of 1870 as merely a first step, to be followed by subsequent laws strengthening the scope of city self-government. As a whole, the public received the reform favorably and placed great hope in it. The public anxiously awaited decisive changes in municipal finances and management from the new agencies of the city administration. Quite logically, these expectations included establishing broader autonomy, the separation of public agencies from the power of the state administration, and the enhancement of their authority and influence in society.[9]

According to the Imperial Decree to the State Senate, only those cities within the Russian territory, Siberia, and Bessarabia fell under the jurisdiction of the law of June 16, 1870. For this reason, the new Municipal Statute was not introduced in all cities of the country simultaneously. The statute went into effect immediately in forty-one provinces and regions and in four port cities important in terms of trade and military considerations. In 1872, laws adapting the Municipal Statute to the capitals and Odessa were adopted. In comparison with the law of June 16, 1870, these changes concerned basic procedural issues and, above all, addressed the need to simplify the functioning mechanism of the city council in major cities with the greatest number of elected members. At the same time, the new law also took into account that the volume of activities in these city administrations was much greater than in other cities.

City council and municipal board elections were the most important features in the realization of the city reforms. Given the councils' powers of independent decision making in economic affairs and independence from the local state administrative-police apparatus, their composition caused the government particular anxiety. In implementing what was essentially a bourgeois reform, the imperial government was being far from consistent. Obliged to acknowledge the growing power of the urban bourgeoisie, the state government tried, as far as possible, to attenuate middle-class influence by opening the elections to voters outside the merchant stratum. To accomplish this, the government tried to attract the nobility into municipal self-government. The autocracy tried to preserve the influence of the class which provided its social bases of support, the nobility, and in this respect the city reform was similar to other bourgeois reforms. Simultaneously, the state pursued the goal of limiting, as far as possible, the access of the nonpropertied, poor stratum of the urban population to the city council.

To evaluate the degree to which the election law fulfilled the hopes of its creators, it is necessary to examine the election results. The Central State Historical Archive in Leningrad has preserved valuable sources for studying the composition of the electorate and municipal public institutions for practically the entire period covering the life of the 1870 Municipal Charter's activity. The Ministry of Interior required uniform statistical reports on elections from all cities. The author has analyzed statistical summaries on elections from the fourth four-year term (1883–84) in the capitals, provincial centers, and major port cities where the City Statute went into effect immediately. The statistics show that, according to the new electoral law, participation in elections was limited to a negligibly small proportion of the urban population. The average percentage of voters (among the residents of forty cities) who participated in the elections was only 5.5 percent. That suggests a pattern: with the increase in the size of the city, the percentage of citizens given the franchise had a tendency to decrease.[10] This can be explained by the fact that in large cities a greater proportion of the inhabitants, such as hired laborers, students, and intellectuals, did not own real estate. In St. Petersburg, of 861,000 residents, only 16,000 (1.9 percent) had voting rights. Statistical data for the forty cities covered by the statute can be supplemented by information on the number of individuals in 501 cities included on the register of eligible voters for the first electoral period. In cities with populations over 20,000, the average percentage of voters did not exceed 4 percent of the general population; 10.4 percent of the urban residents held franchise rights in cities with populations under 5,000.

In the opinion of many prerevolutionary writers, in small cities dominated by the *meshchanstvo,* voting rights actually came close to being general.[11] But analysis of the statistical material does not confirm such an assertion.

The distribution of voters according to type of tax payments allows us to analyze the social composition of the city electoral assembly. The nobility and the clergy (except for *meshchane* and *raznochintsy*) paid taxes on real estate and can be considered landowners in the pure sense. The number of merchants in this group remained insignificant. Individuals paying taxes on trade, and sometimes on both trade certificates and land, made up one single "trade and industry group." This group consisted of the high and the middle bourgeoisie, primarily merchants; the petty bourgeoisie were dispersed across various estates such as the meshchane, peasants, and artisans. The number of voters who received voting privileges based on the payment of taxes for trade certificates also included members of the nobility employed in capitalist free enterprise.

The great majority of city residents granted the franchise were property owners.[12] In those cities included in this study, landowners made up from 60 to 92 percent of the voters. Even in developing trade and industrial centers such as Odessa and Kharkov, taxpayers whose franchise was based on property taxes enjoyed a significant numerical advantage. St. Petersburg represents the sole exception to this rule. There the industrial class made up 76 percent of the voters. It might seem that given such a proportional correlation between the two categories of voters, homeowners would have enjoyed a numerical preponderance. But in fact, matters turned out differently. The outcome of the elections was affected decisively by unequal rates of participation by different blocs of voters. We must bear in mind that the number of voters exercising their right to vote was extremely small. Given the high level of absenteeism apparent in both categories of voters, the industrial class without exception took significantly greater interest in the elections in all cities. The average percentage of active voters from the trade and industry group reached 29.9, while the landowners eligible to vote in each category made up only 9.1 percent of the electorate. Naturally this correlation of forces could not help but affect the results of city elections. The estate composition of forty city councils was as follows: the first category (consisting of nobility, clergy, and raznochintsy) made up 33.2 percent of the elected members; the second category (the merchant class) provided

53.7 percent of the members; and the third category (*meshchane,* artisans, and peasants) accounted for 13.1 percent of the members.[13]

One-third of the seats in the city councils were occupied by members elected from the first curia. We can tentatively label this group the noble-bureaucratic bloc. Since only a sprinkling of the clergy and raznochintsy were included among the homeowners, due to their professional affiliations they were predominantly affiliated with the bureaucracy. The high proportion of elected members from the first category, when compared with its proportional weight in the urban population, testifies to their eagerness to take part in municipal government. It also reflects a flight of the nobility from the countryside to the city that began after the reforms.

The proportion of the merchant class in the city councils reached almost 54 percent of all elected members. However, as our calculations have shown, the proportion of seats occupied by persons engaged in trade and industry was significantly higher than that of the merchant estate per se—approximately 68 percent. This information is particularly revealing. It reflects the disintegration of estates and the ongoing process of class formation. For example, it turns out that approximately one-fifth of the nobility elected to the city councils paid duties for trading certificates. Thus the interests of the nobility sitting on the city councils could not but have coincided with those of the merchants. Apparently, in evaluating the results of the elections the bureaucracy issued only figures showing estate representation in the city councils. But even on this basis alone, the state considered the relative weight of the nobility insufficient and was dissatisfied with the results.

The estate affiliation of elected members in each of the three propertied categories remained highly important for the government. Such a distribution had to serve as proof of the effectiveness of the three-curia system, which the state perceived as a barrier preventing voters from the lower classes from penetrating municipal government. This system, as already stated, emphasized the civic inequality of voters assigned to different categories. The average statistics for forty cities prove that in the 1883–84 elections, in the first category one council member was elected for every 2.4 voters; in the second, one for every 8.4 voters; and in the third, one for every 181.3 voters.[14] Information on specific cities not only brings out the unequal number of voters per category but also makes obvious the small number included in the first category. According to the voter registry, in only half of the cities did the number of voters in the first category exceed the number of members to be elected by two times or more. Given voter absenteeism, in practice the twofold quota was maintained only in certain cities. For example, in Tula the twenty-five voters in the first category had to elect twenty-four members and it would seem such occurrences in city elections were common.[15]

Did the three-curia system justify the expectations of the government? To evaluate this question, we must look at the distribution of the elected delegates according to category. Of 2,940 elected members in forty city councils, the first category accounts for 759, the second for 1,031, and the third for 1,051 (39 percent of the total). Electors of the third curia, who represented a far larger bloc of voters than did delegates in the other two curia, made up only 39 percent of the members elected to the duma. Thus the three-curia system undoubtedly played its prescribed role by limiting participation by small property owners in the city council, but even the third category's modest representation of voters was too much for the ruling elite. To aggravate the situation, it soon became obvious that the three-curia system worked in favor of the merchant class.

Less detailed statistical sources provide information for a greater number of cities and confirm the basic conclusions drawn from our forty cities. Election results displeased the ruling elite. By the beginning of the 1880s, cities were compelled to reexamine the election laws. The review was designed to guarantee weakening of the influence of the bourgeoisie in city administration, exclusion of the lower classes in urban society from the elections, and inclusion of townspeople not owning real estate, the so-called apartment renters, in the ranks of those receiving "half-rights."

The municipal reform created institutions of a completely new character and with new duties. With the reform, the functions carried out by public administrative bodies underwent fundamental changes. If earlier their responsibilities centered on levying taxes and collections, carrying out various types of duties, and subsidizing a series of government institutions, now the city government moved into purely municipal affairs. The state abdicated all responsibility for the development and management of city finances. The state gradually concentrated responsibility for public services such as city planning and maintenance *(blagoustroistvo)*, municipal health and sanitation, transportation, elementary education, and medical services in the hands of city government agencies.

In the twenty years from 1871 to 1890, city revenues grew from nineteen million to fifty-six million rubles. In 1871, ten cities had revenues exceeding 200,000 rubles, and in 1890, forty-three cities exceeded that amount. The opportunities were now greater for meeting city needs, such as lighting, sewer systems, and waterworks. In truth, cities did not have complete discretion in the distribution of their monetary resources. A significant part of the city budget was designated for "obligatory expenditures." In 1890 up to 22 percent of the budget went for the support of the police, military posts, lighting and heating prisons, and so forth. Expenditures for the support of hospitals, charities, and education were considered "optional." But it was precisely in these areas that the city councils achieved their greatest success. In 1871 city councils funded charities to the amount of 581,000 rubles and schools in the amount of 500,000 rubles. By 1890, expenditures in these areas had reached 5.2 million and 4.7 million rubles respectively.

In St. Petersburg several striking changes occurred in a relatively short period, particularly in the area of public education. In 1877, when the St. Petersburg municipal administration assumed the right to manage city elementary schools, only sixteen state-supported, one-room schools existed. In 1883 the number of city elementary schools was 156 and in 1893, 300. The St. Petersburg city council allocated one-tenth of its discretionary resources to education in city schools. With the goal of disseminating culture and enlightenment among the lower-class adult population, the St. Petersburg city council embarked on several undertakings, such as opening Sunday schools and free city reading rooms. With varying success, similar projects were carried out in other cities throughout the country.

Of course, truly significant progress in the development of the municipal economy remained impossible. Many of the city governments' projects remained unrealized dreams. General city interests were often sacrificed to a claque of city bosses; there were abuses in the distribution of municipal funds; and the majority of the elected council members were characteristically indifferent.[16] Many of the city council's deficiencies can be explained by the lack of a tradition encouraging participation in municipal affairs. But the primary defect in the Municipal Statute of 1870 was that although it singled out a broad range of obligations and placed great responsibilities on the new public institutions, it did not create favorable conditions for implementation. We must also bear in mind the limited budgets, the absence of a mechanism of compulsion, and the lack of experience at working with the local bureaucracy. Nonetheless, city government was not inactive. At the close of the 1880s, liberal society regained influence and spoke up in defense of municipal self-government. Liberals stressed that it was not surprising that city government had accomplished so little, but rather, given the circumstances, that it had achieved any results at all.[17]

The City Statute of 1870 strictly limited the scope of the municipal administration to economic *(khoziaistvennye)* affairs. Legally, this ruled out any manifestation whatsoever of political activity. Besides, the merchant classes with their inherent political indifference predominated in the majority of the city councils. In many ways this fact shaped the political character of city councils' activities. During the 1870s and 1880s, speeches or declarations on political matters were rare within the dumas' walls. The liberal address of the Moscow city council in 1870 and the speech of Moscow's mayor Boris N. Chicherin on the occasion of Alexander III's coronation in 1883 must be considered among those rare episodes in the history of city self-government. The Moscow address of 1870 was written on the initiative of a group of Slavophiles who played an influential role in the city council. It raised the issue of liberal reforms, meaning essentially freedom of speech, press, and religion. Alexander II interpreted the very desire to undertake further reforms as an attack on the absolute powers of the autocracy, and scandal ensued. The mayor of Moscow, Prince V. A. Cherkasskii, was forced to resign. The government's reaction is explained not only by the content and tone of the document but also by the fact that the proposal had originated in the city council, an institution which up to that time had played no role in the political life of the country.

The speech given by Chicherin at a banquet for city mayors in May 1883 evoked a similar response. The mayor expressed the hope that this meeting of mayors "would not pass without leaving a trace" but would serve instead as "a beginning of the unification of zemstvo men." Higher state circles strongly disapproved of Chicherin's speech, which they regarded as "constitutional." They explained to Chicherin that His Imperial Highness regarded the mayor's actions "out of line," and he was dismissed. The situation in the Moscow city council deteriorated. Several nominees to the post of mayor in the pending election were not confirmed in office.

In 1884 Chicherin was once again elected to the council. At the very first meeting of the new group on December 29, 1884, the members expressed their gratitude to Chicherin for his previous service to the city. The ruling circles, for good reason, interpreted this act as a demonstration of antigovernment sentiment. With undisguised worry, the government awaited the mayoral election in January 1885. Almost daily the Moscow governor-general reported to St. Petersburg on the council's mood and on his fear that Chicherin would be nominated. Despite the measures taken by the governor-general, Chicherin's name was included on the ballot; however, at the very last moment he refused to run.

The liberal address of 1870 and the Chicherin affair can be taken as the most significant incidents of the intrusion of city councils into the political arena. In truth, during these two episodes the speeches of individual elected members did justify the state bureaucracy in considering them antigovernmental. In St. Petersburg, discussions concerning a proposal to elect former minister of the interior M. T. Loris-Melikov an honorary citizen of the city attracted the state's attention. During the course of the discussion, the council members allowed critical debate on recent internal policies of the government. Several of the speeches were extremely critical. The government took every measure within its power to guarantee that information about the goings-on in the St. Petersburg city council did not appear in the press.[18] It is known that in certain provincial city councils oppositional sentiment mounted. After the death of Emperor Alexander II, for example, a proposal introducing a Russian constitution was brought forth in the city of Nikolaev.

In general, the city councils over a twenty-year period did not overstep or even try to exceed the boundaries of their designated economic activities. Nonetheless, misunderstandings between the city governments and the state administration gradually arose. In an overwhelming majority of cases, the provincial administration continued to see itself as the sole "master of the province," equally subordinating both local bureaucrats and the leaders of the new municipal government agencies. This high-handedness undercut the standing of the city leaders and often caused serious conflicts between governors and city mayors. At the beginning of 1873, as a result of just such conflicts, the mayors of Moscow, Riazan, and Perm submitted their resignations.[19]

The state government did not always support the local bureaucracy in such altercations. In the majority of cases, however, the state decisively censured the city councils' slightest attempts to increase their influence at the expense of the bureaucracy. At all levels of the bureaucracy the tendency was to work to reduce the influence of the city council to nothing, particularly when the council concerned itself with general city interests going beyond the scope of purely economic activities. A request by the St. Petersburg city council to borrow three thousand rubles for the funeral of the famous Russian author Ivan S. Turgenev, who had died in France, was considered illegal and transferred to the provincial administration.

Conflicts between city governments and the state bureaucracy sometimes were quite bitter and proved extremely embarrassing for the state government. At the beginning of the 1880s, a dispute arose between the St. Petersburg city council and the Ministry of the Interior over a review of the city budget. The conflict continued for several years, and, in the end, the city council appealed against the minister of the interior to the State Senate. Government circles viewed this act as extraordinary.

As already noted, the city governments in actuality seldom ventured beyond narrow economic concerns. But within the range of duties permitted them, the city councils tried to act with complete autonomy, independent of the powers of the bureaucratic apparatus. The limits of the councils' authority were vaguely defined, and this situation led to interminable conflicts over jurisdiction on management issues. Furthermore, the provincial authorities often violated clearly spelled-out terms of the law as well. Administrative abitrariness reached its height in the second half of the 1880s. In 1888 a conflict arose between the Odessa city government and the local state administration. The governor-general of Odessa, Kh. Kh. Roop, considered hospital affairs outside the provenance of the city government and attempted to force a new statute concerning city hospitals on it. In response to objections from the city council, Roop issued an "obligatory decree" introducing the new statute and turning hospital control over to the police administration. When he received a delegation from the city, Roop announced that he was prepared to use extreme measures and deploy force in order to establish order. He threatened anyone who opposed his decisions on city management with administrative exile.

Even the government disapproved of Roop's blatant contempt for the law. The minister of the interior, D. A. Tolstoi, who could hardly be considered sympathetic to the city government, reported to the tsar that the activities of the Odessa governor-general were "not in accordance with the City Statute" and requested instructions to countermand the orders issued by Roop. In response to Tolstoi's request, the tsar wrote that "the governor-general's orders, of course, are illegal, but there is nothing else that he can do. The city council serves no one and has become too arrogant." The tsar proposed that the orders of the Odessa governor-general "temporarily remain in force."[20] This episode convincingly testifies to the fact that under the autocratic regime the rights of city self-government were tenuous indeed.

The gradual shift from tolerating self-government can be traced in the changing stance of the government on the issue of confirming elected city leaders in office. According to the Municipal Statute, in cities which were not provincial capitals, mayors and their replacements were approved by governors; in provincial capitals they were approved by the minister of the interior; and in both capitals by the tsar. During the 1870s the government refrained from interfering in city council decisions, even when, for whatever reason, the candidate for mayor did not suit the state administration. The only basis for vetoing a candidate was if the elections had not followed the formal requirements outlined in the Municipal Statute. By the first half of the 1880s, however, confirmation in office became completely abitrary. The refusal to approve the famous journalist and editor of the liberal *Vestnik Evropy,* M. M. Stasiulevich, as an assistant to the St. Petersburg mayor serves as an example. Stasiulevich had been elected to the city council twice. He took an active part in council activities and, in May 1884, was elected to the post of deputy mayor. However, Minister of the Interior Tolstoi refused to approve the appointment "in light of the fact that M. M. Stasiulevich's way of thinking and actions do not correspond to the goals of the government." The tsar confirmed the decision.[21] That same year the state refused to confirm the selection of the former exile B. N. Shostakovich (grandfather of the composer Dmitri D. Shostakovich) to the position of deputy mayor for the city of Tomsk. Similar incidents occurred in subsequent years.

At the end of 1880s the notion that city government was incapable of solving serious urban economic issues enjoyed widespread currency within the state administration. Accusations of this sort leveled at specific dumas in a number of instances served as the basis for violating one of the cardinal tenets of the Municipal Statute, the election of city governments. The circumvention of this basic criterion of self-government resulted in the practice of appointing city mayors according to the government's dictates.

The city councils by no means stood idly by when the state adminstration trammeled on their rights. Council protests against this breach of the City Statute were not always passive, and many went beyond mere formal complaints to the Senate. The protests took many forms, such as the repeated election of people who had not been confirmed by the government and demonstrative disruptions of elections.

Many conflicts arising in the 1870s and 1880s between the state administration and agencies of muncipal government were largely ignored by society at large. Although the causes of the conflicts often seem insignificant, they nonetheless provoked deep concern on the part of the administration. Each conflict attracted the government's undivided attention. The state considered any incident of noncompliance with demands by the local bureaucracy oppositional, and thereby illegal activity. In all of these petty incidents, the squabbles are extremely telling. They testify to the fact that contrary to existing opinion, the city councils often "incited rebellion." During the course of the conflicts, political developments within the new institutions revealed the rudiments of political consciousness, of a corporate identity among elected council members and the councils' readiness to oppose the monarchy's bureaucratic apparatus.

The state's attitude toward city government changed over time. For the first decade after the reforms, the central bureaucracy assumed a protective attitude toward the municipal administration. But even during these years the ruling elite doggedly avoided any legal changes in the Municipal Statute that might enhance city self-government. The autocracy viewed the Municipal Statute as the final limit of permissible concessions. Therefore many of the basic flaws in the law of 1870 cannot be viewed as the results of oversight or accident; they reflected the state's original intent to accommodate municipal self-government within the structure of the autocratic regime.

At the end of the 1870s and the beginning of the 1880s, new public awareness forced the ruling elites to take unavoidable steps to resolve the problems confronting city government. A commission headed by M. S. Kakhanov prepared a project outlining partial changes for the electoral law of 1882. But scarcely had the government succeeded in establishing its position in these matters when all further activity in this area was cut off.

In the 1880s the state advanced a series of legal proposals to limit self-government. In 1886 Minister of the Interior Tolstoi presented a comprehensive program reviewing the municipal reforms of the 1860s and 1870s. Tolstoi's "counterreforms" attempted to maximize the city government's subordination to the bureaucratic apparatus of the autocracy. First Tolstoi proposed expanding the Ministry of the Interior's authority to oversee the activities of zemstvo, city, and peasant institutions. Then he attempted to limit "the elective principle" by creating a system of state appointments to local government. At the same time he sought to expand the nobility's participation in local government. The reorganization of city government was to take shape after the adoption of the peasant and zemstvo reforms, and the city reforms were to conform to the spirit, as well as the letter, of the new zemstvo reforms.

The need for a basic reform of city government was substantiated by the indefensibility of trying to maintain the former status of municipal institutions, given the changes wrought by the zemstvo reforms and the unsatisfactory conduct of city management. The state's reasons for revision may be found in the unwarranted autonomy assumed by the city councils, the inadequacy of state supervision, and the nobility's feeble participation in city government. Changing the distribution of forces, particularly increasing the participation of the nobility, became one of the major goals in revising the Municipal Statute.

Adopted on June 11, 1892, the counterreform marked the end of a definite stage in state policy toward municipal self-government. The revolutionary situation of the 1860s and 1870s had forced the ruling elite to the edge of an abyss, and the reforms provided a ledge upon which the government could regain a foothold. In addition, the government itself was concerned to adapt the autocratic order to new economic conditions and therefore was interested in achieving positive results with the reforms. The city reform had an essentially bourgeois character, but its implementation had been far from consistent. As already stated, the Municipal Statute did not create the conditions necessary for success on the part of city institutions. The ruling elite's unwillingness to enter on a path of reform, which would have guaranteed solutions to the problems confronting it, serves as one of the most telling aspects of the crisis of the Russian autocracy.

NOTES

This essay is based on excerpts from V. A. Nardova, *Gorodskoe samoupravlenie v Rossii v 60-kh-nachala 90-kh godov XIX veka* (Leningrad, 1984).

1. See Walter Hanchett, "Tsarist Statutory Regulation of Municipal Government in the Nineteenth Century," in Michael Hamm, ed., *The City in Russian History* (Lexington, Ky., 1976), 91–114.

2. TsGIA, f. 1961, no. 1, s. 80, "Zapiska P. A. Valueva Aleksandru II."

3. V. N. Mironov, "Russkii gorod vo vtoroi polovine XVIII–pervoi polovine XIX veka," *Istorii SSSR,* 1988, no. 4, 150–68.

4. *Otechestvennye zapiski,* 1882 no. 4, 206 (163).

5. Nardova, *Gorodskoe samuopravlenie,* 75.

6. Article 5 of *Gorodskoe Polozhenie.*

7. *Materials Relating to the New Public Administration (Ustroitsvo) in Imperial Cities* (St. Petersburg, 1877), vol. 3, 461.

8. Nardova, *Gorodskoe samoupravlenie,* 49.

9. Ibid.

10. Ibid., table 2a, 62–63.

11. G. I. Shreider, *Nashe gorodskoe obshchestvennoe upravlenie* (Moscow, 1902), vol. 1, 62; A. G. Mikhailovskii, *Reforma gorodskogo samoupravleniia v Rossii* (Moscow, 1908), 19. According to the information for the period under consideration, in those states where general electoral rights existed, for example in France, the percentage of eligible men reached 25–30 percent of the population.

12. Nardova, *Gorodskoe samoupravlenie,* table 4, 66–68.

13. Ibid., table 6, 70.

14. Ibid., table 8, 75.

15. Ibid., table 9, 76.

16. For more on the indifference of city council members, see Anatole Leroy-Beaulieu, *Empire of the Tsars and the Russians* (New York, 1969), vol. 2, 235.

17. V. A. Nardova, "Gorodskoe samoupravlenie v zhurnalistike 70-80-kh gg. XIX veka," *Obshchestvennaia mysl' v Rossii* (Leningrad, 1986), 159–80.

18. P. A. Valuev, *Dnevnik. 1877–1884* (Petrograd, 1919), 167.

19. Nardova, "Gorodskoe samoupravlenie," 168.

20. Pavel A. Zaionchkovskii, *Rossiiskoe samoderzhavie v kontse XIX stoletiia* (Moscow, 1970), 157–58.

21. TsGIA, f. 1284, op. 241, d. 86, l. 144.

XI

CROWNING THE EDIFICE

THE ZEMSTVO, LOCAL
SELF-GOVERNMENT, AND
THE CONSTITUTIONAL MOVEMENT,
1864–1881

Fedor A. Petrov

Translated by Robin Bisha

The history of the zemstvo has long attracted the attention of researchers. Before 1917 a considerable literature was published on it; the best of these publications is the unsurpassed work of B. B. Veselovskii, *Forty Years in the History of the Zemstvo* (4 vols., St. Petersburg, 1909–11). Since the late 1950s Russian historians have often turned to the history of the zemstvo. V. V. Garmiza and L. G. Zakharova published monographs devoted to the preparation of the zemstvo reform of 1864 and the zemstvo counterreform of 1890; E. G. Kornilov and N. M. Pirumova wrote on the activities of the zemstvo democratic intelligentsia; and many others described the history of individual zemstvos.[1] American researchers have also taken up the history of local self-government. S. Frederick Starr and Thomas Pearson published monographs, and Terence Emmons and Wayne Vucinich edited a collection of articles on the history of the zemstvo. Bruce Lincoln's monograph deals with the zemstvo reform in the context of the other Great Reforms.[2]

These works concentrate on the *preparation* of the zemstvo reform or on certain aspects of the activities of the zemstvo institutions. Recently scholars have turned to another question in the study of self-government in prerevolutionary Russia: the zemstvo and its place in the state apparatus. This can be elucidated only by tracing the zemstvo reform in practice and the first steps of the zemstvo in the political arena. This essay is an attempt at such an analysis; it also introduces little-known archival materials.

The abolition of serfdom unavoidably entailed alterations in the governing mechanism of autocratic Russia. In the 1860s reformers did not consider complete alteration of the autocratic-bureaucratic system but rather the introduction into that system of an all-estate institution of self-government— the zemstvo. Liberal publicists bitterly joked that "new wine was poured into old bottles." The power of the Russian emperor remained unlimited, and the higher state institutions retained their feudal character. However, the reform placed elective agencies which had an independent sphere of activity alongside the local institutions of state administration.

On January 1, 1864, Alexander II approved the Statute on Provincial and District *(Uezd)* Zemstvo Institutions, which introduced the zemstvo. This statute remained in force a quarter century, until the Statute of 1890 (the Zemstvo counterreform). The introduction of institutions of local self-government was a significant step on the path of political education of a country in which the majority of the population had only recently been emancipated from serfdom. Elected by the various estates of Russian society, the zemstvo institutions differed in principle from such corporate-estate organizations as the noble assemblies. Advocates of serfdom were indignant that "yesterday's slave sits next to his former owner" on the bench of the zemstvo assembly. And it is true that members of various estates were called upon to serve in the zemstvos—nobles, bureaucrats, clergy, merchants, industrialists, lower-class urban people, peasants.

According to the Statute of 1864 all electors were divided into three curiae. The first curia consisted of uezd landholders, including those who owned at least 200 desiatinas of land, other immovable property with a value of not less than 15,000 rubles, or trade and industrial enterprises with an annual income of 6,000 rubles or more. This curia also included small land-holders who held one-twentieth of the full qualification. Not only noble landholders were allowed into this curia but also landowners of other estates, including peasants. Merchants of the first and second guilds took part in the second curia, as did owners of urban immovable property valued at 500 to 3,000 rubles.

There was no property qualification for participation in the elections to the third curia, the rural societies. However, these elections were indirect. In the *volost'* assemblies, peasants selected electors who went on to special meetings to elect delegates. In this way the institutions of peasant self-government created in 1861 were willy-nilly built into the structure of all-estate local self-government. Landowners and parish priests also had the right to be elected from this curia.

Uezd zemstvo assemblies determined the number of delegates elected from each curia by their own formulae. As a result, the representation of the estates in the institutions of local self-government was not proportionate to their representation in the Russian population.

Thus in the first elections to the uezd zemstvos, on average, gentry made up 41.7 percent, clergy 6.5 percent, merchants 10.4 percent, and peasants

38.4 percent. Insofar as the delegates to the provincial assemblies were selected rather than directly elected from the membership of the uezd zemstvo assemblies, it is not difficult to see that the landed gentry would dominate. Of the 2,055 delegates to provincial assemblies (for the same period), nobles and bureaucrats made up 74.2 percent, clergy 3.8 percent, merchants 10.9 percent, and peasants 10.6 percent.

Later, in the central, southern, and southeastern provinces, the industrial and new landowning bourgeoisie from the merchant estate and peasantry began to gradually displace the nobility in the uezd zemstvos. L. G. Zakharova provides some statistics which analyze this process in detail.[3] So, for example, the proportion of merchants in the uezd zemstvo assemblies of Kostroma Province increased over twenty years from 9.8 percent to 25.4 percent, of Nizhnii Novgorod from 7.2 to 14.5, of Vladimir from 16.3 to 29.1, and of Moscow from 14.9 to 23.9. Representation of peasant landholders in the assembly of Tauride Province increased from 1 percent to 14.1 percent, and of Saratov from 0.9 to 5.4. While the percentage of gentry delegates to provincial assemblies increased overall (in 1883–86 it reached 81.6), especially in Kursk, Poltava, Samara, and several other provinces, the number of gentry delegates to the Moscow provincial zemstvo assembly declined by almost 7 percent. And in the provincial zemstvos of northeastern European Russia, Olonetsk, Vologda, Viatka, and Perm, the gentry were a minority of the delegates. Russian publicists called them "peasant zemstvos."

Delegates met annually in provincial and uezd capitals for regular zemstvo assemblies (there were also extraordinary sessions). The chairman of these meetings was the local marshal of the nobility, evidence that the nobility retained a leading role in the activities of the all-estate institutions of self-government. These assemblies elected the executive organ of the zemstvo, the zemstvo board, and its chairman (who could be from any social estate). This board managed the day-to-day activities of the zemstvo. The governor approved the chairman of the uezd zemstvo board, and the minister of internal affairs approved the provincial chairman.

The activities of the new institutions of all-estate self-government were limited to economic and cultural affairs. The zemstvo worked in the fields of communications, medicine, popular education (activity in this sphere was supposed to be limited to expenses for the construction and creation of schools, since the Ministry of Education retained control of the educational process), and charity. It cooperated in the development of local trade and industry, supported peasant crafts, and so on. The zemstvo had the right to petition the government "in areas of economic needs and benefit to the province and uezd."[4]

The government created conditions by which the zemstvos received the slighting appellation "the fifth wheel of the cart" of the Russian governmental apparatus. As can be seen, the new institutions of all-estate self-government were introduced only at the level of the province and uezd. There was no central zemstvo representation; neither were there small zemstvo units in the volosts. Contemporaries wittily called the zemstvo "a building without a foundation or a roof," and the slogan "the crowning of the edifice" became from that time the main slogan of Russian liberals for forty years, right up to the creation of the state duma. The government kept local administrative and political power in its own hands, and the institutions of local self-government were forced to turn to government officials to fulfill their resolutions and to collect zemstvo dues. Moreover, according to the 1864 statute the governor had the right "to stop the fulfillment of any resolution of the zemstvo institutions which was against the law and the general welfare" (article 7).

Up to the beginning of the twentieth century the establishment of new institutions of self-government was limited to thirty-four provinces of European Russia. Zemstvo institutions were not introduced in the Baltic provinces, Belorussia, the right bank Ukraine, the Caucasus, Central Asia, Astrakhan and Arkhangel'sk provinces, Siberia, or the Far East. In 1876 a zemstvo opened in the area of the Don Cossacks, but within six years it was closed.

And so in all respects, including geography and sphere of competence, the reach of the zemstvos was limited. But even in such a truncated form, local self-government was incompatible with autocracy. Russia's gradual and complicated evolution from absolutist to constitutional monarchy was accompanied by the struggle of these two tendencies in policy toward the zemstvo.

In the period under study the basic tendency was of constant assault by the bureaucracy on the rights of the zemstvo. Only two years after the Zemstvo reform, the law of November 21, 1866, inflicted a serious blow on the zemstvo budget processes. The zemstvos could now collect dues based only on the value of the buildings owned by trade and industrial enterprises, not including assessments on the equipment located there or the trade and industrial income. When the St. Petersburg provincial zemstvo assembly approached the government to allow it to take part henceforth in preliminary discussions of pertinent legislation, it was closed by the government for six months and its most active leaders were exiled. A law of July 13, 1867, limited the activity of the zemstvo in three directions. First, chairmen of zemstvo assemblies received the right, at their personal discretion, to deprive any of the delegates of their right to vote, to forbid discussion of questions considered "outside the competency of the assemblies," to close the meetings to the public, and to shut down assemblies which had posed questions not in accord with the law in the opinion of the administration. Second, the 1867 law categorically forbade any sort of contacts among provincial zemstvos, even in questions which demanded urgent cooperative decisions, such as combating epidemics. Finally, the law required the submission of all zemstvo publications (journals, reports, collections of resolutions, etc.) to the provincial censor. Subsequently, *glasnost'*—oral and in print—of the new institutions of all-estate self-government proved to be heavily dependent on the governmental administration on one hand and the estate-corporate organizations on the other. Many other resolutions and ministerial circulars significantly encroached upon the rights of the zemstvo.[5] A revised statute on public schools of May 23, 1874, limited the rights of the zemstvo in the sphere of public education.

Despite these repressive measures, liberal tendencies can periodically be observed in governmental policy, especially in periods of crisis for the autocracy. The most farsighted statesmen in Russia understood that sooner or later it would be necessary to restructure both local and central administration, and they worked up projects which on one hand should have won over liberal society and on the other should have resulted in only a minor diminution of autocratic power. While the Zemstvo reform was still in preparation, the minister of internal affairs, P. A. Valuev, proposed the reorganization of the highest state legislative consultative body in Russia, the State Council. Valuev suggested that representatives of the zemstvos, mostly nobles, should be included in it. But his idea was never realized. The same fate befell the Grand Duke Konstantin Nikolaevich's project of 1866. The notion of including zemstvo representatives in deliberations of state was also reflected in the so-called Loris-Melikov Constitution, drawn up by the all-powerful minister of the last months of Alexander II's reign. As P. A. Zaionchkovskii stresses, given the example of the brilliant analysis of the projects of the liberal bureaucracy in the late 1870s and early 1880s, "on its own, Loris-Melikov's project did not infringe on the principles of autocracy, but given the evolving circumstances and with the right correlation of forces, it could have been the beginning of a parliamentary system in Russia."[6] However, the assassination of Alexander II on March 1, 1881, not only buried the hopes of the liberals for the "crowning of the edifice" but also brought about the reactionary policies of the government of Alexander III. One element of this policy was the zemstvo counterreform.

What was the role of the new institution of all-estate self-government in the life of the country? It is hardly necessary to provide the American reader details on the role of the zemstvos in the development of health care and public education in Russia, since major works by Nancy Frieden and Ben Eklof have covered zemstvo activity in those areas.[7]

Zemstvo economic measures had fewer results. "One will scarcely find," B. B. Veselovskii fairly assessed, "any other area of zemstvo activity so rich in promising beginnings and suffering to the last from such a striking lack of systematization as that of economic measures."[8] The "agrarian question" provided the stimulus to action in this area. We sometimes encounter the opinion that before the 1890s the zemstvo assemblies rarely discussed the deficiency of arable land in the peasants' allotments. Such is not exactly the case. Famines affecting millions of peasants were frequent in Russia. The sharp decline in the economic situation of the peasants in most of the provinces of European Russia in 1880 brought the agrarian question to the fore at sessions of zemstvo assemblies. The Voronezh provincial zemstvo assembly stated straightforwardly in December 1880 that "after study by many institutions, such as the zemstvo assemblies, government commissions, academic societies, and independent researchers, everyone has finally recognized that peasant allotments are deficient in arable land."[9] Other zemstvos, such as those of St. Petersburg and Novgorod, Kursk, Khar'kov, and Samara, discussed the food supply question. And the Tver provincial zemstvo assembly directly raised the question of a reassessment of the statute of February 19, 1861, as "a temporary, transitional compromise" between "the often completely opposing interests of the peasants and the landlords." It called for the participation "of the most interested parties, and especially the peasants, as the absolute majority of the population" in this reassessment.[10]

Zemstvos in many areas organized small-scale credit to facilitate the purchase and leasing of land by peasant communes. Many zemstvos organized savings and loan associations and handicraft cooperatives (kustarnye arteli). They granted food and financial assistance to malnourished peasants and petitioned for reduction of the peasants' redemption payments, replacement of the poll tax with an all-estate progressive income tax, and assistance in the resettlement of peasants. This is just a sample of the economic activities undertaken by the zemstvos that deserve, in our opinion, further research.

The activities of the zemstvo institutions in Russia were not limited to cultural and economic problems. The zemstvos strove to play a role in the political life of the country as well. By their nature the new institutions of all-estate self-government inevitably inclined toward nationwide forms of self-government, parliamentary forms in particular. Therefore it was in the framework of the zemstvos that political opposition to autocracy, the zemstvo liberal movement, originated. In an article devoted to Russian liberals, the U. S. journalist George Kennan, who visited Russia several times, wrote: "The sole basis for them to lean on was the institution of the zemstvo since they, being by law members of the established corporation, were called by the government to be representatives of the population."[11] And the Russian liberals actually believed, as one of them, the founder of the special newspaper Zemstvo, V. Iu. Skalon, wrote that "once local self-government is put into good order the entire system of government must be reorganized" and the government will call zemstvo representatives "to more important positions in government."[12]

The history of zemstvo liberalism, an important component in the history of Russian liberalism in general, has attracted a great deal of attention recently. N. M. Pirumova and K. F. Shatsillo have published specialized monographs focusing attention on the speeches of the zemstvo in the 1890s and the early 1900s.[13] Here I would like to draw the attention of the reader to the initial efforts of the zemstvo in the political arena toward the end of the 1870s. It was in this period that the basic points of the zemstvo liberal political program took shape. These included widening the sphere of zemstvo activity by transferring local administrative and political functions to it, expanding the principles of self-government to the upper reaches of the

Russian state apparatus, and supporting the elemental civil freedoms of person, speech, press, and assembly.

The Russo-Turkish War of 1877–78 played a significant role in activating liberal-constitutional ideas in Russian society. As a result of this war Bulgaria became a free constitutional democratic state. "The Balkan war shook up all strata of the people," stated the leader of the left wing of the zemstvo movement, I. I. Petrunkevich. "We went to Bulgaria as liberators, turned a Turkish province into a free and constitutional state, made yesterday's slaves into free citizens, granted them all constitutional rights and guarantees, but we ourselves returned home slaves as before." A member of the revolutionary circle of "Southern rebels," V. K. Debogorii-Mokrievich, recalled that after the war "talk about the necessity of a constitution was ubiquitous. The zemstvos came to life and set to work preparing addresses to present to the emperor."[14]

An occasion for addresses soon arose. In the same year that the Russo-Turkish War ended Russian revolutionaries perpetrated a series of terrorist acts. The most important of them were Vera Figner's attempt on the life of the St. Petersburg governor Trepov on January 24 and the assassination of the chief of the gendarmes Mezentsov by Sergei Kravchinskii on August 4. Intimidated by terror, the government twice appealed to society for assistance in the struggle with the revolutionary movement.[15] The zemstvos hurried to respond to the government's call. The majority of them limited their addresses to expressions of indignation toward the revolutionaries and boundless devotion to the tsar; however, a few appealed to the government with petitions hinting at the necessity of continuing the reforms of the 1860s and the granting of a constitution. At the December session of the Khar'kov provincial zemstvo assembly, delegate E. S. Gordeenko (Khar'kov's city head and professor of Khar'kov University) submitted a note in which he linked success in the struggle with the revolutionary terrorists to the introduction of a nationwide zemstvo representative body. However, the official response to the government, which the Khar'kov zemstvo approved December 14, made no mention of that opinion. In response, Gordeenko published an address in the name of the Khar'kov zemstvo in the Russian émigré newspapers *Obshchee delo* (January 1879) and *Gromada* (no. 4, 1879) and the German *Allgemeine Zeitung* (January 25, 1879). He provocatively addressed the tsar: "Most Gracious Sovereign! Give your loyal people the right to the self-government which is natural to them; give them graciously that which you gave the Bulgarians."[16] The address of the Poltava provincial zemstvo assembly (we were lucky to discover a copy in the archive of the Third Section) stressed that "only by joint efforts of the government and the entire zemstvo can we decisively overcome the propaganda undertaken by the enemies of government and society."[17] Such hints about the necessity for "crowning the edifice" of zemstvo self-government were combined in these addresses with a clearly expressed preparedness to assist the autocracy in its struggle with the revolutionary movement at the slightest concession on its part to the zemstvos.

The Chernigov and Tver zemstvos expressed the consistent aspiration of the liberals to hold to the "golden mean" between the government and the revolutionaries. In the 1870s zemstvo activists had formed a circle in Chernigov with the aim of "turning the zemstvo institutions into a school for self-government and thus preparing the country for a constitutional system."[18] This circle, which included representatives of the local nobility, the liberal segment of the provincial bureaucracy, and the urban intelligentsia, was led by I. I. Petrunkevich. Petrunkevich was a local landholder, chairman of the *mirovoi s"ezd* of Borzensk uezd, and a delegate to the Chernigov provincial zemstvo. He was a leader of the zemstvo liberal movement until 1905, then sat on the Central Committee of the Constitutional Democratic party. Other members of the circle included A. P. Karpinskii, director of the city bank and, from 1879, chairman of the provincial zemstvo board; A. F. Lindfors, a delegate to the Gorodnia uezd and Chernigov provincial zemstvos; V. M. Khizhnizkov, Chernigov city head and zemstvo activist, by profession a teacher; and V. A. Savich, justice of the peace of Borzna uezd. Those who cooperated with the revolutionary populists, such as the doctor Ia. M. Belyi, rural teachers G. Ia. Erchenko and I. P. Chudnovskii, and a peasant delegate to the provincial zemstvo, M. N. Maistrenko, also supported the constitutional plans of the Chernigov zemstvo activists. The success of the agitation for a constitution was hindered by the existence of a reactionary group, headed by Marshal of the Nobility N. I. Nepliuev, alongside the liberals in the assembly. These two groups constantly clashed; these clashes reached their apogee at the end of the 1870s.

On January 13, 1879, liberal delegates brought up the question of composing "an answer to the government's appeal." The Chernigov address, written by I. I. Petrunkevich, sharply differed from the Khar'kov and Poltava addresses. Petrunkevich opined that the reactionary course taken by the government had provoked the growth of the revolutionary movement and fostered "the flourishing of ideas contrary to the governmental structure, contrary to the wishes of the government and of the people, who recognize that only the peaceful development of societal institutions is sound and reliable." The address expressed indignation at the corruption of the peasant, zemstvo, and court reforms, the violation "of legal guarantees, equally necessary for all individuals and for all spheres of the state," and "the irresponsibility and unchecked nature of the bureaucracy." Petrunkevich paid special attention to the lack of glasnost. He pointed out that as a consequence of censorship society had been deprived of the opportunity to express its opinion "at the same time that anarchist ideas are being widely disseminated by the clandestine press and by word of mouth." In conclusion he stated that the Chernigov zemstvo members flatly refused to support the government in its struggle with the revolutionaries and hinted that restructuring the system on a constitutional basis was necessary.[19]

The frightened local authorities ordered the hall where the zemstvo meetings were held surrounded by gendarmes and police and declared the meeting of January 23, at which the address was to be discussed, closed to the public. Nepliuev cut short Petrunkevich's attempt to read the address, then he and twenty other delegates walked out of the meeting.[20]

When the events at the Chernigov provincial zemstvo assembly were reported to Alexander II he demanded that no further deliberations or debate on answers to the government's communication be allowed in the zemstvo assemblies.[21] Later the government dealt with Petrunkevich by demanding that the local gendarmes submit information about him to the Third Section. Remarkably, they accused Petrunkevich of being "too much and too hotly interested in public education" and of harboring excessive sympathy for peasants, which he had expressed by proposing reductions in redemption dues and resettling impoverished peasants and by defending them from police abuse. The main charge was authorship of the address. The chief of the gendarmes, A. R. Drentel'n penciled in the margin of the report: "This is an unconditional protest against the government and the Russian state."[22]

Petrunkevich had foreseen the danger of his actions in a letter to Countess A. S. Panina of April 1879 (this letter was perlustrated) when he wrote that "we people who believe in peaceful progress might be lumped together with the revolutionary party, and under this cover we may experience all the delights of administrative exile."[23] Drentel'n proposed to the minister of internal affairs, L. S. Makov, to send Petrunkevich, "a person of extreme opinions," as far from Chernigov province as possible. Makov ordered Petrunkevich arrested on April 26 and sent him to the city of Varnavin in Kostroma Province under police surveillance. His term of exile lasted until 1886.

Petrunkevich's arrest and exile made a great impression on his contemporaries. Students of St. Petersburg University sent him a letter saluting "one of those very few Russian zemstvos in which people can be found capable of honest, independent deeds." The émigré newspaper *Gromada* (1879, no. 4) and the censored publications *Russkaia mysl'* (1880, no. 2) and *Russkaia rech'* (1880, no. 10) expressed solidarity with the Chernigov zemstvos. The liberal delegates of the Chernigov zemstvo elected Petrunkevich to the Borzna uezd and the Chernigov provincial zemstvos in the winter session of 1880–81 as an expression of protest against his administrative exile. They also drew up a petition requesting that he be allowed to resume his position.[24]

Petrunkevich did not rest content with composing what was by necessity a moderate address in Russia. Even before his arrest he had anonymously published a brochure abroad. Contrary to the opinion that this brochure, "The Immediate Tasks of the Zemstvo," was written "by a group of zemstvo constitutionalists as a result of a discussion of issues of program" at the first zemstvo congress,[25] Petrunkevich wrote it before the zemstvo congress, held April 1, 1879. Comparison of its contents with Petrunkevich's memoirs dates the brochure to sometime between February 9 and 16.

"The Immediate Tasks of the Zemstvo" can be seen as a radical version of the Chernigov zemstvo address (Petrunkevich himself remembered later that he argued the same points in the brochure). In addition he evaluated the situation in contemporary Russia in far more barbed terms: "The welfare of the people was blighted by the war and we need many years to heal the open sores. The poverty of the poorest classes, the weight of taxes, popular ignorance, the embezzlement of public funds, the misappropriation of state property, squandering of public resources, financial bankruptcy, persecution of students, the frequent resort to political denunciations, administrative exile by the hundreds—such is the picture of Russia. There is no reason to expect that the government will overcome these problems. On the contrary, it has proved itself unable to deal with the situation of its own making. In begging us for help it has proved its impotence in the struggle with a small but energetic party. Now it is society's turn."[26]

Petrunkevich's brochure claimed to be the program of the entire zemstvo liberal movement, setting out its "immediate tasks," its ultimate goals, and its tactics in the face of the growth of the revolutionary movement and the crisis of the autocracy. Petrunkevich pointed to certain goals which would require the unity of all zemstvo liberals: societal control over state expenditures, "freedom of speech and person, an end to administrative exile and arbitrariness in administration, independence of the peasant estate from the police, tax reform and education reform in line with popular needs, and, finally, the observance of laws by the very government which has enacted them." Rejecting "any constitution handed down from above," Petrunkevich demanded the convocation of a constituent assembly, "since after the experience of Chernigov there could be no doubt the government was incapable of limiting itself in any way or of granting a constitution until compelled to do so."[27]

The realization of this program, especially the convocation of a constituent assembly, would have been an appreciable step toward the rule of law in Russia. But it was exactly that aspect which prevented "The Immediate Tasks of the Zemstvo" from becoming a statement of general zemstvo policy. For the majority of the zemstvo liberals, who could not bring themselves to utter the word *constitution*, this program was far too radical. Comparison of Petrunkevich's brochure with the projects of other ideologists and zemstvo liberals also published abroad in 1877–79 makes this evident. K. D. Kavelin, the renowned public figure and founder of the "state school" of Russian historiography, advanced an original idea for the reorganization of Russian governmental institutions. He suggested the replacement of the single senate with three senates (administrative, legislative, and judicial), one-third of the members of each to be elected in the provincial zemstvo assemblies, and elimination of most of the higher and central bureaucratic institutions, such as the State Council and the ministries. The like-minded B. N. Chicherin, a delegate to the Tambov zemstvo, however, considered it necessary to strengthen the State Council by conscripting zemstvo representatives into it. This was similar to the projects of the liberal bureaucracy already discussed. The Slavophiles A. I. Koshelev and the less-well-known D. V. Voeikov, delegates to the Riazan and Simbirsk zemstvos, proposed the idea of the convocation of a general zemstvo duma.[28] Although these proposals differed in form they shared the idea that zemstvo representatives would be allowed to take part in state activities only in an advisory capacity, in no way encroaching on the unlimited power of the Russian autocrat.

The Tver zemstvo was the last to put forth an address in the spirit of its own earlier activities of the late 1850s and early 1860s. Its leaders in the late 1870s were Aleksandr and Pavel Bakunin, brothers of the famous anarchist Mikhail Bakunin and delegates of the Novotorzhskii uezd zemstvo as well as the Tver provincial zemstvo; Vasilii Lind, a relative and the chairman of the Novotorzhsk uezd board; Ivan Petrunkevich's cousin Mikhail, senior doctor at the Tver provincial hospital; T. N. Povalo-Shveikovskii; N. P. Olenin, chairman of the provincial zemstvo board; F. I. Rodichev, friend and confederate of I. I. Petrunkevich and marshal of the nobility of Ves'egonsk uezd (Rodichev later became one of the leading activists of the Kadet party and a deputy to every convocation of the State Duma); P. A. Korsakov, chairman of the Ves'egonsk mirovoi s"ezd and provincial delegate, who worked fruitfully in the zemstvo in public education, medicine, and small land credit; the positivist philosopher and delegate from Staritsa uezd E. V. de Roberti; and others. Like the members of the Chernigov circle, the Tver zemstvo activists strove "to prepare themselves for a future role as the local elect in a central representative assembly. That institution was never out of their thoughts."[29]

The famous Ukrainian publicist M. P. Dragomanov noted that "the Tver address seems like a continuation of Chernigov's, but surpasses it in the positive nature of its demands, and is superior to the Khar'kov address in merit."[30] The Tver zemstvo delegates began by repeating verbatim the critique of the government put forward in the Chernigov address but went further. Their address concluded with a request that the tsar grant Russia "genuine self-government, the right of the inviolability of the person, an independent judiciary, and freedom of the press" following the example of Bulgaria, which had been liberated from the Turkish yoke.[31] Until recently we did not know the identities of the signers of the Tver address. We can now ascertain their names from the copy of this document discovered in the archives.[32]

The Tver liberals attempted to gain approval for this address at an extraordinary session of the provincial zemstvo assembly on February 21, 1879. The primary topic of this session was the cholera epidemic then threatening Russia.

Since the governor of Tver prohibited the publication of the protocol of that meeting, it is worth saying a few words about the speeches of the liberal delegates based on archival sources. The provincial board proposed to elect a special commission to examine sanitary conditions in the areas most threatened by cholera and to petition for permission for representatives of this commission to meet "with their counterparts of other provinces in Moscow, since it was the main center of all paths of communication, to work out general measures to defend the population from infection." This proposal evoked lively discussion, since it not only pointed out the necessity of consolidating zemstvo efforts against the epidemic but also broached the question of the legal status of the zemstvos and guarantees of person. Thus F. I. Rodichev declared that this address expressed "the only conditions under which peaceful and legal development of society is now possible—those of societal autonomy and personal freedom." However, the attempt to discuss the address in the assembly was unsuccessful. As in Chernigov, the chairman of the assembly even forbade the reading of the text. That limited the Tver liberals to a proposal "to petition for permission for a congress of health commissions from all the zemstvos." The head of the Tver provincial gendarmes noted in his report that "in the petition for permission for a zemstvo congress in Moscow it is impossible not to see aspirations for the introduction, even if only in principle, of all-Russian Zemstvo congresses."[33]

In January and February 1879 the question of a general zemstvo congress on the cholera to be held in Moscow actually came up in five other provincial zemstvo assemblies: Chernigov, Moscow, Riazan, Iaroslavl, and Nizhnii Novgorod.[34] The liberal delegates of these provinces apparently were trying to legalize the secret general zemstvo congress they were planning to hold in Moscow.

Why did the liberals, standing, as A. A. Bakunin expressed, "on the legal terrain," turn to illegal political activity? The government declined the numerous petitions of the zemstvos for permission to hold congresses to discuss issues of medicine, public education, agriculture, etc., stating that such congresses did not conform "with one of the fundamental principles of the Zemstvo statute, by which the zemstvo institutions were conferred an exclusively local character."[35] Petitions for permission to hold congresses on the cholera epidemic were no exceptions. Therefore individual radical zemstvo activists of various regions of the country decided to conduct a secret general zemstvo congress. The goal of this congress was to unite the fragmented liberal opposition and consolidate a petition campaign and other legal means of influencing the government.

The first zemstvo congress took place April 1, 1879, in Moscow, in the apartment of the jurist Prince S. M. Kropotkin on Novinskii Boulevard. M. M. Kovalevskii, Moscow University professor, famous Russian scholar, and social activist, chaired the congress. We have established the names of twenty-two participants. Four were representatives of the Chernigov zemstvo and seven were from Tver. Maxim Kovalevskii's colleagues and like thinkers from the juridical faculty of Moscow University, at that time a center of constitutionalism, also attended: V. A. Gol'tsev, who a year later would become a delegate of the Tver zemstvo; the leading Russian economist A. I. Chuprov; and representatives of the Ukrainian and Polish intelligentsia.[36] I. I. Petrunkevich, a main organizer of the clandestine congress, recalled that "we discussed measures which would further a constitution in Russia, . . . lead the country out of the situation in which terror, on the one hand, and rampant reaction, on the other, pushed aside the country's cultural needs."[37] The question of a constituent assembly surfaced. The notes of F. I. Rodichev, found in the archive of the well-known historian V. Ia. Bogucharskii, indicate that Ukrainian activist V. L. Berenshtam "proposed that we form a society to work toward obtaining a constituent assembly. The 'southerners' and Gol'tsev were in support. The 'northerners' were against."[38] In the end, the participants did no more than proclaim the necessity of a constitutional structure for Russia. They made no decision about forming an effective zemstvo organization. They decided to continue periodic zemstvo congresses, but even this decision remained unimplemented. The next zemstvo congress took place fourteen years later, in 1893, under different circumstances and with a different alignment of forces in society.

An important part of the illegal activity of the zemstvo liberals at the end of the 1870s was their attempt to establish contacts with the revolutionary populists with the goal of joint political struggle. We have already seen that in their addresses the zemstvos condemned terrorist acts and expressed their readiness at the least concession to aid the autocracy in the struggle with the revolutionary movement. The leaders of the left wing of zemstvo liberalism, such as Petrunkevich, Lindfors, and others, had not lost hope that they could talk the revolutionaries out of a terrorist struggle with autocracy and involve them in the peaceful petition campaign for constitutional reforms.

In the same period the revolutionaries' relations to the liberals changed. In May 1878 the populist newpaper *Nachalo* could still write that revolutionaries were indifferent "to the replacement of autocratic with constitutional government" and none of them were planning "to help liberals in the struggle for a constitution." But gradually the revolutionary populists, as one of them, M. Iu. Ashenbrenner, recalled, "understood that their main enemy was the government itself, which would not allow the development of a public movement, that the immediate tasks of the fighting party was to obtain political guarantees to receive the freedom to propagandize the people. . . . Thus the socialists established contacts with liberals, zemstvo radicals, writers, and advocates, and began negotiations."[39]

The most favorable moment for negotiations on joint political activity was the brief period at the end of 1878 and the beginning of 1879 when the revolutionary populists had made the transition to a struggle for political freedoms and the liberal monarchist public had not yet been frightened by the attempts on the emperor's life. Such negotiations took place twice in the winter of 1878–79, in Kiev and St. Petersburg.[40] The questions discussed at the Kiev meeting were of a general character, and the negotiations did not lead to any concrete results.

The negotiations between radical representatives of the liberal camps and members of the revolutionary party the People's Will, which took place in February 1879 in St. Petersburg, have never been treated in the historical literature. The revolutionary Dmitrii Klements, who had wide connections in capital circles, initiated these negotiations. Materials from the Third Section archives and memoir sources show who participated in these negotiations. On the revolutionary side were Klements; N. K. Bykh, organizer of the People's Will press; his brother Lev; the editors of *Nachalo*, V. V. Lutskii, N. I. Zhukovskii, and A. A. Astaf'ev. On the other side were the zemstvo activists A. F. Lindfors and P. A. Aleksandrov, representatives of the Nizhnii Novgorod provincial zemstvo; the liberal publicist A. A. Golovachev (author of *Ten Years of Reform*); the editor of the journal *Slovo*, A. A. Zhemchuzhnikov, who was closely linked to the circle of liberals in the Samara zemstvo headed by A. N. Khardin; the writer A. I. Ertel'; and others.[41]

Unlike the Kiev meeting, the St. Petersburg negotiations had one concrete question on the table: publication of a joint illegal newspaper, by which the zemstvo liberals (who had virtually no opportunity to propagandize their ideas because of increasing disregard for freedom of speech in the censored Russian press) hoped "to acquaint society with the needs of the zemstvo and its right to widen its sphere of activities." However, due to a disagreement over who should play the leading role in the proposed edition, the newspaper was never published.

Thus the forces in opposition to autocracy at the end of the 1870s failed to unite in a general onslaught against the established system. It seems to us that the failure of the negotiations of 1878 and 1879, which further alienated the revolutionary camp from the zemstvo liberal opposition, helped make inevitable the tragedy of March 1, 1881.

A. K. Solov'ev's attempt on the life of Alexander II (April 2, 1879) frightened monarchist zemstvo activists away from any sort of link with the revolutionary underground and led to renewed reaction. The government instituted the office of temporary governor-general on April 5, 1879. The governor-general received extremely broad powers, including the power to suspend the activities of zemstvo assemblies. A law of August 19 of the same year required the preliminary consent of the governor for "filling permanent vacancies in the zemstvo and city institutions whether by election or appointment." "Antizemstvo" laws brought the political activity of the zemstvos to an abrupt halt. The regular winter session of the zemstvo assemblies in 1879–80 were uncommonly colorless. The zemstvo liberal movement came to life again only in the epoch of the so-called dictatorship of the heart. This was a qualitatively new phase in the political history of the zemstvo.

We will venture a few conclusions. The new institution of all-estate self-government was introduced in Russia in the epoch of the 1860s within a very limited framework. Nevertheless, the zemstvos, in their very first steps, achieved significant successes in public education, medicine, and, to a lesser degree, economics. As to their political activities, it was only fifteen years after the reforms of 1864 that they entered the historical arena as organs of public opinion with a specific program for the restructuring of the political life of the country. One short period, lasting less than a year, from August 1878 through April 1879, was rich in manifestations of zemstvo liberalism. Precisely in this period, in the words of V. I. Lenin, "political relations took an appreciable step forward."[42] The political program of zemstvo liberalism contained various shades of social thought, from the moderate plans of veteran Westernizers and Slavophiles to the radical ideas of a new generation of Russian liberals, Petrunkevich and his comrades, whose program demanded a constituent assembly. All zemstvo liberal plans aspired to expand the application of the principles of all-estate self-government, as laid out in the Zemstvo reform, into the entire Russian state apparatus.

This aim presupposed the movement of the country further along the path of reform. But if the speeches of the liberal gentry in the late 1850s furthered the reforms of the 1860s and to a certain degree determined the character of these reforms, the speeches of the zemstvo liberals twenty years later had no immediate impact. The evolution of the Russian state in a constitutional direction was delayed by a quarter of a century until the first Russian revolution of 1905.

NOTES

1. V. V. Veselovskii, *Istoriia zemstva za sorok let,* 4 vols. (St. Petersburg, 1909–11); V. V. Garmiza, *Podgotovka zemskoi reformy 1864 goda* (Moscow, 1957); L. G. Zakharova, *Zemskaia kontrreforma 1890* (Moscow, 1968); E. G. Kornilov, *Zemskaia demokraticheskaia intelligentsiia i ee uchastie v revoliutsionnom dvizhenii 70–x gg. XIX v.,* candidate diss. (Moscow, 1973); N. M. Pirumova, *Zemskaia intelligentsiia i ee rol' v obshchestvennoi bor'be do nachala XX v.* (Moscow, 1986).

2. S. Frederick Starr, *Decentralization and Self-Government in Russia, 1830–1870* (Princeton, N.J., 1972); Thomas S. Pearson, *Officialdom in Crisis: Autocracy and Local Self-Government, 1861–1900* (Cambridge, Mass., 1989); Terence Emmons and Wayne S. Vucinich, eds., *The Zemstvo in Russia: An Experiment in Local Self-Government* (Cambridge, Mass., 1982); W. Bruce Lincoln, *The Great Reforms: Autocracy, Bureaucracy, and the Politics of Change in Imperial Russia* (DeKalb, Ill., 1990).

3. L. G. Zakharova, *Zemskaia kontrreforma 1890 goda,* chap. 1.

4. *Polozhenie o gubernskikh i uezdnykh zemskikh uchrezhdeniiakh. 1 ianvaria 1864 g.* (Sergiev Posad, 1915), 3–4.

5. See B. B. Veselovskii, *Istoriia,* vol. 3 (St. Petersburg, 1909), 120–35.

6. P. A. Zaionchkovskii, *Krizis samoderzhaviia na rubezhe 1870-kh-1880-kh godov* (Moscow, 1964), 477.

7. Nancy Mandelker Frieden, "The Politics of Zemstvo Medicine," in Emmons and Vucinich, eds., *Zemstvo in Russia,* 315–43, and *Russian Physicians in an Era of Reform and Revolution 1856–1905* (Princeton, N.J., 1981); Ben Eklof, *Russian Peasant Schools: Officialdom, Village Culture, and Popular Pedagogy, 1861–1914* (Los Angeles, 1986).

8. Veselovskii. *Istoriia*, vol. 2, 13.

9. *Zhurnaly Voronezhskogo gubernskogo zemskogo sobraniia ocherednogo 1880 goda* (Voronezh, 1881), 168–69.

10. *Protokoly ocherednogo Tverskogo gubernskogo zemskogo sobraniia 1880 g.* (Tver', 1881), 28–30, 296–300.

11. George Kennan, *Poslednee zaiavlenie russkikh liberalov*, trans. from the English (Rostov-on-Don, 1905), 15–167. The original article reads: "The only basis upon which they could proceed in legal form was that furnished by the zemstvos, or provincial assemblies. These were legally authorized bodies, representative of the people, and recognised by the government, and it was decided to have these zemstvos adopt and simultaneously forward memorials or petitions to the Crown setting forth the grievances of the people and asking for a constitutional form of government." *Century*, 1887, no. 11, 54.

12. *Zemstvo*, 1880, no. 27.

13. N. M. Pirumova, *Zemskoe liberal'noe dvizhenie. Sotsianlnye korni i evoliutsiia do nachala XX veka* (Moscow, 1977); K. F. Shatsillo, *Russkii liberalizm nakanune revoliutsii 1905–1907 gg.* (Moscow, 1985).

14. I. I. Petrunkevich, "Stranichka iz vospominanii," in *Pamiati Gol'tseva* (Moscow, 1910), 102–3; V. K. Debogorii-Mokrievich, *Vospominaniia* (St. Petersburg, 1906), 308.

15. The appeals came in the semiofficial newspaper *Pravitel'stvennyi vestnik* of Aug. 20 and in a speech by Alexander II in Moscow on Nov. 20.

16. See F. A. Petrov, "Zemskoe liberal'noe dvizhenie v period Vtoroi revoliutsion-noi situatsii (konets 1870-kh—nachalo 1880-kh gg.)," candidate diss. (Moscow, 1975), 52–55, 223–24.

17. TsGAOR, f. 109, 3 eksp., 1879, d. 178, l. 4. Twelve delegates signed the address including the well-known activist for peasant reform G. P. Galagan. But the board decided to consign the address immediately to its files *(Svod zhurnalov Poltavskogo gubernskogo zemskogo sobraniia XVI. ocherednogo sozyva 1878* (Poltava, 1879).

18. I. I. Petrunkevich, *Iz zapisok obshchestvennogo deiatelia* (Prague, 1934), 41–42. See also V. M. Kh[izhniakov], "O zemskikh delakh i deiateliakh. Pis'ma iz Chernigova," *Slovo*, 1878, nos. 10–20, and *Vospominaniia zemskogo deiatelia* (Prague, 1916); S. F. Rusova, "K 40-letiiu Chernigovskogo zemstva," *Russkaia mysl'*, 1904, no. 12, and "Moi spomini," *Za sto let*, bk. 2 (Kiev, 1928); Ia. M. Belyi, *Vospominaniia zemskogo vracha* (Novgorod, 1907).

19. *Mneniia zemskikh sobranii o sovrmennom polozhenii Rossii*, compiled by V. Iu. Skalon (Berlin, 1883), 91–98.

20. TsGAOR, f. 109, kopiia s protokola zasedaniia 23 ianvaria, 3 eksp., op. 1879 g., d. 75, ll. 16–25.

21. TsGIA, f. kantseliarii ministra vnutrennykh del. op. 1, ll. 612 and 18.

22. TsGAOR, f. 109, 3 eksp., op. 1879, d. 75, ll. 3, 32–50.

23. TsGAOR, f. 109, prilozhenie k delam, op. 214, d. 610, l. 13.

24. The Committee of Ministers rejected this petition. *Zhurnaly Chernigovskogo qubernskogo zemskogo sobraniia ocherednykh sessii 1880 i 1881 gg.* (Chernigov, 1881–82); tsGIA, f. Komiteta ministrov, 4 maia 1882 g., op. 356, ll. 48, 249.

25. Pirumova, *Zemskoe liberal'noe dvizhenie*, 131, 185.

26. *Iubileinyi zemskii sbornik* (Moscow, 1914), 434.

27. *Iubileinyi zemskii sbornik*, 432–35; Petrunkevich, *Iz zapisok obshchestvennogo deiatelia*, 110.

28. K. D. Kavelin, "Politicheskie prizraki, 1877," in *Sobranie sochinenii*, vol. 2 (St. Petersburg, 1898), 927–94; B. N. Chicherin, *Konstitutsionnyi vopros v Rossii, Rukopis' 1878 goda* (St. Petersburg, 1906); A. I. Koshelev, *Chto zhe teper' delat'?* (Berlin, 1879); Zemstvo delegate (Zemskii glasnyi) D. V[oeikov], *Zemstvo i prizyv pravitel'stva k bor'be s revoliutsionnoi propagandoi* (Leipzig, 1879).

29. K. F. Golovin, *Moi vospominaniia*, vol. 1 (St. Petersburg, n.d.), 269.

30. M. P. Dragomanov, *Sobranie politicheskikh sochinenii*, vol. 2 (Paris, 1905), 807.

31. *Mneniia zemskikh sobranii*, 85–90.

32. The following men signed the address: A. A. and P. A. Bakunin, A. P. Balavenskii, M. A. Voloskov, A. B. Vrasskii, I. A. Kaliteevskii, S. D. Karasenskii, I. D. Karaulov, N. D. Kvashnin-Samarin, I. A. and P. A. Korsakov, P. P. Maksimovich, I. N. Mamontov, S. A. Nedoveskov, M. I. Oknov, N. P. Olenin, M. I. Petrunkevich, T. N. Povalo-Shveikovskii, E. V. de Roberti, D. I. and F. I. Rodichev, L. A. Ushakov, and N. A. Chaplin; TsGAOR, f. 109, 3 eksp., op. 1878 g., d. 201, l. 49.

33. TsGAOR, f. 109, 3 eksp., op. 1878 g., d. 201, ll. 12, 25–52.

34. TsGIA, f. kantseliarii ministra vnutrennikh del, op. 2, d. 1827, ll. 2, 34–39.

35. *Sbornik pravitel'stvennykh rasporiazhenii po delam, do zemskikh uchrezhdenii otnosiashchimsia (1879–1880)*, vol. 11 (St. Petersburg, 1889), 79.

36. A complete list of attendees is in F. A. Petrov, "Nelegal'nye obshchezemskie soveshchaniia i s"ezdy kontsa 70-kh—nachala 80kh godov XIX v.," *Voprosy istorii*, 1974, no. 9, 41–42.

37. I. I. Petrunkevich. "Stranichka iz vospominanii," 110, and *Iz zapisok obshchestvennogo deiatelia*, 112.

38. TsGALI, f. V. Ia. Bogucharskogo, d. 169, l. 62.

39. ORIGIM, f. 282, d. 419, l. 41.

40. The meeting in Kiev on December 3, 1878, is the subject of an article which compares the evidence of representatives of the three participating sides: zemstvo liberals, revolutionary populists, and Ukrainian social activists who participated as mediators. F. A. Petrov, "Iz istorii obshchestvennogo dvizheniia v period Vtoroi revoliutsionnoi situatsii v Rossii. Revoliutsionery i liberaly v kontse 1870-kh godov," *Istoriia SSSR*, 1981, no. 1, 144–45.

41. See D. A. Klements, *Iz proshlogo* (Leningrad, 1925); N. K. Bukh, *Vospominaniia* (Moscow, 1928), 127–28; *Arkhiv "Zemli i voli"* (Moscow, 1925); and TsGAOR, f. 109, 3 eksp., op. 1879 g., d. 138, ll. 127–30.

42. V. I. Lenin, *Polnoe sobranie sochinenii*, vol. 5 (Moscow, 1972), 39.

XII

JURORS AND JURY TRIALS IN IMPERIAL RUSSIA, 1866–1885

Alexander K. Afanas'ev
Translated by Willard Sunderland

The abolition of serfdom in Russia prepared the way for the subsequent zemstvo, muncipal, and military reforms of the 1860s and 1870s. As a result of these reforms, several new societal institutions were created based on principles of self-government. The creation of these new institutions was accompanied by the democratization of different branches of the state administration. The judicial reform of 1864 eliminated the old feudal court system and thus removed a serious obstacle from Russia's path to capitalist development.

The jury court was the single most important institution associated with the judicial reform. Though the form of the jury court was somewhat more limited in Russia than in Europe and North America, the Russian court nevertheless embodied the fundamental principles of Western jurisprudence: an independent court, an oral and public legal process, the equality of all citizens before the court, and public involvement in the administration of justice. Jury courts in Russia decided three-fourths of all recorded criminal cases.

Numerous historical works discuss the judicial reform and its central institutions. Almost all of them, however, were written by contempories of the reform itself and thus tend to be polemical in tone. More recent studies of the subject have been primarily concerned with preparations for the reform and with the organization of the new court system in accordance with legal statutes. To date there has been no monographic study of the history of the Russian jury system.[1]

In examining the history of any state or societal institution, the question of social composition is of central importance. After all, it is the institution's composition which largely determines its character, function, and relationship with society and the state. In the case of the Russian jury system, the question of social composition is primarily a political issue. It involves determining the degree of democracy obtaining in the jury system and assessing the extent to which popular participation affected the juridical process. Furthermore, the most significant characteristic of the new court—its willingness to convict, or *repressivnost'*—also stems directly from the social composition of the juries.

The distinctive importance of the composition of the juries was well recognized by contemporaries. Statistical information pertaining to the juries, however, has never been published. In fact, the judicial record-keeping system did not even prepare for the collection of statistical data on the juries. Due to this lack of hard data, most conclusions about the composition of the juries have been based either on the personal experiences of jury members or on a reading of the legal statutes.

According to the statutes, those eligible for jury service were required to be Russian citizens from twenty-five to seventy years of age who had resided for at least two years in the *uezd* in which the jury selection was to take place. Convicted criminals, dissolute persons, spendthrifts, and insolvent debtors were not allowed to participate in the jury courts. Also excluded were the blind, deaf, and dumb; the insane; and those not competent in the Russian language.

To establish who was eligible for jury service, lists were drawn up at the *uezd* level. Priority was given to justices of the peace, judges, and civil servants (not higher than the fifth class), as well as to all elected local officials. Peasant elders and peasants elected to various posts within the volost commune were also included within this category of privileged representatives.

Those remaining who were eligible for jury service were expected to meet a property requirement. Potential jury members had "to own no less than 100 desiatinas of land; or to possess other real estate of commensurate value amounting to a sum of no less than 2,000 rubles in the capitals, no less than 1,000 rubles in provincial cities, and no less than 500 rubles in other localities; or to earn income from capital revenue, professional work, handicraft, or other industry amounting to an annual sum of no less than 500 rubles in the capitals and 200 rubles in other localities."[2]

It is worth noting that the property requirement was not excessively high. As A. F. Koni remarked, "In order to perform jury service in a large provincial town, a gross annual income of 200 rubles was required. Such a yearly income, amounting to an average of 16.66 rubles a month, reflects a level of extreme poverty. Only clerical workers of the lowest level earned this kind of income, and they appear to have lived on the very edge of need as a result of it."[3] Still, despite the fact that it was comparatively low, the property requirement nevertheless effectively excluded the great majority of the Russian population, the half-destitute peasantry of the Russian countryside, from participation in the jury court system.

Other groups were officially excluded from the lists of potential jury members: priests and monks, military officers, civil servants serving in the defense and judicial ministries, ecclesiastical treasurers, forestry wardens, police officers, public school teachers, and all those "employed in the service of private persons [domestic servants?]."[4]

The general lists were to be compiled by the first of September each year by "Special Provisional Commissions, consisting of representatives elected annually at uezd zemstvo meetings or, in the capitals, elected at the joint sessions of municipal duma and local zemstvo organizations."[5] For a month after the first of September, requests to exclude or include names on the lists could be submitted to the special commissions. Alterations of any kind, however, had to be reviewed and confirmed by the governor, who was then required to publish the approved lists by the beginning of November.[6] It was from these lists that the special commissions—now presided over by the local marshal of the nobility and justices of the peace—were required to pick individuals for jury service during the coming year.

The selected individuals were then included in primary lists and informed of the length of time during which their appearance in court was required.[7] In addition to the primary lists, reserve lists were drawn up in towns where trials were expected to be held during the coming year. Individuals from these reserve lists were called for jury service if jurors from the primary lists were for some reason unable to appear in court. "Primary lists of jury members will include the following: in the cities of St. Petersburg and Moscow and their uezds, 1,200 individuals; in uezds with more than 100,000 residents, 400 individuals; in uezds with less than 100,000 residents, 200 individuals. . . . Reserve lists of jury members will include: in the cities of St. Petersburg and Moscow, 200 individuals; and in other cities, 60 individuals."[8]

The judicial code prohibited the state administration from participating in the selection of jury members. The provincial governor's role in the process was clearly limited. If he chose to exclude an individual from the general list, he was required to submit a well-grounded explanation for his decision to the special commission. Furthermore, as noted above, the lists themselves were compiled by representatives of the zemstvos and municipal dumas, a practice which only reinforced the significance of those institutions of local self-government created during the reform period. The fact, however, that the special commissions were chaired by marshals of the nobility and included local justices of the peace meant that the general all-*soslovie* principle of the new court system was, in practice, somewhat restricted.

Differing interpretations of the jury selection law frequently led to contradictory conclusions about the actual composition of the juries. In 1862, in an analysis of the new judicial statutes, N. P. Ogarev came to the conclusion that "there will likely be few peasants on the juries," suggesting instead that "the great majority of jurors will be drawn from the ranks of the government bureaucracy."[9] In response to a claim put forward by the newspaper *Vest'* in the spring of 1867 that the new jury system included too many representatives from the lower classes, the publisher M. N. Katkov retorted, "on the contrary, the majority of jurors are members of the highest social strata."[10] An observer from the newspaper *Delo,* basing his conclusions on demographic data, suggested that most jurors would be drawn from within the peasant estate.[11]

Practicing jurists, such as A. M. Bobrishchev-Pushkin, A. F. Koni, and N. I. Timofeev, noted that there were peasant majorities on most provincial juries. These jurists, however, did not provide any concrete data to support their observations. As for the jury representation of other estates, the existing literature does not provide even approximate figures.

In 1896, K. K. Arsenev, a lawyer and public figure, lamented in an address to the St. Petersburg Juridical Society: "We do not have even the most elementary information about the jury courts, about the proportional representation of different classes and estates, about the number of educated persons, and so on. The jurymen are still the mysterious strangers that A. F. Koni once spoke about."[12]

To this day jury composition in late Imperial Russia remains clouded in mystery. In Soviet historiography, it has become a commonplace to stress the antidemocratic nature of the jury courts. This conclusion, however, has little basis in fact. Instead it reflects the study in isolation of the legal statutes relating to the selection of jury recruits. And, of course, from the point of view of these statutes, the composition of the juries does indeed appear to have been extremely restricted. The noble leadership of the special commissions certainly intended for measures such as the property requirement to limit the extent of popular participation in the jury system. Russian realities, however, thwarted these intentions, forcing changes both in the initial designs of the architects of the reform and in a priori decisions about jury composition.

The need to collect and publish data on the juries was frequently noted in the legal literature of the late nineteenth century.[13] During this period the Tsarist government was also concerned with the issue of jury composition, due no doubt to the alarm it felt at the excessively high number of acquittals rendered in public malfeasance trials in the early 1870s. An important document relating to this issue—a list of the jury members of Vladimir Province for 1874[14]—has been preserved in the archive of the Ministry of Justice. The list is attached to the governor's report for that year, an illustration of the direct relationship between the *repressivnost'* of the courts and the composition of the juries.

In June 1884 a law was passed introducing "changes to the jury code."[15] This law was known to contemporaries simply as "the novel on the juries." In the course of drawing up this "novel," a special commission under the chairmanship of M. N. Liuboshchinskii[16] was established to oversee the systematic collection of jury data. The commission received jury registers from various localities. Unfortunately, however, only the registers for 1883 have been preserved. They make up three enormous volumes, appended to a report entitled "Amendments Relating to the Selection of Jurors for the

General and Primary Lists."[17] These registers appear in the form of tables which provide information on the quantity of jurors in each locality, their estate membership, their level of literacy, and their religious affiliation. In some cases the names of military personnel, office workers, and peasants who had met the property requirement are noted.

The majority of the registers were compiled carelessly and do not conform to the format requested by the special commission. In fact, an examination of the registers reveals that their figures do not always add up. Because of these discrepancies, I have chosen to use only the most reliable and internally consistent registers—twenty-two out of a total of sixty-two—as source material for this study. Despite their small number, these registers are sufficient to provide a general picture of the country as a whole, for the social composition of the juries tended to vary little from one district court to another (the exception being the district courts of the capital cities). Statistical data on the juries of late Imperial Russia are published here for the first time.

Official provincial newspapers (*gubernskie vedomosti*), which annually published both primary and reserve juror lists, also provide important information about the composition of juries. Unfortunately, complete runs of these newspapers remain for only a few provinces. For this study, I have used data drawn from the official newspapers of Vladimir, Kazan, and Nizhnii Novgorod provinces for 1873.

In this essay, tabular data are presented on primary and reserve jurors selected for service in the capital and other provinces in 1883. From a comparison of these data with data on the juries from 1873, it is possible to determine the changes in jury composition which took place over the decade. When examining the two tables, it is important to remember that jury composition tended to vary considerably within a given province, with the most noticeable differences occurring between the provincial capital and outlying rural uezds, or districts. I have arranged the tables to reflect this variety, providing separate columns for the provincial capital district, for the remaining uezds, and for the province as a whole.

I have grouped the jurors in rows according to their social estate. The first row in each table gives the percentages of noble and civil servant jury members. Judging from the sources, approximately one-fifth of those listed in this category nationwide appear to have been nobles, the rest civil functionaries of one sort or another. It is important to keep in mind, however, that state bureaucrats in Russia largely descended from the noble estate. The second row provides information on the merchant jurors. Close to 20 percent of the individuals represented in this category nationwide were honorary citizens, having either acquired this status themselves or inherited it. The third row represents the *meshchane* (burgher) jurors and includes a small group of factory workers (approximately 10 percent nationwide) who were eligible for jury service as members of the meshchanin estate. *Raznochintsy* (commoners, or, lit., "diverse ranks") make up another 10 percent

TABLE 1. **Jury Composition in Russian Capital Provinces by Percent, 1883.**

	St. Petersburg Province			Moscow Province		
Social Estate	Capital District (N=2,900)	Other Districts (N=2,279)	Total (N=5,179)	Capital District (N=2,160)	Other Districts (N=3,300)	Total (N=5,460)
Nobles, Civil Servants	53.0	15.6	36.6	46.2	8.2	23.2
Merchants	13.4	8.6	11.3	32.4	15.7	22.3
Meshchane	29.0*	21.9	25.8	13.2	20.4	17.6
Peasants	4.6	53.9	26.3	8.2	55.6	36.9

*Includes a large number of razhnochintsy, who made up almost one-fifth of all jurors in official St. Petersburg.

Sources: "Vedomost' o prisiazhnykh zasedateliakh po okrugu Sankt Peterburgskogo okruzhnogo suda za 1883 g. s raspredeleniem ikh po chetvertiam goda," TsGIA, f. 1405, op. 73, d. 3656(a), ll. 2-3; "Svodnaia vedomost' o prisiazhnykh zasedateliakh po akrugu Moskovskogo okruzhnogo suda za 1883 g.," ibid., ll. 23–27.

of the *meshchane* jurors nationwide. Concerning the fourth row, peasant jurors, more will be said below.

The difference in jury composition between the capital districts and outlying uezds is immediately apparent in table 1. In St. Petersburg District in 1883, nobles and merchants accounted for 66.4 percent, nearly fifteen times greater than the percentage of peasants (4.6). In other districts in the same province, by contrast, the percentage of peasant jurors was greater than the percentage of nobles and merchants by more than two to one (53.9 vs. 24.2). A similar distribution can be seen in Moscow Province (55.6 vs. 23.9).

To provide a comparison, some information is available on jury composition for the St. Petersburg District for 1873.[18] At that time, 54 percent of the jurors on the primary and reserve lists were either noblemen or civil servants, 14.6 percent merchants, 26.4 percent meshchane, and 5 percent peasants. It is evident that little change occurred in jury composition over the decade.

Because civil servants accounted for a large proportion of the jurors of St. Petersburg District, it is appropriate to note their position according to the table of ranks. Information on this exists for 1873. Of 756 civil servants—representing approximately 54 percent of the total number of jurors in the capital district in 1873[19]—four persons possessed no rank at all, while 107 stood at lower than the tenth rank. All the remaining civil servant jurors (645) had higher ranks. In other words, functionaries with a rank of ten or higher outnumbered the rest by more than six to one. Among the most highly ranked civil servants, there were three privy councilors, ninety state councilors, and fifty-nine titular ones. Thus a significant majority of the capital's civil servant jurors were drawn from high and middle levels within the state bureaucracy.[20]

In 1873, as noted, peasants accounted for only 5 percent of the capital's jurors, despite the fact that they made up approximately one-third of the population of St. Petersburg in the early 1870s.[21] Peasant jurors were just as rare in Moscow's municipal district. According to figures for 1882, peasants accounted for 49.2 percent of Moscow's population, while nobles and civil servants, who made up virtually half of the city's jurors, accounted for only 7.4 percent.[22]

Judging from table 1, there were no serious discrepancies in jury composition between St. Petersburg and Moscow. Nonetheless, the percentages do reflect the different character of the two cities. St. Petersburg's official capacity as the national capital is clearly revealed by the fact that over half (53 percent) of the city's jurors were nobles or civil servants. The older commercial and patriarchal character of Moscow is reflected in the city's larger percentage of merchants (32.4 as opposed to 13.4 in St. Petersburg) and peasants (8.2 as opposed to 4.6) and in its relatively small percentage of nobles and civil servants (46.2 as opposed to 53).

Although differences between the two major cities in the percentage of literate jurymen were small, in general the literacy rate among jurors in the capital districts was rather high (89.2 in Moscow). Almost all of the jurors in the capital districts were Russians by nationality, a fact that is reflected in the overwhelming number of jurors adhering to the Russian Orthodox Church: 90.4 percent in St. Petersburg and 95.4 percent in Moscow.

The nondemocratic character of the jury courts stands out particularly clearly in the districts of St. Petersburg and Moscow, where peasants made up a combined total of only 6.4 percent of the jurors. This extremely low percentage can be explained by the fact that elected peasant officials did not live in the cities and thus were obviously not included in municipal jury lists. Furthermore, the property requirement for jury service in the capital districts was two times higher than the requirement in other uezds, a clear reflection of the fact that the special commission members who drew up jury lists preferred to exclude representatives from "lower" estates whenever it was possible to select jurors from "higher" social categories.

The overwhelming majority of city dwellers were denied the right to serve on the jury courts. In Moscow in 1875, out of a population of 200,000 men between the ages of twenty-five and seventy, only about 10,000 (or 5 percent) were registered on the city's jury lists.[23]

It is important to remember, however, that together the two capital cities accounted for only about 2 percent of the population of European Russia.[24] Jurors in these cities represented no more than one-twentieth of the total number of jurors in the country as a whole.[25] Without data on the juries in provincial Russia, therefore, it is impossible to draw conclusions about the jury courts on a national level.

Now let us examine the composition of juries in other provinces. Table 2

TABLE 2. **Jury Composition in Russian Provinces (Except St. Petersburg and Moscow) by Percent, 1883.**

Social Estates	Capital Districts (N = 8,509)	Other Districts (N = 47,855)	Total (N = 56,364)
Nobles, Civil Servants	35.9	11.1	14.9
Merchants	15.1	8.4	9.4
Meshchane	23.8	17.3	18.3
Peasants	25.2	63.2	57.4

Source: "Vedomost' o prisiazhnykh zasedateliakh" for 1883, TsGIA, f. 1405, op. 73, d. 3656(a), ll. 2–3, 10–11, 13, 23, 28, 30–31, 50, 54–56, 58, 68, 84, 130–31, 141–42, 162, 175, 180, 191–92, 197, 201–2, 205, 227, 232–33, 243, 245, 247–48, 259–60, 268–69, 271.

gives data on the jurors in twenty district courts in provinces other than St. Petersburg and Moscow.[26]

The composition of provincial juries differed markedly from juries in the capital provinces. More than half of the jurors in the noncapital provinces were peasants, while nobles, civil servants, and merchants made up only one-fourth of the jurors. Once again, as in the case of the capital provinces, there is a clear difference between juries in provincial capital districts and those in the remaining uezds, where close to two-thirds of the jurors were peasants. It is important to note that jurors in the remaining uezds outnumbered jurors in the provincial capitals by almost six to one. This ratio was more or less constant throughout the country.

In the case of three provinces, it is possible to compare jury data for 1873 and 1883. In 1873, peasants on the primary lists made up 73.7 percent of the jurors in Vladimir Province, 78.1 percent in Nizhnii Novgorod Province, and 72.2 percent in Kazan Province. Over the next ten years, the proportional share of peasant jurors dropped somewhat but still remained the highest of all the estates: 64.8 percent in Vladimir, 73.1 percent in Nizhnii Novgorod, and 70.6 percent in Kazan. In 1883, as a result of the slight drop in peasant jurors, the number of *meshchane* on the primary lists increased: in Vladimir by 10 percent, in Nizhnii Novgorod by 3 percent, and in Kazan by 8 percent. This rise in the representation of *meshchane* jurors was no doubt a reflection of the quickening pace of economic development in Russia, the effects of which had brought about a notable increase in the size of the urban population.[27]

I noted above that the composition of juries in the capital provinces changed little between 1873 and 1883. This is also the case with the three noncapital provinces that I have just reviewed. These observations suggest, then, that in the remaining provinces there was also little change in jury composition over the course of the decade.

Now a few words about worker participation in the jury courts. According to the judicial codes, worker participation was permitted. To qualify for jury service, however, a worker had to have a monthly income of at least 16.66 rubles in the provinces or two and a half times more—41.66 rubles—in the capitals. An adult worker's average monthly earnings at this time amounted to 14.16 rubles. Only workers in high-paying industries such as metal-working and textile production could expect to meet the income requirement in the provinces. In the capitals, a similar situation prevailed. Due to relatively low wages—on average, 18.41 rubles per month[28]—workers in the capitals were completely excluded from participation in the juries. From worker figures published in the provincial jury lists, it is clear that, just as in the capitals, workers in other cities in European Russia were also effectively denied the right to jury service.

There are data on *tsekhovye* (guild workers) from Nizhnii Novgorod Province for 1873. *Tsekhovye* in the capital district accounted for 2.8 percent of the jurors, in Balakhna uezd for 0.5 percent, in Ardatov for 4.7 percent, and in Arzamas for 4 percent. The total number of *tsekhovye* serving on the juries in these districts was half the number of civil servant jurors, with the latter making up the most sizable minorities on the primary lists. In the remaining districts of the province, there were no *tsekhovye* jurors at all.[29]

Almost all the civil servants who served on juries in the provinces possessed civil rank. As a result, simple nonranking clerical workers rarely served as jurors in the provinces, and never at all in the capitals.

In the twelve provinces for which data are available,[30] it appears that almost half the jurors could neither read nor write. This is readily understandable considering that there was no literacy requirement for jury service and that peasants, who made up the majority of the jurors, were largely illiterate. The literacy rate was especially low in noncapital districts. During judicial inquests in these districts, it was not uncommon for juries to be disbanded and reselected because none of the standing jurors was qualified to serve as chairman, a position whose occupant was required by law to be able to read and write. Nonetheless, the literacy rate of provincial jurors was more than twice the average literacy rate of males in the fifty provinces of European Russia. Of those called up for military service in 1883, only 24.5 percent were literate.[31]

The nationality of the jurors is not directly indicated in the sources, but it can be determined to some extent by looking at religious affiliation. Jurors adhering to the Orthodox faith were usually Russians. Lutheran jurors were generally either Germans or ethnic Balts, Catholic jurymen were Poles, Jewish jurors were Jews, and Moslem jurors were Tatars.

The jurors of the central provinces were Russian almost without exception. In the borderlands of European Russia, where "alien" (*inorodtsy*) peoples were in the majority, the picture is somewhat different. In certain districts in Kazan Province, Moslems counted for almost a fourth of all jurors, yet in the province as a whole, Tatar jurors made up only about 12 percent of the total. Likewise, in the district courts of Simfiropol, Tatars represented roughly 18 percent of the jurors, whereas in the provinces of Perm and Simbirsk, which were part of the Kazan judicial district, they accounted for little more than 4 percent.[32] These figures reflect the general policy of russification pursued by the imperial government in the late nineteenth century.

Jews, who made up a significant part of the population in the western and southwestern regions, suffered the greatest discrimination. It was established by law that the representation of Jews on the jury courts in nine western provinces (the provinces of Kiev, Volyn', Kamenets-Podolsk, Vitebsk, Vilna, Kovno, Grodno, Mogilev, and Minsk) could not exceed the percentage of Jews in the local population. Only Christians could serve as jury chairmen, and Jews were not permitted to participate on juries considering cases of sacrilege ("crimes against the faith").[33] As a result of these measures, in Kiev Province, where Jews accounted for half of the population, only 10 percent of the jurors were Jews. A similar situation prevailed in Volyn' province.[34]

The numerical predominance of peasant jurors played an important role in the new jury courts. Therefore it is necessary to consider how this predominance was obtained, who the peasant jurymen were, and what influence their broad representation on the juries had on the development of the new court system.

The officials who drew up the judicial statutes must have foreseen that peasants would represent a significant share of the jurors in a largely peasant country such as Russia. However, judging from a review of the pertinent legislation, it seems clear that the authors of the judicial reform did not anticipate that peasants would constitute the absolute majority of the country's jurors.

The basic reason for the overwhelming number of peasant jurors undoubtedly had to do with the very structure of the Russian population, 90 percent of which belonged to the peasant estate.[35] In addition, the working conditions of the new courts and deficiencies in the juror selection process contributed to the large peasant representation on the juries.

Even during the honeymoon period of the judicial reform, when the jury courts had just been formed and were enjoying immense popularity, members of the upper classes often tried to avoid serving on the juries. After the very first sessions of the jury courts in St. Petersburg, the liberal newspaper *Golos* reported a rumor that the city's aristocrats had decided to boycott the jury courts altogether.[36] In Herzen's newspaper *Kolokol,* a commentary on this subject ran under the dramatic headline "Those who are slaves in their own hearts cannot be made into free men."[37] All too familiar were stories like the one about an individual who argued that he was exempt from jury service because his noble heritage accorded him the right not to serve at all.[38]

During the first months of jury service in St Petersburg, eighteen people were indicted for intentional evasion of their jury duties.[39] With time, this number grew. Disgruntled aristocrats were joined by defectors from other privileged social groups.

In 1874 the chairman of the Moscow circuit court, writing to the city's mayor, lamented that "the number of educated persons serving on the juries is dropping continuously from year to year. . . . The jury lists for 1866 and 1867 were composed almost exclusively of educated persons, and the lists for 1868, 1869, and 1870 likewise abounded with such citizens. In recent years, however, and especially this year, the name of an educated person appears on the lists as a rare exception."[40] A similar process took place in St. Petersburg, where "in 1886 only 36 percent of the total number of jurors were representatives of the most advanced and educated social classes."[41]

In the provinces, evasion of jury service, which was regarded with some prestige, was insignificant in the first years of the reform. A contemporary observer wrote: "The jurors in our first years were people of choice. Our intelligentsia served among the jurors and indeed all of the best people within the locality sought this honor. There were, of course, merchants and townspeople and even peasants, but they were all literate and intellectually mature. It would have been inconceivable to permit an illiterate person to serve on the juries."[42]

Gradually, evasion of jury duty became rather widespread in the provinces. In Kazan in 1883, for example, truancy among jurors reached 22.5 percent. This sometimes led to the postponement of court sessions, for if seven out of thirty-six jurors summoned failed to appear, the chances for subsequently electing a twelve-man jury from the remainder were reduced. In all of Kazan Province that year, 13 percent of the jurors failed to report for duty.[43] According to the data for the Pskov district court for 1884, this percentage reached 12.[44] In other places, the situation was no better. During the first six-and-a-half years of the jury courts (1866–72), legal proceedings for evasion of jury duty were initiated against 2,358 persons.[45] It should be noted that in this period approximately half a million jurors participated in the new courts.

The elite's purposeful evasion of its jury duties drew the attention of the Tsarist government. The ministries of justice and internal affairs sent inquiries to their provincial offices concerning the reasons for this development. The responses from the provinces led to the conclusion that "evasion of jury duty among persons belonging to educated estates frequently stems from (1) the long duration of sessions in a great many district courts and (2) the extremely unsatisfactory living quarters provided for the jurors, not only in those outlying areas where circulating courts are held but also in the permanent courthouses of the district courts."[46]

By law jurors were not permitted to leave the courthouse until the conclusion of the trial on which they were serving. It was not uncommon for complicated trials to last several days, sometimes even several weeks. District courts were usually situated in old, dilapidated buildings that were cold or noxious in the winter and hot and stuffy in the summer. There were no dining halls or sleeping quarters. Jurors were often forced to spend the night on bare benches in the public courtrooms alongside gruesome pieces of material evidence from the cases in process. In addition, in "noisy" cases, which were often discussed in the press before they went to court, unpopular verdicts could bring down a hail of abuse and unfounded recriminations upon the heads of the jurors.

It is understandable that people who were accustomed to a certain level of comfort and of prominence in social affairs, as well as those who were at best uninterested in legal matters, would want to avoid performing onerous jury duties. By the opening date of the court session, in the words of a contemporary, "a veritable epidemic of different illnesses would befall the rich merchants and noblemen who had been selected for jury service; rich landowners would be overrun with unexpected misfortunes on their estates, and civil servants would become suddenly imbued with an exceptional desire to carry out their official assignments. As a result, instead of all of these people showing up for jury duty, the court would receive doctors' reports and requests, petitions, and announcements from a number of different authorities. Only peasants and townspeople, those for whom jury service was hardest of all, were dutiful in carrying out their obligations."[47] Rich people sometimes simply bought themselves out of their duties by paying a fine. Others used contacts on the jury selection commissions to have their names deleted from the lists. In the end, the weight of jury duty came to rest squarely on the shoulders of simple people, usually peasants.

The Russian peasantry was far from a monolithic social group. For this reason, it is necessary to determine precisely which categories within the peasantry were recruited for jury service. The law on the selection of jurors was designed to ensure that only the richest and most "trustworthy" of the peasants would serve. It should be recalled that the jury lists included only those peasants who met the property requirement and those who occupied specific posts within peasant government. Peasants who fell within the second category were not required to have a certain amount of property or level of income. Judging from the source data, it is clear that the overwhelming majority of peasant jurors belonged to this category.

According to "Information on the Jurors of Velikiie Luki Uezd," 85 percent of the peasants included on the jury lists for the period 1879–82 were village elders, volost supervisors, etc.[48] Peasants who owned at least 100 desiatinas of land amounted to only 11 percent of the peasants on these lists, while peasants with at least 200 rubles in yearly income accounted for a mere 4 percent. Information concerning the peasant representatives on the juries is available for Mogilev and Letichev uezds, as well as for eight uezds in Orel Province.[49] In all of these areas, one finds a breakdown similar to the one in Velikiie Luki uezd. In the eight uezds of Orel Province, 85 percent of peasant jurors did not meet the property requirement.[50] Approximately two-thirds of the peasant jurors were village elders, only a few of them in any sense well-off. Out of the 224 village elders who appeared on the jury lists for Mogilev *uezd,* only 56 could show proof of the legally required amount of property or income.[51]

In the central and western provinces, where the majority of jurors served, only an average of 5 percent of the peasant jurors owned 100 or more desiatinas of land. In several non-Black Earth provinces (Novgorod, Samara, Perm, Simbirsk) the proportion of these peasants sometimes exceeded 50 percent. This, however, did not mean that even there all of these peasants were rich farmers. Rather, the 100-desiatina property requirement, "which was rather significant in the Black Earth region, represented in other areas only the very lowest of incomes."[52]

In freeing a portion of the peasantry from meeting the property requirement, the authors of the judicial reform were apparently proceeding on the assumption that the peasants would elect the most "trustworthy" and well-to-do people to serve as their representatives in peasant government. In practice, however, the richest peasants usually avoided service in the posts that accorded the right to jury service. As a result, the notion of the "strong peasant" as juror was not realized. The majority of peasants who qualified to serve as jurors because they met the service requirement belonged to the poorest group in peasant society.

In one report submitted to the minister of justice, it was noted that "the majority of our jurors come from the poor, sometimes starving, illiterate peasantry, the half-literate lower middle classes (*meschanstvo*), and petty officialdom."[53] On occasion, one could find jurors such as those described in a report by the magistrate of the Vladimir district court: "In October 1870 in the town of Shuia, a peasant juror by the name of Petr Leontievich Dubynkovo was called up for service and promptly announced that if he were not immediately released from jury duty he would likely die of hunger. This peasant was wearing an old threadbare prisoner's smock which he had been forced to purchase for lack of means. On the smock, one could still see the letters of the convict's name."[54]

As the minister of internal affairs noted, it was all too common for there "to appear among [the jurors] people who had to be released from [jury] service because their meager means required that they work as day laborers in their free time. . . . sometimes there are crowds of jurors in the street petitioning for exemption from service."[55]

The poverty of the jurors was a widespread phenomenon that constantly attracted attention. Newspapers carried dozens of articles on the starving "judges of conscience." Several zemstvos took the initiative to distribute small stipends to needy jurors. The Senate, however, outlawed such aid with the law of September 5, 1873, declaring that the law on zemstvo organizations (which had, of course, been passed prior to the judicial statutes) did not allow for such a use of funds.

The numerical majority of peasants among the jurors had a double meaning both for the peasants themselves and for the new court system in which they were serving. For the peasants, jury duty was an onerous obligation which they could not throw off. At the same time, peasant participation in the juries raised the legal awareness of the *narod* and had a considerable educational impact. For the courts, peasant jurors had the advantage of knowing firsthand the social milieu and everyday motives for the majority of the crimes that came before the courts. This was due to the simple fact that peasants constituted the majority of the defendants in criminal cases. In 1873, for example, peasants accounted for 86.8 percent of the population in the six areas with acting district courts and for 61.9 percent of all those sentenced.[56] In addition, peasant jurors, who successfully coped with a large number of "everyday" cases (murder, robbery, etc.), could be relied on as the most conservative element in special cases involving crimes with political overtones or offenses against the church.

Despite their preponderance on the juries, peasants were not always responsible for deciding the jury's final verdict. Sometimes they would fall under the influence of eloquent representatives of the privileged estates who were able to convince the uneducated and rough-speaking peasant majority of the need to hand down one verdict or another.

Yet in the great majority of cases, the verdicts of the jury courts were simple and just. These verdicts expressed the people's view of Russian reality and led to the withdrawal of a number of obsolete and inhumane laws which were not compatible with popular notions of the correlation between justice and punishment. There were, however, clear examples of a lack of fairness and justice in the treatment of certain crimes: merciless cruelty was shown toward horse thieves and persons convicted of sacrilegious offenses, while excessive tolerance was shown in cases involving crimes against women and official corruption or malfeasance. A marked rise in the number of acquittals would occur on the eve of large peasant holidays. As a result, the *repressivnost'* of the jury courts during the period in question was 12 percent less than that of the state courts.[57]

The preponderance of "dark," impoverished peasants on the juries was seen by the authorities, with some justification, as one of the main reasons for the court's often unsatisfactory performance. It was thought that the way to "rectify" the functioning of the court lay in increasing the number of jurors from educated social classes. To ensure the participation of more educated people, however, it was necessary to contend with what caused these potential jurors to evade their duties. In other words, working and living conditions for the juries had to be improved. Unfortunately, the authorities found it impossible to allocate the necessary funds for this purpose. Instead, in a move characteristic of the Tsarist government, the authorities decided to enforce the service of educated jurors by inaugurating stronger administrative and restrictive methods. On June 12, 1884, the law on changes in the jury code was issued, allowing for police officials to assist in the formation of juries, cutting by half the number of jurors who could be excluded from service, and reducing the number of jurors placed on reserve lists. The number of jurors was sharply increased in the capitals and decreased in the provinces. On April 28, 1887, another law was introduced entitled "On Changes in the Rules for Jury Selection."[58] The terms of this law doubled the property requirement for jury service, accorded provincial governors the right to exclude any person from the jury lists without explanation, and required that jurors demonstrate an ability to read—thus establishing what amounted to, in G. A. Dzhanshiev's phrase, "a semi-literacy requirement," inasmuch as full literacy involved the ability to both read and write.[59]

Although there are no quantitative data to reveal the effect this law had on the composition of the juries, it is reasonable to suppose that it was not particularly significant. After all, the composition of the Russian population remained the same and the problems that had originally prompted educated jurors to evade their duties had not been resolved.

After the assasination of Alexander II, the Tsarist government embarked on a new course to strengthen the nobility's position as the principal upholder of state policy. This was done largely by reducing the representation of the lower middle classes and the peasantry in governmental and societal organizations. The level of this representation had by the mid-1880s become quite sizable: peasant and meshchane constituted approximately 40 percent of the uezd zemstvos[60] and almost 50 percent of the uezd dumas,[61] the locus of the main body of Russia's municipal electorate. It must be noted, however, that the 1890 zemstvo statute and the 1892 municipal statute, which had both been issued to restructure the composition of these organizations, were not particularly successful.

The jury courts, judged by their societal composition, were the most democratic of all the institutions created by the Great Reforms. Their political character was more sharply expressed than that of either the zemstvos or the dumas. The jury courts had the right to grant pardons, previously the exclusive domain of the state government; their verdicts influenced the changing of legal statutes; and their activities provided an example of majority rule in judicial matters, undisputably one of the most important spheres of state administration.

Because the courts had such a clearly progressive and democratic character, the reactionary Tsarist government of the 1880s moved to bring them back into line with autocratic rule. The reactionary press, mouthing the government view, used isolated examples of unfair verdicts to accuse the courts of meting out "street justice" and to call for their abolition. *Moskovskie vedomosti, Grazhdanin,* and other publications constantly baited the jury courts. As one law journal wrote, "The jury courts in their first quarter century have borne the brunt of more attacks than any other institution founded during the reign of Emperor Alexander II."[62] The laws of 1884 and 1887 were the first links in a whole chain of measures intended to restrict popular participation in government and to strengthen the autocracy's support within the nobility and the bureaucracy.

NOTES

1. For the history of the first period of the Russian jury courts, see my dissertation "Sud prisiazhnykh v Rossii. Organizatsiia, sostav, i deiatelnost' v 1866–1885 godakh" candidate diss. Moscow State University, 1979.

2. *PSZ* 2d ser., n. 41475, 84.

3. A. F. Koni, *Sobranie sochinenii* (Moscow, 1965), vol. 4, 263.

4. *PSZ*, 2d ser., n. 41475, 85, 86, 89, 97–99, 107, 100, 102.

5. Ibid.

6. Ibid.

7. Ibid.

8. Ibid.

9. *Kolokol*, Dec. 1, 1862.

10. *Moskovskie vedomosti*, Mar. 31, 1867.

11. *Delo*, 1868, no. 5, 104.

12. *Zhurnal iuridicheskogo obshchestva pri imperatorskom Sankt-Peterburskom universitete*, kn. 2, November 1896, 11.

13. *Iuridicheskii vestnik*, kn. 1, 1871, 51; *Zhurnal grazhdanskogo i ugolovnogo prava*, kn. 2, 1882, 84; ibid., kn. 3, 1885, 18–19.

14. TsGIA, f. 1405 (Ministerstvo iustitsii), op. 69, d. 7033(v), ll. 212–13.

15. *PSZ*, 3d series, n. 2314.

16. TsGIA, f. 1405, op. 73, d. 3655(a), l. 119.

17. TsGIA, op. 73, d. 3656(a), 3656(b), 3656(v).

18. LGIA, f. 53 (Petrogradskii istoriko-filologicheskii institut), op. 1, d. 460, l. 9.

19. In St. Petersburg uezd, 1,200 names were placed on the primary lists and 200 on the reserve lists. This was far from a sufficient number for a city numbering 700,000 (and almost one million a decade later). It therefore was decided to double the number of the city's jurors. In 1883 there were 2,400 on the primary lists and 500 on the reserve lists. *PSZ*, 2d ser., n. 54751. The number of jurors was raised in Moscow as well.

20. The legal statutes released officials of the fifth rank and higher from having to perform jury service. *PSZ*, 2d ser., n. 41475, p. 84. The statutes, however, did not prohibit high-ranking officials from serving on the juries if they desired to do so.

21. A. G. Rashin, *Naselenie Rossii za sto let 1811–1913. Statisticheskie ocherki* (Moscow, 1956), table 91.

22. Ibid., table 88.

23. TsGIAM, f. 16, op. 225, d. 1132, l. 2.

24. Rashin, *Naselenie Rossii*, tables 19 and 69.

25. In the first half of the 1880s, approximately 160,000 jurors were placed on primary lists every year; TsGIA, f. 1405, op. 86, d. 3007, l. 85. Together with the persons on reserve lists, the number of potential jurors in the country numbered 200,000. The capital provinces, however, accounted for only 10,500 of this total.

26. The provinces are Vladimir, Voronezh, Volyn' (Lutski district court), Ekaterinaslav, Kazan, Kiev, Bessarabia (Kishniev district court), Nizhnii Novgorod, Novgorod, Penza, Perm (Perm and Ekaterinaslav district courts), Pskov (Velikolutski district court), Riazan, Simbirsk, Smolensk, Taurida (Simfiropol district court), Tambov, Tver, Chernigov, and Iaroslavl.

27. For more detailed information on the jurors in these three provinces, see my article in *Voprosy istorii*, 1978, no. 6.

28. N. Balabanov, *Ocherki po istorii rabochego klassa v Rossii* (Kiev, 1924), pt. 2, 94–95.

29. *Nizhegorodskie vedomosti*, 1872, nos. 48–49; 1873, nos. 2, 5, 11.

30. Vladimir, Kazan, Kiev, Bessarabia Oblast, Penza, Perm, Simbirsk, Taurida, Voronezh, Tambov, Tver, and Iaroslavl.

31. Rashin, *Naselenie Rossii*, table 253.

32. TsGIA, f. 1405, op. 73, d. 3656(a), ll. 192, 175, 202, 227, 232–33.

33. *PSZ*, 2d ser., n. 57589, 5, 7–8.

34. TsGIA, f. 1405, op. 73, d. 3656(a), ll. 248, 260, 268–69.

35. In 1897, peasants accounted for 85 percent of the Russian population; see Rashin, *Naselenie Rossii*, table 205.

36. *Golos*, Sept. 2, 1866.

37. *Kolokol*, Oct. 1, 1866.

38. *Golos*, Aug. 31, 1866.

39. *Ochet Ministerstva iustitsii za 1866 god* (St. Petersburg, 1869), 21.

40. TsGIAM, f. 16, op. 225, d. 1132, l. 1.

41. *Iuridicheskaia gazeta*, Jan. 6, 1902.

42. I. P. Timofeev, *Sud prisiazhnykh v Rossii. Sudebnye ocherki* (Moscow, 1882), 91.

43. TsGIA, f. 1405, op. 73, d. 3656(a), ll. 1, 179.

44. Ibid.

45. TsGIA, f. 1405, op. 521, dd. 88–90, 94; op. 68, d. 1894; op. 69, d. 889; op. 71, dd. 2638, 2639.

46. TsGIA, f. 1405, op. 69, d. 7033(b), l. 108.

47. *Delo*, 1884, no. 3.

48. TsGIA, f. 1405, op. 73, d. 3656(b), ll. 14, 182; d. 3656(v), l. 91; d. 3656(b), l. 182.

49. Ibid.

50. Ibid.

51. Ibid.

52. *Russkii vestnik*, 1885, no. 176.

53. TsGIA, f. 1405, op. 69, d. 7033(v), ll. 24, 213.

54. Ibid.

55. TsGIAM, f. 16, op. 225, d. 1132, l. 12.

56. *Svod statisticheskikh svedenii po delam ugolovnym, voznikshim v 1873 g.* (St. Petersburg, 1874), 53.

57. For the working history of the jury courts in Russia, see my article in *Trudy gosudarstvennogo istoricheskogo muzeia* 67 (1988); 56–74.

58. *PSZ*, 3d ser., n. 4396.

59. G. A. Dzhanshiev, *Osnovy sudebnoi reformy* (Moscow, 1891), 177–78.

60. L. G. Zakharova, *Zemskaia kontrreforma 1890* (Moscow, 1968), 153.

61. L. F. Pisar'kova, "Moskovskoe gorodskoe obshchestvennoe upravlenie c serediny 1880kh godov do pervoi russkoi revoliutsii," candidate diss. (Moscow, 1980), 11.

62. *Zhurnal grazhdanskogo i ugolovnogo prava*, November 1889, 1.

XIII

POPULAR LEGAL CULTURES
THE ST. PETERSBURG *MIROVOI SUD*

Joan Neuberger

The Judicial Reform of 1864 has been considered the most successful of the Great Reforms. Yet its primary goal was to instill a respect for law in Russian society, and there is wide agreement that after the reform Russia remained deficient in precisely this area. The specific goals of the Judicial Reform were to eradicate the convoluted and corrupt old judicial system and to replace it with a modern, independent judiciary, modeled on Western institutions and based on the principle of equality before the law.[1] In social and cultural terms reformers hoped that exposure to the rule of law, institutionalized in the new courts, would create a legally literate population that could be assimilated into a unified, orderly, civil society.

To their credit the reformers realized how difficult their task would be. They recognized that the majority of Russians lived according to their own ideas about justice. It should be noted that customary law, unlike statutory law, was not a written code of prohibitions and punishments. The phrase itself is an abstraction that refers to sets of highly localized, consensual rules and ideas that were anything but abstract. Popular customs regarding justice and governing behavior were embedded in the practice of everyday life.[2] Generally speaking, the reformers' goal was to wean the people from the amorphous and variable customary law and to teach them the new, uniform, statute law. The weaning and teaching were to occur differently in different institutions. The jury, at one extreme, had the people fully involved in applying statute law, and the *volost'* (after 1861, a unit of peasant administration comprising several villages and hamlets) customary court, at the other, denied peasants access to statute law altogether. The *mirovoi sud*—the Justice of the Peace court—stood in between these two.[3]

In fact, nothing exemplifies the spirit of the Judicial Reforms better than the mirovoi sud. More than any other institution, it was designed explicitly to "teach the law to the people" and to bridge the gap between *narod* (commoners) and *obshchestvo* (educated society). Created to deal with the most common, petty criminal cases and civil suits, the mirovoi sud was considered an ideal classroom.[4] To win the trust of the people and ease the transition to the new legal system, mirovoi sud hearings were to be carried out with as little formality as possible. People of all classes appearing before the court had the right to explain their positions in their own words and to address justices of the peace or other litigants directly. Everyone was guaranteed equal treatment under the law.

Most important, the justices of the peace (JPs) were endowed with exceptionally broad powers of interpretation; cases brought to them were to be decided according to a unique blend of statute and custom. JPs were expected to make decisions on the basis of simple mediation between civil disputants or on the basis of common sense and personal conviction in criminal cases. In assessing the merits of a case, JPs were to take into consideration local legal customs and traditional practices when they conflicted with statute. They were "to decree a resolution" only when mediation failed. In that case the JP still had the authority to base his decision either on statutes of the mirovoi sud code or on his own "conviction" or "conscience."[5] The justice of the peace was envisioned as a kind of local Solomon, bringing wisdom and a knowledge of local customs to the interpretation of statutory law and the mediation of disputes.

In practice, the mirovoi sud's mission to teach the law to the people was hampered by restrictions imposed on it by the more cautious members of the reform commission.[6] Since volost courts had been established outside the regular legal system to deal with the majority of peasant cases, rural justices of the peace only encountered peasants in cases involving members of other estates. Then in 1889 the rural mirovoi sud was abolished entirely when the new land captains usurped the JPs' legal jurisdiction. In contrast, the urban mirovoi sud, which survived the attack of the counterreformers, was an all-class court in those cities where no purely peasant legal institution existed. The St. Petersburg court was further distinguished by the dedication of many of its justices of the peace, who saw their institution as a model for the courts (and the legal order) throughout the empire and fought ardently to protect its democratic features. The capital's mirovoi sud enjoyed as much success as any court in establishing its authority, so it illustrates especially clearly the contradictions and limitations inherent in the reformers' original vision, as well as the legal cultures their vision helped create.

The combination of paternalism and institutionalization that characterized the mirovoi sud typified the Judicial Reform and was responsible for the kind of legal culture that appeared in Russia after 1864. The reformers' sensitivity to the existence of traditional legal culture and their determination to replace it (as well as their appreciation of the difficulty of doing so) generated the successes as well as the limitations of the new legal system. Most observations about the deplorable state of late Imperial Russian legal culture focus on the radicals' distrust of the law or the autocrats' willingness to bend the law at whim.[7] But the Judicial Reform touched the lives of millions of imperial subjects. Everyday in the mirovoi sud, local custom confronted modern Western legal statute to produce a new legal culture. It is in these courtrooms that the reform had its widest impact. The ideas about law and justice that issued from both sides of the bench and the rituals, everyday practices, and language used to enact those ideas exhibit for us the formation of postreform legal culture.

The mirovoi sud succeeded in establishing the authority of legal norms to an extent that forces us to reconsider the common wisdom about legal consciousness in Russia. But it was a mixed success. The reformers, in their effort to avoid abruptly imposing the new legal system on an unprepared population, produced a system that ultimately undermined their attempt to wean the people from their traditional legal customs. The creation of local Solomons empowered to combine customary wisdom with statutory law did indeed allow assimilation to occur, but it occurred alongside a heightened awareness of segregation and difference.

At the beginning, hopes for the new mirovoi sud ran exceptionally high. In typically exuberant tones a Moscow province JP wrote:

> The immensity of the moral and practical consequences of such a revolution is obvious—it facilitates the gradual reeducation of every stratum of our society. . . . The introduction of the mirovoi sud, by virtue of its immediate repercussions, represents the most portentous facet of the judicial reform.[8]

This unalloyed optimism was matched by the bureaucratic reformers' confidence that "by virtue of its closeness to the litigants and the simple form of its procedure, [the mirovoi sud] will correspond to the judicial needs of the urban and rural people" and will transmit to the people modern legal concepts and respect for individual personal and property rights.[9]

These hopes contained the contradiction at the heart of the reform. On one hand, the members of the State Council believed that the majority of the people had no need of a formal legal system because the majority of them do not

> know the laws, cannot endure formalism, respect only natural fairness [*estestvennaia spravedlivost'*], and value their time, therefore they only care about a decision that is quick, and to their way of thinking, fair, . . . the main task of the mirovoi sud is to satisfy the urgent needs of the people in a court of conscience.[10]

On the other hand, the JPs were created expressly to introduce modern legal concepts. As I. V. Gessen made clear in his analysis of the government debates over judicial reform, the justice of the peace was expected to be more than a government agent enforcing the law. To teach the law to the people (who already possessed their own, rudimentary, sense of justice), the JP had to possess common sense, wisdom, and good will toward people, as

well as familiarity with local customs and broad practical experience. These
qualities were a matter of serious discussion because they were considered
essential for the JP to win the trust of the local population, to mediate fairly
among them, and at the same time to convey the concepts of legal order.[11]

Given these contradictory and extravagant expectations, the chorus of
praise that greeted the opening of the mirovoi sud in 1866 is astonishing.
The minister of justice, D. N. Zamiatin, expressed at length his satisfaction
with the court in his annual report for that year.[12] A. F. Koni, the eminent
Russian jurist, wrote that the court

> immediately gained popularity among the people and within a month after
> the introduction of the reform the nickname "mirovoi" had come to sound
> like something long familiar, habitual, something that had entered the flesh
> and blood of daily life while still conferring an instinctual respect.[13]

The majority of newspapers from all over the country added their voices to
the chorus during the mirovoi sud's first year.[14] Even thirty-five years later,
an editorial in the popular commercial daily *Peterburgskii listok,* which was
often critical of official judicial actions, commented that "from the first moment of its existence to the present day, the mirovoi sud enjoyed and still
enjoys the sympathy of the population, which sees in it a court that is open
and accessible to everyone."[15]

Most observers credited the justices of the peace themselves with the
court's success. Koni extolled the first JPs as people who saw their work as
"more than service [*sluzhba*]; as an occupation that enriched life and gave
it particular value."[16] M. P. Chubinskii, another prominent jurist, claimed
that the JPs deserved credit for popularizing the new judicial system as a
whole, because they were the ones who made justice accessible and the law
understandable.[17]

Mirovoi sud proponents took as evidence of this success the enormous
number of cases brought to the justice of the peace courts from the day
they opened their doors. The volume of cases far overwhelmed expectations.[18] The number of litigants was seen as proof of popular trust in the JPs
and trust in the new system. One Petersburg justice of the peace, who ended
up serving for over thirty years, called the opening of the mirovoi sud a time
of "celebration . . . for those for whom harmonious legal equality and lack
of hypocrisy were an unprecedented marvel, . . . the masses regarded the
justices with complete trust.[19]

Popular trust, then, was supposed to make it possible for the mirovoi sud,
in the words of one journalist, to become "a school for teaching respect for
individuality and the law."[20] In the provinces and in the capitals, JPs, other
jurists, and journalists all expressed their elation at the ability of the court
to raise the cultural level of the population by providing people with legal
experience. A provincial JP reported that

in the beginning the mirovoi sud was unintelligible to the majority of illiter-
ates. . . . Then, as a result of the first open acts of the justices of the peace,
law and legal matters apparently began to make some sense; and now, after
two years, the general understanding of the court has reached such a level
that the observer cannot help but be surprised at how, in such a short time,
our simple folk, with their native sensibility and common sense, acquired not
only trust but full respect for the court.[21]

There were some hurdles, however. The JPs' ability to teach the law to
the people was hindered by material and political problems. Funding for JP
salaries was inadequate in many districts, and everywhere it was difficult
to find clerks willing, for the low salaries offered, to do the enormous amount
of paperwork required by the unexpectedly high caseload.[22] Rooms suitable
for the dispensation of justice were often difficult to find, even in provincial
and national capitals. The Ekaterinoslav mirovoi sud reported in 1877 that
its chambers were located in a "simple hut" with only a clay floor, parti-
tioned from the zemstvo post station by a small canopy. One of the first JPs
in Petersburg, F. N. Ustrialov, recalled that after he opened his court in
1866 the police located a prostitute inspection station in the basement of the
building; Ustrialov found that offensive both to his litigants and to the cause
of mirovoi justice.[23] In St. Petersburg things had improved little by the turn
of the century. Newspaper columnists and court reporters as well as JPs
complained about the court's deplorable surroundings. According to one
columnist, the "pitiful, miserable, beggarly" mirovoi chambers did not influence the quality of "mercy and justice reigning in the courts," but they did

to a significant degree reflect [the official lack of] respect for justice, even
the attitude of the population toward it. A filthy, black stairway, a dark little
corridor, a convictlike servant dressed like a prisoner, a low ceiling . . . and
the justice of the peace, squeezed in all around in his suit jacket. . . . Justices,
and indeed justice, require more majestic conditions.[24]

Clearly the Tsarist government did not feel the need to surround its local
judicial system with symbols of royal power the way the British, as Douglas
Hay demonstrated, considered essential for the exercise of local legal authority.[25] While most of the supporters of the mirovoi sud would argue that
heavyhanded symbols of authority would defeat the mirovoi's educational
goals, they would all agree that material neglect undermined the same purpose by exhibiting the government's lack of regard for the court.[26]

And of course there were critics. When criticism of the mirovoi sud began
to surface in the 1870s it took two diametrically opposed forms: friendly
criticism from jurists and JPs trying to correct its shortcomings and hostile
criticism from government officials and conservatives (including some newspapers) trying to restrict its independence. Direct attacks on the mirovoi sud
began immediately after the court began operation in 1866 and culminated in
the abolition of the rural mirovoi in 1889.

One of the main problems facing the new system was that JPs, it turned out, needed some legal knowledge despite having power to refer to custom and conscience. Yet people with higher legal education were few, especially in rural Russia. The reformers tried to circumvent this problem by insisting that JPs be elected. Election, rather than appointment, was intended to guarantee that JPs were popular and responsible local figures, capable of winning the people's trust and familiar enough with local customs to base decisions on them.[27] While official surveys of the 1870s and 1880s show the court functioning relatively smoothly, an inevitable number of corrupt, inefficient, or incompetent JPs also surfaced in these years.[28] Local administrative officials, irritated by their inability to appoint JPs (and thereby control the court) attacked the personal shortcomings of the rural justices in order to malign the entire system. Proponents of elected justices of the peace countered that appointing JPs would neither improve the quality of personnel nor prevent corruption, the two ostensible concerns of the critics.[29]

After the rural mirovoi sud was abolished, opponents of elected JPs continued to attack the remaining urban courts. Many St. Petersburg JPs saw themselves as defenders of a heroic project, but they also had fewer operational and personnel problems than their rural counterparts. Fewer cases of misconduct, a lower rate of appeals, and much greater efficiency characterized the Petersburg courts from the beginning. More Petersburg JPs had juridical training or some higher education, more incumbents were re-elected, and far more were considered dedicated, "quality" personnel.[30] The commercial press represented the justices of the peace as well known, respected figures all the way up to 1914.[31]

The problem in St. Petersburg was that the court functioned, in a sense, too well. The Petersburg mirovoi sud provided accessible and equitable legal services to the capital's population. By the turn of the century it was thoroughly entrenched in city life. Its JPs, on the whole, were both dedicated to the cause of mirovoi justice and professional in the performance of their duties, if not in their training. But the excessive caseload that had plagued the whole system since 1866 made informal mediation increasingly difficult. Did the sacrifice of the informal, personal mediation make it impossible to win sufficient trust to "teach the law to the people"? The mirovoi sud had contact with hundreds of thousands of Petersburgers each year (and many more who read about cases in the newspapers); did that mean that it had taught the law to the people?

These questions can be answered in part by turning to the exercise of mirovoi justice itself. Because the mirovoi experiment attracted so much attention and because court sessions quickly became popular entertainment, newspapers published detailed reports of court cases and JP memoirs were numerous. The St. Petersburg court found a devoted chronicler in V. N. Nikitin, who reported on mirovoi sud cases for various newspapers. A year after the court opened he collected the reports of cases he considered typical, instructive, and representative of all strata of society and published them for the benefit of inexperienced JPs who might see how the capital's justices combined custom with statute and coped with the complexities of mediation. These verbatim reports of court proceedings convey the popular experience of mirovoi justice in ways that modify the initial, wholly positive conclusions drawn about the court's success.[32]

Generally speaking, most of the early Petersburg JPs did what they could to spread the word about the new court and to teach the law to the people. Some JPs "advertised the mirovoi" by inviting reporters to their courtrooms and even providing them with special seats. Others tried to make the law more accessible by playing to their audience, making their hearings as entertaining as possible with humorous asides and references to the Old Testament.[33] Many tried to make it clear that legal settlement in a mirovoi sud was preferable to the individual settling of scores. Nikitin related a case in which a landlord stole a lodger's possessions to prevent his vacating the premises without paying his rent. When the landlord argued that he had no other way of guaranteeing payment the JP exclaimed, "That's not true! You have the most reliable guarantee: the mirovoi sud."[34]

Access to the court and equality before its law were considered critical to the court's mission to teach the law to the people. The court's informality and oral, vernacular proceedings were designed to provide the poor and uneducated with full access to justice, equal to that of the elite. Most Petersburg JPs bent over backward to treat everyone with equal respect, in the belief that equality before the law extended beyond the resolution of cases to the treatment of individuals in the public sphere.[35] By all accounts this caused considerable resentment among members of Russia's old elite. As one prerevolutionary court historian observed,

> They were known to have considered it incompatible with their station to stand before the eyes of the court on the same level as a "muzhik." On losing a case, they would reproach the justice for his "willingness to trade a brother noble for a peasant."[36]

I. A. Galov, one of the first Petersburg JPs, recalled that in the early years JPs were called "reds" and "revolutionaries" by members of the gentry chagrined at having to appear in court alongside commoners *(prostoliudina)*.[37] The journal *Vest'* published a series of indignant articles denouncing the equality of all before the law as an abrogation of the principles of a society of orders (which of course it was) and as the first step toward anarchy *("vsiakomu svoe")*.[38] While most elite resistance to mirovoi leveling was rooted in class prejudice, some early JPs, as D. M. Wallace noted, "in seeking to avoid Scylla, came dangerously near to Charybdis" by going out of their way to humiliate or injure the well born.[39] Others used the new office in a more legitimate crusade to track down those who expected privilege to protect them from the court's justice. Nikitin recounted a number of cases in which JPs punished people who tried to bribe or otherwise influence them and sought out people who tried to evade the court's authority.[40]

The JPs' zealous adherence to the principle of equality before the law was, however, not as straightforward as it appears at first glance. In practice, equality before the law was limited by popular ignorance of the law and by class hostility, but also by the JPs' own, often unrecognized, class prejudices. In the majority of Nikitin's cases, JPs listened to the long-winded explanations of petty grievances between neighbors, commercial acquaintances, relatives, *zemliaki,* and so on with admirable patience. But in many cases involving people at the very bottom of the social ladder, even the most conscientious JPs faltered. When a homeless peasant was accused of stealing two coats and a pair of boots, the JP interrogated the accused rather than letting him tell his own story. The manner of interrogation made the JP's suspicions clear from the start. The JP's manner differed not only from his treatment of defendants and litigants in other cases who were allowed to tell their own stories, but also from his treatment of the witnesses in this case. The arresting policeman and main witness were permitted to narrate their version of events without interruption and without the warnings to "speak truthfully" made to the peasant-defendant.[41] In another case, brought by one peasant migrant worker against his *zemliak* (fellow countryman), the JP repeatedly and angrily expressed his frustration with the defendant's inability to express himself in proper Russian. Although the peasant's remarks do not seem as obscure as the justice claimed, he was fined two rubles for continuing to speak in the same idiosyncratic manner.[42]

For the most part, however, ordinary people found the JPs more accessible and more respectful than prereform authorities. Accessibility and equality were considered critical because they were supposed to create an environment of trust that would allow the people to see the benevolence of the new legal system and to adopt the standards defined in its laws. People did indeed flood into the court from every corner of society, and many came away satisfied with their first experience. Nikitin related one case in which a landlord sued his lodger for three rubles and fifty kopeks in unpaid rent. The lodger did not dispute the charge and agreed to repay the debt then and there. After hearing the way the JP negotiated the case—clearly, quickly, fairly, and "without any paperwork"—the landlord forgave the debt, then revealed that he had read about the mirovoi sud in the newspaper and had decided to bring the case just to test the new system, which he found to be "fine."[43] But did efficiency, equality, and respect lead to a thorough or even positive appreciation of the legal system? One worker, asked in 1866 to compare the new court with the old, suggested that it did:

> How can the new one not be better? [In the old court] some cop interrupts you right off. You try to give an explanation and he roars at you with some nonsense that rubs you the wrong way. But now, no way—everything's been shaken up, and it's all right this mirovoi. Someone starts to mouth off and

he's stopped by a law and a fine. A ruble is a lot of money, and if that's the law that means it has to be that way, so you don't regret it. No, no, this court is okay.[44]

Certainly the mirovoi sud sparked popular interest everywhere. Its sessions were well attended and numerous newspapers reported its cases. But JPs and other observers drew extremely broad conclusions from the volume of attention. One provincial JP (among many others) called the mirovoi "truly . . . a school for the people," because,

> on leaving the court, the audience gathered in small circles and discussed everything they had heard: they carried on arguments about the credibility of the accusation and of the evidence produced, about the worthiness of the decision.[45]

The extent to which such discussions generated legal consciousness or respect for judicial authority rather than a great deal of local gossip is difficult to gauge.

The kinds of cases people brought to the JPs in the years before the court's jurisdiction was widely understood are one indicator of what people wanted the court to do for them. Members of all urban social groups came (or were summoned) to the JPs for settlement of a wide variety of public and domestic disputes. At first the JPs were presented with a high number of cases involving conflicts between husband and wife, including requests to dissolve marriages, a power reserved for church authorities. A mother came to have a JP prevent her son from drinking. Women came for protection against their husbands or fathers. Mothers complained about the loose behavior of their daughters.[46] Numerous cases involved personal insults of one kind or another. A baker sued a customer for defaming her in front of other customers. Another woman brought charges against her neighbor for calling her a loose woman because she had not married the man she lived with for eight years. A Jewish artisan brought charges against a Russian artisan for grabbing him by the beard and calling him a "Yid."[47] P. M. Maikov, an early Petersburg JP, recalled that many of his first cases were trivial ones brought by peasants, workers, servants, and so forth for the sole purpose of exhibiting their new right to stand side by side with a high official and have it publicly explained that they were now equal citizens.[48]

Many of these conflicts were outside the court's competence, the limits of which JPs explained over and over again during the early years. By the turn of the century, as many observers noted, people stopped bringing frivolous cases, domestic quarrels, or cases without proper proof. As evidence of rising legal consciousness, however, this is ambivalent at best. The shift in suits filed might signify popular acceptance of the official definition of appropriate matters, but it might only mean that people understood where the court drew the line. To some extent this was nothing more than an acceptance of the fact that the court's definition of legal matters was differ-

ent from some popular definitions. The court would prosecute certain forms
of domestic and workplace violence previously considered private matters.
It would try to reconcile some disputes according to law and some based
on negotiated compromise. But it would not accept cases in which neither
material evidence nor reliable witnesses could be produced, and most mari-
tal and family matters for which so many people sought the court's aid
during the early years remained outside the JPs' scope.

In the capital, statute came to dominate mirovoi sud practice for pragmatic
reasons. Many JPs and other observers noted that the essential informality
of the mirovoi sud was sacrificed soon after it opened to the high caseload,
which demanded more speed and impersonality. By 1891 Petersburg JPs
were required to judge an average of 3,500 cases per year; ten years later
that figure had risen to more than 4,300 cases per year.[49] In addition, some
degree of formality was forced on the mirovoi sud by Senate cassation rul-
ings that usually rejected cases decided by "conscience," without reference
to statute.[50] The decline of informality caused considerable regret, as late as
the 1900s, among many JPs who felt that time-consuming, personal mediation, which allowed custom to influence decisions, was still desirable in
many cases. On the other hand, one writer noted that Petersburg JPs rarely
had to deal with people who expected their cases to be decided according
to customary law. And after the first few years of its existence an increasing
number of people *requested* decisions based on statute rather than mediation, a sure sign, one prerevolutionary historian thought, of "cultural
consciousness," "self-esteem," and "knowledge of the law" among the Petersburg population.[51]

While statutory law may have been an alien standard for many Petersburg
inhabitants, one should not assume its predominance was disadvantageous
to those outside the educated elite. Many poor Petersburgers benefited from
the application of statute law and the principles underlying it. The abused
women and children who managed to have their cases heard and the poor
victims of petty crime certainly benefited from legal protection.[52] After the
turn of the century the mirovoi sud prosecuted thousands of shopkeepers
for selling spoiled and dangerous food (a serious problem before refrigera-
tion). And beginning in 1901 increasing numbers of workers brought grievances against their employers to the mirovoi.[53]

Nor does the alienness of statute imply that mirovoi justice was simply
imposed on the people from above. To be sure, it was imposed in the sense
that the Judicial Reform was state policy, but it was accepted without much
resistance, even eagerly by many. Mirovoi sud practice shows that the court
was able to satisfy a popular desire for institutionalized justice and that
many people accepted the authority of the justices of the peace and the law
they enforced. Over time, many of the problems of the 1860s, such as confusion over the JPs' jurisdiction, were ameliorated. Even in the absence of
informality, the mirovoi sud thrived: during the twentieth century the number of mirovoi sud cases increased more quickly than the rate of population

growth.[54] These are all signs that a legal culture of some kind was firmly implanted in late Imperial urban society, with perhaps deeper roots than we are accustomed to thinking.

Beneath the surface, however, one can see the limits of mirovoi sud success: in its accessibility, equity, usefulness, and authority. The litigants and defendants in the majority of Nikitin's cases showed themselves willing to accept JP authority to mediate their disputes, and the high number of cases confirms this. But people often responded to the specific decisions with more confusion or irritation than comprehension. Thus it is difficult to determine whether people brought disputes to JPs and accepted JPs' decisions because they trusted the JPs and respected the authority of the law or because the mirovoi sud was the only game in town and they were displaying habitual submission to authority in a new form. The peasant-worker fined for his outbursts of peasant dialect was typical in concluding (apparently without sarcasm):

> So it's really true. A verdict fair and square, that's right, and along the way I got burned for two rubles. Farewell, sir. We're heading out to the village now, and when we get there we'll discuss everything about this court of yours; it's okay, it didn't do me much good, but it's interesting.[55]

Historians of the mirovoi sud often pointed to the low percentage of decisions that were appealed as evidence of the people's satisfaction with the court. But in Nikitin's two collections of Petersburg cases from the 1860s, almost every case ends with the loser proclaiming his or her intention to seek appeal. It is possible that on reflection people were satisfied with the court's decisions. But it is also possible that they changed their minds because of the additional time and expense the appeal would take. The low rate of appeals might signal popular acceptance of the law or of the court's authority, but it might signal only resignation to the court's power.

There were times when the access and informality of the court, which reformers considered the cornerstone of mirovoi sud success, was viewed as intrusion. In their zeal to bring the law to the people, some JPs forced the law on the people. N. A. Nekliudov, who became the chairman of the Petersburg mirovoi conference (its governing body and instance of first appeal), was JP for the Haymarket district, well known for "sheltering the dregs of society."[56] Nekliudov advertised the new court in 1866 by strolling around his district at various times of day and night, listening to the complaints of the local population, and resolving their disputes right on the street. A. N. Matveev, another of the first JPs, responded aggressively to reports of disorders occurring on the streets of his district. He would hurry out to the street, ask various people what was going on, and, after satisfying himself as to the legitimacy of the complaints, fling open his coat to reveal the sign of his office (JPs wore special chains around their necks) and propose that the crowd of people follow him to his chambers. I. O. Kvist, another prominent JP, was known to drag people off the streets, conduct them to his court, and fine them on the spot.[57]

These incidents were reported as evidence of the passion with which the first JPs approached their positions, but such ardor on their part might well have been viewed, from the other side of the bench, as an invasion. The JPs not only extended the arm of the law into relatively lawless public spaces; they also redefined acceptable private behavior as well. Naturally, the increased ability of the state to police its streets was applauded by the minister of justice.[58] But the people who found themselves in court for public rowdiness, wife abuse, and maltreatment of apprentices, for example, were "almost always naively surprised" to discover that their habitual public behavior or private abuse was against the law.[59] In these cases, traditional justifications for customary behavior—customary law—were simply disregarded by the court.

From the reformers' point of view, not to mention that of the abused, the court would have served its purpose if it had prevented future public rowdiness or violence. Since people continued to bring similar complaints to JPs for resolution, we can assume that at least some people favored statute over custom in these cases. But we also know that the "naive surprise" with which wife abusers, masters who tormented apprentices, and street revelers responded to their first court appearances turned bitter after a few days' reflection in detention. Those newly defined as criminals resented the abrogation of their own customary disciplinary powers, and the continuation of such cases suggests that they did not view the statute as a legitimate deterrent.[60] It seems likely that such resentment extended to at least some law-abiding Petersburgers who retained a strong sense of customary justice in place of, or even alongside, acceptance of statutory norms.

The mirovoi sud's successes make it clear that hundreds of thousands of people living in the capital adapted to the official legal culture relatively easily, even in the absence of informal mediation. This strongly supports the view that while the official Westernized legal culture was new, the concept of law—zakon—was no more alien to people outside the educated elite than the concepts of justice—pravo. But we do not know how far the JPs' influence spread. In the working-class periphery, more disputes were settled with a fist or a bottle than with mirovoi mediation, even at the end of the century. And popular skepticism (even among those who entered the court more or less deliberately) reveals limits to people's willingness to adopt the official legal culture. While many people learned to use the legal system to their advantage, there is no evidence that they were willing to swallow the official legal culture whole. It is more likely that people maintained a bifurcated legal culture in the postreform period, a mixture that contributed to the overall urban-rural amalgam of lower-class culture in the capital.

Ironically, it was the reformers' sensitivity to the existence of popular justice (if not of law) that perpetuated the bifurcation of legal cultures. The mirovoi sud existed in a kind of judicial limbo. Its informality and openness to customary law separated it from the rest of the judicial system. This made the court accessible but also allowed it to legitimize the coexistence of legal cultures. The reformers' efforts to eradicate paternalism led them to devise a new form of paternalism, which undercut their mission to create a unified and orderly civil society.

NOTES

1. The Judicial Reform, issued as *Sudebnye ustavy* 20 noiabria 1864 goda (henceforth, *SU*), 4 vols. (St. Petersburg, 1864), structured the new institutions and delineated the regulations governing them. Vol. 4 contained the only new *laws* published—the civil and criminal codes of the mirovoi sud: *Ustav o nakazaniiakh, nalagaemykh mirovymi sud'iami.*

2. For an introduction to Russian customary law, see the discussion among Moshe Lewin, Christine Worobec, George Yaney, and Michael Confino in *Russian Review* 44 (1985), no. 1; Peter Czap, Jr., "Peasant Class Courts and Peasant Customary Justice in Russia, 1861–1912," *Journal of Social History* 1 (1967), no. 2; and Stephen Frank, "Popular Justice, Community and Culture among the Russian Peasantry, 1870–1900," *Russian Review* 46 (1987), no. 3.

3. Standard modern histories of the Judicial Reform have paid little attention to the mirovoi sud, especially the urban mirovoi, but between 1866 and 1917 several good histories and numerous memoirs appeared. This essay is drawn from those histories that relied most on citations from official debates, government inspections, publicistic works, and case reports from the 1860s and 1870s: *Petrogradskii mirovoi sud za piat'desiat' let* (henceforth, *PMS*), (Petrograd, 1916); G. A. Dzhanshiev, "Vvedenie mirovogo suda," *Epokha velikikh reform*, 8th ed. (Moscow, 1900); I. V. Gessen, *Sudebnaia reforma* (St. Petersburg, 1904); S. P. Mokrinskii, "Vybornyi mirovoi sud," *Sudebnye ustavy 20 noiabria 1864 g. za piat'desiat' let* (henceforth, *SU*50), (Petrograd, 1914); N. N. Polianskii, "Mirovoi sud," *Sudebnaia reforma*, ed. N. V. Davydov and N. N. Polianskii (Moscow, 1915).

4. *SU*, vol. 4, *Ust. o nak.*, art. 1; *Zhurnal soedinennykh departamentov zakonov i grazhdanskikh del Gosudarstvennogo soveta za 1862 g.*, no. 65, 17–20, cited in F. I. Korsakov, "Praktika Petrogradskogo mirovogo s"ezda po grazhdanskim i ugolovnym delam v otsenke pravitel'stvuiushchego senata," *PMS*, 1062; M. Brun, "Mirovye sud'i," *Entsiklopedicheskii slovar' Brokgauz-Efrona*, vol. 19 (St. Petersburg, 1896), 428–29; Polianskii, "Mirovoi," 205.

5. On civil "decrees," see *SU*, vol. 1, *Ust. grazh. sud.*, art. 70. Decisions in criminal cases might be rendered according to a JP's "inner conviction" *(po vnutrennemu ikh ubezhdeniiu)* or, in civil cases, his "conscience" *(po ubezhdeniiu sovesti)*. See *SU*, vol. 2, *Ust. ugol. sud.*, art. 119, and vol. 1, *Ust. grazh. sud.*, art. 129. For the reformers' discussion on the formality of JPs' decision making, see I. V. Gessen, *Sudebnaia reforma* (St. Petersburg, 1904), 73–75.

6. There was a great deal of discussion about the jurisdiction of peasant affairs during the editing process; to judge by complaints after implementation, many ambiguities remained unresolved. Jurisdiction over specific cases was unclear; similar crimes brought different penalties in the different courts. A peasant who stole two rubles from a city dweller at market earned a sentence of six months in prison when the case was tried in the mirovoi. But when a volost court tried a peasant for stealing thirty rubles from another peasant at home in the village, the sentence was only a few days' detention; for these and similar cases, see V. Nazar'ev, "Sovremennaia

glush': Iz vospominanii mirovogo sud'i," *Vestnik evropy*, 1872, kn. 2; Baron Korf, "Mirovoi sud v provintsii," *Vestnik evropy*, 1869, kn. 1, and 1870, kn. 1. These incidents were reported both as criticism of the reality of "equality before the law" and to indicate the difficulty, if not the futility, of attempting to teach the law to the people when the law seemed irrational and unfair.

7. Samuel Harper, "Exceptional Measures in Russia," *Russian Review* (London) 1 (1912), no. 4; Richard Pipes, *Russia under the Old Regime* (New York, 1974); Bogdan Kistyakovsky, "In Defense of Law: The Intelligentsia and Legal Consciousness," *Landmarks* (New York, 1977); Leonard Shapiro, "The Pre-Revolutionary Intelligentsia and the Legal Order," in *The Russian Intelligentsia*, ed. Richard Pipes (New York, 1961).

8. V. P. Bezobrazov, "Mysli po povodu mirovoi sudebnoi vlasti," *Russkii vestnik*, October 1866, 369, 373.

9. *Zhurnal soedinennykh departamentov zakonov i grazhdanskikh del Gosudarstvennogo soveta*, 1862, no. 65, 43, cited in B. V. Vilenskii, *Sudebnaia reforma i kontrreforma v Rossii* (Saratov, 1969), 167.

10. Cited in Korsakov, "Praktika," 1063.

11. Gessen, "Sudebnaia," 73; *Ob"iasnitel'naia zapiska k proektu uch. sud. ustanovleny*, cited in Mokrinskii, "Vybornyi," 3–5; Brun, "Mirovye," 428; F. N. Ustrialov, "Mirovoi sud v S-Peterburge v 1868–1872 g.," *Istoricheskii vestnik*, 1885, no. 19, 117. This image was widely discussed in the press in the 1860s; see press survey in A. A. Pushnov, "Vvedenie mirovykh sudebnykh ustanovlenii," *PMS*, 13–14.

12. Cited in Mokrinskii, 55.

13. A. F. Koni, "Novye mekha i novoe vino," *Sobranie sochinenii*, vol. 4 (Moscow, 1966), 253; Polianskii, "Mirovoi," 198; P. M. Maikov, "Vospominaniia," *PMS*, 1362.

14. See Pushnov, "Vvedenie," 34–51, for a survey of responses to the opening of the mirovoi sud in the press.

15. *Peterburgskii listok*, May 15, 1901.

16. A. F. Koni, "Mirovye sud'i," *Sobranie sochinenii*, vol. 1, 289; D. F. Domozhirov and A. N. Beliaev, "Proizvodstvo del u mirovykh sudei i v s"ezde," *PMS*, 246–47; Mokrinskii, "Vybornyi," 52–53, 60; Gessen, "Sudebnaia," 182; *Sudebnyi vestnik*, July 2, 1866, and Sept. 2, 1866, cited in Pushnov, "Vvedenie," 34–37.

17. M. P. Chubinskii, "Sudebnaia reforma," *Stat'i i rechi po voprosam ugolovnogo prava i protsessa*, vol. 2 (St. Petersburg, 1912), 186–87, 233–34.

18. In 1867, the first full year of operation, JPs were established in sixteen provinces; they heard 237,176 civil cases and 147,651 criminal cases, an average of 939 per JP. In St. Petersburg alone, however, twenty-eight JPs heard 56,144 cases in their first *half year* at work, averaging more than 2,000 cases per JP, many of whom worked more than twelve hours a day. See E. N. Tarnovskii, "Statisticheskie svedeniia o deiatel'nosti sudebnykh ustanovlenii, obrazovannykh po ustavam Imperatora Aleksandra II za 1866–1912 gody," *SU50*, vol. 2, 339, 342; I. V. Krasovskii, "Lichnyi sostav," *PMS*, 189.

19. N. G-e, "Proshloe i nastoiashchee mirovogo suda v Peterburge (Beseda so stareishim mirovym sud'ei d. s. s. I. A. Galovym," *Peterburgskaia gazeta*, May 23, 1901.

20. Cited in Pushnov, "Vvedenie," 34.

21. *Svod zamechanii o deiatel'nosti novykh sudebnykh ustanovlenii po primeneniiu Ustavov 20 noiabria 1864 g.*, 4–5, cited in Polianskii, "Mirovoi," 203; see also I. V. Gessen, "Istoriia mestnogo suda i zadachi preobrazovaniia," *Reforma mestnogo suda* (St. Petersburg, 1910), 24–25; Dzhanshiev, "Vvedenie," 461–62; D. M. Wallace, *Russia on the Eve of War and Revolution* (Princeton, N.J., 1984), 79.

22. Polianskii, "Mirovoi," 227; Mokrinskii, "Vybornyi," 34–37; M. Grebenschchikov, "Mirovoi sud v S-Peterburge, v poslednem desiatiletii," *Zhurnal grazhdanskogo i ugolovnogo prava*, 1887, kn. 7, 6–7.

23. Mokrinskii, "Vybornyi," 35; Ustrialov, "Mirovoi sud," 102.

24. Aborigen, "Stolichnyi den'," *Peterburgskii listok,* Mar. 8, 1901.

25. Douglas Hay, "Property, Authority and the Criminal Law," in *Albion's Fatal Tree: Crime and Society in Eighteenth-Century England,* ed. Douglas Hay et al (New York, 1975), 26–31.

26. V. I. Likhachev, "K tridtsatiletiiu mirovykh sudebnykh ustanovlenii," pt. 2, *Zhurnal Ministerstva iustitsii,* 1895, no. 12, 13.

27. *SU,* vol. 3, *Uchrezh. sud. ustan.,* arts. 19–40; Gessen, *Reforma,* 24.

28. Mokrinskii cited local inspections, governors' reports, and reports of the senatorial inspection of 1880. He claimed that critics exaggerated accusations of misconduct for political reasons. Mokrinskii, "Vybornyi," 4–5, 8, 14–21, 47–49, 52, 57–60; Polianskii, "Mirovoi," 219–20; Gessen, *Sudebnaia,* 182. Grebenschchikov, "Mirovoi sud," 1–2, cited inspections of the 1860s and 1880.

29. William Wagner, "Tsarist Legal Policies at the End of the Nineteenth Century: A Study in Inconsistencies," *Slavonic and East European Review* 54, no. 3; Theodore Taranovski, "The Aborted Counterreform: Murav'ev Commission and the Judicial Statutes of 1864," *Jahrbücher für Geschichte Osteuropas* 29, no. 2; V. Fuks, *Sud i politsiia* (Moscow, 1889), summarized the critics' position; the proponents' position was represented in *Vybornyi mirovoi sud. Sbornik statei* (St. Petersburg, 1898).

30. V. V. Menshutkin, "Proekty preobrazovanii mirovogo s"ezda," *PMS,* 983–1047; Wagner, "Tsarist," 385–89; Baron Korf, "Mirovoi sud v provintsii," *Vestnik Evropy,* 1869, kn. I, 913; V. D. Nabokov, "Polveka mirovoi iustitsii," *Russkaia mysl',* 1917, no. 7–8, 102–3; Krasovskii, "Lichnyi," 189ff.; Bezobrazov, "Mysli," 371; *Vybornyi mirovoi sud,* 83–93.

31. This was true of the middle-class commercial newspapers *Peterburgskii listok* and *Peterburgskaia gazeta* as well as the working-class *Gazeta-kopeika,* though none of these refrained from exposing cases of corruption or misconduct in the mirovoi sud; see, for example, *Peterburgskii listok,* Apr. 29, 1901, and June 1, 1911; *Gazeta-kopeika,* Feb. 15, 1909.

32. V. N. Nikitin, *Mirovoi sud v Peterburge. Stseny v kamerakh sudei i podrobnye razbiratel'stva zapisannye s podlinnykh slov* (St. Petersburg, 1867). He published another collection of mirovoi sud cases as *Oblomki razbitogo korablia. Stseny u mirovykh sudei shestidesiatykh godov* (St. Petersburg, 1891).

33. Maikov, "Vospominaniia," 1360–61.

34. Nikitin, *Mirovoi,* 18.

35. Maikov, "Vospominaniia," 1355.

36. Mokrinskii, "Vybornyi," 23.

37. G-e, *Peterburgskaia gazeta,* May 23, 1901. Wallace confirmed this, *Russia,* 82; also Polianskii, "Mirovoi," 198, 203; Dzhanshiev, "Vvedenie," 462–63; Pushnov, "Vvedenie," 41.

38. Pushnov, "Vvedenie," 44–49. Domozhirov and Beliaev, "Proizvodstvo," 253–54, noted that the JPs' addressing everyone with the respectful "vyi" provoked a heated polemic in the press.

39. Wallace, *Russia,* 81.

40. Nikitin, *Oblomki,* 87–88, 96–98.

41. Nikitin, *Mirovoi,* 60–67.

42. Nikitin, *Oblomki,* 98–101. As a counterexample, Maikov's memoirs include a case in which a JP sympathized with workers who used the court to win an increase in wages, even after they broke the season-long contract they had signed; Maikov, "Vospominaniia," 1363–66.

43. Nikitin, *Oblomki,* 1–3.

44. *S.-Peterburgskie vedomosti,* June 26, 1866, cited in Domozhirov and Beliaev, "Proizvodstvo," 254; see also Polianskii, "Mirovoi," 205.

45. *Svod zamechanii,* 6; cited in Polianskii, "Mirovoi," 206.

46. Nikitin, *Oblomki,* 3–6; Domozhirov and Beliaev, "Proizvodstvo," 244–47; L. P-l', "K iubileiu mirovogo suda," *Novosti,* May 22, 1901; G-e, *Peterburgskaia gazeta,* May 23, 1901.

47. See Nikitin, *Mirovoi,* 97–104 and 163–69, on criminal suits, and 135–200 on civil suits of a similar nature; see also his *Oblomki,* 88–92.

48. Maikov, "Vospominaniia," 1362.

49. *S-Peterburgskie stolichnye sudebnye mirovye ustanovleniia i arestnyi dom za 1902 god. Otchet* (St. Petersburg, 1903), 58.

50. Korsakov, "Praktika," 1067–69.

51. Domozhirov and Beliaev, "Proizvodstvo," 245; G-e, *Peterburgskaia gazeta,* May 23, 1901; Iks, "Rechi konservatory," *Grazhdanin,* Mar. 30, 1900; Korsakov, "Praktika," 1069. JPs' discussions of these problems can be found in their annual reports nearly every year and other judicial publications, such as *Sudebnoe oboz-renie,* May 20 and 29, 1905.

52. Newspaper court reporting at the turn of the century was full of such cases; for example, "V kamerakh mir. sudei," *Peterburgskii listok,* Jan. 25 and Feb. 21, 1901.

53. "Ist metel'schchikov," *Peterburgskii listok,* Mar. 17, 1901.

54. *S-Peterburgskie stolichnye sudebnye mirovye ustanovleniia i arestnyi dom za 1913 god. Otchet* (St. Petersburg, 1914), 102.

55. Nikitin, *Oblomki,* 101.

56. Domozhirov and Beliaev, "Proizvodstvo," 264.

57. Ibid., 264–65.

58. Count Palen's annual report cited in Mokrinskii, "Vybornyi," 55–56.

59. Pushnov, "Vvedenie," 40; Bezobrazov, "Mysli," 374.

60. *Golos* published a survey of such cases, in which workshop masters and others insisted on their right to commit the acts for which they were charged; cited in Pushnov, "Vvedenie," 40.

XIV

THE UNIVERSITY STATUTE
OF 1863
A RECONSIDERATION

Samuel D. Kassow

Writing from exile in 1929, Professor A. A. Kizevetter recalled the annual celebrations marking Tat'iana Day, the traditional founding day of Moscow University. Long before the tedious official ceremony started, officials, students, professors, and alumni from all over Russia filled the main auditorium. After sitting through the obligatory prayers, the long scholarly paper, and the rector's remarks, the throng would rise, sing the national anthem, then depart for a day of festive partying in Moscow's restaurants. This was one day in the year when the police would look the other way as crowds of students in their distinctive uniforms sauntered down the Tver and Strastnois boulevards to the Romanovka and other favorite hangouts. Meanwhile, the alumni-professors, doctors, lawyers, civil servants, even a few industrialists and businessmen, would leave for smaller, more intimate gatherings all over Moscow. In the late afternoon they would start making their way toward a tavern, the large hall of the Bolshoi Moskovskii Traktir in the center of town. After more speechmaking and drinking, *troiki* (traditional drinking groups of three males) would begin taking the alumni to the Iar'. On this day (January 12), the famous restaurant served only revelers from the university. All the rooms would be packed. New guests would arrive to cheers from the crowded rooms inside. V. O. Kliuchevskii, the great historian, would recite humorous couplets, while the famous lawyer Plevako improvised speeches on topics shouted from the audience.

This was a joyous holiday. It was very pleasant for everyone to feel, even once a year, that he belonged to a larger group of cultured individuals bound by common memories and sharing the same mood. All the barriers that separated people—age, politics, occupation—were swept away. . . . What was this, this one-day Moscow carnival? Was it just revelry and merrymaking? No, this was a celebration of the conscious unity of cultured Russia.

That cultured Russia was divided by many disputes . . . but on Tat'iana Day
the feeling of belonging to the same alma mater outweighed all the divisions.[1]

Not everyone shared Kizevetter's lyrical view of the "one-day carnival."
There were years when ugly brawls broke out between the carousing students and the tough butcher boys from the nearby Hunters' Row market.
Student organizations crusaded against the public drunkenness of Tat'iana
and issued appeals for the students to uphold the traditions and the honor
of the student body, preferably by attendance at speeches discussing the
terrible plight of the dark masses who stood totally outside the university
world. For many, Kizevetter's family of "cultured individuals," the alumni
of Moscow University, actually bore a closer resemblance to a panoply of
characters from Chekhov's plays: bored and ineffectual doctors and civil
servants, for whom university days indeed seemed like a faded dream.

Thus even Tat'iana symbolized the ambiguities of the universities' position
in Tsarist Russia. The clashes between privileged students and their poorer
contemporaries, the uneasy conscience which led many students to reject
merrymaking in order to express concern about the underprivileged masses,
the very uncertainty as to whether the university produced a class united
by common culture or only the pale imitation of a civil society which would
disintegrate under the pressures of Russian life—all underscored the para-
doxes of Russian higher education.

The root paradox was that institutions like Moscow University were the
creatures of a Russian state which had a profound mistrust of that very
"conscious unity of cultured Russia" which Tat'iana was celebrating. Almost
until the very end of the autocracy, there was no alternative agent—no
churches, individuals, or cities—which could develop and support higher
educational institutions without state participation. And ironically, this Russian state, in many respects so reactionary, was also a most powerful source
of revolutionary change, as its higher educational policy proved. Putatively
dedicated to preserving the principle of estates, the inviolability of Russian
Orthodoxy and the prerogatives of the aristocracy, the autocracy founded
universities and institutes which directly undercut the principle of privilege
and status determined by birth. Open to young people from all estates, the
higher educational institutions, especially the universities, posed yet another
long-term threat to the state, even as they imbued ever-growing numbers of
civil servants with new values of public service and liberal education.[2] Their
dedication to the principle of education based on pursuit of scientific truth
(nauka) implied an openness to inquiry and a connection to a cosmopolitan
academic culture. This culture would defy all attempts at strict regimenta-
tion and control and would clash with an ideology based on the personal
authority of the tsar and official Orthodoxy.

The relationship between the universities and the Russian state was not
easy. But were the constant conflicts inevitable? Was it foreordained, as
some historians have argued, that "self-governing," if not autonomous, uni-

versities were inherently incompatible with the Tsarist state?[3] Or was there some way of conceptualizing a stable relationship between the institutions of higher learning and the government?

The 1863 University Statute came closest, for all its flaws, to reflecting the views of the majority of the Russian professoriate.[4] It provided for faculty elections of rectors and deans; faculty disciplinary jurisdiction over student offenses; faculty election of new professors, subject to certain procedural conditions and ministerial approval; a doubling of financial support for the universities; broader provision for supporting and training graduate students; and broad faculty authority over course content and teaching schedules.

The statute also contained two major flaws: it denied the students corporate rights and refused to recognize their collective identity, and it failed adequately to define the jurisdiction and prerogatives of the state-appointed curators and thus opened the way for dangerous ambiguities and misinterpretations. While early in the drafting process it seemed that women might win admittance as full students, this proposal fell by the wayside in the final drafts.

But despite its flaws, the reform era produced a statute which gave the faculty at least as many rights as were enjoyed by faculties in France, Great Britain, the United States, and Germany. The 1863 statute gave Russian professors no less academic freedom than their counterparts at most U.S. universities, no more reason to complain about overcentralization and government interference than their counterparts in France. If the vaunted German university system was still a preferred model, there were still Russian academics ready to point out the weaknesses lurking behind its facade of academic excellence. The nineteenth century saw intensive ferment in the world of higher education.[5] Russian professors had problems, but they were certainly not alone.

If by comparison with foreign examples the 1863 statute had many positive features, why did it last such a short time? And why did so many educated Russians consider the "university question" to be a problem, a case of the glass being half empty, not half full? It would be true to say that part of the problem lay in the nature of the beast. The university was a complex institution that discharged diverse, simultaneous tasks and answered to many potentially incompatible constituencies. This did not make for a happy situation, especially in Russian circumstances.

But that is only a partial answer. In another sense the universities challenged the tsars and the bureaucracy to modify their most basic political concepts in order to make room for anomalies like universities that were both state and "public" institutions, that relied on government allocations but demanded some measure of autonomy and self-governance to carry out their mission. Institutionally and intellectually the universities challenged the Russian government to rethink its relationship to societal institutions.[6] The government for the most part failed that challenge.

The 1863 statute, while it contained many positive measures, suffered from basic flaws already apparent in the drafting process, in the "politics" of the reform. The immediate impact of Russia's first large-scale student disorders overshadowed all steps of the drafting process. The process itself was disjointed.[7] Its integrity suffered from the revolving-door nature of the Russian Ministry of Education. Between 1858, when the reform process started, and 1863, there were three different ministers of education, none of whom had actually studied at a university.[8]

The deliberations produced many useful measures but did not lay down procedural precedents which would guide state-university relations in the future. Professors were appointed, not elected, to the educational reform commissions. The tsar seemed to have little interest in the complexities of university reform but insisted on strict measures to deal with the student issue. That Alexander II could turn the final drafting over to Count S. G. Stroganov, who two years before had called for the closing of the universities, shows how little he understood the actual problem of university-state relations. And even relatively conservative professors like Moscow's Boris Chicherin resented the fact that the ministers of education had no educational expertise.[9] G. A. Dzanshiev, in his panegyric to the Great Reforms, called the university statute an "unprincipled compromise."[10]

But in one important sense the drafting process had far-reaching ramifications. Various actors in the reform process—especially E. F. von Bradtke—encouraged glasnost and published dozens of comments on the "university question." This facilitated a serious public debate, ostensibly about educational reform but actually about the future contours of Russian public life. N. I. Pirogov's article "Voprosy zhizni" ("Questions posed by life") sounded a ringing call for a total rethinking of Russian education, a shift of purpose from narrow utilitarian training to broad humanism.[11] The intense discussions which soon filled the press about the nature of the university or the relative merits of *vospitanie* and *obrazovanie* reflected serious attempts to understand the complex interplay of such issues as higher education, discipline, authority, and the rise of a civic culture.

The one major source of controversy was the debate about the French versus the German model of higher education. N. I. Kostomarov wanted "open universities" modeled after the French system, and he crossed swords in several heated articles with Boris Chicherin, who favored retaining the German model. According to Kostomarov, lectures should be open to the public. Attendees who felt like it could take exams. Such a university would supposedly eliminate the dysfunctional role of a "student caste."[12] It would also remove any excuse for bureaucratic interference by renouncing any claim to impart moral education *(vospitanie)* or train civil servants. According to Kostomarov, civil society could only develop by *supplanting* traditional estate and corporate identities. Only an "open," nonutilitarian university would serve a Russian public which needed to free itself from state tutelage and obsession with rank.[13] Specific estate and corporate allegiances and a tendency to confuse the acquisition of knowledge with its alleged moral or career benefits thwarted the process of societal development and legitimized unwarranted state interference in the development of a mature public and its vital institutions.

Chicherin felt differently. He argued that turning students into "individual visitors" was tantamount to the destruction of the university. Unless students retained some special status and identity, the universities would degenerate into public places of entertainment, a pathetic reflection of all the alleged faults of the Russian public: lack of seriousness, a low level of culture, and an inability to undertake serious, disciplined work. Chicherin's argument implied that the task of the Russian university was to help *create* a civic culture which was sorely lacking, not to mirror the faults and immaturity of the surrounding society. The universities were to be an oasis where scientific research would combine with respect for hard work and civility to inculcate new and better values in an amorphous and confused Russian public. Strongly implied here was the necessary interaction of knowledge, discipline, authority, and hierarchy in the creation of an effective civic culture and the education of professional and civil service elites.[14]

Never had a university statute been preceded by so much public debate. Never had the issue of the student body received such attention.[15] The public discussion and the emergence of the student problem were themselves symptoms of a fundamental change in the nature of the "university question" since the statutes of 1804 and 1835. The universities had reached a level of achievement, social acceptance, and complexity which would henceforth preclude easy management of the "university question" by fiat. On the other hand, the "student movement" had only just begun, and the very concept of an intelligentsia, much less such a revolutionary one, was in its infancy.

So the 1863 statute marked a "plastic, fluid moment." Positions had only begun to harden. From that point on, discussions of the university question would be dominated by one of its components, the student problem. It would be hard to remember that only a short time before, at the beginning of the nineteenth century, the main worry of the Russian state had been finding enough students to attend the universities!

Alexander I's Secret Committee, in laying the groundwork for the 1804 statute, and Sergei Uvarov, the main force behind the 1835 statute, acted within a context dictated by the need to establish and consolidate a stable higher educational system in very unfavorable conditions.[16] They faced several challenges. By the onset of the reform era, most of these challenges had been overcome. But the process shaped the formative period of the Russian universities and helped determine the discourse of university policy. What were these major questions faced by the framers of the first two statutes?

The first question was whether the Tsarist government, at the beginning of the nineteenth century, would choose the basic model of the university as the capstone of the nation's higher educational system or would follow the French in erecting a system based on centrally controlled, specialized schools. At the time there were solid reasons for emulating the French model. In England and in France the university as an institution was in headlong decline. Nevertheless, the 1804 statute made a decision which determined the future direction of Russian higher education: it chose the model of the German university. But since Russia was not Germany, crucial differences would emerge which would fan many controversies and help ensure the emergence of a nettlesome "university question."

Russian students were not German students and behaved differently, especially after 1848. And Russia did not enjoy the abundant supply of academics who staffed the provincial universities and served as privatdocents. That meant that for practical reasons, let alone political ones, Russia would be following a model of higher education whose basic core—*lehrfreiheit* and *lernfreiheit*—was unworkable in Russian conditions. The Russian universities would have less "competition" between teachers and could afford to give students much less freedom in choosing courses. As Paul Miliukov aptly remarked, the 1863 statute therefore reflected a compromise between the German theory of university study and the French system of regimented study plans.[17] That tension between theory and practice, combined with the intractable student problem, began to undermine the statute from the moment of its inception.

A second question facing the framers of the first university statute, once they chose the university model, was whether they should opt for a Göttingen-type system of academic governance, which stressed wide-ranging faculty autonomy, or insist on tight outside control over the faculty council by curators and ministers. The initial dearth of native accomplished professors naturally strengthened the tendency for powerful curators and ministers to whip fractious, unwieldy, and incompetent faculty councils into line and take the hard decisions necessary to build strong universities.[18]

This conundrum—that to build strong universities in a country which did not have them, one needed strong outside control—would also haunt the future course of faculty-state relations. Once faculty councils gained more self-assurance, conflicts over their proper role in determining academic appointments and other governance issues were unavoidable. For example, would financial matters and student disciplinary problems fall to the jurisdiction of appointees responsible to the curator or a rector elected by the faculty council? The 1804 statute was overoptimistic in giving the faculty councils extremely wide powers. A basic principle of Sergei Uvarov's 1835 statute was that faculty councils should not handle disciplinary and budgetary matters (although they still had the right to elect rectors). By 1863 many professors were once again calling for a return to the principles of 1804 and explicitly attacking the 1835 statute.[19] While scholars such as Nikolai Pirogov and V. D. Spasovich joined the Kharkov Faculty Council in calling for a sharp curtailment of the curator's power, the final draft of the statute straddled the issue. Thus there remained an ominous vagueness in the delineation of the powers of the curator, rector, and university council, especially in times of emergency.[20] But professors regained many of the administrative powers they had lost in 1835. The faculty council had new financial authority, especially over the spending of tuition fees and, through disciplinary courts, more jurisdiction over student affairs.

A third question was whether the universities, indeed the entire educational system, should be open to all classes, with education a major lever of social mobility, or should conform to the state's estate division of society. Alexander's Secret Committee supported the former policy, and although Nicholas I made strong noises about "closed universities," the Ministry of Education never entirely relinquished the all-class principle.[21]

Fourth, if the universities were indeed to be the top rung of an integrated, all-class "ladder" stretching from the village school through the gymnasium to the very top, then what should be their administrative relationship to the lower tiers of the educational system? The 1804 statute insisted that the universities administer the lower rungs of the educational ladder, but this feature fell by the wayside in 1835,[22] and did not emerge in the 1863 debate.

Fifth, should the content of university education be "professional" and "utilitarian," conforming to the putative proposition that the purpose of higher education was to train civil servants and professionals? Or should the universities embrace the Humboldtian view that the universities would better serve the nation (and provide better civil servants and professionals in the bargain) by combining teaching and research and stressing "pure" rather than "applied" education?[23] The 1863 statute remained true to Humboldtian tradition, at least in theory. It greatly strengthened the educational range of the universities, although its financial provisions fell far short of many professors' hopes.[24] On the other hand, calls by Pirogov for a more imaginative relationship between "pure" and "applied" knowledge in the universities went largely unanswered in the statute.[25]

Sixth, given the gentry's initial suspicion of higher education, how could the nobility be induced to send its sons to the universities? If it refused, then the state faced the unpleasant choice of either staffing the civil service with nonnobles or admitting that university education was somehow unnecessary for the bureaucracy. By the early 1860s this question was largely solved, as a large proportion of the *studenchestvo* consisted of young men from the nobility.[26] But the reform era saw a lot of debate about eliminating the "service rights" attached to the university degree, an incentive which the government had originally used to attract nobles. On this issue, as on so many others, there was no clear "liberal" or "conservative" position.[27] Service rights remained.

Seventh, how could the universities most quickly end an overreliance on foreign scholars and train talented, Russian faculties? While finding enough professors remained a problem right up to 1917, by the middle of the nineteenth century the ministry could report astounding progress. Between 1855 and 1862 there was a remarkable transformation of the Russian professoriate. By the fall of 1861, 47.5 percent of university teachers had entered the profession within the preceding five years.[28] This influx had an extraordinary effect on the vitality of the universities.[29]

In short, the Ministry of Education could point to some striking successes between 1804 and 1863. The universities had taken hold; Uvarov, for all his faults, had done much to improve educational quality; the Russian professoriate was now producing native scholars with solid credentials; and a growing proportion of the civil service had a higher education. In fact, in his 1862 memorandum to the Voronov commission, Professor Andreevskii of St. Petersburg University asserted that the universities, in achieving the moral regeneration of the ruling elites, had made the Great Reforms possible.[30]

One of the most intriguing and potentially significant aspects of the public debate about the reform was N. I. Pirogov's suggestion to junk the very concept of an all-inclusive statute as the basic regulator of university-state relations.

The financial dependence of the universities on the state dictated the central place of the *ustav,* the statute which tried to govern and regulate virtually all the manifold relationships of a devilishly complex institution. Even in better-situated and wealthier countries, the relationship of the universities to the surrounding society was a complicated matter that did not easily lend itself to clear conceptualization and neat categorical questions. Indeed the mid–nineteenth century marked a period of intense questioning of the nature and goals of higher learning in Europe and the United States. But at least in Britain and the United States, the universities could rely on the sheer diversity of private support and well-entrenched traditions. Russia was not England. There was no long tradition of university education where public opinion might act as a bulwark against excessive state interference. Statute replaced trust, and without trust, the ustav had to spell out the interconnections of university governance, student discipline, financial jurisdiction, the establishment and division of specific chairs, procedures for hiring retired professors, the powers of the minister and the curator, and many other matters. The dangers were obvious.

There was, of course, a constant tension between the implicit rigidity of the statute and the fluid nature of the universities. Like those in any other country, the Russian universities had to answer to several different constituencies and perform a variety of often conflicting functions. Government bureaucrats wanted them to train obedient and loyal civil servants and professionals. Many professors resented the government's emphasis on the teaching function of the universities, arguing instead that the primary purpose of the universities was to serve the nation by promoting independent research—only a research university could train a self-reliant professional class and an enlightened civil service. To complicate matters further, there was no unanimity within the professoriate on what the term *research university* really meant.

But Nikolai Pirogov pointedly questioned the need for a detailed statute. It was easier, he stressed, to define the universities by what they were *not* than by what they were:

> If it is difficult to define the West European universities, then it is even more difficult to define ours. . . . The Russian university is not an institution of applied learning, but it is also not a scientific research institution *(svobodno-nauchnoe uchrezhdenie)*. It does not impart general education, but neither is its main purpose moral education. In character it is not based on the estate principle; nor is it a church institution, a private-philanthropic institution, a purely bureaucratic institution, or an institution modeled along the lines of a medieval corporation. And yet, in varying degrees, each of the above principles is incorporated into our university structure.[31]

In the end, he stressed, not even the best ustav could substitute for autonomy, mutual trust, and professional and scientific competence. His hope was to make the universities "less bureaucratic" and give them the chance to adjust to local and regional circumstances.

But as the story of the 1863 statute shows, trust was in short supply. Not just the government but most of the professoriate felt the need for a statute. If the government wanted to make sure of its ultimate power to regulate the universities, professors wanted to ensure that the government was committed to a specific number of chairs *(shtat)* or to a specific enumeration of faculty council or department rights. There was also widespread support for the notion that a statute guaranteed a certain minimum level of knowledge for the civil service and the professions. In short, on the question of a statute, Pirogov did not represent the majority of the Russian professoriate.[32]

Especially after enactment of the 1863 statute, student unrest, more than anything else, determined government policy toward the universities. No matter how important other matters were—defining faculty power; delineating the relationship between the universities, the curators, and the state; adjusting to the growth of scientific knowledge by creating new chairs and institutes; deciding on the qualifications for faculty status—the student movement became the primary factor determining educational policy. And here many professors shared the government's concerns about student unrest.

Russian universities were the incubators of a student subculture, a meeting place where thousands of provincial youths, often poor but having little in common with the popular masses and even less with the ruling elite, joined a proud new social group, the student body, and then left, to become teachers, doctors, lawyers, civil servants, or, in a few cases, embittered revolutionaries. Had these students accepted the professors' view of the university, had they been content to sit quietly for five years and leave with their diplomas in hand, there would have been no student movement. But the dream shared by both professors and government that the student movement would somehow disappear clashed with some obvious differences between Russia and other West European countries. While the Russian student movement was quite distinct from the revolutionary movement, it shared with it a basic refusal to accept the "liberal" model of the university.[33] It was not so much student poverty as the "nonmodel" status of the roles the "elite" universities were preparing the students to fill which pushed the student movement toward constant confrontation.[34]

The student demonstrations of 1858–61 not only challenged government authority. The students, especially when they demanded the removal of unpopular professors, also challenged *faculty* authority. Even "liberal" professors such as N. I. Kostomarov and K. D. Kavelin learned that student moods were quite fickle. Most professors would be happy with a statute that gave more rights to themselves but not to the students. This failure to deal with the student problem emerged as the Achilles heel of the statute.[35]

In the end, the 1863 statute reflected a much less focused, much less coherent vision of the Russian university than did the 1884 statute. This is not to defend the 1884 ustav, which began to self-destruct almost immediately. The point is that Dzanshiev was basically right. There was a *policy* behind the 1884 counterreform; the 1863 statute was a compromise. What kind? Professors got much of what they wanted; students lost much of what they already had. Lines of authority between government and faculty remained ominously blurred, a sign of serious trouble in the future. And what of the visions of Chicherin, Kostomarov, and Pirogov? Although the final outcome bore a superficial resemblance to Chicherin's vision of the university, the future of the "university question" would show the fragility of his faith in the university's ability to combine instruction and moral education, replace the hierarchy of *soslovnost* with the hierarchy of achievement, and legitimize a new professional ethos.

Fundamentally, the 1863 statute was a missed opportunity to define the prerogatives of the Russian universities and lend them a modicum of stability. This is not to deny the achievements of the 1863 statute. It provided an important structure for the professionalization of the Russian professoriate and the advancement of Russian science; the rise of learned societies, the recognition of faculty primacy in appointments, and authority over budgets and student discipline were a big improvement over the 1835 statute.[36]

But the 1863 statute failed to legitimize the right of the Russian universities to the "special treatment" so cogently implied by Pirogov's essay. Professors were to be appointed, not elected, to the special consultative boards of the Ministry of Education. Safeguards on academic freedom were not sufficiently spelled out. The ultimate power of the curator to intervene in university affairs remained. The point here is not to argue that the drafting commissions rode roughshod over the wishes of the professoriate. Indeed, the statute gave the faculty councils and the departments as much power in some vital areas as their German counterparts. But the actual *process* of formulating the statute failed to establish some important precedents. The appearance of the statute followed an extraordinary transformation of Russian student life which began in 1855 and saw the rapid development of a student corporate spirit. Yet in the final statute, Stroganov struck down recommendations by Kavelin and Spasovich on recognizing student rights. From the students' point of view, therefore, the statute was a step back, an annulment of the concessions they had won in the 1850s. As Pirogov observed, "When I read these rules, the words of Napoleon regarding the Bourbons suddenly comes to mind. Clearly the Bourbons are not alone in being unable to forget the past."[37] The faculty seemed happy that it had won university courts (although a minority of Moscow professors preferred the old inspector system) and was sufficiently jaded by the student movement to abandon any idea of fighting the restrictions on student organizations.

The 1863 statute quickly ran into trouble. Many professors charged that the minister of education had overstepped his authority in staffing the newly established Odessa University. In Moscow University, the messy Leshkov Affair prompted several professors, including Boris Chicherin, to resign from the faculty.[38] There was insufficient faculty consensus or professional identity to prevent unseemly scandals on the faculty councils. Legitimate questions arose about the quality of university education. Squabbling between faculty and the failure of either government or university authorities to squelch student unrest undermined the legitimacy of the statute and paved the way for the counterreforms that followed.

The stage was set for a new attempt at redefining the university. After the appointment of Dmitri Tolstoi as minister of education in 1866, a concerted assault began on the 1863 statute. It should be emphasized that this was not an anti-intellectual assault on higher education but an alternative vision of a higher educational system which would solve the student problem by raising academic standards and curtailing the powers of the professoriate in university governance. Appointed curators should run the universities, professors teach and write, students study. All would then be well. The case received added impetus from the recurring student problems, including the 1869 St. Petersburg demonstrations, and the abortive 1866 assassination attempt on the tsar.

M. N. Katkov, editor of *Moskovski vedomosti,* Professor N. A. Liubimov, and Tolstoi led the attack. Their indictment of the statute made several points. First, the professors' disciplinary courts were too lax and had failed to deal with the student problem. Second, the statute (read, the professoriate) had failed to raise academic standards, which itself aggravated the student problem. Third, the state, which funded the universities and depended on them for an effective civil service, had lost effective control over standards and teaching content. Fourth, the universities were admitting too many unprepared students. Fifth, the professors had abused their hiring powers and had allowed political criteria and croneyism to determine appointments.

The conservatives called for a new statute, based on more state control and a more consistent application of the German university model. One reason, they emphasized, for the alleged failure of the 1863 statute was that it was an unwieldy hybrid of the French and the German systems. That resulted in the worst of all worlds. Students had no real *lernfreiheit* but had to follow set study plans. Too few seminars and too many large, boring lecture courses left them with excessive time on their hands. The faculty had too much power over their charges. But, the conservatives emphasized, there was a remedy—state examinations. This would give the government some measure of control over the curriculum.

State examinations, *lernfreiheit,* and honoraria would supposedly put things right. Professors would find it harder to pander to fads or court cheap popularity. After all, Katkov reasoned, if students knew that they had to pass a strict state exam, they would take the courses that best prepared them for it. Professors not teaching what students needed would fall by the wayside. To keep their feet to the fire, Katkov proposed implementing another feature of the German system—parallel courses taught by privatdocents. The "competition" would supposedly force faculty members to hew closely to the state examination agenda or lose their audience.

Tolstoi and Katkov also called for a return to a basic feature of the Uvarov 1835 statute, taking away from the faculty councils their powers over university administration and student discipline. Professors would concentrate on what they were supposed to do: research and teaching. In 1876 Tolstoi appointed a formal commission to reexamine the 1863 statute. In 1879 he abolished the professors' disciplinary courts and replaced them with state appointed inspectors.

The faculty councils fought back in the press and in the 1876 commission meetings.[39] In a hard-hitting article published in the February 1876 issue of *Vestnik Evropy,* V. I. Guerrier expressed the views of the majority of the Russian professoriate in attacking Liubimov's proposals on transplanting key features of the German system to Russia.[40] In the commission the faculty councils fiercely defended the statute.

A brief period of liberalization in 1880–81 gave the faculty councils a respite. But the handwriting was on the wall. Despite stiff opposition in the 1876 commission and from the majority of the State Council, Tsar Alexander III approved the 1884 University Statute, which largely reflected the views of Katkov and Liubimov. In the event, almost all the predictions of the State Council majority came true. The state examinations proved unworkable. The government restored the professors' disciplinary courts in 1902 and openly admitted that the 1884 statute was in shambles.[41]

A fundamental determinant of the government's university policy was the tension between the state's efforts to ensure control and the fact that in

many ways the development of the universities was influenced and shaped
by factors that resisted such manipulation and control. The development of
new academic disciplines, the achievements of Russian scientists, the growing conviction of Russian parents and young people that any kind of higher
education was essential to social and economic success—all of these resulted in pressures and changes which kept the universities in flux. The
state could regulate an institution whose professors wanted to do nothing
but teach and whose students wanted only to study hard and become doctors, lawyers, teachers, and civil servants. It could not so easily control an
institution where students were much surer about what they did not want
to be—provincials with useless high school diplomas—than they were settled on future career choices. Nor could it regiment a professoriate that was
coming to believe that questions of university governance were an essential
part of its professional prerogative.

The state was almost always ready to recognize professors as teachers
and scholars. What it could never do was to concede them a professional
identity which linked them across disciplines in a common relationship of
shared responsibility for university governance and structural safeguards of
academic freedom.[42] And in truth, many Russian professors were not interested in such an identity. The basic problem was not the state's inability to
agree temporarily to periods of university autonomy but its lack of willingness to accede to some form of permanent and manifest institutionalization
of such autonomy. The state's "ideology of order" helped cripple its political
vision and its ability to govern a rapidly changing society. Certainly the
universities were critical nodal points where many of the tensions generated
by the clash of official paternal authoritarianism and autonomous social
developments converged in a pattern of misunderstanding and confrontation.

The ultimate significance of the 1863 statute is twofold. In recognizing the
principle of some degree of faculty council power, it helped bolster a view
of university governance which would always attract some support in the
civil service elite. The 1883–84 State Council deliberations are examples.
But the statute failed to *conceptualize* a proper balance between state, faculty, and student power. Perhaps this is a moot point, especially if we assume
that the "university problem" was "insoluble."

But the time to create a strong precedent which would have recognized
and institutionalized the *unique* nature of the universities was during the era
of the Great Reforms. Later on, with the rise of a large urban proletariat,
the ruling elites would become even less likely to take a lenient view of
student unrest. Maybe it is too much to hope that what was still a non-
university-trained elite could have understood the issues. That a more far-
reaching statute would have put Russia far ahead of any other country is
no excuse for the failure of the reform process to grasp this opportunity.

NOTES

1. A. A. Kizevetter, *Na rubezhe dvukh stoletii* (Prague, 1929), 315–18.
2. See Dominick Lieven, *Russia's Rulers under the Old Regime* (New Haven, Conn., 1989), 84–121; Walter Pintner, "The Russian Civil Service on the Eve of the Great Reforms," *Journal of Social History,* Spring 1975, 55–68; Richard S. Wortman, *The Development of a Russian Legal Consciousness* (Chicago, 1976), 34–51, 197–236; P. A. Zaionchkovskii, *Pravitel'stvennyi apparat samoderzhavnoi Rossii v 19-om veke* (Moscow, 1978). For an eloquent defense of the universities' mission to improve the civil service, see Paul Vinogradov, "Uchebnoe delo v nashikh universitetakh," *Vestnik Evropy,* 1901, no. 10. Also see the comments of Professor I. E. Andreevskii in *Zhurnaly zasedanii Uchenogo komiteta Glavnogo upravleniia uchilishch* (St. Petersburg, 1863), addendum to meeting of Aug. 14, 1862.
3. See, for example, Klaus Meyer, "L'histoire de la question universitaire au XIX siecle," *Cahiers du Monde Russe et Sovietique,* 1978, no. 3, 301–2. For an explicit faculty statement to the contrary, see the 1901 memorandum of the Kharkov Faculty Council to Minister of Education Vannovskii, *TsGIA,* f. 733, op. 226, d. 95.
4. There has been relatively little study of the drafting of the statute. William Mathes gives a good account but does not use archival materials; see Mathes, *The Struggle for University Autonomy in Russia during the First Decade of the Reign of Alexander II (1855–1866),* Ph.D. diss., Columbia University, 1966. For Soviet scholarship, see R. G. Eimontova, "Universitetskaia reforma 1863-ogo goda," *Istoricheski zapiski,* 1961, no. 70; "Revoliutsionnaia situatsiia i podgotovka universitetskoi reformy v Rossii," *Revoliutsionnaia situatsiia v Rossii v 1859–1861 gg.,* vol. 6 (Moscow, 1974); and "Universitetskii vopros i russkaia obshchestvennost' v 50-kh 60-kh godakh 19-ogo veka," *Istoriia SSSR,* 1971, no. 6. The factual base is good, but one cannot accuse Professor Eimontova of ignoring Marxist-Leninist conceptual frameworks. For an interesting account of the universities on the eve of the Great Reforms, see R. G. Eimontova, *Russkie universitety na grani dvukh epokh: ot Rossii krepostnoi k Rossii kapitalisticheskoi* (Moscow, 1985). Prerevolutionary accounts of the 1863 statute include G. A. Dzanshiev, "Universitetskaia avtonomiia," in *Epokha Velikikh Reform* (St. Petersburg, 1907); I. M. Solov'ev, "Universitetskii vopros v 60-kh godakh," *Vestnik vospitaniia,* 1913, no. 9; B. B. Glinskii, "Universitetski ustavy," *Istoricheskii vestnik,* 1900, nos. 1–2; P. N. Miliukov, "Universitety v Rossii," *Entsyklopedicheskii Slovar' Brokhauza i Efrona,* vol. 68 (St. Petersburg, 1902). See also S. V. Rozhdestvenskii, *Istoricheskii obzor deiatel'nosti Ministerstva narodnogo prosveshcheniia 1802–1902,* (St. Petersburg, 1903).
5. See Laurence R. Veysey, *The Emergence of the American University* (Chicago, 1965); Sheldon Rothblatt, *The Revolution of the Dons* (London, 1968); Fritz Ringer, *The Decline of the German Mandarins* (Cambridge, England, 1969); George Weisz, *The Emergence of Modern Universities in France, 1863–1914* (Princeton, N.J., 1983).
6. See Alan Sinel, *The Classroom and the Chancellery* (Cambridge, 1973), 115.
7. The formulation of the 1863 statute reflected several contradictory influences. The first stage in the reform process began in 1858 when curator G. A. Shcherbatov of the St. Petersburg Educational District asked the university's Faculty Council to draft a model statute. The "young Turks" on the council, led by K. D. Kavelin, drafted a model statute which featured strict limitations on the curator's power, a major expansion in the role of the council and the elected rector, and, most significantly, recognition of student rights. It remained a dead letter. Angered by recurrent

student protests, Tsar Alexander II fired E. O. Kovalevskii and installed a new minister of education, Admiral E. V. Putiatin. Putiatin hoped to crush the incipient student movement by restricting scholarships and banning most student organizations. This policy failed miserably, and major new student unrest broke out in the fall of 1861. The tsar replaced Putiatin with A. V. Golovnin and authorized the formation of a commission chaired by E. F. von Bradtke, curator of the Dorpat Educational District. This commission produced a draft statute. More important, it published dozens of essays on the university question by Russian and foreign professors, curators, and journalists. These materials then went to the Main School Administration, which established a second commission under A. S. Voronov. It commissioned several professors, mainly from St. Petersburg University, to collate the von Bradtke materials and make recommendations concerning the various sections of the proposed statute. In a telling indication of his essential ambivalence about university reform, Alexander then empowered a commission under Count S. G. Stroganov to vet the Voronov recommendations. The final product, modified in several significant ways, was the 1863 statute.

8. The ministers were E. P. Kovalevskii, E. V. Putiatin and A. V. Golovnin.

9. Boris Chicherin, *Vospominaniia: Moskovskii Universitet* (Moscow, 1929), 25.

10. Dzhanshiev, "Universitetskaia," 285.

11. N. I. Pirogov, *Izbrannye pedagogicheskie sochineniia* (Moscow, 1985), 28–52.

12. R. G. Eimontova, *Russkie Universitety,* 316–17.

13. *Zamechaniia na proekte obshchego ustava, Imperatorskikh russiiskikh universitetov* (St. Petersburg, 1862), vol. 2, 155–68.

14. Ibid., 341–63. To all this Kostomarov replied that if one really believed Chicherin's arguments about the immaturity of Russian society, then why not move the universities to the north woods and the Pinsk marshes, where their isolation would be guaranteed? It was ridiculous, Kostomarov asserted, to maintain a distinction between "student" and "citizen." The universities were not there to remake society but to serve it. This debate provided another example where the distinction between "liberals" and "conservatives" broke down. "Conservatives" such as Nikitenko and Korf supported the basic principles of Kostomarov's scheme, while "liberals" such as Kavelin sided with Chicherin.

15. Between 1853 and 1860, student enrollment in the five Russian universities (St. Petersburg, Moscow, Kiev, Kharkov, and Kazan) climbed from 2,809 to 4,935. There are several good treatments of the student movement: S. Ashevskii, "Russkoe studenchestvo v epokhu 60-kh godov," *Sovremennyi mir,* 1907, nos. 6–11; Daniel Brower, *Training the Nihilists: Education and Radicalism in Tsarist Russia* (Ithaca, N.Y., 1975); Alain Besancon, *Education et société en Russie dans le second tiers du 19me siècle* (Paris, 1974); William L. Mathes, "The Origins of Confrontation Politics in Russian Universities: Student Activism, 1855–1861," *Canadian Slavic Studies,* 1968, no. 2.

16. The best studies of this period are James T. Flynn, *The University Reform of Tsar Alexander I 1802–1835* (Washington, D.C., 1988), and Cynthia Whittaker, *The Origins of Modern Russian Education: An Intellectual Biography of Count Sergei Uvarov, 1786–1855* (DeKalb, Ill., 1984).

17. Miliukov, "Universitety v Rossii," 793. Pirogov strongly defended *lernfreiheit* and was critical of the 1863 statute for not doing more to allow students freer choice; see his *Izbrannye pedagogicheskie sochineniia,* 404. Chicherin, on the other hand, defended the restrictive provisions of the statute as being more attuned to the real needs of Russia's students; see his "Chto nuzhno dlia russkikh universitetov?" *Zamechaniia na proekt obshchego ustava,* vol. 2, 354. For a highly negative view of the French model of higher education, see K. D. Kavelin, "Izvlecheniie iz pis'ma ot 4(16) oktiabria iz Parizha," *Sobranie sochinenii,* vol. 3, 213–26. It should be added that Kavelin was not entirely uncritical of the German universities. Or, at the very

least, he was much less enthusiastic than Pirogov. See his "Svoboda prepodavaniia v Germanii" and "Ustroistvo i upravleniie nemetskikh universitetov," in *Sobranie sochinenii*, vol. 3, 5–212.

18. See Flynn, *The University Reform of Alexander I*, esp. 216–59. For a strong defense of curatorial powers by the curator of the Kharkov Educational District, see D. S. Levshin, *Zamechaniia na proekt*, vol. 1, 361–89.

19. See the memorandum of the Kharkov University Faculty Council to von Bradtke's commission, *Zamechaniia na proekt*, vol. 1, 280–319, and the comments of A. N. Pypin, ibid., 153–61.

20. Piotr Kapnist called this one of the major drawbacks of the 1863 statute. See P. Kapnist, "Universitetskie voprosy," *Vestnik Evropy*, 1903, no. 11, 189–90. The debate on the issue of curators is recorded in the minutes of the 1862 Voronov commission. See *Zhurnaly zasedanii Uchenogo komiteta Glavnogo upravleniia uchilishch po proektu obshchego ustava Imperatorskikh rossiskikh universitetov* (St. Petersburg, 1862).

21. See Flynn, *The University Reform of Alexander I*, esp. 253–55. In April 1861 Count Stroganov proposed solving the student problem by turning the universities into "closed schools," open only to students from the nobility and the "propertied classes." According to A. V. Nikitenko, almost the entire State Council rejected the plan. See Nikitenko, *Dnevnik*, vol. 2 (Moscow, 1955), 189–90. This in no way diminished Tsar Alexander's faith in Stroganov's abilities, for in 1863 the tsar appointed Stroganov to head a committee to review the draft statute.

22. Glinskii regrets this. See "Universitetskie ustavy," 1900, no. 1, 341.

23. James McClelland makes a strong argument that the government made a big mistake in following the German ideal of "pure learning." See his *Autocrats and Academics* (Chicago, 1979). The vast majority of the Russian professoriate, "liberal" and "conservative," would have disagreed violently. Typical is Professor Andreevskii's memorandum to the 1862 Voronov commission: "the universities have prepared a whole generation which turned away from serfdom . . . a generation which can reform the judicial system and which waits ready to help the government put this idea into action. . . . This generation is developing all branches of pure science *(nauki)* which are so necessary to society and to the government. Only the universities offer the possibility of the independent and consistent advance of science." *Zhurnaly zasedanii Uchenogo komiteta Glavnogo upravleniia uchilishch*, addendum to meeting of Aug. 14, 1862.

24. Whereas the 1835 statute theoretically provided for thirty-four chairs *(kafedry)* and thirty-nine professors in each university, the 1863 statute raised those numbers to fifty-three and fifty-seven. In reality, finding enough candidates who met the two-degree requirement (the Russian professoriate insisted on this) remained a huge problem, and many teaching posts remained "vacant," filled by those without the doctorate or by professors who had passed the statutory retirement age. This remained a problem right up to the end of the Tsarist regime. See Miliukov, "Universitety v Rossii," 794.

25. See Pirogov, *Izbrannye pedagogicheskie sochineniia*, 346.

26. By 1857 about two-thirds of Russian university students were sons of nobles or civil servants. See Eimontova, *Russkie universitety na grani dvukh epokh*, 242.

27. For example, "liberals" such as Pirogov joined "conservatives" such as Putiatin in advocating the end of linking service rights to the university degree. The "conservative" argument was that ending this incentive would reduce the influx of careerists and poor students and thus lessen student unrest. "Liberals" saw the attraction of freeing "science" from state tutelage. On the other hand, professors from opposite ends of the political spectrum argued that linking service rights to the diploma was an essential prerequisite of a strong and honest civil service.

28. Eimontova, *Russkie universitety na grani dvukh epokh*, 108.

29. There is a good discussion of this in Mathes, *The Struggle for University Autonomy*, 86–94.

30. *Zhurnaly zasedanii Uchenogo komiteta Glavnogo upravleniia uchilishch*, addendum to meeting of Aug. 14, 1862.

31. Pirogov, *Izbrannye pedagogicheskie sochineniia*, 322.

32. Mathes, *The Struggle for University Autonomy*, 150.

33. For a more extended discussion of this point, see Samuel D. Kassow, *Students, Professors and the State in Tsarist Russia* (Berkeley, Calif., 1989), esp. chap. 2.

34. I have borrowed the notion of "elite" and "expert" universities from a highly suggestive theoretical article by Joseph Ben-David and Randall Collins: "A Comparative Study of Academic Freedom and Student Politics," in S. M. Lipset, ed., *Student Politics* (New York, 1970), 148–95. "Elite" universities did not try to give their graduates practical training; "expert" universities did. The authors also distinguish between "model" and "nonmodel" systems. In the former, the universities train graduates for positions and responsibilities which have clear models in the wider society. In the latter, universities "are created by a traditional, or at any rate uneducated, elite for the purpose of eventually reforming themselves or increasing their efficiency through training new and better qualified people of a kind that do not yet exist in the country."

35. In fact, many professors, especially in St. Petersburg, argued for allowing students to have *skhodki;* maintain libraries, self-help funds, and other organizations; even elect delegates to the university court. The draft statute worked out in 1858 by the St. Petersburg faculty council provided for this, and K. D. Kavelin wrote a forceful memorandum urging that the concessions won by the students after 1855 not be revoked. He especially defended their right to hold skhodki. Recognition of student rights was also urged by Professor Spasovich in the Voronov commission; see *Zhurnaly zasedanii Uchenogo komiteta*, 141–63. But as Mathes points out, many professors, especially in Moscow, had been shocked by the students' claim to a de facto veto of faculty appointments and wanted a tougher policy. Faculty attitudes also hardened after the fall of 1861. See Kavelin, "Zapiska o bezporiadkakh v Sankt Peterburgskom universitete," *Sobranie sochinenii*, vol. 2 (St. Petersburg, 1904) 1192–1206; Eimontova, "Revoliutsionnaia situatsiia," 63–64; Mathes, *The Struggle for University Autonomy*, 120.

36. See Alexander Vucinich, *Science in Russian Culture*, vol. 2 (Stanford, Calif., 1970), 66–104.

37. Quoted in Mathes, *The Struggle for University Autonomy*, 449.

38. The issue concerned the procedures for allowing Professor Leshkov to serve past retirement age. Chicherin charged that the rector and curator ignored the procedural rules of the statute.

39. The voluminous journals of the 1875 commission to consider the revision of the 1863 statute are especially valuable in following attempts to solve university problems by introducing *lernfreiheit*, honoraria, etc. See *Zhurnaly kommissii dlia peresmotra obshchego ustava Imperatorskikh rossiskikh universitov* (St. Petersburg, 1875).

40. V. I. Guerrier, "Svet i teni universitetskogo byta," *Vestnik Evropy*, 1876, no. 2.

41. See Kassow, *Students, Professors and the State*, chap. 1.

42. On the concept of cross-disciplinary professional identity, see Walter Metzger, "Academic Freedom and Scientific Freedom," *Daedalus*, Spring 1978.

XV

THE RISE OF VOLUNTARY ASSOCIATIONS DURING THE GREAT REFORMS
THE CASE OF CHARITY

Adele Lindenmeyr

One of the most striking characteristics of Russian society during the era of the Great Reforms was its new spirit of voluntarism. The contrast with past years was dramatic. Habitually suspicious of private initiative, Nicholas I intensified his government's repression of any independent thought or action after the outbreak of revolution in Europe in 1848. Even Mikhail Pogodin, once an apologist for Nicholas I's policy of Official Nationality, condemned the government in the last years of that reign for imposing on Russia "the quiet of a graveyard, rotting and stinking, both physically and morally."[1] Russia's defeat in the Crimean War broke that silence. During the reign of Alexander II, Russians established growing numbers of voluntary associations of various kinds—professional and philanthropic, educational and cooperative, moderate and radical. For all their diversity, these associations reflected the emergence of independent public opinion, a new civic consciousness, and a new commitment to autonomous social action. What is more, in twenty-five years the spirit of voluntarism acquired enough vitality to survive more suspicious government policies after 1881, and voluntary associations continued to grow in numbers and diversity right up to the October Revolution.[2]

In the words of Nicholas Berdyaev, "there is something mysterious in the growth of movements in public life in Russia in the 1860s."[3] Was the new voluntarism truly a spontaneous movement from below? What was it about those post–Crimean War years that stimulated so many Russians to unite for the sake of social betterment? Or did the voluntarism of this era owe its existence to initiatives from above? What role did a more liberal tsar, the Great Reforms themselves, and changes in government policy toward voluntary associations play? This essay seeks to answer these questions by exploring the rise of one of the most popular outlets for the new voluntarist spirit: private charitable associations.

The Spread of Charitable Associations

The twenty-five years between 1855 and 1880 witnessed a dramatic increase in the number of charitable societies and institutions. An approximate picture of this growth can be found in an 1880 Ministry of the Interior report on public and private poor relief during the reign of Alexander II. According to this report, at the start of the new reign there were only forty private charitable societies and seventy-three private charitable institutions in the Empire. "But subsequent government measures," the report boasted, "together with the constantly growing voluntarism [*samodeiatel'nost'*] of society itself, yielded extensive results": by 1880 there were 348 private charitable societies and 225 institutions.[4] Surveys of charities conducted in the 1880s, though far from complete, also attest to the vigorous development of private organized charity during the preceding three decades.[5]

A more detailed portrait of charitable societies formed during the Great Reform era can be obtained by analyzing the information collected in the most comprehensive survey of Russian charity, conducted by the Department of the Institutions of Empress Maria (*Vedomstvo uchrezhdenii Imperatritsy Marii*) at the turn of the century.[6] Naturally, this survey only included private charitable societies in existence in 1901, the year it was conducted; no doubt many of the societies founded in earlier decades did not survive to be counted in the 1901 survey. Nevertheless, the data collected on those charitable associations founded between 1855 and 1881, and still in existence in 1901, reveal some interesting characteristics of organized charity during the reform period.[7]

The 1901 survey unearthed even more reform-era societies than the Ministry of the Interior reported in 1880. Of 3,700 private charitable societies in 1901 which provided information on their date of founding, 753, or 20 percent of the total, had been established between 1856 and 1880. By comparison, only 101 of the societies still in existence in 1901 had been established between 1801 and 1855 (and only nine before 1801). The numbers of societies rose throughout the period, though at an uneven rate:

1856–60	24
1861–65	61
1866–70	153
1871–75	188
1876–80	327

Not surprisingly, the overwhelming majority of the charitable societies at this time were founded in St. Petersburg, Moscow, or provincial capitals (ninety-five St. Petersburg charities existing in 1901 opened between 1861 and 1880, and forty-four Moscow charities opened during the same period):

	1856–60	1861–65	1866–70	1871–75	1876–80	Total
Provincial capital	11	40	75	128	141	395
District town	8	12	55	45	143	263
Countryside						
("v uezde")	2	4	10	8	22	46
Other town	3	4	11	7	19	44

The 1901 survey also provides insight into particularly popular kinds of charity at this time. One of the most striking characteristics of this period is the Orthodox orientation of many of the societies. Between 20 percent and 40 percent of the societies which opened in each half-decade between 1856 and 1875, for example, restricted their aid to members of the Orthodox Church. More than a third of the societies established during the 1860s, and still in existence in 1901, came under the jurisdiction of the Holy Synod. Touched by the reformist spirit of the 1860s, the Church and a number of individual priests launched projects aimed at making parishes the center of organized assistance to impoverished clergy and the parish poor.[8] The movement for the revival of the parish also had the support of the Slavophile writer and publisher Ivan S. Aksakov, who used his journal Den' to advocate the spread of traditional Orthodox forms of individual and collective charity.[9]

The survey also reveals that two new kinds of charitable activity emerged during the reform period. The great majority of societies founded between 1856 and 1865—from two-thirds to three-fourths—identified themselves as "general purpose" charities that did not specialize in the kind of need they addressed. In the following decade, however, many new societies addressed themselves either to assisting needy students or to aiding wounded or sick soldiers and the victims of natural disasters, usually in affiliation with the newly established Russian Red Cross. Aid to needy students, usually at gymnasiums, was a popular cause in the 1870s. During this decade at least 129 such societies were established.[10] Local branches of the Red Cross began to be established in the late 1860s, and by the mid-1870s fifty-five had been founded (that were still in existence in 1901, that is). With the outbreak of the Russo-Turkish War, the establishment of local Red Cross committees to aid families of draftees took off. At least eighty-eight local branches were established between 1876 and 1880, usually in district towns (this was more than one-quarter of all charitable societies established during that half-decade).[11] The proliferation of Red Cross committees during the Russo-Turkish War was linked to the Panslav movement; by organizing a local committee, anyone could help liberate Russia's Slavic brothers. Inspired by Aksakov and other Panslav theorists, Russians also founded numerous Slavonic assistance committees during the 1860s and 1870s.[12]

The Autocracy's Policy

Founding a voluntary association during the reign of Nicholas I was far from easy. Voluntary associations of all kinds had to receive Imperial confirmation through the Committee of Ministers in order to exist legally. A small number of charitable and other kinds of associations received Imperial confirmation each year until 1848, when the outbreak of revolution in Europe halted even that cautious policy.[13] Declaring that "everyone has the opportunity to give aid to the poor by individual doles or [by contributing to] the social welfare boards," Nicholas ordered a ban on all new charitable associations in March 1848. The ban was not officially lifted until 1859.[14]

Despite the ban, however, an upsurge of voluntary initiative from educated society became apparent as early as the Crimean War. The government itself appears to have sponsored at least some of these early manifestations of a new voluntarist spirit. Perhaps the best-known examples are the communes of sisters of mercy and "compassionate widows" *(obshchiny sester miloserdiia, serdobol'nykh vdov)* who, like their French and English sisters, volunteered to serve as nurses in battlefront hospitals during the Crimean War. Their efforts enjoyed the patronage of the Imperial family: in 1854 the Grand Duchess Elena Pavlovna founded the Krestovozdvizhenskaia Obshchina, whose sisters participated in the siege of Sevastopol and other battles, and the Empress Alexandra sponsored a similar order of "compassionate widows" to serve in the war.[15]

Another association established in the early part of the reign of the new tsar also had close ties to the government. The group that launched the Society for the Improvement of Workers' Housing in St. Petersburg in 1857 drew from the highest court and government circles and enjoyed the patronage of the Duke of Mecklenburg, husband of a grand duchess.[16] The society imported a hybridized form of organized charity popular in Europe, especially in England, where it was known as "five percent philanthropy": the creation of joint-stock companies to raise funds for improved housing for the urban poor.[17] Like its European counterparts, the society proposed to sell shares promising a modest but regular and low-risk return to finance the building of model low-cost housing. The founders' high connections no doubt helped the society receive the tsar's blessing and praise from the *Journal of the Ministry of the Interior,* which remarked: "In this matter, important for the public good, it is left to the government to wish complete and rapid success to the enlightened founders of so useful and long-awaited an enterprise."[18]

The autocracy's sponsorship of early efforts such as these suggests that a new attitude toward voluntary associations was already developing in the mid-1850s. But the formulation of a more lenient policy toward associations under the new tsar did not result from thoughtful consideration of the role of voluntarism in an autocracy, or, in the case of charitable associations, any study of the proper organization of poor relief. Rather, it evolved out of a series of ad hoc decisions on particular cases, in response to pressure from a public increasingly interested in organizing for various socially useful purposes.[19] By the end of the 1850s, for example, the Ministry of the Interior had received a large number of petitions to establish charitable societies. The elderly minister of the interior, Count S. S. Lanskoi, who had been an active participant in organized philanthropy during the reign of Alexander I, persuaded Alexander II in 1859 to approve all the petitions received thus far by the government. This action effectively rescinded the 1848 ban.[20]

Further relaxation of government policy came during consideration in late 1861 and early 1862 of a petition from Orenburg, where a group of local residents wished to establish a charitable society. In recommending approval for the Orenburg Charitable Society to the Committee of Ministers, Minister of the Interior P. A. Valuev expanded on the subject of charitable associations in general. Valuev argued that by being able to investigate the needs of poor families and provide more flexible and informed assistance, private charitable societies acted as a necessary supplement to the social welfare boards *(prikazy obshchestvennogo prizreniia),* which offered only impersonal aid in institutions. Moreover, he continued, charitable societies relieved the government of a significant part of its responsibility for public relief, while they usually did not seek any state financial help. For these reasons, Valuev's report claimed, the ministry tried to cooperate with the founders of such societies as far as possible. The present procedure of confirmation, however, which required Imperial permission for each society after consideration in the Committee of Ministers,

> burdens the government with the examination of superfluous matters while it delays the opening of such organizations, which . . . should be encouraged in every possible way by the government, since their aim is the most beneficent and they make it easier for the government to fulfill its public relief obligations.[21]

Valuev recommended that the minister of the interior be given the authority, after consultation with other pertinent agencies, to grant permission to new charitable associations.[22] With the consent of the committee and Alexander II, the new policy became law at the beginning of 1862.[23]

The 1862 law had an immediate positive impact on the development of charitable associations in Russia.[24] It accelerated the bureaucratic procedure of confirmation (in the first month after it was issued at least nine new charitable societies officially opened).[25] In addition, by signaling the government's approval of this kind of voluntarism, the new law encouraged public interest in charitable associations. Between 1861 and 1863 the Ministry of the Interior received petitions for official confirmation from forty-three charitable and mutual aid societies—more than it had received during the entire reign of Nicholas I.[26] The government was apparently satisfied with the results of the new procedure, for it issued another law in 1869 that transferred authority to approve privately founded charitable institutions from the tsar and Committee of Ministers to the minister of the interior. In his 1868 report to the Committee of Ministers recommending this new policy, Minister Timashev noted that the number of public and private charitable institutions had been growing rapidly in recent years, a development which he, like his predecessor, felt the government should encourage.[27]

The autocracy's more lenient attitude and general good will toward voluntary associations did not signify that it would dispense approval with an open hand, however. According to a Ministry of the Interior report for the early 1860s, all cases where a proposed society "could have any kind of political or social significance" were passed on to the Committee of Ministers or rejected outright. For example, the ministry denied permission for charitable societies in Vilnius, Zhitomir, and Kamenets;[28] it was probably particularly sensitive to voluntary association in these western border areas after the Polish rebellion in 1863. In fact, the 1862 policy on charitable associations explicitly excluded Russian Poland; there, mutual aid and charitable societies continued to need to obtain Imperial permission through the Committee of Ministers.[29] The brief history of the Sunday school movement (1859–62), too, illustrates how government tolerance for some social initiatives could quickly turn into repression.[30] Finally, two statutes issued during this period tightened the definition of an illegal association. These statutes banned all "secret"—that is, unconfirmed—societies, regardless of their purpose. In addition, any legal society that deviated from its original purpose or used permitted activities to disguise antigovernment activity was also considered illegal.[31]

The government's actions on private organized charity formed part of its general policy toward the role of society in the reform period. The autocracy tolerated, even facilitated, voluntary initiative when it shifted the financial burden for some relatively low-priority problem, such as aiding the Empire's needy and impoverished, from the state treasury to the public. Minister of the Interior Valuev had used the same approach toward the question of improving the material condition of Russia's wretched parish priests: ruling out any state aid to the clergy, his reform commission shifted the burden back to the parish.[32] Such a policy suffered from what Gregory Freeze has called an "enervating contradiction in Great Reform politics: the desire to stimulate autonomous social development versus the fear that this initiative might go too far or swerve in an unanticipated, undesirable direction."[33] While praising charitable activity for its moral virtue and social usefulness, the government tried to ensure that it stayed within the boundaries it set. Participation in local self-government, freedom of association, and other civil liberties doled out to Russians by a cautious Alexander II were only meant, as Alfred Rieber has said, "to increase the opportunities of the people to serve and obey him."[34] Granting complete freedom of action to Russian society remained out of the question.

An Ethos of Philanthropy: The Generation of the Sixties

The government's more tolerant policy toward voluntary associations facilitated but did not create the voluntarism of the reform era. The rise in voluntarism also had roots in the unique ethos that developed in educated society in this period. The "generation of the sixties" prized compassion and a social conscience, and regarded service to society as a personal moral duty. Young, educated Russians dedicated themselves to raising the cultural and material level of the population. Although they sometimes clothed themselves in nihilist fashions of scientific rationalism and utilitarianism, men and women of this generation shared a passion for social change. "The sixties can be called the spring of our lives, an epoch of the flowering of spiritual forces and social ideals, a time of passionate strivings for light and for new, previously unknown social activity," one woman wrote in her memoirs. To understand the times, she continued, one must understand

> how Russian people were seized by a feverish movement forward, how the youth yearned to educate themselves and enlighten the people, what unbending resoluteness it showed in order to shake off immediately the old person, to begin to live a new life and make all needy and burdened people happy. This unprecedented yearning of society for moral and intellectual renewal had a tremendous influence on changing the entire world view of Russians, and at the same time on many aspects of life, on the relationship of one class of society to another.[35]

Though often overlooked in favor of the more radical communes, study circles, and nihilist groups of the day, the unprecedented opportunity to form legal voluntary associations offered Russians another outlet for their passion for renewal.

The ethos of the 1860s left its imprint on many who became leaders of Russian philanthropy in the late Imperial period. The lives of three individuals, all born in 1837, illustrate how youthful experiences during the period of the Great Reforms turned into a lifelong dedication to organized charity. One representative of this generation was the leading feminist and philanthropist Anna Filosofova (1837–1912). The jurist A. F. Koni described her as sensitive, quick to respond to injustice, activist and energetic, angered by backwardness and ignorance, and full of hopes for a "bright future"—all qualities prized by her contemporaries.[36] Filosofova and her circle in Petersburg revitalized the routine charity long practiced by well-born ladies with their "genuine enthusiasm for charity" and "unfeigned respect" for the poor.[37] Another charity leader who embodied the spirit of the decade was the jurist Petr N. Obninskii (1837–1904). A *mirovoi posrednik* at the time of the Emancipation, Obninskii gave his own former serfs his best land for free. In 1866 he became the justice of the peace for his district in Kaluga.

Later, as a Moscow procurator, Obninskii became a leader in charitable work on behalf of children, starting Russia's movement to protect children against cruelty.[38] Another contemporary was the liberal historian Vladimir Ger'e (Guerrier) (1837–1919), best known for his services to women's higher education as the founder of the Higher Women's Courses in 1872. Active in urban affairs as a delegate to the Moscow City Duma from 1876, Ger'e was also one of Russia's leading charity reformers, helping to create Moscow's new municipal welfare system in 1894 and serving on the government commission to reform the Russian poor law in the 1890s.[39]

The origins of the distinctive ethos of the "generation of the sixties" are not easy to explain. The reforms themselves, of course, had a powerful effect on society. The abolition of serfdom in particular invited the hope that the entire old order, characterized by poverty, ignorance, corruption, patriarchy, and cultural backwardness, could be banished by the efforts of right-minded, dedicated individuals. As the government eased the procedures for establishing charitable societies and institutions in the 1860s, organized charity became a relatively accessible means of working for social progress—one which, moreover, appeared to enjoy complete government support. After decades of government suspicion of voluntary activity, the government of Alexander II seemed to be calling on educated society for help in the task of renewal. The tsar's own example encouraged the social service ethic; to loyal Russians, Alexander's reforms reflected a deep humanitarian concern for his subjects that they should try to emulate. As the history of one provincial charity founded in the late 1860s recalled,

> In the sixties Russia was called by the will of the late tsar to a new life, to new, great activity. The liberation of the peasants, local self-government, the judicial reform—all these questions could not but excite, awaken. . . . There was a feeling of a common life, common cares, a common necessity to become acquainted, to join together, to work in friendship, to extend a helping hand to the beginning zemstvo, to the poor. . . . These new trends, this new direction, served as the reason or rather the stimulus for the founding of our Mozhaisk Charitable Society.[40]

Guilt over their privileged status probably also played a part in the motives of some members of the "generation of the sixties." An 1858 article in the *Zhurnal zemlevladel'tsev* reproached the "idle district nobility: for its "egoism and apathy" and called upon it to form charitable societies.[41] Anna Filosofova wrote her husband in 1872: "I cannot see the suffering [*strazhdushchie*], especially in our village, without reproving myself, without reproaching myself for it. *We must help them,* it is our duty!"[42] In the moral atmosphere of this period, service to society offered personal satisfaction and fulfillment, especially at a time when conventional roads to happiness, like a career in state service or marriage and a family, were being challenged.[43]

At the beginning of the reform era, at least, philanthropy found favor even in radical circles, as one way to work for social progress. Writing in *Sovremennik* in 1857, Nicholas Chernyshevsky praised the accomplishments of the Odessa Women's Charitable Society (founded in the early years of the reign of Nicholas I) and went on to expound on several schemes which charitable societies could implement to lower the cost of living for the urban poor. While gently mocking the vanity that often motivated individual givers, Chernyshevsky's article supported rational philanthropy to relieve, if not eradicate, the sufferings of the working poor.[44] Two issues later, *Sovremennik* reprinted the article from the *Journal of the Ministry of the Interior* describing the Society for the Improvement of Workers' Housing, whose organization and goal conformed closely to the kind of philanthropy Chernyshevsky had recommended in his earlier article.[45] In the early reform period, radicals and moderates maintained close ties and cooperated in launching various civic endeavors, such as the philanthropic Literary Fund and the Sunday schools.

Philanthropy was particularly important as an outlet for women touched by the *Zeitgeist* of the 1860s. As a writer on the history of women in Russian charity explained, "since the sphere of activity for women in our country is much narrower than for men, all this pent-up energy was turned to public charity."[46] Women launched many of the most prominent or innovative charitable endeavors of the 1860s; some of them, like day nurseries, sewing workshops, and other projects designed to enable women to earn their own living, bore a progressive stamp. The sewing collective for poor women run by Vera Pavlovna, heroine of Chernyshevsky's enormously influential novel *What Is to Be Done?* (1863), is well known. Efforts to help working women preceded Chernyshevsky's famous fictional workshop, however. According to L. P. Bogoslovskaia, Chernyshevsky modeled his heroine's project after existing sewing workshops set up as early as 1859 by the Society for Inexpensive Lodgings, founded by the feminists Filosofova, Nadezhda Stasova, and Maria Trubnikova.[47] At the same time, Chernyshevsky's support of enlightened philanthropy, especially by women, and his positive depiction of sewing workshops in *What Is to Be Done?* inspired and gratified these women.[48] Philanthropic work by women on behalf of poor working women did not belong exclusively to feminists or progressive-minded activists, however. In Moscow, for example, the deeply religious Alexandra Strekalova opened her Society to Encourage Industriousness to provide sewing work and instruction to poor girls in the very year Chernyshevsky's novel was being serialized in *Sovremennik*.[49]

The links between philanthropy and radicalism did not survive long, at least in St. Petersburg. Philanthropy became discredited in radical eyes after plans for a society for women's work in St. Petersburg, a joint effort of Peter Lavrov (later a major radical theoretician) and moderate feminists, foundered on the rocks of acrimonious conflict between the "nihilists" and the "aristocrats."[50] Different paths opened up before members of the generation of the sixties. Some, disillusioned by the reforms and rejecting faith in gradual change, turned to the radical doctrines of nihilism and populism and underground political activity. Others, men and women, took advantage of expanding professional opportunities in medicine, teaching, law, and other fields. Still others, however, continued to find in organized charity a way to address society's problems and work for progress.

Charity in the Polemics of the 1860s

The reform era also witnessed the emergence of the first real public discussion of problems of poverty and charity since the reign of Alexander I, when the *Journal of the Imperial Philanthropic Society* (1817–26) reported on new initiatives in Russian and Western poor relief. In fact, almost four thousand books and articles on charity and related subjects were published between 1855 and 1881, reflecting unprecedented interest in the subject.[51] Newspapers and journals in the capitals and provinces printed the annual reports of charitable societies and institutions, discussions of the history of charity, and descriptions of innovative forms of aid. For the first time, too, the Russian press began to discuss in some depth the problems of poverty, begging, slums, unemployment, and juvenile delinquency. The first specialized journals dealing with charity since the demise of the *Journal of the Imperial Philanthropic Society* in 1826 also appeared during the period of the Great Reforms.[52]

Journals and other literature of the day did more than report on charity. The topics of begging, almsgiving, and the proper form and goal of charitable giving generated considerable controversy. Begging and charity, especially almsgiving, became the subjects of a polemic between progressive and late-Slavophile publicists and journals.[53] The debate weighed personal, individual giving against organized philanthropy, and moral against utilitarian motives for helping the poor.

Progressive and radical writers in journals such as *Sovremennik* and *Iskra* attacked the ancient Russian custom of almsgiving for encouraging begging, idleness, and parasitism, and its Slavophile defenders for romanticizing poverty.[54] Having labeled almsgiving "patriarchal" and old-fashioned in his article on philanthropy in 1857,[55] Chernyshevsky returned to the subject in *What Is to Be Done?* The character Katerina Vasil'evna Polozova, a sheltered, gentle girl, gave money to the poor "like every good woman." After reading and thinking, however, she came to the conclusion that the aid she gave did much less good than it should. "She began to see," Chernyshevsky continues, "that too often sham or worthless poor people deceived her; and that this money almost never was of lasting benefit to people who deserved help, who knew how to use the money given them: for a time it brings them out of misfortune, but in six months or a year, these people are again in the same misfortune."[56] In the novel, Katerina Vasil'evna finds the answer to her questions about wealth, poverty, and the purpose of her life in a new friendship with Vera Pavlovna and support for her sewing collective.

A particularly vehement opponent of begging and traditional forms of giving was the eccentric populist Ivan Pryzhov. His 1862 book on Moscow's beggars sought to expose the deceit that he felt lay behind most begging, and stressed the harmfulness of the casual dole. "Kopeck almsgiving is fatal," Pryzhov proclaimed, "both for beggars and for those who give it."[57] Still another attack on begging and conventional charity came from the pen of Petr Tkachev, whose 1864 article "Poverty and Charity" asserted that while the number of beggars and paupers in Russia was growing, both government authorities and societies "dozed." Even worse, he declared, some people "even find an extremely good side to begging, namely the stimulation in us of a spirit of humanitarianism and charity."[58]

Defenders of individual charity rejected social betterment as the purpose of charity, emphasizing instead the moral value of helping one's neighbor. The Slavophile critic N. N. Strakhov, for example, writing in Fedor Dostoevsky's journal *Vremia,* praised personal, direct charitable giving, which he believed elevated rather than degraded the morality of giver and recipient and united rich and poor.[59] Dostoevsky, an inveterate almsgiver himself, continued the debate over the value of individual charitable giving in his novels. *The Idiot* (1869) contains a particularly long passage on the subject, in the form of a monologue by the character Ippolit. "Anyone who would attack individual charity . . . is attacking human nature and holding man's personal dignity in contempt," Ippolit declares. He goes on to describe "an old man, a 'general'" in Moscow, famous for his generosity toward criminals and convicts, and especially for the personal concern he showed them as people. Dostoevsky had in mind the real prison doctor F. P. Gaaz (1780–1853), known for his extraordinary charity and dedication to his patients. In words reminiscent of Strakhov's, Ippolit concludes:

> In planting your seed, in offering your "alms," your good deed in whatever form, you are giving away part of your individuality and receiving part of another's; you are communing one with another already with a certain mutual consideration, and you will be rewarded by knowledge and by the most unexpected discoveries.[60]

Dostoevsky caricatured Pryzhov's condemnation of begging and almsgiving in his next novel, *The Possessed* (1872), in a lecture Varvara Petrovna gives Stepan Trofimovich. Almsgiving, she says, "corrupts both the giver and the recipient, and moreover, does not achieve its goal, because it only increases begging. . . . Almsgiving in present-day society should be prohibited by law. In the new order there will be no poor people."[61]

As the identities of the participants suggest, this debate was only partly about begging and almsgiving. Pryzhov, Chernyshevsky, Tkachev, and the other radicals who attacked almsgiving regarded not well-organized charitable societies but basic changes in the social order as the ultimate solution to poverty. At the same time Strakhov, Dostoevsky, and Aksakov used alms-giving to substantiate their ideas about the Russian character and the nature of human goodness. Consequently, the effect of this debate on the public is difficult to gauge.

Did the debate stimulate the formation of charitable associations? Prob-ably so—since the form of a voluntary association could accommodate com-peting views on how to deal with poverty. People inspired by the Slavophiles' defense of individual good deeds and traditional charity could respond by forming one of the many parish-based or Church-related charitable societies that were particularly popular in the 1860s. On the other side, opponents of almsgiving tended to regard charitable associations as an improvement, at least, over random almsgiving. Even those influenced by arguments that charity was a weak palliative could, as many did, use the form of a charitable association to pursue a progressive aim, be it independent work for women or education for the masses. In any case, the debate over begging and alms-giving stimulated public interest in charitable activity.

Can Berdyaev's "mystery" of the origins of voluntarism during the Great Reform era be solved? New laws and more lenient government policies, as we have seen, really explain only why so many associations and movements of the period—though far from all—received legal sanction. Yet the example set by Alexander II and the reforms themselves inspired many Russians to work for social progress. Other factors that stimulated the development of voluntary charitable associations range from the specific, like the establish-ment of the Russian Red Cross in 1867, to broader social and cultural cur-rents of the time: social activism in the Orthodox Church, the Panslav movement, the entry of women into public life. The distinctive ethos of the 1860s, too, with its belief in the possibility of progress, commitment to selfless service to country and *narod,* and hope of creating if not complete equality, then at least closer ties between classes, nourished the upsurge of voluntarism.

Another reason lies in the form of the voluntary association itself, whose flexibility enables it to accommodate widely different political and social agendas. Perhaps that is why organized charity in particular, and voluntary associations in general, continued to grow in Russia through the late nine-teenth and early twentieth centuries. In that sense the era of the Great Reforms did not end for Russian voluntarism with Karakozov's attempt on the tsar's life in 1866, or the last military reform in 1874, or the assassination of Alexander in 1881. One of the strongest legacies of the reform era was surely the training it gave Russians in organization and civic involvement.

NOTES

1. Quoted in Nicholas V. Riazanovsky, *Nicholas I and Official Nationality in Russia, 1825–1855* (Berkeley, Calif., 1959), 219.

2. One of the first historians to pay attention to the development of voluntary associations in Imperial Russia was Jacob Walkin, *The Rise of Democracy in Pre-Revolutionary Russia: Political and Social Institutions under the Last Three Tsars* (New York, 1962), chap. 6.

3. Quoted in ibid., 127.

4. TsGIA, f. 1287 (Khoziaistvennyi departament Ministerstva vnutrennikh del), op. 15, 19–go fevralia 1880, d. 127, "Obozrenie obshchestvennogo prizreniia za 1-e dvadtsatipiatiletie nastoishchego tsarstvovaniia," ll. 3-30b. According to this report, similar growth had taken place in the numbers of mutual aid societies—460 had been founded since 1862; l. 4. The report does not state how these statistics were compiled, but they probably came from the ministry's records of officially approved charters.

5. Between 1875 and 1886 the Imperial Philanthropic Society published the results of its survey of charitable associations and institutions in the Empire, conducted with the assistance of the Central Statistical Committeee; Imperatorskoe Chelovekoliubivoe Obshchestvo, *Sbornik svedenii po obshchestvennoi blagotvoritel'nosti,* 7 vols. (St. Petersburg, 1875-86). The survey was flawed, however, largely because of careless responses and the refusal of some private charities to cooperate. More successful surveys were done by the Moscow and St. Petersburg city governments in the 1880s; though still incomplete, they reveal an extensive network of private charities in these cities: Iu. E. Ianson, ed., *Sbornik spravochnykh i statisticheskikh svedenii o blagotvoritel'nosti v S-Peterburge za 1884 god* (St. Petersburg, 1886), and *Sbornik svedenii o blagotvoritel'nosti v S-Peterburge za 1889 g.* (St. Petersburg, 1891); *Sbornik statisticheskikh svedenii o blagotvoritel'nosti Moskvy za 1889 god* (Moscow, 1891).

6. Sobstvennaia ego Imperatorskogo Velichestva Kantseliariia po uchrezhdeniiam Imperatritsy Marii, *Blagotvoritel'nost' v Rossii,* 2 vols. (St. Petersburg, [1907]).

7. The statistics presented are taken from my analysis of the data on 4,199 charitable societies surveyed in 1901; the survey data are in vol. 2 of *Blagotvoritel'nost' v Rossii.* The cross-tabulations and other operations in the analysis were carried out with the use of the Statistical Package for the Social Sciences (SPSS).

8. A. A. Papkov, *Tserkovno-obshchestvennye voprosy v epokhu Tsaria-osvoboditelia* (St. Petersburg, 1902); Gregory L. Freeze, *The Parish Clergy in Nineteenth-Century Russia: Crisis, Reform, Counter-Reform* (Princeton, N.J., 1983), 286–97.

9. Nicholas V. Riasanovsky, *Russia and the West in the Teaching of the Slavophiles: A Study of Romantic Ideology* (Cambridge, Mass., 1952), 131. A founder and leader of the Slavonic Benevolent Society, Aksakov also found the form of the philanthropic association ideal for the promotion of his Panslav ideas. On Aksakov's ideas concerning the leading, progressive role educated society should play in postreform Russia, see N. I. Tsimbaev, *I. S. Aksakov v obshchestvennoi zhizni poreformennoi Rossii* (Moscow, 1978).

10. This is almost 26 percent of the societies established in this decade and still in existence in 1901 that provided information on both their date of founding and their purpose.

11. One hundred three, or almost one-third, of the societies established between 1876 and 1880 came under the jurisdiction of the Main Committee of the Red Cross.

12. S. A. Nikitin, *Slavianskie komitety v Rossii v 1858–1876 godakh* (Moscow, 1960).

13. According to one historian, only twenty-five charitable, learned, and agricultural societies were established under Nicholas I; Nikolai Anufriev, "Pravitel'stvennaia reglamentatsiia obrazovaniia chastnykh obshchestv v Rossii," *Voprosy administrativnogo prava,* bk. 1, 1916, 24. A search through the *Polnoe Sobranie Zakonov* (ser. 2) for this period revealed only twenty new charitable associations, including six mutual aid societies, that received official confirmation.

14. Nicholas's order was not made public at the time. Minister of the Interior P. A. Valuev mentions it in an 1862 memorandum on charitable associations. TsGIA, f. 1263 (fond Komitetov ministrov), alf. 51, 1862, d. 2953, "Prilozhenie k zhurnalam k. m. [Komiteta ministrov] za ianvar' m-ts," l. 250b.

15. John Shelton Curtiss, "Russian Sisters of Mercy in the Crimea, 1854–1855," *Slavic Review,* March 1966, 84–100; Brenda Meehan-Waters, "From Contemplative Practice to Charitable Activity: Russian Women's Religious Communities and the Development of Charitable Work, 1861–1917," in Kathleen McCarthy, ed., *Lady Bountiful Revisited: Women, Philanthropy and Power* (New Brunswick, N.J., forthcoming).

16. "Ob uchrezhdenii v S-Peterburge obshchestva dlia uluchsheniia pomeshchenii rabochego naseleniia," *Zhurnal Ministerstva vnutrennikh del,* pt. 24 (1857), 19–28. The founders included Senator D. P. Khrushchev, the Petersburg Marshal of the Nobility Count Shuvalov, A. A. Abaza (who became minister of finance in 1880), and the banker Baron Stieglitz.

17. See John Nelson Tarn, *Five Per Cent Philanthropy: An Account of Housing in Urban Areas Between 1840 and 1914* (London, 1973).

18. Ibid., 28.

19. A Ministry of the Interior report in the early 1860s described society's "general propensity [*naklonnost'*] toward the development of associational public activity in all forms and for all kinds of purposes." *Izvlechenie iz otcheta Ministra nutrennikh del za 1861, 1862, i 1863 gg.* (St. Petersburg, 1865), 134–35.

20. TsGIA, f. 1263, alf. 51, d. 2953, ll. 250b–260b.

21. Ibid., ll. 27–28.

22. Ibid., ll. 28–280b.

23. *PSZ,* ser. 2, vol. 37, no. 37852 (Jan. 12, 1862). A similar devolution of authority was introduced for other types of societies at this time; in 1863, for example, the authority to permit learned societies was transferred to the Ministry of Education, and in 1866 the Ministry of State Domains received the same authority for agricultural societies; Anufriev, "Pravitel'stvennaia reglamentatsiia," 26.

24. The new law, and the government's positive assessment of organized charity, were explained in the report "Ustroistvo obshchestvennogo prizreniia v Rossii," which the Ministry of the Interior's Economic Department prepared for the commission working on the reform of local government. This report, announcing the new policy, received fairly wide publicity: it was published in the newspapers *Severnaia pochta,* special supplement to 1862, nos. 181 and 191, and *Nashe vremia,* 1862, nos. 181, 183, 197, 201, and 203. Copies of it were also sent to governors with the recommendation that its contents be made widely known among people interested in poor relief in the province; *Sbornik tsirkuliarov i instruktsii Ministerstva Vnutrennikh Del za 1862, 1863 i 1864 gody,* D. Chudovskii, comp. (St. Petersburg, 1873), 105–6.

25. E. Maksimov, "Obshchestvennaia pomoshch' nuzhdaiushchimsia v istoricheskom razvitii ee v Rossii," in *Blagotvoritel'nost' v Rossii,* vol. 1, 75.

26. *Izvlechenie iz otcheta Ministra vnutrennikh del za 1861, 1862, i 1863 gg.,* 135.

27. TsGIA, f. 1263, op. 1 (45), 1868, No. 3361, "Zhurnal [Komiteta Ministrov] za dekabr' m-ts," No. 803 (24 dek. 1868), ll. 70100b–703. Reviewing the entire reign of Alexander II in 1880, the Ministry of the Interior expressed satisfaction with the expansion of public and private relief. The report lists the government measures that it considered responsible for the expansion of public and private welfare; they included the 1862 law on charitable societies, a government policy of strictly implementing the will of donors to charity, the Emancipation Statute (which gave communes the right to run their own charitable institutions), the Municipal Statute of 1870, and measures granting the ministry, zemstvos, and town governments au-

thority to accept charitable donations—but oddly enough, not the Zemstvo Statute. TsGIA, f. 1287, op. 15, d. 127.

28. *Izvlechenie iz otcheta Ministra vnutrennikh del za 1861, 1862, i 1863 gg.*, 135.

29. *Svod zakonov*, vol. 13, 1892 ed., art. 441, primechanie. Draft charters submitted for ministerial confirmation were routinely sent to the ministry's Department of Police for its opinion.

30. On the Sunday school movement and other "small deeds," see Reginald E. Zelnik, *Labor and Society in Tsarist Russia: The Factory Workers of St. Petersburg, 1855–1870* (Stanford, Calif., 1971), chap. 5.

31. *PSZ*, ser. 2, vol. 42, no. 44402 (Mar. 27, 1867), and vol. 49, no. 53606 (June 4, 1874).

32. Freeze, *The Parish Clergy in Nineteenth-Century Russia*, 251.

33. Ibid., 254.

34. Alfred J. Rieber, "Alexander II: A Revisionist View," *Journal of Modern History* 43 (1971): 55.

35. E. N. Vodovozova, *Na zare zhizni: Memuarnye ocherki i portrety*, (Moscow, 1987), vol. 2, 25–26.

36. A. F. Koni, "Pamiati A. P. Filosofovoi," *Sbornik pamiati Anny Pavlovny Filosofovoi*, vol. 2 (Petrograd, 1915), 1–10.

37. Richard Stites, *The Women's Liberation Movement in Russia: Feminism, Nihilism and Bolshevism, 1860–1930* (Princeton, N.J., 1978), 65; the first phrase is Stites's own, the second is quoted from a biography of one of the early feminist leaders.

38. A. F. Koni, "Pamiati Petra Narkizovicha Obninskogo," in P. N. Obninskii, *Sbornik statei* (Moscow, 1914), 5–18.

39. Christine Johanson, "Ger'e (Guerrier), Vladimir Ivanovich," *Modern Encyclopedia of Russian and Soviet History*, Joseph L. Wieczynski, ed., vol. 12 (Gulf Breeze, Fla., 1979), 149–51; Adele Lindenmeyr, "A Russian Experiment in Voluntarism: The Municipal Guardianships of the Poor, 1894–1914," *Jahrbücher für Geschichte Osteuropas*, vol. 30 (1982), 429–51.

40. *Otchet Mozhaiskogo blagotvoritel'nogo obshchestva za pervye 25 let ego sushchestvovaniia* (Moscow, 1893), 1.

41. A. Z. . .n [A. I. Zabelin], "Mysli ob obshchestvennoi blagotvoritel'nosti," *Zhurnal zemlevladel'tsev* 2 (August 1858): 86, 91.

42. A. Miliukova, "Obshchestvennoe nastroenie 60-kh godov i Anna Pavlovna Filosofova," in *Sbornik pamiati Anny Pavlovny Filosofovoi*, vol. 2, 44; emphasis in the original.

43. See Stites, *The Women's Liberation Movement*, pt. 2. The code of service to society often rested upon an assumption of moral superiority over the culture—or lack of one—of the "ignorant masses" and over the selfish, unenlightened prereform generation. Radical or liberal, the members of the generation of the sixties constituted themselves as a new kind of moral elite, entrance into which required dedication to others.

44. "Otchet pravleniia Odesskogo zhenskogo blagotvoritel'nogo obshchestva za 1856 god," *Sovremennik* (1857, no. 5), in N. G. Chernyshevsky, *Polnoe sobranie sochinenii v piatnadtsati tomakh*, vol. 4 (Moscow, 1948), 592–605. Chernyshevsky's authorship of this unsigned article is affirmed by the editors of the volume; see 944.

45. Chernyshevsky, *Polnoe sobranie sochinenii*, vol. 4, 801–5.

46. P. Ariian, "Zhenshchiny v istorii blagotvoritel'nosti v Rossii," *Vestnik blagotvoritel'nosti*, 1901, no. 9, 48.

47. L. P. Bogoslovskaia, "'Chto delat'' N. G. Chernyshevskogo i zhenskie arteli 60-kh godov XIX v.," *Revoliutsionnaia situatsiia v Rossii v 1859–1861 gg.*, ed. M. V. Nechkina (Moscow, 1974), 128. See also Barbara Alpern Engel, *Mothers and Daughters: Women of the Intelligentsia in Nineteenth-Century Russia* (Cambridge, England, 1983), 58–59, and Stites, *The Women's Liberation Movement*, 69.

48. Bogoslovskaia, "'Chto delat'"," 127, 132. Vera Pavlovna's sewing enterprise in the novel is more ambitious than most real-life sewing workshops of the time; she turns it into a producers' and consumers' cooperative whose profits are shared by the worker-partners. On efforts by women to establish sewing workshops following Chernyshevsky's fictional model, see Vodovozova, *Na zare zhizni*, vol. 2, chap. 22.

49. Sergei Iakovlev, "Aleksandra Strekalova (Biograficheskii ocherk)," *Trudovaia pomoshch'*, September 1904, 215–16. Strekalova also established a society to publish "useful books" for the masses in the early 1860s.

50. Engel, *Mothers and Daughters*, 59–60; Stites, *The Women's Liberation Movement*, 69–70.

51. V. I. Mezhov, *Blagotvoritel'nost' v Rossii. Bibliograficheskii ukazatel' knig i statei na russkom iazyke, vyshedshikh v Rossii v period tsarstvovaniia Imperatora Aleksandra II* (St. Petersburg, 1883).

52. *Vestnik blagotvoritel'nosti* (1870, seven issues); *Nuzhda i pomoshch'* (1871, five issues); *Vestnik nuzhdy i pomoshchi* (1871, four issues). The journal *Dukh Khristianina* (1861–65), a leader in the parish revival movement, frequently reported on charity.

53. I. Iampol'skii, *Satiricheskaia zhurnalistika 1860-kh godov: Zhurnal revoliutsionnoi satiry "Iskra" (1859–1873)* (Moscow, 1964), 117–18. According to Iampol'skii, the argument had roots in the 1840s, in an exchange about charity between Vissarion Belinsky and Konstantin Aksakov.

54. For example, see M. N. Kurbanovskii, "Nishchenstvo i blagotvoritel'nost'," *Sovremmenik*, September 1860, 249–304, a lengthy critique of begging and the lack of rational and effective aid in Russia. An article by V. S. Kurochkin, a member of *Zemlia i volia*, titled "Dilentantizm v blagotvoritel'nosti," in *Iskra*, 1860, caricatured the Slavophile romanticization of almsgiving; Iampol'skii, 117.

55. "Otchet pravleniia Odesskogo zhenskogo blagotvoritel'nogo obshchestva," in Chernyshevskii, *Polnoe sobranie sochinenii*, vol. 4, 593.

56. Chernyshevskii, *Chto delat'*, in *Polnoe sobranie sochinenii*, vol. 11 (Moscow, 1939), 307.

57. Ivan G. Pryzhov, *Nishchie na sviatoi Rusi. Materialy dlia istorii obshchestvennogo i narodnogo byta v Rossii* (Moscow, 1862), 122.

58. P. Tkachev, "Statisticheski etiudy. (Etiud tretii.) Bednost' i blagotvoritel'nost'," *Biblioteka dlia chteniia*, 1864, no. 10–11, 19.

59. N. Kositsa [N. Strakhov], "Tiazheloe vremia," and "Nechto ob avtoritetakh," reprinted in N. Strakhov, *Iz istorii literaturnogo nigilizma 1861–1865* (St. Petersburg, 1890), 149–99; see also F. M. Dostoevsky, *Polnoe sobranie sochinenii*, vol. 9 (Leningrad, 1974) (notes to *The Idiot*), 450. Articles attacking almsgiving, however, also appeared in *Vremia;* see V. S. Nechaeva, *Zhurnal M. M. i F. M. Dostoevskikh "Vremia"* (Moscow, 1972), 199.

60. F. M. Dostoevsky, *The Idiot*, pt. 3, chap. 6; editors' notes to the novel in *Polnoe sobranie sochinenii*, vol. 9, 343–44, 450–51.

61. *The Possessed*, pt. 2, chap. 5; notes to the novel in *Polnoe sobranie sochinenii*, vol. 12 (Leningrad, 1975), 300.

BIBLIOGRAPHY
Compiled by Abbott Gleason

In compiling this bibliography of works on the Great Reforms published between 1953 and 1990, I have become aware of how difficult certain lines are to draw. Studies of the countryside, peasant disturbances, and radicalism all lie in terrain contiguous to that of the reform of institutions. The existence of the "revolutionary situation" concept, which linked institutional reform to these other subjects for many Soviet historians, makes the line even more difficult to draw. Nevertheless, the many Soviet and American works on Russian radicalism and on the peasantry have been omitted, unless they bear directly on the reforms themselves. In the same way, studies of social and economic change in rural Russia have been included only if they bear on the genesis or the concrete character of reform activities.

My thanks to Gareth Cook and the Center for Foreign Policy Development of Brown University for significant assistance on this project.

Abbott, Robert. "Police Reform in the Russian Province of Iaroslavl, 1856–1876," *Slavic Review*, 32, no. 2 (Summer 1973): 292–302.

Adler, Charles C., Jr. "The Promulgation of Serf Emancipation in St. Petersburg 5/17 March 1861: An Eyewitness Account," *Canadian Slavic Studies*, 1967, no. 1, 271–75.

———. "The Revolutionary Situation 1859–1861: The Uses of an Historical Conception," *Canadian Slavic Studies*, 1969, no. 3, 383–99.

Afanas'ev, A. K. "Sostav suda prisiazhnykh v Rossii," *Voprosy istorii*, 1978, no. 6, 199–203.

Balmuth, Daniel. *Censorship in Russia.* Washington, D.C.: University Press of America, 1979.

———. "Origins of the Russian Press Reform of 1865," *Slavonic and East European Review* 47 (1969): 369–88.

Baraboi, A. Z., et al., eds. *Otmena krepostnogo prava na Ukraine. Sbornik dokumentov i materialov.* Kiev, 1961.

Bestuzhev, I. V. "Krymskaia voina i revoliutsionnaia situatsiia," *Revoliutsionnaia situatsiia v Rossii v 1859–1861 gg.*, Moscow, 1963.

Beyrau, Dietrich. "Agrarstruktur und Bauernprotest: Zu den Bedingungen der russischen Bauernbefreiung von 1861," *Vierteljahresschrift für Sozial- und Wirtschaftsgeschichte*, vol. 64, bk. 2, 1977, 179–236.

Brooks, E. Willis. "Reform in the Russian Army, 1856–1861," *Slavic Review* 43, no. 1 (Spring 1984): 63–82.

Budaev, D. I. "Izmeneniia v zemlepol'zovanii krest'ian Smolenskoi gubernii v rezultate provedeniia reformy 1861 goda," *Nauchnye doklady vysshei shkoly. Istoricheskie nauki*, 1959, no. 4.

———. *Krest'ianskaia reforma 1861 goda v Smolenskoi gubernii.* Smolensk, 1967.

Burzhuaznye reformy v Rossii vtoroi poloviny XIX veka. Voronezh, 1988.

Chernukha, V. G. "Problema politicheskoi reformy v pravitel'stvennykh krugakh Rossii v nachale 70-kh godov XIX v.," in Akademiia Nauk SSSR, Institut Istorii SSSR, Leningradskoe otdelenie, *Problemy krest'ianskogo zemlevladeniia i vnutrennoi politiki Rossii: dooktiabrskii period*, 138–91, Leningrad, 1972.

———. "Konstituirovanie Soveta ministrov (1861 g.)," *Vspomogatel'nye istoricheskie distsipliny*, 1976, no. 8, 164–84.

———. *Krestianskii vopros v pravitel'stvennoi politike Rossii (60–70 gody XIX v.)*. Leningrad, 1972.

———. *Pravitel'stvennaia politika v otnoshenii pechati 60–70-e gody XIX veka*. Leningrad, 1989.

———. "Sovet Ministrov v 1857–1861 gg.," *Vspomogatel'nye istoricheskie ditsipliny*, 1973, no. 5, 120–36.

———. *Vnutrenniaia politika tsarizma s serediny 50-kh do nachala 80-kh gg. XIX v.* Leningrad, 1978.

———. "Vsepoddaneishii doklad komissii P. A. Valueva ot 2 aprelia 1872 g. kak istochnik po istorii podatnoi reformy v Rossii," *Vospomogatel'nye istoricheskie ditsipliny* 2 (1969): 262–69.

Davletbaev, Bulat Sabirovich. *Krestianskaia reforma 1861 goda v Bashkirii*. Moscow, 1983.

Dneprov, E. D. "Proekt ustava morskogo suda i ego rol' v podgotovke sudebnoi reformy (aprel' 1860 g.)," in *Revoliutsionnaia situatsiia v Rossii v 1859–1861 gg.*, 57–70. Moscow, 1970.

Druzhinin, N. M. "Agrarnaia reforma 1866 g. i ee posledstviia," in Iu. V. Bromlei et al., eds., *Slaviane i Rossiia*, 148–63. Moscow, 1972.

———. "Byvshie udel'nye krest'iane posle reformy 1863 g. (1863–1883 gg.)," *Istoricheskie zapiski* 85 (1970): 159–206.

———. "Glavnyi komitet ob ustroistve sel'skogo sostoianiia," in N. E. Nosov et al., eds., *Issledovaniia po sotsial'no-politicheskoi istorii Rossii*, 269–86. Leningrad, 1971.

———. *Gosudarstvennye krestiane i reforma P. D. Kiseleva*. 2 vols. Moscow-Leningrad, 1946–58.

———. "Krest'ianskoe dvizhenie 1857–1861 gg. po dokumentam tsentral'nykh istoricheskikh arkhivov SSSR," *Voprosy istochnikovedeniia*, 1961, no. 1, 17–26.

———. "Likvidatsiia feodal'noi sistemy v russkoi pomeshchichei derevne (1862–82 gg.)," *Voprosy istorii*, 1968, no. 12, 3–34.

———. "Mirovye posredniki 1860–1870 godov (k voprosu o realizatsii reformy 1861 g.)," *Trudy instituta ekonomiki i prava*, 1968, no. 15, 114–27.

———. "Moskva i reforma 1861 g.," AN SSSR, *Istoriia Moskvy*. Moscow-Leningrad, 1952–67. Vol. 4, 13–57.

———. "Senatorskie revizii 1860–1870-kh godov (K voprosu o realizatsii reformy 1861 g.)," *Istoricheskie zapiski*, 1966, no. 79, 139–75.

———. "Vliianie agrarnykh reform 1860-kh godov na ekonomiku russkoi derevni," *Istoriia SSSR*, 1975, no. 5.

———. *Russkaia derevnia na perelome 1861–1880 gg.* Moscow, 1978.

Eimontova, R. G. "Revoliutsionnaia situatsiia i podgotovka universitetskoi reformy v Rossii," *Revoliutsionnaia situatsiia v Rossii v 1859–1861 gg.*, 60–80. Moscow, 1974.

———. "Universitetskaia reforma 1863 g.," *Istoricheskie zapiski* 70 (1964): 163–96.

———. "Universitetskii vopros i russkaia obshchestvennost' v 50–60-kh godakh XIX v.," *Istoriia SSSR*, 1971, no. 6, 144–58.

Emmons, Terence, ed. *Emancipation of the Russian Serfs*. New York, 1970.

———. "The Peasant and Emancipation," in Wayne Vucinich, ed., *The Peasantry in Nineteenth-Century Russia*, 41–71. Stanford, Calif., 1968.

———. *The Russian Landed Gentry and the Peasant Emancipation of 1861*, Cambridge, England, 1968.

Emmons, Terence, and Wayne S. Vucinich, eds. *The Zemstvo in Russia: An Experiment in Local Self Government*. Cambridge, England, 1982.

Eroshkin, N. P. *Istoriia gosudarstvennykh uchrezhdenii dorevoliutsionnoi Rossii*. Moscow, 1968.

Field, Daniel. *The End of Serfdom: Nobility and Bureaucracy in Russia, 1855–1861*. Cambridge, Mass., 1976.

——. "The Reforms of the 1860s," in S. H. Baron and Nancy Heer, eds., *Windows on the Russian Past*, 89–104. Columbus, Ohio, 1977.

Freeze, Gregory. "P. A. Valuev and the Politics of Church Reform (1861–1862)," *Slavonic and East European Review* 56, no. 1 (January 1978): 68–87.

Fridman, M. B. "Podgotovka otmeny krepostnogo prava v Belorusii," *Uchenye zapiski Belorusskogo gosudarstvennogo universiteta*, no. 36, *Voprosy istorii B.S.S.R.*, 73–107. Minsk, 1957.

——. *Podgotovka zemskoi reformy 1864 goda*. Moscow, 1957.

——. "Zemskaia reforma i zemstvo v istoricheskoi literature," *Istoriia SSSR*, 1960, no. 5, 82–107.

Frieden, Nancy Mandelker. *Russian Physicians in an Era of Reform and Revolution 1856–1905*. Princeton, N.J., 1981.

Garmiza, V. V. "Iz istorii razrabotki zakona o vvedenii zemstva v Rossii," *Vestnik MGU* 1 (1958): 131–45.

Gerasimova, Iu. I. *Iz istorii russkoi pechati v period revoliutsionnoi situatsii 1850-kh nachala 1860-kh gg*. Moscow, 1974.

——. "Krizis pravitel'stvennoi politike v revoliutsionnoi situatsii i Aleksandr II," *Revoliutsionnaia situatsiia v Rossii v 1859–1861 gg.*, 93–106. Moscow, 1962.

——. "Otnoshenie pravitel'stva k uchastiiu pechati v obsuzhdenii krest'ianskogo voprosa v period revoliutsionnoi situatsii kontsa 50-kh–nachala 60-kh godov XIX v.," *Revoliutsionnaia situatsiia v Rossii*, 81–105. Moscow, 1974.

Gindin, I. F. *Gosudarstvennyi bank i ekonomicheskaia politika tsarskogo pravitel'stva (1861–1892 godu)*. Moscow, 1960.

Gorlanov, L. R. *Udel'nye krest'iane*. Smolensk, 1986.

Gorovoi, F. S. "Dvorianskie gubernskie komitety o podgotovke otmeny krepostnogo prava na Urale," *Uchennye zapiski Sverdlovskogo pedagogicheskogo Instituta*, 1966, no. 38, 49–65.

Kaiser, F. B. *Die russische Justizreform 1864. Zur Geschichte der russischen Justiz von Katharina II. bis 1917*. Leiden, 1972.

Kakhk, Iu. Iu. "Estoniia v obshcherossiiskoi revoliutsionnoi situatsii kontsa 1850-kh–nachala 1860-kh godov," *Revoliutsionnaia situatsiia v Rossii v 1859–1861 gg.*, 259–83. Moscow, 1965.

——. "Krest'ianskie volneniia 1858 g. v Estonii," *Istoriia SSSR*, 1958, no. 3, 129–44.

Kerblay, Basil. "La Réforme de 1861 et ses effets sur la vie rurale dans la province de Smolensk," in Roger Portal, ed., *Le Statut des paysans libérés du servages, 1861–1961*, 267–310. Paris, 1961.

Kil'miashkin, A. E. *Podgotovka krest'ianskoi reformy 1861 g. v gubernskikh komitetakh (Penzenskoi, Simbirskoi i Tambovskoi gubernii)*, Trudy NII iazyka, literatury, istorii i ekonomiki pri Sovete ministrov Mordovskoi ASSR 1971, *Trudy*, Saransk, 1971, no. 40, 182–212.

Kimball, Alan. "Revolutionary Situation in Russia (1859–1862)," in *The Modern Encyclopedia of Russian and Soviet History*, vol. 31, 54–57.

——. "The Russian Peasant Obshchina in the Political Culture of the Great Reforms: A Contribution to *Begriffsgeschichte*," *Russian History* 17, no. 3 (Fall 1990): 259–80.

Kipp, Jacob. "Consequences of Defeat: Modernizing the Russian Navy, 1856–1863," *Jahrbücher für Geschichte Osteuropas* 20, no. 2 (June 1972): 210–25.

——. "M. Kh. Reutern on the Russian State and Economy: A Liberal Bureaucrat during the Crimean Era, 1845–1860," *Journal of Modern History* 47, no. 4 (September 1975): 438–59.

Koval'chenko, I. D. "K voprosu o sostoianii pomeshchichego khoziaistve pered otmenoi krepostnogo prava v Rossii," *Ezhegodnik po agrarnoi istorii Vostoch-noi Evropy 1959 g.*, 192–227. Moscow, 1961.

———. *Russkoe krepostnoe krest'ianstvo v pervoi polovine XIX v.* Moscow, 1967.

———. "Agrarnoi rynok i kharakter agrarnogo stroia Rossii v kontse XIX–nachale XX v.," *Istoriia SSSR*, 1973, no. 2, 42–74.

Krutikov, V. I. *Otmena Krepostnogo prava v Tul'skoi gubernii.* Tula, 1956.

Kucherov, Samuel. "Sudebnaia reforma Aleksandra II (1864–1964)," *Novyi zhurnal* 78 (1965): 231–52.

Leshchenko, N. N. "Krestianskaia reforma 1861 v Kharkovskoi gubernii," *Ezhegodnik po agrarnoi istorii Vostochnoi Evropy za 1964 god*, 603–14. Kishinev, 1966.

———. *Krest'ianskoe dvizhenie na Ukraine v sviazi s provedeniem reformy 1861 goda (60-e gody XIX st.).* Kiev, 1959.

———. "Reforma 1861 goda v Khersonskoi gubernii po ustavnym gramotam," *Ezhegodnik po agrarnoi istorii Vostochnoi Evropy za 1966 god*, 424–35. Tallin, 1971.

———. "Rezul'taty provedeniia reformy 1861 g. v Ekaterinoslavskoi gubernii po ustavnym gramotam," *Ezhegodnik po agrarnoi istorii Vostochnoi Evropy za 1965 god*, 381–88. Moscow, 1970.

———. "Vykupnaia operatsiia na iuge Ukrainy," *Ezhegodnik po agrarnoi istorii Vostochnoi Evropy za 1968 god*, 224–35. Leningrad, 1970.

Lincoln, W. Bruce. *In the Vanguard of Reform: Russia's Enlightened Bureaucrats, 1825–1861.* DeKalb, Ill., 1982.

———. "The Circle of the Grand Duchess Yelena Pavlovna, 1847–1861," *Slavonic Review* 48 (1970), no. 112: 463–70.

———. "The Editing Commissions of 1859–1860: Some Notes on Their Members' Backgrounds and Service Careers," *Slavonic and East European Review* 56, no. 3 (July 1978): 346–59.

———. "The Karlovka Reform," *Slavic Review* 28 (September 1969): 463–70.

———. "The Genesis of an 'Enlightened' Bureaucracy in Russia, 1825–1856," *Jahrbücher für Geschichte Osteuropas* 20 (1972): 321–30.

———. *The Great Reforms: Autocracy, Bureaucracy and the Politics of Change in Imperial Russia.* DeKalb, Ill., 1990.

———. *Nikolai Miliutin: An Enlightened Russian Bureaucrat of the Nineteenth Century.* Newtonville, Mass., 1977.

———. "A Profile of the Russian Bureaucracy on the Eve of the Great Reforms," *Jahrbücher für Geschichte Osteuropas* 28, no. 2: 181–96.

———. "Russia on the Eve of Reform: A Chinovnik's View," *Slavonic and East European Review* 59, no. 2 (April 1981): 264–71.

———. "Russia's Enlightened Bureaucrats and the Problem of State Reform, 1848–1856," *Cahiers du monde russe et soviétique*, 1971, no. 12, 410–21.

Litvak, B. G. "K istorii formuliara ustavnoi gramoti 19 fevralia 1861 g.," *Arkheograficheskii ezhegodnik. 1957.* Moscow, 1958.

———. "O nekotorykh priemakh publikatsii istochnikov statisticheskogo kharaktera," *Istoricheskii arkhiv*, 1957, no. 2.

———. "O nekotorykyh spornykh voprosakh realizatsii reformy 1861 g.," *Istoricheskie zapiski*, 68 (1961).

———. "Predvaritel'nye itogi obrabotki ustavnykh gramot shesti gubernii chernozemnogo tsentra," *Ezhegodnik po agrarnoi istorii Vostochnoi Evropy. 1960 g.* Kiev, 1962.

———. *Russkaia derevnia v reforme 1861 goda.* Moscow, 1972.

———. "Sovetskaia istoriografiia reformy 19 fevralia 1861 g.," *Istoriia SSSR*, 1960, no. 6, 99–120.

L'vova, T. N. "Zemskie vybory i sotsial'nyi sostav glasnykh zemskikh uchrezhdenii

Moskovskoi gubernii 60–70-kh gg. XIX veka," *Uchennye zapiski Moskovskogo pedagogicheskogo instituta im. V. I. Lenina,* 1964, no. 200, 41–60.

McCauley, Martin, and Peter Waldron. *The Emergence of the Russian State.* London, 1988.

McNeal, Robert H. "The Reform of Cossack Military Service in the Reign of Alexander II," in Bela Kiraly and Gunther Rothenberg, eds., *War and Society in East Central Europe: Special Topics and Generalizations on the Eighteenth and Nineteenth Centuries,* 409–11. New York, 1979.

McReynolds, Louise, "Imperial Russia's Newspaper Reporters: Profile of a Society in Transition, 1865–1914," *Slavonic and East European Review* 68 (1990), no. 2: 277–93.

Malloy, James A. "N. A. Miliutin and the Zemstvo Reform of 1864," *Etudes slaves et est européennes* 14 (1969): 83–102.

Miller, Forrestt. *Dmitrii Miliutin and the Reform Era in Russia.* Nashville, Tenn., 1968.

Mironenko, S. V. "Krestian'skii vopros v poslednom Sekretnom komitete (1857 god)," *Problemy istorii SSSR,* Moscow, 1976, no. 5, 271–94.

Mironov, B. N. "The Russian Peasant Commune after the Reforms of the 1860s," *Slavic Review* 44 (1985), no. 3: 438–67.

Mukhina, E. N. "Nachalo podgotovki krest'ianskoi reformy v Rossii (1856–1857 gg.)," *Vestnik Moskovskogo universiteta,* ser. istoriia, 1977, no. 4.

———. "Otkliki dvorianstva na pervye reskripty ob uchrezhdenii gubernskikh dvorianskikh komitetov po krest'ianskomu delu," *Vestnik Moskovskogo universiteta,* ser. istoriia, 1983, no. 4.

Nardova, V. A. *Gorodskoe samoupravlenie v Rossii v 60-kh–nachale 90-kh godov XIX v.* Leningrad, 1984.

Nechkina, M. V. "Reforma 1861 goda kak pobochnyi produkt revoliutsionnoi bor'by," *Revoliutsionnaia situatsiia,* 7–17. Moscow, 1962.

Neupokoev, V. I. "Podatnoi vopros v khode reformy 1861 goda," *Revoliutsionnaia situatsiia v Rossii v 1859–1861 gg.,* 212–29. Moscow, 1978.

———. "Podgotovka 'krest'ianskoi' reformy 1861 g. v Litve (gubernskie komitety 1858 g.)," *Uchenye zapiski Vil'niusskogo gosudarstvennogo universiteta,* vol. 2, no. 6, 1955, 169–212.

———. "Resheniia dvorianskikh komitetov 1857 goda v Litve o lichnom 'osvobozhdenii' kresti'ian (K voprosu o nachale 'krest'ianskoi reformy' v Litve)," *Uchenye zapiski Vil'niusskogo gosudarstvennogo universiteta,* vol. 1, 1955, 59–87.

Orlovsky, Daniel T. *The Limits of Reform: The Ministry of Internal Affairs in Imperial Russia, 1802–1881.* Cambridge, Mass., 1981.

Orzhekhovskii, I. V. *Iz istorii vnutrennei politiki samoderzhaviia v 60–70kh godakh XIX veka.* Gorkii, 1974.

———. "Osushchestvlenie vykupnoi operatsii v Nizhegorodskoi gubernii," *Uchennye zapiski Gor'kovskogo gosudarstvennogo universiteta,* vol. 65, 1964.

Pearson, Thomas S. *Russian Officialdom in Crisis: Autocracy and Local Self-Government, 1861–1900.* Cambridge, England, 1989.

Pereira, Norman. "Alexander II and the Decision to Emancipate the Russian Serfs, 1856–1861," *Canadian Slavonic Papers* 22 (1980): 99–115.

Pintner, Walter M. "Reformability in the Age of Reform and Counterreform, 1855–1914," in Robert O. Crummey, ed., *Reform in Russia and the USSR: Past and Prospects.* Urbana, Ill., 1989.

———. "The Russian Higher Civil Service on the Eve of the 'Great Reforms,'" *Journal of Social History,* 1975, no. 8, 55–68.

Pirumova, N. M., *Zemskaia intelligentsiia i ee rol' v obshchestvennoi bor'be do nachala XX v.,* Moscow, 1986.

————. *Zemskoe liberal'noe dvizhenie: Sotsial'nye korni i evoliutsiia do nachala XX v.* Moscow, 1977.

Portal, Roger, *Le Statut des paysans libérés du servage, 1861–1961.* Paris, 1961.

Pushkarev, Sergei. "The Russian Peasants' Reaction to the Emancipation of 1861," *Russian Review,* 27 (1968): 199–214.

Rieber, Alfred J. "Alexander II: A Revisionist View," *Journal of Modern History* 43 (1971): 42–58.

————. *The Politics of Autocracy: Letters of Alexander II to Prince A. I. Bariatinskii 1857–1864.* Paris/The Hague, 1966.

Rogger, Hans. "Government, Jews, Peasants and Land in Post-Emancipation Russia. The Pre-Emancipation Background; Stirrings and Limits of Reform," *Cahiers du monde russe et soviétique* 17 (1976), no. 1: 5–25.

Rozov, E. K. "Oppozitsionnoe dvizhenie tverskogo liberal'nogo dvorianstva v period podgotovki i provedeniia reformy 1861 g.," in A. A. Kondrashenkov et al., eds., *Voprosy agrarnoi istorii tsentra i severo-zapada RSFSR,* 192–204. Smolensk, 1972.

Ruud, Charles. "Censorship and the Peasant Question: The Contingencies of Reform under Alexander II (1855–1859)," *California Slavic Studies* 5 (1970): 137–67.

————. "A. V. Golovnin and the Liberal Russian Censorship, January–June 1862," *Slavonic and East European Review* 50, no. 119 (April 1972): 199–219.

————. "The Russian Empire's New Censorship Law of 1865," *Canadian Slavic Studies* 3 (1969), no. 2: 369–88.

Scheibert, Peter. *Die russische Agrarreform von 1861.* Cologne, 1973.

Shcherbina, P. F. *Sudebnaia reforma 1864 goda na pravoberezhnoi Ukraine.* L'vov, 1974.

Shepelev, L. E. *Tsarizm i burzhuaziia vo vtoroi polovine XIX veka.* Leningrad, 1981.

Shepeleva, O. N. "Zapiski P. A. Valueva Aleksandru II o provedenii reformy 1861 g.," *Istoricheskii arkhiv* 7 (January-February 1971).

Shevchenko, M. M. *Istoriia krepostnogo prava v Rossii.* Voronezh, 1981.

Shuvalova, V. A. "K voprosu o sudebnoi reforme 1864 goda," *Voprosy istorii,* 1965, no. 2, 209–12.

Sinel, Allen. "Educating the Russian Peasantry: The Elementary School Reforms of Count Dmitrii Tolstoi," *Slavic Review* 28, no. 1 (March 1968): 49–70.

————. *The Classroom and the Chancellery: State Educational Reform in Russia under Count Dmitrii Tolstoy.* Cambridge, Mass., 1973.

Skerpan, Alfred. "The Russian National Economy and Emancipation," in Alan Ferguson and Alfred Levin, eds., *Essays in Russian History,* 160–229. Hamden, Conn., 1964.

Starr, S. Frederick. *Decentralization and Self-Government in Russia.* Princeton, N.J., 1972.

Suny, Ronald Grigor. *The Making of the Georgian Nation.* Bloomington, Ind., 1988.

————. "'The Peasants Have Always Fed Us': The Georgian Nobility and the Peasant Emancipation, 1856–1871," *Russian Review* 38 (1979), no. 1: 27–51.

Troitskii, N. A. *Tsarskie sudy protiv revoliutsionnoi Rossii.* Saratov, 1976.

————. *Tsarizm pod sudom progressivnoi obshchestvennosti, 1866–1895.* Moscow, 1979.

Ulashchik, N. N. *Predposylki krest'ianskoi reformy 1861 g. v Litve i Zapadnoi Belorussii.* Moscow, 1965.

————. "Vvedenie obiazatel'nykh inventariei v Belorussii i Litve," *Ezhegodnik po agrarnoi istorii Vostochnoi Evropy: 1958 g.,* 256–77. Tallin, 1959.

Vilenskii, B. V. *Podgotovka sudebnoi reformy 20 Noiabria 1864 g. v Rossii.* Saratov, 1963.

————. *Sudebnaia reforma i kontrreforma v Rossii.* Saratov, 1969.

Violette, Aurele. "Judicial Reforms in the Russian Navy during the 'Era of Great

Reforms': The Reform Act of 1867 and the Abolition of Corporal Punishment," *Slavonic and East European Review* 56 (1978), no. 4: 586–603.

———. "The Grand Duke Konstantin Nikolayevich and the Reform of Naval Administration, 1855–1870," *Slavic and East European Review* 52 (1974), no. 129: 584–601.

Von Wahlde, Peter. "Dmitrii Miliutin: Appraisals," *Canadian Slavic Studies* 3 (1969): 400–414.

———. "Russian Military Reform: 1862–1874," *Military Review* 39, no. 10, 60–69.

Walkin, Jacob. *The Rise of Democracy in Pre-Revolutionary Russia*. New York, 1962.

Wcislo, Francis W. *Reforming Rural Russia: State, Local Society, and National Politics, 1855–1914*. Princeton, N.J., 1990.

Wortman, Richard. *The Development of a Russian Legal Consciousness*. Chicago, 1976.

———. "Judicial Personnel and the Court Reforms of 1864," *Canadian Slavic Studies* 3, no. 2 (Summer 1969): 224–34.

Zaionchkovskii, P. A. "D. A. Miliutin (Biograficheskii ocherk)," *Dnevnik V. A. Miliutina. 1873–1875*, vol. 1, 1–72. Moscow, 1947.

———. "K voprosu o deiatel'nosti Sekretnogo komiteta po krestianskomu delu v 1857 g.," *Istoricheskie zapiski*, vol. 58, 1956.

———. *Otmena krepostnogo prava*. Moscow, 1954, 1960, 1968.

———. "P. A. Valuev (Biograficheskii ocherk)," in P. A. Valuev, *Dnevnik*, vol. 1, 17–54. Moscow, 1961.

———. "Podgotovka i priniatie zakona 24 noiabria 1866 g. o gosudarstvennykh krest'ianakh," *Istoriia SSSR*, no. 4 (July 1958): 103–13.

———. *Provedenie v zhizn' krest'ianskoi reformy 1861 g*. Moscow, 1958.

———. "Sovetskaia istoriografiia reformy 1861," *Voprosy istorii*, 1961, no. 2, 85–104.

———. *Voennye reformy 1860–1870 godov v Rossii*. Moscow, 1952.

Zakharova, L. G. "Dvorianstvo i pravitel'stvennaia programma otmeny krepostnogo prava v Rossii," *Voprosy istorii*, 1973, no. 9, 32–51.

———. "Itogi i zadachi izucheniia krest'ianskoi reformy 1861 g. v Rossii," *Sel'skoe khoziaistvo i krest'ianstvo SSSR v sovremennoi sovetskoi isotriografii (Materialy XVI sessii simpoziuma po izucheniiu problem agrarnoi istorii*, 85–94. Kishinev, 1978.

———. "Otechestvennaia istoriografiia o podgotovke krest'ianskoi reformy 1861 goda," *Istoriia SSSR*, 1976, no. 4, 54–76.

———. "Perepiska ministra vnutrennikh del P. A. Valueva i gosudarstvennogo sekretaria S. N. Urusova v 1866 g.," *Istoriia SSSR*, 1973, no. 2, 115–27.

———. "Pervoe issledovanie po istorii krest'ianskoi reformy 1861 g. v Rossii," *Vestnik MGU*, seriia istoriia, 1977, no. 1, 34–50.

———. "Podgotovka krest'ianskoi reformy v Rossii 1861 g. i krest'ianstvo," in *Sotsial'noekonomicheskie problemy rossiiskoi derevni*, 121–37. Rostov-na-Donu, 1980.

———. "Pravitel'stvennaia programma otmeny krepostnogo prava v Rossii," *Istoriia SSSR*, 1975, no. 2, 22–47.

———. "Programma otmeny krepostnogo prava redaktsionnykh komissii i dvorianstvo. Iz istorii krest'ianskoi reformy 1861 g. v Rossii," *Vestnik MGU*, 1979, no. 2, 22–37.

———. "Redaktsionnye komissii 1859–1860 gg.: uchrezhdenie, deiatel'nost' (k probleme krizisa 'verkhov' nakanunie padeniia krepostnogo prava v Rossii," *Istoriia SSSR*, 1983, no. 3, 53–71.

———. "Samoderzhavie, biurokratiia, i reformy 60-kh godov XIX v. v Rossii," *Voprosy istorii*, 1989, no. 10, 3–24.

————. *Samoderzhavie i otmena krepostnogo prava v Rossii 1856–1861*. Moscow, 1984.

————. "Zapiska N. A. Miliutina ob osvobozhdenii krest'ian (1856)," in *Voprosy istorii Rossii XIX–nachala XX veka,* 24–33. Leningrad, 1983.

Zenkovsky, Serge A. "The Emancipation of the Serfs in Retrospect," *Russian Review* 20 (1961), no. 4: 280–292.

CONTRIBUTORS

Alexander K. Afanas'ev is a Senior Researcher at the State Historical Museum in Moscow. He holds the *kandidat* degree in history and is the author of a series of articles on nineteenth-century Russian history, dealing with the internal policies of the autocracy, the court reforms, and cultural history.

John Bushnell is Professor of History at Northwestern University and author of *Mutiny amid Repression* and *Moscow Graffiti: Language and Subculture.*

David Christian teaches Russian and World History at Macquarie University, in Sydney, Australia. His publications include *Bread and Salt: A Social and Economic History of Food and Drink in Russia* (with R. E. F. Smith), *"Living Water": Vodka and Russian Society on the Eve of Emancipation,* and *Power and Privilege: Russia and the Soviet Union in the 19th and 20th Centuries.* He is presently working on a history of Inner Asia.

Ben Eklof, Associate Professor of History at Indiana University, is author of *Russian Peasant Schools* and *Soviet Briefing: Gorbachev and the Reform Period*, editor of *School and Society in Tsarist and Soviet Russia*, and co-editor (with Stephen Frank) of *The World of the Russian Peasant* and (with Edward Deprov) of *Democracy in the Russian School.*

Daniel Field is Associate Professor of History at Syracuse University and Fellow of the Russian Research Center. He is author of *The End of Serfdom* and *Rebels in the Name of the Tsar* and served as editor of the *Russian Review* from 1982 to 1989.

Peter Gatrell is Senior Lecturer in Economic History at the University of Manchester and author of *The Tsarist Economy, 1850–1917* and *Government, Industry, and Rearmament in Russia, 1900–1914: The Argument of Tsarism.* He is currently writing an economic and social history of Russia during the First World War.

Abbott Gleason is Professor of History at Brown University and author or coeditor of several publications, including *Ivan Kireevsky and the Origins of Slavophilism; Young Russia; Bolshevik Culture: Experiment and Order in the Russian Revolution;* and *Shared Destiny: Fifty Years of Soviet-American Relations.* He is currently researching the concept of "totalitarianism" in Europe and the United States from 1920 to the present.

Samuel D. Kassow is Professor of History at Trinity College, in Hartford, Connecticut. He is the author of *Students, Professors, and the State in Tsarist Russia* and a co-editor of *Between Tsar and People.*

Jacob W. Kipp, a Senior Analyst for the Foreign Military Studies Office at Ft. Leavenworth, Kansas, serves as Research Coordinator for European Military Studies. He is also an Adjunct Professor of History at the University of Kansas, where he teaches in the Russian and East European Studies Program. He has published extensively in Russian and Soviet military and naval history, and is the American editor of the journal *European Security*.

Adele Lindenmeyr is Associate Professor of History at Villanova University. She has published numerous articles on the history of charity and social reform movements in Imperial Russia, and recently completed a book on charity and public welfare in Russia from the eighteenth to the twentieth centuries.

Valeriia A. Nardova is a Senior Researcher at the St. Petersburg branch of the Institute of History of the Russian Academy of Sciences, a doctor of history, a specialist in nineteenth-century Russian history, and author of many articles and books, including *Gorodskaia semiia v Rossii v 60-kh-nachale 90-kh godov XIX veka* [The Urban Family in Russia from the 1860s to the 1890s].

Joan Neuberger teaches Russian history at the University of Texas at Austin. She has published *Hooliganism: Crime, Culture, and Power in St. Petersburg, 1900–1914* and is now working on a book entitled *The People's Court: Popular Legal Cultures in the Urban Justice of the Peace Courts, 1864–1917*.

Fedor A. Petrov is a Senior Researcher at the State Historical Museum in Moscow. He holds the *kandidat* degree in history and is a specialist in nineteenth-century Russian history. He is the author of *Muzei "Staraia Moskva"* [The "Old Moscow" Museum] and of a number of articles about the zemstvo and the public movement in Russia.

Alfred J. Rieber is Alfred L. Cass Term Professor of History at the University of Pennsylvania. He is author or editor of eight books on Russian and Soviet history, including *The Politics of Autocracy: Letters of Alexander II to Prince A. I. Bariatinskii, 1857–1864* and *Merchants and Entrepreneurs in Imperial Russia*. He is currently working on a book-length study of interest-group politics in the era of the Great Reforms.

Natalia F. Ust'iantseva is an Assistant Professor *(dotsent)* at the Cheliabinsk Institute of Culture, holds a *kandidat* degree in history, and is author of a number of articles on nineteenth-century Russian history, primarily concerning the Great Reforms.

Larissa Zakharova is a Professor of History at Moscow State University, a doctor of history, and a specialist in Russian history from the 1860s to the early twentieth century. She is the author or editor of numerous articles, editions of original sources, and monographs, including *Samoderzhavie i otmena krepostnogo prava v Rossii, 1856–1861* [Autocracy and the Abolition of Serfdom in Russia, 1856–1861].

INDEX

Abaza, A. A., 69
Abolition of Serfdom (Zaionchkovskii), 9
Adams, Arthur, 3
Aksakov, Ivan, 68, 266, 275
Alaska, sale of, 67
Aleksandr Aleksandrovich, Grand Duke. *See* Alexander III
Aleksandr Nevskii (frigate), 124
Aleksandrov, P. A., 210
Aleksandrovskii plant, 122, 129
Alexander I, 60, 251, 273
Alexander III (Grand Duke Aleksandr Aleksandrovich), 155, 201, 258
Allgemeine Zeitung, 203
Alma, battle of the, 116
Amendments Relating to the Selection of Jurors for the General and Primary Lists, 217–18
Amosov, Colonel, 121
Andreevskii, Professor, 254
Anti-Semitism, 76, 223, 239
Archangel (Arkhangel'sk), 120, 178, 200
Ardatov District, 222
Arkhimed (frigate), 121
Armand, 124
Arsenev, K. K., 217
Artillery Academy, 72
Artseulov, N. A., 128
Artsimovich, V. A., 44, 174
Arzamas District, 222
Ashenbrenner, M. Iu., 209
Ashworth & Stevens plant, 122, 123, 127
Astaf'ev, A. A., 210
Astrakhan Province, 178, 200

Baird of Merseyside, 122, 123, 124, 127, 131
Bakunin, Aleksandr, 207, 208
Bakunin, Mikhail, 207
Bakunin, Pavel, 207
Balakhna District, 222
Baltic provinces, 24, 26, 65, 73, 103, 110, 200
Baranov commission, 61
Bariatinskii, A. I., 10, 23, 117, 145, 151, 155
Barshchina, 46, 52, 53, 91, 92
Beketov, A. N., 171
Belgium, 20
Belinsky, Vissarion, 171
Belorussia, 200
Bel'sk District, 165
Belyi, Ia. M., 204
Benardaki, D. E., 107
Berdyaev, Nicholas, 264
Berenshtam, V. L., 209

Bessarabia, 187
Bezak, A. P., 74
Bezdna village, 45
Birzhevye vedomosti, 65
Bismarck, Otto von, 1, 3, 35
Black Sea, 120, 124, 125, 132, 133, 139
Black Sea Steamship and Navigation Company, 125
Bobrinskoi, A. P., 76, 78
Bobrinskoi, V. A., 69
Bobrishchev-Pushkin, A. M., 217
Bogoslovskaia, L. P., 272
Bogucharskii, V. Ia., 209
Bordeaux, 124
Bornholm, 121
Borovkov, N. A., 171, 177
Borzna District, 204, 205
Bosnia-Herzegovina, 139
Botkin, V. P., 172
Bourbons, 257
Bradtke, E. F. von, 250
Britain, 98, 115–16, 118, 120–22, 150, 249. *See also* England
Bronevskii, D. D., 173
Brown and Co., of Sheffield, 127
Bulgaria, 139, 141, 142, 203, 207
Bulygin Duma, 63
Bunge, N. Kh., 29
Butakov, G. I., 118–19
Buturlin Committee, 20
Bykh, Lev, 210
Bykh, N. K., 210
Bykhov District, 173

Captain, HMS, 133
Carr & MacPherson of St. Petersburg, 126, 127, 129
Catherine II, 181
Caucasus, 145, 147, 155, 200
Central Asia, 73, 74, 150, 200
Central State Historical Archive in Leningrad, 187
Chekhov, Anton, 248
Cherkasskii, V. A., 25, 28, 29, 191
Chern' District, 164
Chernigov, 47, 167, 204, 205, 206, 207, 208
Chernukha, V. G., 11
Chernyshevskii, Nikolai, 5, 9, 26, 272, 273
Chevalier, Michel, 69
Chicherin, B. N., 184, 191, 250, 251, 256, 257
Chizhov, F. V., 68
Chubinskii, M. P., 234
Chudnovskii, I. P., 204

Chuprov, A. I., 209
Clayperon, 69
Cold War, 2
Coles, C. P., 129, 133
Committee of Ministers, 34, 61, 267, 268, 269
Commune (peasant), 50, 51, 94
Constantinople, 141, 143
Constitutional Democratic party, 204, 207
Corps of Engineers, 71
Cossacks, 103. *See also* Don Cossacks
Council of Ministers, 34, 36, 61, 77
Council of State, 97, 110, 126, 151; and Alexander II, 20, 32; and Nicholas, 42; as proto-parliament, 61; and Konstantin Nikolaevich, 64; factional strife in, 77; conservatives in, 162, 164, 185, 186; proposed reorganization of, 201, 206

Danube, crossing of, 139–41, 142
Davydov, Denis, 171
Debogorii-Mokrievich, V. K., 203
December Uprising, 60
Decembrists, 23, 25, 27, 28
Delo, 217
Den', 266
Derviz, Von, 69
Devastation, HMS, 132
Dmitrii Donskoi (frigate), 124
Dobroliubov, N. A., 171
Dobrudja, 141
Dolgorukov, V. A., 32, 74
Dolgorukov, V. V., 75, 76
Don Cossacks, 200
Dondukov-Korsakov, Prince, 74
Donets basin, 72
Dostoevsky, Fedor, 274, 275
Dragomanov, M. P., 207
Dragomirov, Mikhail, 152
Drentel'n, A. R., 205
Druzhinin, N. M., 6, 107
Dubynkovo, P. L., 226
Dvorakovskii, Constable, 45
Dzhanshiev, G. A., 228, 250, 256

Editorial Commissions, 29–34, 36; legislation in, 11; establishment of, 28
Eidel'man, N. Ia., 5
Ekaterinoslav, 235
Eklof, Ben, 201
Eko, 5
Elena Pavlovna, Grand Duchess, 27, 64, 69, 267
Emmons, Terence, 6, 10, 197
End of Serfdom (Field), 10
Engels, F., 8
Engineering Academy, 72
England, 1, 120–22, 124–27, 252
Erchenko, G. Ia, 204
Ericcson, 128
Ertel', A. I., 210

Estates. *See* Sosloviia
Estonia, peasant uprisings in, 11, 26

Far East, 200
Fathers and Sons (Turgenev), 170
Field, Daniel, 4, 7, 10
Figner, Vera, 203
Filosofova, Anna, 270, 271, 272
Finance Ministry, 73
Finance Committee, 68
Finland, yards in, 124
First Duma, 63
First World War, 2
Forty Years in the History of the Zemstvo (Veselovskii), 197
France, 1, 21, 30, 70, 115, 116, 118, 249, 250, 252
Franco-Prussian War, 147, 151
Free Economic assembly, 59
Free Russian assembly, 59
Free Russian Press in London, 21
Freeze, Gregory, 269
French Revolution of 1789, 23
Fricke, 122, 123
Frieden, Nancy, 201

Gaaz, F. P., 274
Galernyi Isle, 123, 126, 127, 129
Galov, I. A., 237
Galvano-Plastic Works, 123
Garmiza, V. V., 197
Ge, N. N., 171
General-Admiral (cruiser-frigate), 124, 129
General Staff Academy, 152
Geographical Society. *See* Imperial Russian Geographical Society
Germany, 1, 98, 222, 249, 250, 252, 258. *See also* Prussia
Gerschenkron, Alexander, 85, 134
Gessen, I. V., 233
Glasnost' and perestroika, 1, 5
Goldsmith, Raymond, 86
Golokhvastov, D. P., 36
Golos, 62, 223
Golosa iz Rossii, 22
Golovachev, A. A., 210
Golovnin, A. V., 23, 64, 76
Gol'tsev, V. A., 208, 209
Golubtsov, F. A., 105
Gorbachev, Mikhail, 4, 5
Gorchakov, A. M., 67, 74
Gordeenko, E. S., 203
Gornyi Dubniak, 155
Gorodnia District, 204
Gorvits, 144
Got'e, Iu. V., 7
Grande Société des chemins de fer russes, 68
Grazhdanin, 228
Gregor, 144
Grodno, 174, 223

Gromada, 203, 205
Grot, K. K., 109
Gulf of Finland, 119, 122
Gurko, I. V., 141, 144

Halevy, Elie, 1
Hay, Douglas, 235
Herzen, A. I., 9, 21, 223
Holy Alliance, 21
Holy Land, 125
Holy Synod, 266

Iaroslavl, 208
Idiot, The (Dostoevsky), 274
Ignat'ev, P. I., 24
Imperial Russian Geographical Society, 26, 60
Institute of Transportation Engineers, 69, 70
Isherwood, 122
Iskra, 273
Istoriia SSSR, 7
Ivan "Kalita," 104
Izhora, 121

Johnson, R. E., 50
Jones, Eric, 96
Journal of the Ministry of Internal Affairs, 2, 267, 272
Journal of the Imperial Philanthropic Society, 273
Judicial Codes of 1864, 33, 162, 231, 240
Junkers' schools, 148, 149

Kakhanov, M. S., 195
Kaluga, 40, 169, 172, 174, 270
Kamenets, 269
Karakozov, D. V., 75, 76, 275
Karamzin, N. M., 171
Karlovka, 27, 28
Karpinskii, A. P., 204
Katkov, Mikhail, 62, 63, 65, 75, 77, 216, 257, 258
Kaufman, K. P. fon, 74
Kavelin, K. D., 27, 28, 38, 171, 206, 256, 257
Kazan', 45, 218, 221, 222, 223, 224
Kennan, George, 202
Kennedy, Paul, 116
Khardin, A. N., 210
Kharkov, 46, 188, 202, 204, 207
Khilkov, A. M., 172
Khizhnizkov, V. M., 204
Khodkevich, 164
Kholmsk District, 164
Kiev, 24, 148, 175, 209, 210, 223
Kiselev, Count, 155
Kizevetter, A. A., 247, 248
Klements, Dmitrii, 210
Kliuchevskii, V. O., 7, 247
Kniazhevich, A. M., 112
Kochubei, V. A., 169
Kogan, 144

Kokorev, Vasilii, 111
Kolokol, 22, 26, 223
Kondrat'ev, N. D., 86
Koni, A. F., 215, 217, 234, 270
Konstantin Nikolaevich, Grand Duke, 20, 23, 36, 37, 66, 109, 122, 225; and Alexander II, 20, 22; support of liberals, 26; and Naval Ministry, 27; influence of, 64; eclipse of, 65; as General-Admiral, 124, 130, 132, 134
Kornilov, A. A., 2
Kornilov, E. G., 197
Korolenko, V. G., 36
Korsakov, P. A., 207
Koshelev, A. I., 25, 107, 207
Kostomarov, N. I., 171, 250, 256
Kostroma, 199, 205
Kovalchenko, I. D., 87, 88, 91
Kovalevskii, M. M., 208
Kovno, 163, 174, 223
Krabbe, N. K., 64, 67, 128
Kraevskii, A. A., 62
Kraft, N. O., 70
Krapivna District, 172
Krasnoe Selo, 153
Kravchinskii, Sergei, 203
Kreml' ironclad battery, 127, 129
Krestovozdvizhenskaia Obshchina, 267
Kridener, N. P., 141–42, 143
Kronstadt, 120, 121, 126, 128, 129, 132
Kropotkin, S. M., 208
Kryzhanovskii, N. A., 128
Kudriavtsev, S. G., 122, 123, 129, 131
Kulomzin, A. N., 165, 173
Kuropatkin, A. N., 144
Kursk Province, 96, 163, 199, 202
Kvist, I. O., 241

La Gloire (ironclad), 125
Lame, 69
Landed charters, 9
Lanskoi, S. S., 20, 28, 33, 166, 171, 268
Lavrov, Peter, 272
Lazarevskii, A. M., 167, 169
Lenin, 5, 8, 9, 49, 211
Lent, 42
Leshkov Affair, 257
Leskov, N. S., 119
Lesovskii, S. S., 128
Letichev District, 225
Levshin, A. I., 20
Lievan report, 72
Lincoln, Bruce, 197
Lind, Vasilii, 207
Lindfors, A. F., 204, 209, 210
Literary Fund, 272
Litvak, B. G., 91
Liubimov, N. A., 257, 258
Liuboshchinskii, M. N., 217
London, 65

Loris-Melikov, M. T.: Constitution of, 35, 36, 37, 63, 192, 201
Luker'ia, 40, 41, 42, 44
Lutskii, V. V., 210

Maikov, P. M., 239
Main Committee, 25, 27, 28, 29, 34, 43, 61, 66. *See also* Secret Committee
Maistrenko, M. N., 204
Makhtra War, 26
Makov, L. S., 205
Mamontov, Savva, 111
Manchester, 119
Mansurov, B. P., 125
Marble Palace, 130
Marshal of the nobility, 20, 169, 199, 204, 207
Marx, K., 8
Marxism-Leninism, founders of, 19
Matveev, A. N., 241
Maudsley and Field, 116
Meck, 69
Mecklenburg, Duke of, 267
Mediators of the peace, 33, 40–47, 162–78, 270
Mel'nikov, P. P., 67, 68, 70, 71, 76
Menshikov, A. S., 75
Merrimack, 119
Mershchanskii, 123
Mezentsov, 203
Mikhail Nikolaevich, Grand Duke, 154
Military Law Academy, 149
Military Supreme Court in St. Petersburg, 149
Miliukov, Paul, 252
Miliutin, Dmitrii, 23, 63, 72–75, 142, 144–56; appointment of, 117
Miliutin, Nikolai, 26–29, 35, 62, 63, 68, 74, 150; historian's view of, 5, 7, 11; on peasant reform, 161
Miliutin commission, 32–33, 161, 163, 170, 176
Miller, Forrestt, 147
Minin (ironclad), 133
Ministry of Education, 74, 75, 76, 199, 250, 253, 254, 256
Ministry of Finance, 65, 76, 108, 110
Ministry of Interior, 174, 182, 183, 187, 195, 268
Ministry of Internal Affairs, 26, 32, 60
Ministry of Justice, 76, 217
Ministry of Transportation, 72
Ministry of War. *See* War Ministry
Minsk, 45, 47, 174, 178, 223
Mironov, B. N., 94
Mirovoi posrednik, 169
Mitchell, 126, 127, 129
Mogilev, 174–75, 178, 223
Mogilev District, 225
Mogilevskie gubernskie vedomosti, 173
Molostovka village, 45
Mongol horde, 104
Monitor, USS, 119, 128
Morskoi sbornik, 125, 129

Moscow Entrepreneurial Group, 60, 68
Moscow–Kursk–Kiev railroad, 67
Moscow–Sevastopol railroad, 70
Moskovskie vedomosti, 62, 75, 167, 173, 228, 257
Moskva, 68
Moskvich, 68
Mozhaisk Charitable Society, 271
Municipal Reform of 1870, 77, 183, 186, 187, 191, 195, 196
Musselius, R., 125, 129

Nachalo, 209, 210
Napoleon III, 21
Nauka i zhizn', 5
Naval Ministry, 27, 119–34
Nazimov, V. I.: rescript to, 21, 24
Ne Tron' Menia (ironclad battery), 126
Nechkina, Militsa Vasil'evna, 7–11
Nekliudov, N. A., 241
Nepliuev, N. I., 204, 205
Nepokoichitskii, A. A., 141
Neva yards, 129
New York, 124
Nicholas I, 22, 79, 118, 264; reactionary political course of, 20; and censorship, 21; secret committees under, 24; on abolishing serfdom, 42; societies under, 60; on technological progress, 70; stagnation and obscurantism under, 167; and universities, 253; and societies, 267, 268
Nicolaevan system, 34
Nifontov, A. S., 87
Nikitin, V. N., 236, 237, 238, 241
Nikolaev, 121, 123, 192
Nikolaevskii Academy of the General Staff, 72
Nikolaevskii railroad, 67, 68
Nikolai Nikolaevich, Grand Duke, the elder, 141, 143, 153, 154
Nikolai Nikolaevich, Grand Duke, the younger, 154
Nikopol, 141
Nizhnii Novgorod, 68, 199, 208, 210, 218, 221, 222
Nobel works, 122, 123
Le Nord, 20, 21, 24, 65
Northern War, 118
Novgorod, 202, 226
Novinskii Boulevard, 208
Novotorzhskii District, 207

Obninskii, P. N., 168, 170, 171, 174, 270, 271
Obrok, 52, 53, 91, 92, 93, 98
Obruchev, Nikolai, 141, 144
Obshchee delo, 203
Obukhov, P. M., 129, 131
Obukhov Mill, 129, 130, 131
Odessa, 182, 183, 187, 188, 193, 257
Odessa–Kharkov railroad, 67

Odessa Women's Charitable Society, 272
Ogarev, N. P., 216
Okhta, 123
Old Testament, 237
Olenin, N. P., 207
Olonetsk, 199
Opyt gunboat, 126, 129
Orel, 225
Orel (ship-of-the-line), 121
Orenburg, 178
Orenburg Charitable Society, 268
Orthodox Church, 42, 76, 125, 220, 248, 266, 275
Osman Pasha, 142
Ostrogradskii, M. V., 171

Page Corps, 72
Pahlen, K. I., 76, 77
Panina, A. S., 205
Panslav movement, 266, 275
Paris, 65
Paskevich, F. I., 75
Pax Britannia, 116
Peace of Paris, 21
Pearson, Thomas, 197
Peasant dues. *See* Barshchina; Obrok
Peasant Land Bank, 95
People's Will, 210
Pereire brothers, 69
Perestroika. *See* Glasnost' and perestroika
Perm, 166, 176, 192, 199, 223, 226
Pervaz-Bakhri (frigate), 118
Pervenets (ironclad battery), 126, 128, 129
Pestich, F. N., 128
Peter the Great, 5, 49, 118, 120, 134, 172
Peterburgskii listok, 234
Petersburg Medical-Surgical Academy, 75
Petr Velikii (battleship), 132
Petrashevtsy, 23, 25
Petropavlovsk (frigate), 127
Petrunkevich, I. I., 203, 204, 205, 206, 207, 209, 211
Pipes, Richard, 104
Pirogov, N. I., 74, 171, 250, 252, 253, 254, 255
Pirumova, N. M., 197, 202
Pius IX, 21, 35
Plevako, F. N., 247
Plevna, 142, 143
Podolye, 24, 175, 223
Pogodin, M. P., 22, 264
Pokrovskii, M. N., 4, 9
Poland, 35, 64, 65, 75, 77, 175
Poletika, 127, 129
Poliakov, S. S., 69
Poliarnaia zvezda, 21–22
Polish insurrections, 23, 70, 76, 97, 147, 269
Polish provinces, 73, 74
Politics of Autocracy (Rieber), 10
Polkan (frigate), 121
Poltava, 199, 203, 204

Poltava Province, 27, 47, 48
Popov, A. A., 128, 132
Popov, Gavriil, 5
Popovka (ironclad), 133
Pos'et, Admiral, 72
Povalo-Shveikovskii, T. N., 207
Prussia, 30, 35; lords in, 91
Prussian Municipal Code, 185
Pruth River, 139
Pryzhov, Ivan, 274
Pskov, 164, 170, 224
Pugachev Rebellion, 26, 42
Putilov, N. I., 123, 131
Pypin, A. I., 2

Radetsky, F. F., 144
Raucourt, 69
Red Cross. *See* Russian Red Cross
Reitern, M. Kh., 64–69, 71–74, 76, 78, 97, 117, 127, 146
Revolution of 1905, 34, 38, 49
Revolutionary situation, 7–12
Riazan', 170, 192, 207, 208
Rieber, Alfred J., 6, 7, 9–10, 117, 269
Robert Napier and Penn (engine builders), 121, 122
Roberti, E. V. de, 207
Rodichev, F. I., 207, 208, 209
Romania, 140
Roop, Kh. Kh., 193
Rostovtsev, Ia. I., 27, 28, 29, 32, 109
Rostow, W. W., 84
Royal Navy, 116
Rushchuk, 141, 143, 145
Russell, John Scott, 127
Russian Landed Gentry and the Peasant Emancipation (Emmons), 10
Russian Red Cross, 266
Russian Society of Steam Navigation and Trade, 125
Russian Technological Society, 60, 71
Russkaia mysl', 205
Russkaia rech', 205
Russkii invalid, 73, 78
Russkii vestnik, 65, 167

Saint-Simon, C. H. de, 69, 70
Sakharov, N. V., 40
Saltykov-Shchedrin, Mikhail, 19, 25, 27, 37, 167, 170, 171
Samara, 199, 202, 210
Samarin, Iu. F., 25, 29
Samoderzhavie i otmena krepostnogo prava v Rossii 1856–1861 (Zakharova), 11
San Fransisco, 128
Saratov, 199
Saratov–Dunaburg railroad, 70
Savich, V. A., 204
Sechenov, N. M., 171
Secret Committee, 24, 25, 27, 34, 61, 251, 253

Sejm, 35
Semenov plant, 122
Semenov-Tian-Shanskii, P. P., 29
Semevskii, V. I., 2
Semiannikov, 127, 129
Senate, 164, 165, 168, 176, 226, 240
Serbia, 139
Sevastopol (frigate), 127
Shatsillo, K. F., 202
Sheffield, 119
Shestakov, A. I., 124
Shilder-Shuldner, General, 142, 143
Shipka pass, 141, 142
Shostakovich, B. N., 194
Shostakovich, Dmitrii, 194
Shtakel'berg Commission, 61
Shuia, 226
Shumla, 141
Shuvalov, Count, 62, 64, 66, 67, 73, 76, 77, 78
Shuvalov, A. P., 75
Shuvalov, P. P., 75, 150, 151
Shuvalov group, 73, 74, 75
Siberia, 187, 200
Silistria, 141
Simbirsk, 207, 223, 226
Simfiropol, 222
Sistovo, 139
Skalon, V. Iu., 202
Skobelev, M. D., 143, 144
Slavic Benevolent Society, 59
Slavonic assistance committees, 266
Slavophiles, 25, 207, 211, 266, 273, 274, 275; press, 68
Slovo, 210
Smerch' (ship), 129
Smolensk, 44, 165, 168, 173
Society for Inexpensive Lodgings, 272
Society for the Aid of Russian Industry and Trade, 60
Society for the Improvement of Workers' Housing in St. Petersburg, 267, 272
Society to Encourage Industriousness, 272
Solov'ev, A. K., 210
Solov'ev, S. M., 171
Sosloviia, 51, 256; organizations, 60
Sovremennaia letopis', 168
Sovremennik, 26, 27, 272, 273
Sovremennoe slovo, 73
Spasovich, V. D., 252, 257
Spassk District, 47
Speranskii, M. M., 63, 64; *Discourse on the Laws,* 35
St. Peterburgskie vedomosti, 62, 65
Starchevskii, A. V., 62
Staritsa District, 207
Starr, S. Frederick, 197
Stasiulevich, M. M., 194, 195
Stasova, Nadezhda, 272
State Bank, 98
State Cannon Works at Zlatoust, 129

State Chancery, 61
State Council. *See* Council of State
State Duma, 207
Statute on Liquor Taxes, 102
Statute on Measures to Preserve the Security of the State and Domestic Tranquillity, 36
Steamship Committee, 121, 122, 124
Stock Exchange Society, 60
Stolypin, P. A., 38
Strakhov, N. N., 274, 275
Strekalova, Alexandra, 272
Stroganov, 79
Stroganov, S. G., 250, 257
Strumilin, S. G., 86
Sukhozanet, N. O., 145, 155
Sumy District, 46, 47
Sunday school, 269, 272
Suvorin, A. S., 62
Suvorov, 152, 153
Suvorov school, 73
Svetlana (frigate), 124
Sweden, 118
Syn otechestva, 62

Table of ranks, 219
Tambov, 184, 206
Tatarinov, V. A., 69, 97
Tat'iana Day, 247, 248
Tauride, 199
Ten Years of Reform (Golovachev), 210
Tengoborskii, L. V., 22, 95, 117
Terpigorev, S. N., 177
Thames Iron Works, 126, 127
Third Section, 76, 205
Thomson & Co., 122, 123, 126, 127
Timashev, A. E., 76, 77, 186
Timiriazev, K. A., 171
Timofeev, N. I., 217
Tkachev, Petr, 274
Tolstoi, Dmitrii, 75, 76, 77, 193, 194, 257, 258
Tolstoi, Lev, 19, 23, 171, 172
Tolstoi, Sergei, 171
Tomsk, 194
Totalitarian paradigm, 12
Trans-Siberian railroad, 71
Trepov, 203
Troinitskii, A. G., 166
Trubnikova, Maria, 272
Tugan-Baranovskii, M. I., 86
Tula, 119, 164, 172, 189
Turgenev, Ivan, 170, 171, 193
Tver, 68, 170, 202, 204, 207
Tver' Provincial Committee, 28

Ufa, 178
Ukraine, 200
United States, 117, 133; influence of in railways, 70
Unkovskii, A. M., 25
Ushinskii, Konstantin, 74

Ustrialov, F. N., 235
Uvarov, Sergei, 251, 252, 254, 258

Valuev, P. A., 7, 66, 76, 174; program of, 33; circular sent by, 48; aspiring to leadership, 62; views, 63, 77; on military affairs, 151; on peace mediators, 166, 171, 174; on social welfare, 268
Vannovskii, Petr, 155
Varna, 141
Varnavin, 205
Vedomstvo uchrezhdenii Imperatritsy Marii, 265
Velikie Luki District, 225
Venturi, Franco, 6
Ves'egonsk District, 207
Veselovskii, B. B., 197, 201
Vest', 76, 216, 237
Vestnik Evropy, 194, 258
Viatka, 199
Vidin, 141, 142
Vilnius (Vilno), 24, 148, 174, 223, 269
Virginia, CSS, 128
Vitebsk, 175, 178, 223
Vladimir, 51, 199, 217, 218, 221, 226
Vladimir (frigate), 118
Voeikov, 207
Volkov, M. S., 71
Vologda, 178, 199
Volyn', 175, 223
Volynia Province, 24
Voprosy istorii, 5
Voronezh Province, 171, 173, 201

Voronov commission, 254
Voroponov, F. F., 173
Vremia, 274
Vucinich, Wayne, 197
Vyborg (ship-of-the-line), 121, 122

Wallace, D. M., 237
War Ministry, 68, 74, 117, 146, 148, 150, 151, 155
Warrior, HMS, 125
Warsaw, 147, 175
Webb Yards, 124
Westernizers, 25, 211
What Is to Be Done? (Chernyshevsky), 272, 273
Wheatcroft, S. G., 87
Whistler, Major, 70
Witte, S. Iu., 5, 65, 71, 86
Wolf, Eric, 112

Zablotskii-Desiatovskii, A., 109, 110
Zaionchkovskii, Petr Andreevich, 6–7, 9–12, 117, 201
Zakharova, Larissa, 5, 197, 199
Zamiatin, D. N., 64, 76, 234
Zelinskii, A., 175
Zemstvo, 202
Zhemchuzhnikov, A. A., 210
Zhitomir, 269
Zhukovskii, A. K., 20
Zhukovskii, N. I., 210
Zhurnal Putei Soobshcheniia, 70
Zhurnal zemlevladel'tsev, 271